HM1395

People,
Cities and Wealth

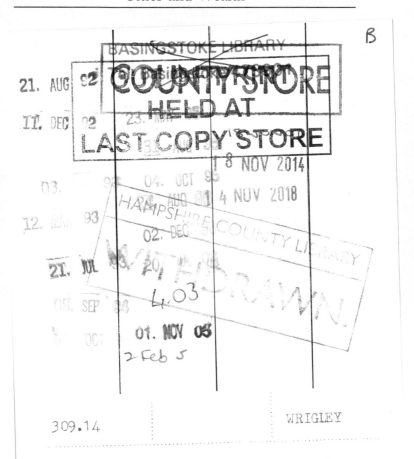

BASINGSTOKE LIBRARY

21. AUG 92

II. DEC 92

COUNTY STORE
HELD AT
LAST COPY STORE

1 8 NOV 2014

4 NOV 2018

03.

04. OCT 95

12. MAR 93

02. DEC

21. JUL

4.03

WITHDRAWN

HAMPSHIRE COUNTY LIBRARY

01. NOV 03

2 Feb 5

B

This book is due for return on or before the last date shown
above; it may, subject to the book not being reserved by
another reader, be renewed by personal application, post, or
telephone, quoting this date and details of the book.

HAMPSHIRE COUNTY LIBRARY

To Marieke, Nick, Tamsin and Rebecca

People, Cities and Wealth

The Transformation of Traditional Society

E. A. Wrigley

Basil Blackwell

First published 1987
First published in paperback 1988
First published in paperback in the US 1989

Basil Blackwell Ltd
108 Cowley Road, Oxford OX4 1JF, UK

Basil Blackwell Inc.
432 Park Avenue South, Suite 1503
New York, NY 10016, USA

British Library Cataloguing in Publication Data
Wrigley, E.A.
  People, cities and wealth: the transformation of traditional society.
  1.Europe – Social conditions
  I.Title
  940.2'2   HN373

  ISBN 0-631-13991-5
  ISBN 0-631-16556-8 Pbk

Library of Congress Cataloguing in Publication Data
Wrigley, E.A. (Edward Anthony), 1931-
  People, cities and wealth.

  Bibliography:p.
  Includes index.
  1. Urban economics – History.   2. Cities and
  towns – Europe – Growth – History.   3. Europe –
  Industry – History.   4. Fertility, Human – Europe –
  History.
  I.Title.
  HT321.W75   1987   307.7'6'09   86-26394
  ISBN 0-631-13991-5
  ISBN 0-631-16556-8 (pbk.)

Typeset in 10 on 11½ Baskerville by Dobbie Typesetting Service, Plymouth, Devon
Printed in Great Britain by
T. J. Press Ltd, Padstow, Cornwall

Contents

Note on References

The reference list at the back of the book provides full details of all the secondary sources to which reference is made in the course of the work. In the footnotes, therefore, when a book or article is mentioned, only the surname of the author and a short title is used, even when the work in question is referred to for the first time.

Acknowledgements

The essays in this volume that have been published previously are the following. They are listed in the order in which they were published.

'The supply of raw materials in the industrial revolution', *Economic History Review*, 2nd ser., xv (1962), pp. 1–16. Reprinted with the permission of the editors.

'Family limitation in pre-industrial England', *Economic History Review*, 2nd ser., xix (1966), pp. 82–109. Reprinted with the permission of the editors.

'A simple model of London's importance in changing English society and economy, 1650–1750', *Past and Present*, xxxvii (1967), pp. 44–70. World copyright: the Past and Present Society, Corpus Christi College, Oxford, England. Reprinted with the permission of the Society.

'The process of modernization and the industrial revolution in England', *Journal of Interdisciplinary History*, iii (1972), pp. 225–59. Reprinted with the permission of the editors and the MIT press, Cambridge, Massachusetts.

'Fertility strategy for the individual and the group', in C. Tilly (ed.), *Historical studies of changing fertility* (Princeton, 1978), pp. 135–54. Reprinted by permission of Princeton University Press.

'The growth of population in eighteenth-century England: a conundrum resolved', *Past and Present*, xcviii (1983), pp. 121–50. World copyright: the Past and Present Society, Corpus Christi College, Oxford, England. Reprinted with the permission of the Society.

'Urban growth and agricultural change: England and the continent in the early modern period', *Journal of Interdisciplinary History*, xv (1985), pp. 683–728. Reprinted with the permission of the editors and the MIT Press, Cambridge, Massachusetts.

'The fall of marital fertility in nineteenth-century France: exemplar or exception?', *European Journal of Population* 1 (1985), pp. 31–60 and 141–77. Reprinted with the permission of the North-Holland Publishing Company, Amsterdam.

In addition, it may be noted that 'Some reflections on corn yields and prices in pre-industrial economies' will also be published in R. S. Schofield and J. Walter (eds), *Death and the social order* (Cambridge, forthcoming).

1

Introduction:
What Was the Industrial Revolution?

Publishing a volume of essays is an exercise with narcissistic undertones.[1] It is difficult not to feel that some justification for such a venture is required. In this introduction I shall suggest that, despite their apparent diversity, the essays in this volume are all related to a common theme which gives them intellectual coherence.

The title of the book indicates that three types of subject matter are covered, reflected in a tripartite division of the essays. The three are population movements and characteristics; urban growth and function; and the processes by which the material wants of society were met, and the circumstances which governed the degree of success experienced in trying to meet them. I hope that, in reflecting on the essays which follow, the reader will be persuaded that the connections between these three topics are intimate, and that a recognition of this fact is essential to a better understanding of the economic and social history of England and other west European countries.

The common theme is the widening of the gap separating the history of western Europe from the history of other developed cultural and political entities in Asia, the Middle East or, indeed, in the European past. The consciousness of such distinctiveness has itself been, of course, one of the main impulses fostering the study of history and of the social sciences during the past 200 years or so. It is an immense topic. Within it, however, there are sub-topics possessing a degree of independence. One of these is particularly appropriate when the object of study is English history. The development of a capacity to raise substantially and progressively the output of material goods, both in aggregate and per head, has been a profoundly important distinguishing mark of west European history. Until late in the nineteenth century England was the setting for many of the most significant developments in this regard. The essays in this book are all linked to this issue, some directly and explicitly, others at one remove.

---

1 Some of the essays have been published elsewhere. Details are given on pp. ix–x.

That the cumulative outcome of massive economic change has been to alter both the habits of life and the preoccupations of people throughout the world is not in dispute. The land and its rhythms impinge relatively little on the lives of most people in developed countries. Even the tiny minority who continue to make a living from farming do so in circumstances that divorce them from their predecessors almost as deeply as those who live in towns and work in offices or factories are separated from their agrarian past. Constraints which once limited and moulded patterns of life and activity have been greatly relaxed. A man may hold a conversation with a friend in Australia as easily as he can chat with his neighbour in the local pub. All constraints imposed by the limitations of transport and communication systems have been radically reduced. People enjoy the casual command of energy on a scale that a Pharaoh might have envied. Poverty may not have been eliminated but its continued presence does not reflect the ineluctable necessities of life in an economy in which output per head was bound to be low and to fluctuate alarmingly from one year to the next, but the characteristics of particular social, economic and political systems. The early decades of life are no longer overshadowed by the likelihood of death from infectious disease. More than nine-tenths of all children born in industrialized countries today can expect to pass their fiftieth birthday, where two centuries ago the comparable figure would have been less than four-tenths.

To assert that material progress has been immense is not to claim that the modern world is 'better' than the traditional world. The cost of the changes has been and remains heavy. The old world, whatever its defects, was durable: the new may yet prove unstable to the point of self-destruction. Uncertainty about the final upshot of the changes, however, enhances the interest attaching to their genesis, for inasmuch as understanding a phenomenon depends upon a knowledge of its development, the history of the changes is not only fascinating in itself but essential to any assessment of the present condition of society.[2]

Defining the industrial revolution

The label conventionally attached to these congeries of changes is that of the industrial revolution. The term is so deeply embedded in both popular and academic usage that it may be too much to hope that it will be superseded. Both adjective and noun, however, represent unfortunate choices, especially when placed in conjunction. To lay exclusive emphasis upon industrial change, thereby by implication relegating changes in agriculture, transport and commerce to minor importance, is unfortunate. Equally, to describe the change as revolutionary is apt to be misleading since it suggests a compressed time-scale and may easily be assumed to imply a period of rapid change flanked on either side by relatively static situations.

2 See, for example, Anderson, 'The relevance of family history'.

Moreover, the fact that the noun is singular compounds the problem since the phenomenon is then likely to be regarded as unitary with all its component elements moving in close sympathy with one another.[3]

Some of the disadvantages of current usage are explored in more detail elsewhere in this book. A brief, general, dogmatic survey of the matter, however, may not be out of place here.

First, deciding the chronology of the industrial revolution, indeed being able to determine whether or not it may be said to have occurred, must obviously depend upon how it is defined. A definition which was linked to attaining a particular level of investment expressed as a percentage of national income, for example, might lead to very different conclusions from one couched in terms of changes in the occupational structure of the population. I shall take real income per head as the central defining characteristic, and regard an industrial revolution as having taken place where real incomes can be shown to have increased substantially and progressively over many decades to levels above those found in pre-industrial economies. Such a definition falls well short of the degree of precision needed at some stage in a fuller analysis, but it is perhaps the definition which commands the widest assent and it places emphasis on the element which deserves to be given the greatest weight.

Using this criterion, a paradoxical feature of conventional treatments of the industrial revolution is at once evident. In the classic chronology of the industrial revolution the crucial early phase is placed in the half-century after about 1780 because during this period there were major advances in production technology in the cotton and iron industries, a very marked acceleration in their rate of growth, a first flush of factory building and, especially at the end of the period, striking improvements in methods of transport. Yet there is more reason to suppose that real incomes per head for the mass of the population were at best at a standstill between, say, 1770 and 1820 than in any other comparable period from the early decades of the seventeenth century onwards. The measurement of real wages is fraught with conceptual problems, technical difficulties and deficiencies in the empirical evidence, but there is a fair measure of agreement about the absence of convincing evidence for improvement during this half-century in contrast with the first half of the eighteenth or the second half of the nineteenth century.[4]

3 There is, of course, an enormous literature devoted to these issues and cognate topics. Much of it was recently surveyed in Cannadine, 'The present and the past in the English industrial revolution'.

4 Phelps Brown and Hopkins have constructed the real wage series with by far the greatest chronological sweep. Using their data, it is possible to construct a 25-year moving average of real wage trends, thus largely eliminating the influence of short-term 'shocks'. This index suggests a slight fall in real wages between 1751 and 1821 (the index falls from 672 to 596), though by 1821 the trend is upwards; at its nadir in 1806 the index stands at 510. Wrigley and Schofield, *Population history of England*, appendix 9, pp. 638–44. Von Tunzelmann's analysis of all available price and wage series suggests that between 1770 and 1820 the trend in real

The margins of error inherent in any attempt to measure real wages over a long period of time, compounded by inadequate data, leave it uncertain how far their apparent trends are to be trusted. But, such as they are, they suggest that a very different construction can be put upon the course of events from that which was once conventional. For example, the process of change which was ultimately labelled the industrial revolution might be depicted as beginning in the early or mid-seventeenth century rather than 150 years later. On this view, the secular rise in real incomes became established in the first century after its inception, was halted for a while towards the end of the eighteenth century, and then resumed in Victorian times. Alternatively, events down to the early decades of the nineteenth century might be regarded as pre-industrial in character on the ground that the pre-industrial economy was characterized not so much by a static uniformity subject only to random shocks as by long, rolling adjustments round an average condition which led to substantial periods both of improving and deteriorating circumstances but with little or no secular change.[5] On this view, neither the many decades of rising incomes before the mid-eighteenth century nor the subsequent reversal constitute evidence of something novel at work. What *is* unusual is that the deterioration should have been relatively brief and mild, and should have been followed by a much more vigorous and sustained rising trend in real incomes. Both interpretations suggest that a longer perspective is desirable in trying to assess what the industrial revolution comprised than has been customary.

Production and population

At this point it is well to stress that the criterion chosen to identify an industrial revolution is essentially a ratio measure. Ignoring the complications associated with changes in the value of money, it is obtained by dividing the flow of income to the population as a whole, or to some group within it, by the number of people in the whole population or group. As a ratio is affected both by movements in the numerator and the denominator, it follows that as much attention may need to be given to population trends as to trends in aggregate income. It is income per head rather than total

---

wages was essentially flat, apart from a sharp dip about 1800. Between 1750 and 1770 the available data are consonant either with a slight fall or a rather more substantial rise in real wages, though on balance the likelihood is of little change. Lindert and Williamson's analysis also suggests little or no change, either in overall real wages or in the wages of major employment categories, over the period 1750–1820; Von Tunzelmann, 'Trends in real wages', figure 1, p. 38 and accompanying text; Lindert and Williamson, 'English workers' living standards', figure 1, p. 12.

5 The view that there were long-term 'oscillations' in the welfare of the labouring classes, rather than a relatively invariant equilibrium level in living standards, was an important and original feature in Malthus's writings from the beginning. He had in mind a concept which bears some resemblance to the notion of an 'immobile history' suggested by Le Roy Ladurie. Malthus, *Essay on population* (1798), pp. 29–34. Le Roy Ladurie, 'L'histoire immobile'.

income that must be estimated, and unravelling any feedback between income changes and population growth rates must be of great importance. To take a limiting case, if it were always the case that a given increase or decrease in the flow of income were matched by an equal proportionate change in the population, incomes per head would never rise or fall. This possibility may seem far-fetched today but it was regarded as a natural assumption by the classical economists. It is one reason why the history of population trends and the attainment of an improved understanding of the relationship between economic and demographic changes are necessarily an important part of the study of the industrial revolution.

It is an obvious corollary of using a real income criterion that rates of growth in aggregate measures of national income or national product may prove deceptive unless taken in conjunction with population growth rates. Divergent views about the period from about 1760 to about 1830 are in part due to the fact that English population growth rates accelerated very sharply over the period to a peak not matched in any earlier or later period.[6] The economy also grew increasingly fast at the time but the interpretation of this spurt of growth will be heavily affected by the degree to which contemporary population changes are taken into account. Of course, if it were invariably true, as Adam Smith, Malthus and Ricardo tended to assume, that an increase in wages, however caused, could be relied upon to provoke demographic changes sufficiently pronounced to restore the previously prevailing equilibrium wage level, an industrial revolution defined by a real income criterion would be *ex hypothesi* virtually impossible, at least for the great bulk of the population dependent upon wages for a livelihood.[7] Only if the economy began to grow at a rate beyond the capacity of human multiplication to match could the difficulty be overcome on such an assumption.

In studying the industrial revolution over the much more extended time-scale which now seems appropriate, the interplay between economic and demographic changes takes on an especial interest. For example, real wages appear to have risen substantially between about 1640 and 1740, even though aggregate economic growth was at a modest pace, because still more modest population growth allowed the ratio which defines real incomes per head to move favourably. In other words, it seems doubtful whether the

---

6 In the quarter-century 1805–30 the annual rate of growth of the population of England was 1.46 per cent. In the preceding quarter-century 1780–1805 it was 1.07 per cent; in the succeeding quarter-century the comparable figure was very similar, 1.17 per cent. Thereafter, until the secular fall in fertility began to cause the birth rate to fall rapidly, the rate of growth did not greatly change. Progressing out from the period of peak growth in the opposite direction, the annual growth rate falls away further: in 1755–80 it was 0.65 per cent; in 1730–55, 0.48 per cent. Wrigley and Schofield, *Population history of England*, table A3.3, pp. 531–5.

7 This characterization of the attitude of the three economists is too starkly phrased to do justice to their positions. Malthus in particular ultimately developed a complex and subtle range of arguments in this connection. See Wrigley, 'Introduction', *Works of Malthus*.

assumption, often made by the classical economists, that population change is dependent on changes in the demand for labour expressed through changes in the level of wages, can be sustained in relation to the two centuries before their era.

Ironically, it was Malthus, though his name is often associated with a rather simplistic view of the dependence of population movements upon prior economic change, who first identified aspects of the behaviour of European populations which have attracted increasing attention in recent years because they suggest social mechanisms whereby the level of real income may have varied considerably in the long run as well as the short.

If a population is to respond to economic stimuli, there must be changes in fertility, or mortality, or both.[8] For example, a reduction in real wages, if there is to be a sympathetic change in labour supply, must increase the death rate, reduce the birth rate or provoke both changes. If one of the two rates is largely inflexible, the pressure for change must be accommodated by alterations in the other. So far as fertility in the past is concerned, if there were to be substantial changes in level in any period before the widespread adoption of family limitation within marriage, they could only be secured by changes in nuptiality; by raising or lowering age at marriage, or by altering the proportion of women who never married.[9] Therefore, only if a population included many couples who were willing to 'look before and after' when contemplating marriage, and to act accordingly, could fertility change be expected to play a major role in modifying population growth rates.[10] Failing this, mortality change had to be the active agent in linking economic signals and demographic responses.

As a young man, Malthus was inclined to be sceptical about the willingness of most prospective brides and grooms to exercise the degree of prudence needed to produce significant reductions in fertility in the face of deteriorating economic circumstances. After the publication of the first *Essay*, he took steps to acquaint himself with such information on the subject as was available in published form and travelled extensively with the same object in view.

---

8 To simplify matters I have not attempted to include migration in the discussion of this topic. In reality, it was often of profound importance in pre-industrial times, especially in relation to small populations and restricted territories.

9 Once again, this is an over-simplification. The level of fertility in a population was much affected by a variety of social, economic and cultural influences, and especially by the duration and intensity of breast-feeding. 'Natural' fertility was to be found in populations in which the absolute level of marital fertility might differ almost by a factor of two. ('Natural' fertility is said to exist wherever the fertility characteristics of couples appear to be unaffected by the number of children already born to them.) Changes in breast-feeding practices might therefore result in substantial alterations in marital fertility. In a fuller discussion, this issue, as also fluctuations in illegitimate fertility, would merit attention.

10 Malthus made reference on several occasions to the immense value to society of those who would 'look before and after'. Where this mentality prevailed there was a fair prospect of raising the standards of welfare among the labouring classes substantially and permanently. Without it, poverty would remain unrelieved. *Works of Malthus*, ed. Wrigley and Souden, v, pp. 183–4.

As a result, he came to appreciate that there were striking differences between nuptiality patterns in western Europe and those to be found elsewhere in the world. The preventive check in western Europe was doing much of the work of maintaining a balance between numbers and their means of support which was elsewhere brought about chiefly by the operation of the positive check.[11]

Malthus's original insight into this range of issues has been much refined and extended in recent years. As a result, any analysis of the divergence of western Europe from the functional and developmental patterns found elsewhere must pay heed to the exceptional character of its demographic and social structural history. Nor is it satisfactory to treat population change as a dependent phenomenon which can be read off from a knowledge of prior economic circumstances. The pioneering work of Hajnal and Laslett has engendered a large volume of research which has identified a new range of commanding heights, so to speak, from which to survey the landscape of social, economic and demographic change during the early modern period.[12]

In relation to the problem of redefining the industrial revolution and the use of real income as the prime criterion in this connection, the crucial considerations relating to west European nuptiality are perhaps the following. First, marriage for women outside western Europe was almost universally a life-cycle stage in a physiological as well as a social sense in that it occurred at or close to menarche. Few women failed to marry and those who married moved into their new state because of physical maturation. In western Europe, in contrast, a significant proportion of each rising generation of women never married, and those who did so were on average a decade beyond menarche. Both the proportions marrying and age at marriage varied substantially. In England, for example, the change in these two aspects of nuptiality was sufficient to increase total marital fertility by about 36 per cent between the late seventeenth and the early nineteenth centuries.[13] Both the restrained scale of nuptiality and its variability are important. *Ceteris paribus*, the former will tend to result in a lower equilibrium population size and higher real incomes than would prevail with early marriage and its accompanying higher fertility, while the latter meant that any response to changing economic circumstances could be mediated via fertility as well as

11 Wrigley, 'Introduction', *Works of Malthus*, i, pp. *20–9*.

12 Hajnal, 'European marriage patterns'; Laslett and Wall (eds), *Household and family in past time*; Wrigley and Schofield, *Population history of England*. Useful summaries of the relevant literature and of the controversies it has provoked may be found in Anderson, *History of the western family*; Smith, 'Fertility, economy and household formation'; Wrigley, 'The means to marry'.

13 This percentage change is derived from the assumption that age at marriage fell from 26.5 to 23.5 years and that the proportion of women never marrying fell from 15 to 7 per cent. Wrigley and Schofield, *Population history of England*, table 7.29, p. 267. Recently, two important articles have been published, further refining the examination of changes in nuptiality and fertility in early modern England: Weir, 'Rather never than late'; Schofield, 'English marriage patterns revisited'.

mortality in western Europe.[14] Furthermore, since marriage decisions were affected by a host of individual and social pressures in addition to economic influences, and since population trends were capable of affecting economic indices no less than vice versa, there was an inherent complexity and richness in the relationship between economic, social and demographic variables in a west European setting which may have been absent or less pronounced elsewhere.

When rates of aggregate economic growth rose above, say, 2 per cent per annum, as they did during the early decades of the nineteenth century, improvements in real income were attainable regardless of fertility or mortality trends. Given the prevailing state of public health provision and medical knowledge, and assuming that marriage practices conformed to the west European norm, maximum population growth rates were then sure to fall short of the rate of economic growth, leaving a margin for improving individual real incomes. But in the two preceding centuries the boot was on the other foot. Rates of population growth in excess of 1 per cent per annum, indeed ranging up to 1.5 per cent per annum, could and at times did occur, but the economy might be regarded as exceptionally buoyant and successful if it reached a rate of growth as high as 0.5 per cent per annum.[15] If, therefore, before 1800 there were long periods of steadily rising real income, it is evident that the expectation that higher wages would always induce more rapid population growth and cause reversion to a 'natural' wage level must have been mistaken. If, as the Phelps Brown and Hopkins series suggests, real wages rose by more than a half almost without interruption between the early seventeenth and mid-eighteenth centuries, then attention to the denominator in the ratio calculation which results in an estimate of real wage per head must be as important as that paid to the numerator.[16] The classical economists were somewhat inconsistent in this regard, emphasizing both the extent of economic change and real wage improvement since Tudor times, and yet asserting the strength of the tendency for changes in wage levels to provoke changes in birth and death rates, but particularly

14 The significance of these interrelationships is perhaps most easily grasped when they are set out diagrammatically. See Wrigley, 'The means to marry', figures 1 and 2, pp. 272–3.

15 The measurement of rates of economic growth in earlier periods is greatly handicapped both by conceptual problems and by data deficiencies, and is possible only subject to wide margins of error. By way of illustration, however, we may note that Crafts has recently estimated that the annual rate of growth of national product between 1700 and 1760 was 0.69 per cent and that this rose to 1.97 per cent in the period 1801–31. The latter figure is comfortably in excess of the highest rates of population growth ever recorded in English history (see note 6 above). The former figure, itself probably exceptional for a pre-industrial economy, is below the population growth rates attainable in pre-industrial times. For example, the population of England rose by 31 per cent between 1560 and 1590, an annual growth rate of 0.92 per cent. Crafts, *British economic growth*, table 2.11, p. 45: Wrigley and Schofield, *Population history of England*, table A3.3, pp. 531–5.

16 The 25-year moving average of real wages based on price and wage data taken from Phelps Brown and Hopkins stood at 401 in 1606, the lowest point reached after a long period of decline in Elizabethan England, and had risen to 690 by 1741. Wrigley and Schofield, *Population history of England*, appendix 9, pp. 638–44.

the latter, which would cause wages to fluctuate only fairly close to an equilibrium level.[17]

It is for this reason, among others, that the study of the institution of marriage has assumed such significance in recent years. It is demonstrable that English population growth rates from Tudor to Victorian times were more heavily influenced by fertility than by mortality changes, and also that *marital* fertility was virtually constant throughout.[18] Fluctuations in nuptiality controlled fertility changes, with some assistance from the closely related changes in illegitimate fertility. The social conventions governing marriage therefore assume great significance. Social rules, like that requiring a newly married couple to establish a new household rather than join an existing one, and institutional forms like service in husbandry with its requirement of celibacy, were not only props of a very unusual marriage system, but were of crucial importance to establishing an economy with relatively high real incomes. The remarkably close relationship between secular changes in real wages and long-term fluctuations in the marriage rate shows that in England not merely was marriage late and fertility therefore low but that nuptiality was responsive to economic circumstances. The possibility existed both to create and subsequently preserve a benign balance between production and reproduction or, in other words, to allow the ratio measure which expresses real income per head to stand at a favourable level and to move favourably over time.[19]

The limits to growth

There were sound reasons, however, for supposing that, no matter how earnestly men and women in the pre-industrial past were willing to 'look before and after', an industrial revolution was impossible. The material technology of the day, though demonstrably capable of substantial development, especially under the spur afforded by increasing specialization of function, was not compatible with the substantial and progressive rise in real incomes which constitutes and defines an industrial revolution.[20]

17 See below, pp. 23–5. This 'model' applied, of course, only in long-settled countries. Knowledge of the situation in North America, where birth rates were very high, death rates low, and both real wages and the return on capital simultaneously excellent by European standards, was one of the most powerful influences on Malthus both in his demographic and economic writings. In this discussion, moreover, I have used real wage and real income as interchangeable terms. This is not the case, of course, but for simplicity's sake in this context, I have assumed that they moved in parallel.

18 On the relative importance of changes in fertility and mortality in influencing the intrinsic growth rate, see Wrigley and Schofield, *Population history of England*, pp. 265–9: on the constancy of marital fertility, Wrigley and Schofield 'English population history from family reconstitution', pp. 168–75.

19 For evidence of the close relationship between changes in real wages and changes in nuptiality, see Wrigley and Schofield, *Population history of England*, pp. 421–30, and the recent review of the topic in Goldstone, 'The demographic revolution in England'.

20 See below, pp. 23–6.

Contemporaries were aware of the limitations to growth, and indeed described and analysed them most persuasively. For an industrial revolution to occur, there had to be not just a quantum leap in the productive capacity of the material technology of the day, but what might be termed a mutation in the economic landscape. However greatly technical and organizational change might improve output per head, in the circumstances governing the operation of a pre-industrial economy, the capacity of the economy to benefit from the change was severely limited by the apparently inescapable fact that the raw materials which formed the input into the productive process were almost all organic in nature, and thus restricted in quantity by the productivity of the soil. The annual flow of vegetable and animal products from the soil set a ceiling to the productive potential of the economy, a ceiling which it appeared impossible to raise indefinitely. Even inasmuch as the ceiling could be inched upward, it seemed unavoidable that progress would be achieved only at the price of greater and greater effort for each unit increase in ouput achieved. Declining marginal returns on the land meant the extinction of any hope of the type of growth which in hindsight was to be christened an industrial revolution.

The mutation in the economic landscape which opened out a fundamentally different range of opportunities and dangers to mankind involved the substitution of inorganic for organic inputs in most branches of industrial production; the associated revolution in the energy sources available for use in productive processes when a way was discovered of converting the energy stored in coal into useful work; and the conversion of farming from an industry engaged in coaxing the maximum net output from ecologically self-sufficient units into one in which mineral-derived inputs from outside the farm were passed through the local ecological system in such quantity as to transform not only the productivity but also the character of farming. In view of the momentous consequence of the transition which occurred, it is important to try to clarify the nature of the continuities and discontinuities between the before and the after.

The English economy of the seventeenth and eighteenth centuries fore-shadowed what came later not only in that real incomes rose quite significantly, but in other ways which deserve equal or greater attention. Real incomes might have been high solely because food was cheap. It dominated the average budget sufficiently to ensure that cheap food must have this effect. But food might be very cheap, and real incomes therefore high, while the economy was yet 'unsophisticated', as in colonial North America. Good land was to be had there at little more than the cost of travelling to the plot in question, and what the classical economists were apt to call 'corn wages' were in consequence at an astronomical level by English standards. Yet in other respects the colonies were scarcely advanced: standards of housing and clothing did not match the high level of real incomes; travel was often slow, difficult and expensive; many goods and services were effectively inaccessible to a large proportion of the population; and the mechanism of trade and exchange operated under severe handicaps.

In England, on the other hand, though corn wages were much lower, the economy grew far more complex and 'sophisticated' between, say, 1600 and 1800. In 1600 there was little to distinguish the structure of the English economy from the structure of other countries in western Europe. Two centuries later, the contrasts were remarkable and instructive. Indeed, it would not be perverse to argue that, whereas in the nineteenth century, the century of the classical industrial revolution, the attempts by other European countries to overhaul England's early lead were so successful that by the end of the century any remaining advantage was on the point of vanishing, in the two preceding centuries the gap between England and other west European states steadily widened. Two aspects of structural change in the English economy deserve particular emphasis: the great strides in agricultural productivity and the remarkable surge in urban growth. The distinctiveness of English experience in these two respects stands out from a comparison of England and France between 1600 and 1800. It is reasonable to suppose that output per head of those engaged in agriculture doubled in England over this period while in France any rise was very much more modest, perhaps about 20 per cent. Meanwhile, the urban population of England increased so rapidly that it comprised 28 per cent of the total population in 1800 where in 1600 it had amounted to no more than 8 per cent: in France, in contrast the comparable figures were 9 and 11 per cent.[21]

Any assessment of economic change in England in the centuries immediately preceding the industrial revolution must pay heed to comparative structural change in England and on the continent. By the late eighteenth century the proportion of the English labour force which was making a living outside agriculture had risen to levels which had no parallel in other European countries with the exception of the Dutch Republic. Only a minority of adult males worked on the land, a strikingly unusual circumstance in a pre-industrial country which remained virtually self-sufficient in all basic foodstuffs.[22] Those not working in agriculture, however, were chiefly engaged in supplying goods and services for local, rather than national or international, markets. Indeed, as late as 1831 total employment in either 'proto-industrial' workshops or factories, whose products reached much wider markets, comprised no more than 10 per cent of the adult male labour force.[23] The cumulative scale of growth and structural change since 1600 was very considerable, but it all fell within the canons of analysis of economic change set out by Adam Smith. Between the late sixteenth and early nineteenth centuries a transformation in the English economy had taken place, but it had entailed only the types of change familiar to the classical economists. Indeed their writings, which in the case

21 For the purposes of these calculations urban population is defined as comprising all those living in towns containing 5000 or more inhabitants. For the estimates themselves, see below, table 7.4, p. 170 and table 7.9, p. 184.

22 See below, table 7.4, p. 170.

23 Wrigley, 'Men on the land', p. 297.

of Adam Smith and Malthus included a large historical component, might be regarded as holding up a mirror to their contemporaries in which they could see reflected the outcome of progressive and sequential change over several generations, and which would make intelligible the extent of the contrast between late Georgian England and their 'feudal' past, or indeed the situation still prevailing elsewhere in the world.

It was also the intent of the classical economists, however, to instruct their contemporaries about the limits to growth, about the nature of the pressures which must result in the 'stationary state'. Viewing events from a vantage point several generations later, it falls to us to show how, and if possible why, their expectations were falsified.

The nature of the breakthrough

The most promising line to pursue in this regard may be summarized in the following terms. It was not a fortuitous accident that the industrial revolution should have occurred in England. The kinds of change briefly listed above constituted a necessary condition for its occurrence, and these changes had progressed further in England than elsewhere in western Europe, with the possible exception of the Dutch Republic. As the Dutch example suggests, however, such changes were not a sufficient condition for what came later. Nor was the shaded pessimism of the classical economists about growth, and especially about the prospects for the standard of living among the labouring masses, misplaced in the economic context familiar to them. The developments that won freedom from the constraints of what might be termed a modernized organic system and transformed it into an industrial inorganic system were unexpected by contemporaries. They depended, in part at least, upon 'external' circumstances, such as the local accessibility of coal, its physical and chemical properties and the upshot of trial-and-error experiment with its use. A similar constellation of prior circumstances in a country with little coal or with a different balance of local resource endowment, such as The Netherlands, where peat proved incapable of playing the role of coal, might very well have failed to result in the changes which pushed England into uncharted territory.[24]

A measure of the extent of the contrast between the modernized organic and the industrial inorganic systems may be found by comparing Adam Smith's discussion of the circumstances governing the progress of national wealth in the *Wealth of nations* with Jevons's comparable disquisition in *The coal question*. Concern about the adequacy of comparative mineral endowment replaces worry about the productivity of agriculture. Other elements in the received wisdom concerning the nature of the industrial revolution may also need scrutiny and revision. For example, the presumption that it was a unitary and progressive phenomenon across a broad band of time has fostered

24 De Zeeuw, 'Peat and the Dutch Golden Age'.

a tendency to suppose that many aspects of society and economy changed in sympathy with the key economic change and with a chronology which reflects the conventional chronology of the industrial revolution. Thus urbanization and industrialization are linked; the demographic transition is associated with the industrial revolution; major changes in family organization are presumed to have occurred under the stresses of rapid economic change; the move towards universal literacy is seen as a function of the rising wealth and new requirements of an industrialized world; and so on.

That economic, demographic and social conditions are intimately linked and that change in any one variable may be expected to be reflected elsewhere in the interlocking system of relationships is a truism. But that the changes listed, and other cognate changes, occurred in the wake, so to speak, of the industrial revolution is a misleading over-simplification, as is the view that the industrial revolution provoked change elsewhere in the system rather than vice versa. For example, the predominance of the small, conjugal family household antedates the industrial revolution by many centuries (indeed it antedates both the modernized organic and industrial inorganic systems to use the jargon introduced earlier). It is uncertain how long a 'modern' family system may have existed in England, but it is clear that it was of great antiquity, at least outside the ranks of the elite.[25] The prior existence of a society composed of small conjugal families – where marriage came late, implied economic independence, involved neolocal residence and was associated with high levels of mobility – was strongly congenial to relatively high real incomes, adaptability and growth. Furthermore, communal provision of help through a system of parochial taxation, such as existed in England from 1598, by providing protection for individuals and families facing old age, hardship and illness, was a further important predisposing factor in encouraging economic growth and efficiency, since it freed individuals to participate in a market economy where a rationality based on immediate self-interest dominated in the manner immortalized in the *Wealth of nations*. In this case, if there is a causal link between family organization and economic development, chronology alone demands that it should run from the former to the latter, not in the opposite direction as was once thought probable.

The other presumptions previously listed are also frail. Literacy was spreading more and more widely through the population for 200 years before the conventional date of the industrial revolution. In the male population

---

25 When Hajnal set the stage for the subsequent surge of work on the European marriage pattern, he was inclined to place its origin in the seventeenth century for the general population and a century earlier for elite groups. Hajnal, 'European marriage patterns', p. 134. Smith has expressed doubt that any major differences between the medieval and early modern marriage patterns can be demonstrated, with a balance of probability that there was little change; while Macfarlane is inclined to see its origins in the customs of Germanic peoples. Smith, 'Origins of the "European marriage pattern" ' and 'La nuptialité en Angleterre'; Macfarlane, *Marriage and love in England*, pp. 328–31.

outside the ranks of the labourers literacy was widespread and in many groups wellnigh universal by 1800.[26] Urbanization also had already progressed a long way by that date.[27] Conversely, the main features of the traditional demographic system appear to have remained largely unchanged until rather late in the day. Levels of fertility, nuptiality and mortality remained within or very close to the 'pre-industrial' range until about 1870, and the nature of the relationships between the main components of demographic behaviour appears to have retained its old pattern until much the same date.[28]

Productivity change and employment structure

If the defining characteristic of the industrial revolution is taken to be a decisive change in real income per head, it goes without saying that one way of tracking the emergence and establishment of the change is to identify industries within which major rises in output per worker took place, and more particularly those where employment was simultaneously expanding. Assuming that mobility of labour between industries was high, the wage rates of those employed in such industries may have reflected only marginally their enhanced capacity to produce; and, equally, those employed in industries in which no change in output per head occurred might none the less benefit despite their unchanging individual productivity. *Ceteris paribus*, individuals throughout the economy in question should derive benefit from increased average individual productivity, whether brought about by a widely diffused and comparatively moderate rise in productivity, or from more spectacular gains confined to those working in particular sectors.

Approached in this way the changes taking place under the modernized organic system might be characterized in the following terms. Very much the largest industry was agriculture. Output per head in farming rose steadily throughout the seventeenth and eighteenth centuries. The increase was slow but, because such a substantial proportion of the labour force worked in agriculture, the overall effect was significant. While English farming continued to meet home food needs, agricultural labour could none the less be released into other occupations and there add to national output and income even though output per head in most non-agricultural work may not have improved significantly. This was probably true of the building trades and of those in a wide range of craft and service employments which collectively employed a large labour force, such as butchers, alehouse keepers, shoemakers, tailors, blacksmiths and bakers. There were, of course, some important exceptions to the rule that productivity outside agriculture changed

26 For the sixteenth and seventeenth centuries, see Cressy, *Literacy and the social order*, especially chapter 7, 'The dynamics of illiteracy'; for the later period, Schofield, 'Dimensions of illiteracy'.
27 See below, pp. 174–9.
28 Wrigley and Schofield, *Population history of England*, chapters 7 and 10.

little. Framework knitting, coastal shipping, some forms of metal goods manufacture, brewing, and perhaps such industries as glassmaking and papermaking, may have constituted exceptions to the general rule. Further research in the topic might prove most instructive, but it would be surprising if better knowledge did not confirm the view that the direct and indirect effects of enhanced agricultural productivity per head dominated the picture down to 1800 or a little later.[29]

In the course of the development of an industrial inorganic system the picture changed. Productivity in agriculture continued to rise in early nineteenth-century England, but agriculture employed a rapidly declining share of the labour force. In 1800 over 40 per cent of all adult males still worked on the land; by 1850 under 25 per cent.[30] The 'weight' of any change in output per head in agriculture within production as a whole therefore fell away sharply. The bulk of the growth in employment outside agriculture continued to be in occupations in which, in the circumstances of the day, there was probably very little change in individual productivity. For example, even as late as the period 1831–41 it seems clear that at least two-thirds of the total increase in adult male non-agricultural employment were of this character.[31] As already noted, only 10 per cent of the adult male labour force in 1831 worked in industries serving distant markets, whether national or international, in which either the process of specialization of function or the use of inanimate sources of power in the production process, or some combination of the two, could secure the possibility of large and progressive gains in output per head.

Self-evidently, the path to an industrial revolution could only appear if such industries grew steadily in importance. Tracing their growth is tracing the revolution itself. Of the two principal causes of rising productivity in this sector of the economy, one had been familiar to the classical economists. For them the clue to promulgating growth in productivity outside agriculture, and indeed to a large extent within agriculture, lay in the extension of the size of the market, which would enable the parable of the pinmakers to have a wider and wider application. Adam Smith and his successors were clear both as to its nature and limits.[32] But the second type of change facilitating a great surge in individual productivity, that which involved using inorganic materials and placing at the elbows of workers quantities of energy without previous parallel, was a novel development, unanticipated by contemporaries and not an obvious extension of earlier changes.[33] Neither source of

29 It is interesting to note that Crafts's recent estimates of total factor productivity growth suggest that such growth in agriculture was as high as in manufacturing in 1760–1800, and higher than in manufacturing in 1800–30 and 1830–60. He also calculates that in agriculture it was probably higher in 1700–60 than in 1760–1800. Crafts, *British economic growth*, p. 84.

30 Wrigley, 'Men on the land', table 11.12, p. 332.

31 Ibid., p. 298.

32 See below, pp. 22–34.

33 This is not to say, however, that coal was not already of the highest importance to English industry. Between 1775 and 1830, coal output in England grew from 4.5 to 27.9 million tons,

increased output per head was a dominant feature of industries employing male labour on a large scale in the early decades of the nineteenth century. Even though impressive increases in output per head were attainable in industries serving large-scale markets, whether using new energy sources or exploiting the possibilities of specialization within the context of traditional production methods, therefore, the collective impact of the new types of employment on the national level of productivity remained modest. Only when employment in the transformed industries began to absorb a substantial fraction of the labour force, and when experience showed that the gains in productivity were not once-and-for-all but indefinitely extensible, did the basis exist for average real incomes throughout the economy to rise substantially and progressively, a feature of the second rather than the first half of the nineteenth century.

Conclusion

The essays in this volume have appeared at intervals over the past 25 years, during which my research interests have extended over a broad terrain. I hope the foregoing will none the less have shown that a common focus upon a set of fundamental and related issues in economic and demographic history is visible throughout, and justifies publication under the same cover. In most cases the titles of the essays will indicate the way in which each one relates to the topics touched on in this introductory essay, though occasionally a change in terminology may make for an initial obscurity. For example, the term modernization has not been used in this introduction, but the essay in which the relationship of the concept of modernization to the industrial revolution is discussed (chapter 3) covers much the same ground as that involved in the discussion of the differences between a modernized organic and an industrial inorganic system.

The essay dealing with fertility in nineteenth-century France (chapter 11) is perhaps the most peripheral of the collection. However, like the essay dealing with fertility strategy (chapter 8), though in a very different manner, it illustrates the flexibility and complexity of the west European nuptiality system and the opportunity which the system afforded for maintaining homeostasis by a wide variety of different expedients. In particular, the

---

or from 0.7 to 2.1 tons per head. A large proportion, certainly, was devoted to domestic use (excluding coal exports, colliery consumption and waste, a total of 50 per cent of production was burnt domestically in 1775, 45 per cent in 1830, with the balance consumed by industry) but, by meeting cooking and heating needs cheaply, the extensive use of coal in the home was an important element in keeping down wage costs and allowing large concentrations of population to develop, as Adam Smith emphasized. In considering the significance of coal to industrial growth, therefore, attention should not be confined to industrial usage. In 1830 output per head in England was more than three times as great as in Belgium, the continental country with the largest output of coal, both absolutely and, by a huge margin, per head. Flinn, *British coal industry*, table 1.2, p. 26; table 7.13, pp. 252–3. Wrigley and Schofield, *Population history of England*, table A3.3, pp. 531–5. Mitchell, *European historical statistics*, tables B1 and E2. Smith, *Wealth of nations*, ii, p. 404.

different regional solutions to exerting control over population trends *by* marriage or *within* marriage, or by some combination of the two, is most instructive. Equally so is the evidence of interaction between mortality, fertility and nuptiality movements; and of the apparent breakdown of the regulatory system in the one region of France that was radically affected by the advent of modern industry on a large scale.

In preparing for re-publication those pieces that have already appeared in print, I have attempted occasionally to clarify the original text and I have removed some passages which now strike me as redundant. I have not, however, made any attempt to change either data or arguments to reflect the impact of publications which have appeared between the date of original publication and the present. Nor have I modified footnotes to take account of work subsequently published.

In some instances the essays have provoked discussion or controversy. For example, the validity of the notion of unconscious rationality, used in the essay on fertility strategy (chapter 8), has been questioned.[34] Or again, there has been debate about the conclusion that the data concerning marital fertility yielded by the family reconstitution of Colyton (chapter 10) suggested that family limitation had been practised there in the late seventeenth and early eighteenth centuries.[35] Equally, some ideas or conclusions embodied in the essays have gained a wide currency without causing wide dissent as, for example, the model of the implications of the growth of London for the transformation of early modern English society and economy (chapter 6), or the discussion of the significance of the nature of the supply of raw materials in the industrial revolution (chapter 4).[36] Both kinds of notice might provide the occasion for further comment, and indeed I hope to return to some of them in due course. At this juncture, however, I shall decline the challenge or resist the opportunity, as the case may be, preferring to include nothing that might distract attention from the general themes summarized in this introductory essay.

34 Lesthaeghe, 'On the social control of human reproduction'.
35 See, for example, Crafts and Ireland, 'Family limitation and the English demographic revolution'; or Morrow, 'Family limitation: a reappraisal'.
36 In relation to the first essay, see, for example, de Vries, *The Dutch rural economy*, pp. 113–18; or Rozman, 'Edo's importance'. In relation to the second, Pollard, *Peaceful conquest*, p. vii; or Freeman, 'Introduction', pp. 7–8.

Part I
The Background to the
Industrial Revolution

2

The Classical Economists and the Industrial Revolution

The opening sentences of the *Wealth of nations* contain a definition of a criterion of economic success closely similar to that used by economic historians today. Adam Smith defined what would now be termed real income per head in the following manner:

> The annual labour of every nation is the fund which originally supplies it with all the necessaries and conveniencies of life which it annually consumes, and which consist always either in the immediate produce of that labour, or in what is purchased with that produce from other nations.
>
> According, therefore, as this produce, or what is purchased with it, bears a greater or smaller proportion to the number of those who are to consume it, the nation will be better or worse supplied with all the necessaries and conveniencies for which it has occasion.[1]

The importance of the distinction between increased aggregate output and increased output per head was familiar to Adam Smith, and he soon turned to the parable of the pinmakers so that he could exemplify one of the most effective ways in which output per head could be increased, thus creating the possibility of a gain in real income per head. Moreover, he was in no doubt that substantial gains in output and income per head had been achieved, notably over the two preceding centuries, stretching back to Tudor times.[2]

In spite of his appreciation both of the concept of heightened individual welfare and of the progress apparent when comparing the present with the past, however, Adam Smith did not suppose that England was about to embark upon a period of unprecedented gain in output per head and living

---

1 Smith, *Wealth of nations*, i, p. 1.
2 Smith's account of pin manufacture is to be found in *Wealth of nations*, pp. 8–9. For his views on England's economic progress over the centuries before his time, see *Wealth of nations*, pp. 100, 365–6.

standards. Nor was his view unusual. Neither Malthus nor Ricardo, perhaps the two most powerful and original minds among the classical economists other than Adam Smith, showed any inkling of the onset of a period of revolutionary progress in society's ability to generate wealth and hence to benefit the living standards of the mass of the population. According to the conventional chronology of the industrial revolution, the period during which these three men dominated economic thought, from about 1770 to about 1835, formed the early decades of the industrial revolution.[3] It is therefore striking that there should be no hint in their writings of any appreciation of the extent of the changes that are supposed to have been in train. Indeed, the irony extends further, for not only was an industrial revolution not expected by them, but they advanced reasons for supposing that what we now term an industrial revolution was impossible. The development which to twentieth-century economic historians has appeared as the most significant feature of their age remained invisible to those contemporaries who might be expected to have been most alive to such a change. Its occurrence was by implication rejected by them as a credible possibility.

Such a paradoxical circumstance can scarcely fail to be instructive, not simply as a curiosity of intellectual history but as providing clues to the nature of the industrial revolution as a mental construct of later generations.

The sources of and limits to growth

In order to clarify the contrast between *ex prae facto* and *ex post facto* views of economic growth in the period, it is convenient to begin by examining the views of the classical economists concerning the sources of growth and the necessary limits to such growth. To focus the discussion, I shall assume that the most significant single feature distinguishing the industrial revolution from other types of economic change is that in the course of an industrial revolution real incomes per head rise substantially and progressively to levels greatly different from those found in pre-industrial societies.

3 Deane and Cole, whose work has been so influential over the past quarter-century, tended to eschew the use of the concept of an industrial revolution, but in their chapter on 'The eighteenth-century origins of economic growth', they noted that, whereas the traditional view was that the 1760s saw the decisive spurt in growth rates, more recently Nef, Ashton and Rostow had all favoured the 1780s. They themselves surveyed foreign trade, industrial change and agricultural growth separately, and concluded that there was evidence for a more gradual acceleration than had once been supposed, including a period of significant growth in, roughly, the middle third of the century. Nevertheless, their survey of total and per caput real output trends led them to write: 'At the end of the century, however, there was a crucial change. After 1785, both total output and population were growing much faster than before, but the former now began to draw decisively ahead of the latter. For the first time, per capita output started to increase by nearly nine per cent per decade – or at more than three times the average rate for the rest of the period under review.' Deane and Cole, *British economic growth*, p. 80. See, however, note 46 below.

The real wage problem

If there is to be a rise in individual living standards it is obvious that, in general, this must be associated with increased output per head. Adam Smith described vividly and incisively how output per head might rise. The proximate cause was a greater specialization of function which, however, was conditional upon two other closely linked phenomena, the extension of the market effectively available to the individual producer, and the accumulation of an increased amount both of fixed and of circulating capital.[4] In favourable circumstances truly sensational increases in output per man were then possible. Whereas a single pinmaker serving a restricted market in isolation could turn out a maximum of 20 pins each day, and those of the crudest type, when a group of men collaborated in pin manufacture, each developing a particular skill to a high pitch of excellence, the average number of pins turned out each day by a member of the group might rise to 4800, and the gain in quality and uniformity of product would be very marked.[5] A 240-fold rise in output per head is well worthy of remark in any economic regime. It might seem to afford the basis for great optimism about the future course of real incomes. If such increases are widely attainable an industrial revolution is unquestionably possible. Why then should the possibility not have suggested itself more strongly to the classical economists?

That Adam Smith, Malthus and Ricardo all discounted the possibility of a sustained, progressive rise in real incomes is readily apparent in their writings. Their conviction stemmed from considerations common to all three with only minor variations. The fundamental point at issue received its classic formulation in Malthus's first *Essay on population*. There Malthus advanced two postulates whose joint implication appeared to limit severely what it was reasonable to expect for the standard of living of the mass of the population. The first was 'that food is necessary to the existence of man'; the second 'that the passion between the sexes is necessary, and will remain nearly in its present state'.[6] Since, in Malthus's view, population tended to grow geometrically while the food supply could at best be expected to increase arithmetically, there was necessarily a constant tension between the

---

4 In his description of Adam Smith's work, O'Brien wrote, 'Economics is seen as providing the statesman's guide to economic growth, and in all this division of labour is given a central role as the mechanism of growth . . . Division of labour is dependent on capital to support it and it does not occur in rude society where this capital is lacking. An enormous load is placed on division of labour, and, via ''progress in the arts'' which proceeds with it, and results from it, it covers virtually all forms of technical progress. National income per head is then dependent on division of labour and the quantity of capital – the former (which determines the skill with which labour is applied) depending on the latter which also determines the proportion between productive and unproductive labourers.' O'Brien, *The classical economists*, p. 34.
5 Smith, *Wealth of nations*, p. 9.
6 Malthus, *Essay on population* (1798), p. 11.

two. By some combination of the positive and the preventive checks population was kept in balance with the available subsistence but there was little prospect of engendering a progressive rise in living standards.

Adam Smith had already taken up a similar stance. Although in his chapter 'Of the wages of labour' he made it clear both that 'In Great Britain the wages of labour seem, in the present times, to be evidently more than what is precisely necessary to enable the labourer to bring up a family', and that, 'The real recompense of labour . . . has, during the course of the present century, increased perhaps in a still greater proportion than its money price', he nevertheless moved towards a conclusion which foreshadows Malthus's formulation.[7] 'Every species of animals', he wrote, 'naturally multiplies in proportion to the means of their subsistence, and no species can ever multiply beyond it. But in every civilized society it is only among the inferior ranks of people that the scantiness of subsistence can set limits to the further multiplication of the human species; and it can do so in no other way than by destroying a great part of the children which their fruitful marriages produce.'[8] Later in the same chapter he suggested that the condition of the labouring poor was likely to be at its best when society was 'in the progressive state . . . advancing to the further acquisition, rather than when it has acquired its full complement of riches . . . It is hard in the stationary, and miserable in the declining state.'[9]

Ricardo did not dissent from the views of Smith and Malthus. On this issue indeed he was happy to pay tribute to Malthus's authority. He expressed himself in his usual trenchant style. 'The natural price of labour is that price which is necessary to enable the labourers, one with another to subsist and to perpetuate their race, without either increase or diminution.' This price depended on the movements in price of the 'food, necessaries, and conveniences . . . essential to him [the labourer] from habit', and the price of labour would follow any movement in these prices.[10] Ricardo distinguished between the market price for labour, which under the influence of comparatively short-term pressures might differ from its natural price,

---

7 Smith, *Wealth of nations*, i, pp. 82, 87.
8 Ibid., p. 89.
9 Ibid., pp. 90–1. It may be noted that Smith repeated the views quoted in this paragraph in very similar terms elsewhere in his book. He opened that part of the chapter on rent entitled, 'Of the produce of land which always affords rent', with the sentence, 'As men, like all other animals, naturally multiply in proportion to the means of their subsistence, food is always, more or less, in demand.' Much later in the same chapter he paraphrased his earlier remarks about the progressive and declining state. 'The wages of the labourer . . . are never so high as when the demand for labour is continually rising, or when the quantity employed is every year increasing considerably. When this real wealth of the society becomes stationary, his wages are soon reduced to what is barely enough to enable him to bring up a family, or to continue the race of labourers. When the society declines, they fall even below this.' Smith, *Wealth of nations*, i, pp. 163, 277.
10 Ricardo, *Principles*, p. 93.

and the natural price itself towards which the market price would always gravitate.[11]

It is when the market price of labour exceeds its natural price, that the condition of the labourer is flourishing and happy, that he has it in his power to command a greater proportion of the necessaries and enjoyments of life, and therefore to rear a healthy and numerous family. When, however, by the encouragement which high wages give to the increase of population, the number of labourers is increased, wages again fall to their natural price, and indeed from a reaction sometimes fall below it.[12]

Like Adam Smith, Ricardo was prepared to concede that for long periods wages might rise. Where Smith had written of the progressive state, he wrote of 'an improving society' where 'for an indefinite period' the market price might remain above the natural rate if 'the increase of capital be gradual and constant' and therefore the demand for labour gave 'a continued stimulus to an increase of people'.[13] Ricardo also emphasized that the natural price of labour was not determined by the biological minimum necessary to support life but was strongly influenced by convention.[14] Nevertheless, Ricardo was a pessimist about the prospects for the remuneration of the labourer in real terms. 'It appears, then, that the same cause which raises rent, namely, the increasing difficulty of providing an additional quantity of food with the same proportional quantity of labour, will also raise wages; and therefore if money be of an unvarying value, both rent and wages will have a tendency to rise with the progress of wealth and population.' However, while the landlord's rent will increase both in money terms and in real value, 'The fate of the labourer will be less happy; he will receive more money wages, it is true, but his corn wages will be reduced [i.e. his real wages will fall]; and not only his command of corn but his general condition will be deteriorated, by his finding it more difficult to maintain the market rate of wages above their natural rate.'[15]

The views of the classical economists on the crucial question of the secular prospects for real wages among the mass of the population may be re-expressed as follows. The scale of any growth of population is determined by the extent of the rise in the demand for labour. In this sense population movements are almost entirely conditioned by prior economic changes. Rapid economic growth may cause the demand for labour to outstrip the

---

11 'The market price of labour is the price really paid for it, from the natural operation of the proportion of the supply to the demand; labour is dear when it is scarce, and cheap when it is plentiful. However much the market price of labour may deviate from its natural price, it has, like commodities, a tendency to conform to it'. Ricardo, *Principles*, p. 94.
12 Ibid., p. 94.
13 Ibid., pp. 94–5.
14 See note 58 below.
15 Ricardo, *Principles*, p. 102.

supply not only for brief periods but in the medium term too. Nevertheless, in the long term population growth may confidently be expected to match, or more than match, any growth in the demand for labour, so that the real incomes of the labouring masses will not rise; or, to use the modern idiom, an industrial revolution was inconceivable.

The land problem and raw material supply

This conviction in turn stemmed from other aspects of economic reality as it was perceived by the classical economists. In particular, it is essential to see the land and agricultural production through their eyes, if the strength of their conviction is to be appreciated. The underlying issue emerges immediately from the way in which Malthus framed his postulates. It would not have mattered that population displayed a tendency to rise geometrically unless checked, provided that it was reasonable to suppose that economic growth could also be induced to increase geometrically and at a higher rate. To the classical economists this was wishful thinking, an abnegation of the sense of responsibility which any thinker of probity should preserve. Malthus expressed the point forcefully when berating Godwin for assuming that an indefinite prolongation of human life was possible as the human mind slowly acquired a greater control over the human body. He deplored Godwin's assertion that this was sound philosophical conjecture, implying that Godwin's speculations were similar to the assertions of the 'Prophet Mr Brothers', and adding, 'I expect that great discoveries are yet to take place in all the branches of human science, particularly in physics; but the moment we leave past experience as the foundation of our conjectures concerning the future; and still more, if our conjectures absolutely contradict past experience, we are thrown upon a wide field of uncertainty and any one supposition is then just as good as another.'[16]

   Malthus had phrased the problem in terms of food supply, arguing that an arithmetic rate of increase was the best that could be hoped for. Later, as his interest in economic questions grew, he offered an analysis of the nature of rent which clarified further the matters at issue. The best land is taken into cultivation first and may initially permit large profits on investment and, by encouraging a rapid accumulation of capital and consequent demand for labour, may for a time also allow wages to be high. But land of less high quality must inevitably be put under the plough, the level of profits and of real wages must both decline and, except in so far as technological change may temporarily arrest the trend, the returns to any additional unit input of capital or labour must fall. At some point it can no longer repay the owner of capital to bring still more marginal acres into cultivation or, alternatively, to invest further capital in raising the output of land already in cultivation.

16 Malthus, *Essay on population* (1798), p. 232.

In the terminology of today, declining marginal returns cannot ultimately be avoided.[17]
Ricardo stood very close to Malthus on this issue:

The natural tendency of profits then is to fall; for, in the progress of society and wealth, the additional quantity of food required is obtained by the sacrifice of more and more labour. This tendency, this gravitation as it were of profits, is happily checked at repeated intervals by the improvements in machinery, connected with the production of necessaries, as well as by discoveries in the science of agriculture which enable us to relinquish a portion of labour before required, and therefore to lower the price of the prime necessary of the labourer.[18]

But Ricardo had no expectation that the problem could be permanently overcome in this fashion. The long-term trends in wages and profits ensured the ultimate failure of the impulse to further growth as investment yielded less and less attractive possibilities.[19]

Malthus's emphasis on food supply as limiting the scope for population growth and preventing a rise in real wages provided a sufficient reason for discounting the possibility of the type of growth later to be termed an industrial revolution, but, though sufficient, it is too limited a point to do justice to the classical economists' understanding of the problem posed by the constraints upon agricultural production.

Adam Smith's discussion of marginal returns and of rent differed from that of his successors. He described the rent of land as a monopoly price and was inclined to censor landlords as loving 'to reap where they never sowed' (though it is clear that he did not consider that this distinguished them from other men since all would behave similarly if opportunity offered).[20] Nor did he formulate his analysis round the point which Malthus and Ricardo regarded as crucial: that at the margin there would be land in cultivation where the price of the produce would yield an aggregate sum just sufficient to pay the wages of labour needed on the land and to service the capital employed, but leaving nothing which could be taken as rent.[21]

---

17 Malthus explicitly contrasted this tendency in agriculture with its opposite in manufacturing. 'The real price of manufactures, the quantity of labour and capital necessary to produce a given quantity of them, is almost constantly diminishing; while the quantity of labour and capital, necessary to procure the last addition that has been made to the raw produce of a rich and advancing country, is almost constantly increasing.' Malthus, *Nature and progress of rent*, p. 45. In this essay as a whole, he concentrated, of course, on rent but the other, more general, attributes of agricultural progress are clearly set out.
18 Ricardo, *Principles*, p. 120.
19 Ibid., p. 126.
20 Smith, *Wealth of nations*, i, pp. 56, 162.
21 Ricardo took Adam Smith to task over this omission, claiming that he had correctly expounded the principle of rent in connection with the question of whether or not a coal mine will

Nevertheless, he covered the wider issues relating to the productivity of the land in a very interesting and influential way.

Although Adam Smith denied that it was possible to obtain increases in output per head in agriculture comparable to those attainable in manufacture because division of labour could not be pushed as far on the farm as in the workshop, he nevertheless insisted that investment to improve the agricultural capacity of a country must always constitute the most beneficial use of capital. He was led to this conclusion by two considerations. Each quantum of capital employed in agriculture put 'into motion a greater quantity of labour than any equal capital employed in manufactures' and, in addition, because nature laboured alongside man on the farm, magnifying the fruits of his labour (and causing a rent to be yielded in a way which had no parallel in other spheres of production), a given quantum of capital 'in proportion . . . to the quantity of productive labour which it employs . . . adds a much greater value to the annual produce of the land and labour of the country, to the real wealth and revenue of its inhabitants.'[22]

In the chapter following that containing his assertion about the superior productivity of capital employed in agriculture, Adam Smith began with a ringing assertion about the central economic activity of all advanced countries (the chapter was entitled, significantly, 'Of the natural progress of opulence'):

> The great commerce of every civilized society, is that carried on between the inhabitants of the town and those of the country. It consists in the exchange of rude for manufactured produce . . . The country supplies the town with the means of subsistence, and the materials of manufacture. The town repays this supply by sending back a part of the manufactured produce to the inhabitants of the country. The town, in which there neither is nor can be any reproduction of substances, may very properly be said to gain its whole wealth and subsistence from the country.[23]

In the context of a discussion of the writings of the classical economists and the industrial revolution, the third sentence quoted is of especial significance. The country is said not only to supply the town with food but with the raw materials of industry. The productivity of the land, in other words, acts in two related but distinct ways to set bounds both to the size of a population and to the individual prosperity of its members. It was common to Adam Smith, Malthus and Ricardo not only to accept that men would naturally multiply in proportion to the means of their subsistence,

---

yield a rent, and only needed to make use of the same logic to provide an equally correct description of rents on land. Ricardo, *Principles*, pp. 329–30.

22 Smith, *Wealth of nations*, i, p. 385.

23 Ibid., p. 401. It is interesting that in an editorial footnote to his edition of the *Wealth of nations*, Cannan, reflecting the experience of a further century refers to 'The error that agriculture produces substances and manufacture only alters them'. Ibid., p. 401.

but also to suppose that the land was the predominant source of industrial raw materials no less than food. Ricardo, for example, remarked:

> There are few commodities which are not more or less affected in their price by the rise of raw produce, because some raw material from the land enters into the composition of most commodities. Cotton goods, linen, and cloth, will all rise in price with the rise of wheat; but they rise on account of the greater quantity of labour expended on the raw material from which they are made, and not because more was paid by the manufacturer to the labourers whom he employed on those commodities.
>
> In all cases, commodities rise because more labour is expended on them, and not because the labour which is expended on them is at a higher value. Articles of jewellery, of iron, of plate, and of copper, would not rise, because none of the raw produce from the surface of the earth enters into their composition.[24]

In a very similar vein, Malthus wrote, 'And it should always be recollected, that land does not produce one commodity alone, but in addition to that most indispensable of all articles – food, it produces the materials for clothing, lodging and firing.'[25] In the circumstances of the day this meant covering the great bulk of all human material needs.

Growth, in the eyes of the classical economists, was subject to dual constraints arising from the place of the land in the overall output scheme. The supply of land was fixed and, while this might not place an absolute ceiling upon agricultural output, it made rising marginal unit costs of production unavoidable at some point in the growth process. In addition, virtually all the raw materials of industry were either animal or vegetable in origin so that industrial expansion, just like population growth, posed insuperable raw material supply difficulties if carried beyond a certain point, hard to identify no doubt, but part of the rational expectations of well-informed men.

The force of the constraints associated with the nature of agricultural production was sufficient to explain why the gain in productivity per head achievable through specialization of function, though it might cause substantial advance, could never lead to a sustained, progressive rise in real wages. It also lent plausibility to the assumption that returns on capital must have a secular tendency to fall, in due course to a level so low as to discourage further investment, thereby ensuring that growth ceased. Societies might reasonably expect to make progress to a plateau of economic prosperity well in advance of that attained in feudal times, but had no hope of indefinite progress.

---

24 Ricardo, *Principles*, pp. 117–18.
25 Malthus, *Principles*, p. 142.

The problem of capital investment

The falling secular trend in the rate of return on capital was an especially prominent feature of the growth process as seen by the classical economists. Adam Smith developed a complex argument in this connection, intermingling empirical with deductive analysis. He observed that capital investment would always tend first to be devoted principally to agriculture, then to manufacture, and only lastly to foreign trade. 'This order of things is so very natural, that in every society that had any territory, it has always, I believe, been in some degree observed. Some of their lands must have been cultivated before any considerable towns could be established, and some sort of coarse industry of the manufacturing kind must have been carried on in those towns, before they could well think of employing themselves in foreign commerce.'[26] In his analysis this sequence springs from a combination of psychological and economic considerations. Where land is readily available, the wish to be independent of other men makes it irresistible to concentrate on the acquisition of land, but in any case capital invested in agriculture is more secure than that invested in manufacture, which in turn is less exposed to random mischance than capital engaged in trade.[27]

The sequence, however, also reflects Adam Smith's view of the nature of the material base which forms the platform for all economic growth. He frequently emphasized how all other economic activities lived on the margin, so to speak, created by the ability of agriculture to produce food beyond the needs of those engaged in its cultivation:

Whatever increases the fertility of land in producing food, increases not only the value of the lands upon which the improvement is bestowed, but contributes likewise to increase that of many other lands, by creating a new demand for their produce. That abundance of food, of which, in consequence of the improvement of land, many people have the disposal beyond what they themselves can consume, is the great cause of the demand both for the precious metals and the precious stones, as well as for every other conveniency and ornament of dress, lodging, household furniture, and equipage. Food not only constitutes the principal part of the riches of the world, but it is the abundance of food which gives the principal part of their value to many other riches.[28]

So firmly did Adam Smith link the possibility of manufacturing growth to the size of the agricultural surplus that he analysed inland urban growth and the development of inland industry in terms of the scale of local agricultural surpluses:

26 Smith, *Wealth of nations*, i, p. 405.
27 Ibid., pp. 404–5.
28 Ibid., p. 194.

An inland country naturally fertile and easily cultivated, produces a great surplus of provisions beyond what is necessary for maintaining the cultivators, and on account of the expense of land carriage, and the inconveniency of river navigation, it may frequently be difficult to send this surplus abroad. Abundance, therefore, renders provisions cheap, and encourages a great number of workmen to settle in the neighbourhood, who find that their industry can there procure them more of the necessaries and conveniencies of life than in other places. They work up the materials of manufacture which the land produces, and exchange their finished work, or what is the same thing the price of it, for more materials and provisions. They give a new value to the surplus part of the rude produce, by saving the expense of carrying it to the water side, or to some distant market; and they furnish the cultivators with something in exchange for it that is either useful or agreeable to them, upon easier terms than they could have obtained it before . . . The corn, which could with difficulty have been carried abroad in its own shape, is in this manner virtually exported in that of the complete manufacture, and may easily be sent to the remotest corners of the world. In this manner have grown up naturally, and as it were of their own accord, the manufactures of Leeds, Halifax, Sheffield, Birmingham and Wolverhampton. Such manufactures are the offspring of agriculture.[29]

Adam Smith was perfectly explicit both about the central importance of the size of the stock of capital to the growth process and to securing an increase in productivity, and also about the tendency of the return on capital to fall to the point where the incentive to accumulate would cease to suffice to maintain the momentum of growth:

The annual produce of the land and labour of any nation can be increased in its value by no other means, but by increasing either the number of its productive labourers, or the productive powers of those labourers who had before been employed. The number of its productive labourers, it is evident, can never be much increased, but in consequence of an increase of capital, or of the funds destined for maintaining them. The productive powers of the same number of labourers cannot be increased, but in consequence either of some addition and improvement to those machines and instruments which facilitate and abridge labour; or of a more proper division and distribution of employment. In either case an additional capital is almost always required.[30]

The devotion of an increased proportion of the national produce to 'replacing a capital' (that is as circulating capital) raised the proportion of the labour

29 Ibid., pp. 430–1.
30 Ibid., p. 364.

force that was 'productively' employed (for example, as manufacturers). In consequence, a lesser proportion was taken as rent or profit, which was only too likely to be expended in the support of 'unproductive' labour (menial servants). As a result, 'We are more industrious than our forefathers', who 'were idle for want of a sufficient encouragement to industry.'[31] However, 'The increase of stock, which raises wages, tends to lower profit. When the stocks of many rich merchants are turned into the same trade, their mutual competition naturally tends to lower its profit; and when there is a like increase of stock in all the different trades carried on in the same society, the same competition must produce the same effect in them all.'[32]

Adam Smith considered that the prevailing rate of interest gave a reliable clue to the average return on capital.[33] He clearly supposed that the different levels of interest rates in the several countries of Europe were a measure of the degree of their development. Rates were higher in Scotland and France than in England, though lowest of all in Holland where the government could borrow at 2 per cent and individuals of good credit at 3 per cent. In general, wages were highest in countries where capital was abundant and the demand for labour consequently strong, so that the rates of interest and wages were inversely related. Exceptionally, as in the colonies of North America and the West Indies, both might be high but this was due to their 'peculiar circumstances'.[34] Ominously, however, the advantages that accrued to labour in a period of increasingly abundant capital, such as English labourers had enjoyed over the two preceding centuries, were essentially transient benefits:

In a country which had acquired that full complement of riches which the nature of its soil and climate, and its situation with respect to other countries, allowed it to acquire; which could, therefore, advance no further, and which was not going backwards, both the wages of labour and the profits of stock would probably be very low. In a country fully peopled in proportion to what either its territory could maintain or its stock could employ, the competition for employment would necessarily be so great as to reduce the wages of labour to what was barely sufficient to keep up the number of labourers, and, the country being already fully peopled, the number could never be augmented. In a country fully stocked in proportion to all the business it had to transact, as great a quantity of stock would be employed in every particular branch as the nature and extent of the trade would admit. The competition, therefore, would everywhere be as great, and consequently the ordinary profit as low as possible.[35]

31 Ibid., p. 356.
32 Ibid., p. 98.
33 Ibid., p. 99.
34 Ibid., pp. 101–4.
35 Ibid., p. 106.

Whether any country had as yet reached that state might be doubtful, but Adam Smith then noted that, 'The province of Holland seems to be approaching near to this state.'[36]Interest rates were so low that very few could afford to live off capital: almost all men must engage directly in business. Events in Holland were a foretaste of what might be expected to happen more generally.

> When the capital stock of any country is increased to such a degree, that it cannot all be employed in supplying the consumption, and supporting the productive labour of that particular country, the surplus part of it naturally disgorges itself into the carrying trade, and is employed in performing the same offices to other countries. The carrying trade is the natural effect and symptom of great national wealth; but it does not seem to be the natural cause of it. Those statesmen who have been disposed to favour it with particular encouragements, seem to have mistaken the effect and symptom for the cause. Holland, in proportion to the extent of the land and the number of its inhabitants, by far the richest country in Europe, has, accordingly, the greatest share of the carrying trade of Europe.[37]

England's recent success in the same field was evidence of similar forces at work. And the English, like the Dutch, increasingly tended to invest abroad for the sake of higher returns even though governmental and societal attitudes to business were less favourable than at home.[38]

Ricardo reached a similar conclusion to that of Adam Smith by a rather different route. In his analysis, wages were principally determined by the price of the necessaries of life.[39] The problem of diminishing returns in agriculture ensured that, in the long run, wages must rise since the price of food must go up. As Ricardo put it:

> with every increased demand for corn, it may rise so high as to afford more than the general profits to the farmer. If there be plenty of fertile land, the price of corn will again fall to its former standard, after the requisite quantity of capital has been employed in producing it, and profits will be as before; but if there be not plenty of fertile land, if, to produce this additional quantity, more than the usual quantity of capital and labour be required, corn will not fall to its former level. Its natural price will be raised, and the farmer, instead of obtaining permanently larger profits, will find himself obliged to be satisfied with the diminished rate which is the inevitable consequence of the rise of wages, produced by the rise of necessaries.[40]

36 Ibid., p. 108.
37 Ibid., p. 395.
38 Ibid., p. 102.
39 See above, p. 24.
40 Ricardo, *Principles*, p. 120.

Although he noted that the tendency of profits to fall was 'happily checked at repeated intervals' both by improvements in agricultural machinery and in agricultural science, towards the end of his chapter 'On profits' Ricardo summarized his findings in a manner which left no grounds for optimism over the long haul about real wages, profit levels or the kind of sustained economic growth which constitutes an industrial revolution:

> Whilst the land yields abundantly, wages may temporarily rise, and the producers may consume more than their accustomed proportion; but the stimulus which will thus be given to population will speedily reduce the labourers to their usual consumption. But when poor lands are taken into cultivation, or when more capital and labour are expended on the old land, with a less return of produce, the effect must be permanent. A greater proportion of that part of the produce which remains to be divided, after paying rent, between the owners of stock and the labourers, will be apportioned to the latter. Each man may, and probably will, have a less absolute quantity; but as more labourers are employed in proportion to the whole produce retained by the farmer, the value of a greater proportion of the whole produce will be absorbed by wages, and consequently the value of a smaller proportion will be devoted to profits. This will necessarily be rendered permanent by the laws of nature, which have limited the productive powers of the land.'[41]

Declining individual productivity, lowered real wages, depressed profits, all imposed by the laws of nature, are scarcely grounds for entertaining an industrial revolution even as a remote possibility.

Malthus's analysis took him over much the same ground with the same result. Having noted that in the early days of settlement of land of high fertility both wages and profits might be high, he added 'But the accumulation of capital beyond the means of employing it with the same returns on lands of the greatest natural fertility, and the most advantageously situated, must necessarily lower profits; while the rapid increase of population will tend to lower the wages of labour.' In short, 'In the natural and regular progress of a country towards its full complement of capital and population, the rate of profits and the corn wages of labour permanently fall together.'[42]

What was missing from the classical analysis?

The classical economists were, of course, entirely mistaken in their expectations. The growth process has proved to be more nearly exponential

41 Ibid., pp. 125–6.
42 Malthus, *Principles*, pp. 149, 158. It should be emphasized, however, that Malthus was on balance considerably more optimistic than is usually recognized and less committed to an 'iron law' view of the future possibilities for real wages than either Ricardo or Adam Smith. See Wrigley, 'Introduction' in *Works of Malthus*, i, pp. 7–39, especially pp. 23–30.

than asymptotic in nature. The living standards of the great mass of the population have improved so greatly that the necessaries of life are widely taken for granted and the conveniences enjoyed by most families cover a range of material objects and service provision which would have appeared utopian six generations ago. The fact that cultivable land is in fixed supply has neither proved an insuperable barrier to increasing food supply, nor has it prevented unit costs of production falling rather than rising. Prospect in 1800 and retrospect in the 1980s are so different that it is tempting either to disregard the views of the classical economists on these matters and concentrate on other aspects of their writings, or to regard them as singularly wrong-headed in their assessments. To do so would be mistaken. The very fact that expectation and the event differed so markedly is itself an important clue to the nature of the changes which constituted the industrial revolution.[43]

Consider the concept whose extension to more and more aspects of production Adam Smith regarded as the *fons et origo* of gains in output per head: specialization of function. As he illustrated with the example of pin manufacture, the scale of potential gains in output per head could be massive. Where the physical nature of the product or success in reducing transport costs by improvements to the transport system permitted the knitting together of a single market embracing a large population, the productivity gains thus unlocked could lower unit costs substantially while at the same time the product itself was of higher quality. In the particular case of the pinmakers the gains arose chiefly because each individual workers was free to concentrate on a single stage within the sequence of operations involved in producing the finished object.[44] Adam Smith also described, however, the way in which an increased scale of production might encourage investment in machinery to raise still further the quantity each worker produced. Indeed, he suggested that the development might reach the point where a viable niche was created for those who specialized in the invention of machines applicable to production processes which had reached a suitable stage of

43 Samuelson's writings illustrate the danger of exploiting the benefit of hindsight without giving sufficient weight to circumstances in the past. 'The classicists', he wrote, 'earned for our subject Carlyle's title of the dismal science precisely because their expositions erred in overplaying the law of diminishing returns and underplaying the counterforce of technical change. They lived during the industrial revolution, but scarcely looked out from their libraries to notice the remaking of the world.' Samuelson, 'The canonical classical model', p. 1428. Smith, Ricardo and Malthus did not lack involvement in the practical economic and political problems of their age and country. It is closer to the truth to regard their immersion in the affairs of a world still deeply affected by the constraints of all pre-industrial economies as an obstacle to making the leap of imagination, one might almost say of faith, necessary to detect a new world in embryo, rather than as a source of knowledge about the future.

44 The increase in productivity achieved by the dexterity acquired from concentration on a single operation was buttressed by the saving in time resulting from not having to lose time moving between different tasks, and by the flow of inventions of appropriate machinery made by workmen whose attention was focused on a single facet of the production process. *Wealth of nations*, i, pp. 11–14.

advancement.[45] Even so, there are limits to the increase in output per head which can be achieved through greater specialization of function by the kinds of change which he envisaged.

If one supposes, for argument's sake, that the degree of elaboration and refinement in the process of pin manufacture that Adam Smith described is attainable by access to a market consisting of one million people, and that this represents a level of productivity unattainable with a market of only a hundred thousand people, it does not follow that the proportional rise in productivity achieved by transition between the two market sizes would be mirrored if the market were to increase to ten million. Particular elements in the manufacturing process, such as cutting the wire into strips of the appropriate length, or sharpening the point, may be incapable of further subdivision. Eventually, indeed, production circumstances will approach the point where a given percentage rise in demand can only be met by an equal percentage rise in the labour force engaged in pin manufacture, and unit costs of production, *ceteris paribus*, instead of falling, will stabilize.

It is true, of course, that the development and introduction of machinery may further complicate matters by enabling gains in productivity to be achieved in addition to those derived from the division of labour. Both the cutting of wire into strips of equal length and the sharpening of a pin, for example, are processes which lend themselves readily to mechanical operations. In reality, the two sources of increased productivity, division of labour and the introduction of machinery, are likely to take place simultaneously and progressively. Between them they may permit the relationship between increasing market size and falling unit costs of production to prevail over a very wide band of absolute market sizes. Even so, it is difficult to envisage productivity changes springing from the combined effect of these two sources providing the momentum for an industrial revolution, unless a third factor is added, and one about which the classical economists had very little to say, in contrast to their full understanding and exposition of the first two factors.[46]

New sources of energy

The third factor is the employment of inanimate sources of power on a large and increasing scale. Machinery, however ingenious, does not offer unlimited

---

45 Ibid., p. 14.

46 The reluctance of the classical economists to envisage the possibility of large gains in individual productivity finds support in the most recent attempt to quantify productivity changes in the period down to 1830. Crafts's estimates of the rise in national product per head per annum in the successive periods 1700–60, 1760–80, 1780–1801 and 1801–31 are 0.31, 0.01, 0.35 and 0.52. There is no consistent or substantial rise in this key statistic before 1830. Crafts's estimates represent a very substantial downgrading of the widely regarded estimates of Deane and Cole, and they lead in turn to much more modest estimates of increase in total factor productivity than earlier equivalents, especially in the early nineteenth century. Crafts, *British economic growth*, table 2.11, p. 45 and tables 4.2 and 4.3, p. 81.

scope for productivity gains as long as it is driven by human or animal muscle. The issue can be elaborated at great length, but the essential point is simple. Individual productivity may be enhanced by the division of labour, by improved machinery or by increasing the amount of work performed through the expenditure of greater quantities of energy appropriately harnessed. The last of the three vastly magnifies the possibilities latent in the first two. For example, the preparation of the soil for crops requires the use of a considerable amount of energy per acre cultivated because soil is heavy and the sod is resistant to disturbance. The area of land that one man can prepare varies enormously according to whether he works with a spade, a horse and a single plough, or a tractor with a multiple plough. His capacity is principally a function of the energy at his command. A man is puny beside a horse, which is in turn feeble compared to a tractor. Similarly, grain can be converted into flour by querns using the power of men or horses, by harnessing the power of a watermill or windmill to turn millstones, or by roller mills using steam or electrical power. What is true of the basic activities involved in growing and processing food is equally true of the manufacture of other necessaries or of luxuries. The progression from distaff spinning to the spinning wheel and so to the spinning jenny, the water frame, the mule and ring spinning, shows a similar trend towards both increasingly complex machinery and, in order to realize its potential, towards larger and larger energy usage, moving from the human muscle to renewable energy sources in the form of falling water and later to the use of a fossil fuel.

In retrospect, it seems tempting to regard changes of the type just described as 'natural'. To contemporaries like Adam Smith, Malthus or Ricardo this was not the case. The beneficial results of division of function were clear to them, and the connection between capital investment, economic advance and improved machinery equally so, but the crucial significance of the scale and type of energy employed in the productive process was not discussed by them. Their pessimism about long-term economic prospects, their views on real wage trends, their insistence on the strictness of the limits to growth should be understood to be closely linked to their implicit belief that the only major sources of energy in the production process were all animate. In such a world the supposition that the productivity of the soil sets limits to the entire productive process is no more than common sense.

No one living in Georgian or Regency England could have been ignorant of the importance of mineral production in general or of coal in particular. Coal was already produced on a massive scale, dominating the coastal shipping trade, and providing the principal traffic on the growing canal system.[47] The homes of most Londoners were warmed by coal fires. Coal

---

47 A recent estimate suggests that in the period 1780–1830 about 40 per cent of coastal shipping capacity was devoted to the coal trade. Armstrong and Bagwell, 'Coastal shipping', p. 155. 'The easier conveyance of coal was, of course,' it has been asserted, 'the primary motive behind the creation of most canals, and cheaper fuel prices were among the first benefits of the canal age to be enjoyed by contemporaries.' Duckham, 'Canals and river navigations', p. 130.

was used by many industries as a source of heat. Newcomen engines had been in use for many decades, chiefly for drainage purposes, and in the later decades of the period true steam engines, reflecting the innovations of Watt, were appearing in numbers. But the significance of these changes was reflected in the writings of the classical economists only to a limited extent. There is a remarkable sentence in the *Wealth of nations* which, at first sight, suggests an astonishing prescience: 'all over Great Britain manufactures have confined themselves principally to the coal countries; other parts of the country, on account of the high price of this necessary article, not being able to work so cheap'. But the reason for this state of affairs was that fuel entered so largely into the budget of labouring men that wages were lower where coal was cheap. 'In a country where the winters are so cold as in Great Britain, fuel is, during the season, in the strictest sense of the word, a necessary of life, not only for the purpose of dressing victuals, but for the comfortable subsistence of many different sorts of workmen who work within doors; and coals are the cheapest of all fuel.'[48]

Coal's weight in the budget of the bulk of the population deserves attention, as does its widespread use in place of wood in individual processes. Similar considerations appear once to have been important in relation to peat in Holland's great age of economic supremacy in the seventeenth century.[49] But there was a far more profound significance to the new coal age. Coal could provide heat and power on a scale previously without parallel. More, it offered the possibility of making the productivity of the land an irrelevance to wider and wider swathes of industrial production. The fear that rising marginal costs of raw material production would hamper and eventually arrest industrial growth for the same reason that the price of food must eventually rise had haunted the classical economists. A predominantly mineral-based industry rendered such fears irrelevant.[50]

Had this point been put to, say, Malthus or Ricardo he might well have conceded that the development of purely mineral-based industries would require some modification of their argument. Adam Smith's exposition of the nature of the trade between town and country would also have needed revision if the scale of industrial output were no longer a function of the size of the surplus of agricultural production in the countryside over its immediate needs. But each or all of the three might still have felt that their fundamental pessimism about the possibility of an industrial revolution was justified, if the defining characteristic of an industrial revolution was a sustained, substantial and progressive rise in the living standards of the mass of the population. Mineral raw materials and inanimate sources of energy might remove the ceiling from industrial output and justify the expectation

48 Smith, *Wealth of nations*, ii, p. 404.
49 De Zeeuw, 'Peat and the Dutch Golden Age'.
50 See chapter 4 below which examines this point in greater detail. The logic of the argument appears to me impeccable, but I am very conscious that the topic cries out for intensive empirical investigation.

that the products of manufacturing industry would experience falling unit costs of production as output volumes rose, but other, and formidable barriers remained.

Two further considerations in particular stood between them and a more general optimism. It remained true that in order to live a man must eat; and it remained plausible to suppose that comparative prosperity would promote more rapid population growth. For an industrial revolution to take root the problem of declining marginal returns in agriculture had still to be overcome and the assumption that, broadly speaking, numbers would grow in parallel to additional output had to be proved false. In the millenniums since hunting and gathering communities had been supplanted by agriculturalists, the historical record, it might be argued, had given much firmer warrant for caution than euphoria under both heads.

Radical change in agriculture

The first of these two considerations, whether in the precise formulation given to it by Malthus and Ricardo, or in the more impressionistic form reflected in Adam Smith's writing, carried especial weight. The constraints upon food supply and upon living standards imposed by the fixed supply of land was regarded as having the status of a law of nature, so that for expectation to be falsified in this regard must occasion far greater surprise even than that arising from access to new sources of energy and industrial raw materials.[51]

In discussing the question, both Malthus and Ricardo emphasized that they had in mind not a mechanical and progressive phenomenon, but a tendency which, though inevitable, might be many times postponed by human ingenuity and by suitable injections of capital.[52] The logical basis for the law of diminishing marginal returns to successive unit inputs of capital and labour seems so compelling that it might seem a work of supererogation to examine its empirical validity, especially when expectations about its operation were as carefully qualified as by Malthus and Ricardo. Yet not only did developments occurring after their lifetime disprove the assumptions of the classical economists, but it also seems doubtful whether the centuries immediately preceding their era offer support to the view that declining marginal returns must inhibit growth except perhaps on a millennial scale. For example, it seems hard to resist the conclusion that output per head had roughly doubled in the English agricultural labour force between about 1550 and about 1800, even though the national population tripled over the period and the area of land in farm did not increase substantially, and in spite of the fact that the country remained effectively self-sufficient in food throughout.[53]

51 See pp. 26–9.
52 See Malthus, *Principles*, pp. 282–3; and Ricardo, *Principles*, pp. 80–3, 120.
53 See below, pp. 167–74.

England's unusually successful showing in economic growth and individual
prosperity from Elizabethan to Regency times, when compared with other
European states, owed more to her achievements in agriculture than to any
other single factor. Her history over this period simultaneously exemplified
the view of the classical economists that growth as a whole was heavily
conditioned by agricultural success, that manufacturing industry lived off
the margin created, so to speak, by a productive agriculture, while yet at
the same time offering a long-sustained and substantial exception to the
supposition that the law of diminishing returns would begin to shackle
economic growth and damage real incomes per head from an early point
in any sustained surge of growth. It is ironic that Malthus should have
pointed out both that England was a conspicuous exception to Süssmilch's
view that there must be a low upper limit to the proportion of the population
making a living from any pursuit other than agriculture, and that even in
the countryside a large proportion of the labour force made its living outside
farming, and yet have been so lucid an analyst of the principle of declining
marginal returns in agriculture.[54]

The logic of the principle is indeed powerful, however, and it remains
important to the understanding of the occurrence of an industrial revolution
to explain how its operation was indefinitely postponed even when
populations doubled, tripled or quadrupled during the nineteenth century.
In a sense the answer is obvious. Technical advance, by creating the
opportunity for profitable investment, could overcome or set at bay the
unfavourable developments that must otherwise be expected. The changes
in question, however, just as in manufacturing industry, owed much to
developments of a new type. Thompson drew attention to their nature, when
he pointed to the contrast between a farming system in which each farm
was an ecologically self-sufficient unit, and one where the physical inputs
to sustain or increase output came increasingly from outside the farm. From
small beginnings with marl, guano, Chilean nitrates, coprolites and tile
drainage, mineral and other industrial inputs played an increasingly
important part in securing increased output per acre in the course of the
nineteenth century. Often this was achieved with declining unit production
costs. Eventually, as in other types of production, inanimate sources of
energy, applied directly or indirectly, became vital to efficient production,
largely supplanting the traditional renewable or animate sources: the tractor
for the horse; artificial fertilizer for farmyard manure; pesticides, alarm guns
and weed-killers for birdscarers and the hoe. It is not too fanciful to depict
the farm as becoming a factory out of doors converting into food energy
and chemicals increasingly derived from mineral sources, much as happened
indoors in conventional factories where mineral raw materials were converted
into useful products in comparable ways.[55]

54 Malthus, *Principles*, p. 335.

55 Distinguishing changes after about 1815 from those occurring earlier, Thompson wrote,
'The essence of the second agricultural revolution was that it broke the close-circuit system

It is an unwritten assumption linked with the classical view of declining marginal returns that there is not merely an unchanging area of cultivable land, but that the annual throughput of energy was also largely fixed as a quantum of insolation assisted by a variable energy input in the form of human and animal labour, itself dependent upon farm produce for sustenance. The restriction on growth explicitly associated with the fact that the supply of agricultural land is constant disappeared when the implicit condition attached to it ceased to hold good. The scale of the change that has taken place in this regard is very striking. Energy inputs and outputs in agriculture can be measured. Such studies show that the energy made available in the form of food by traditional farming methods exceeded the energy input by human and animal labour in a ratio varying according to the product and area between about 10 : 1 and 40 : 1. In contrast, by the late 1960s, when the energy inputs included, of course, petroleum, fertilizers, pesticides etc., the comparable ratio in British agriculture as a whole was 1 : 3.[56] There are difficulties in ensuring a comparison of like with like in such estimates, but there can be no doubt about the extent of the contrast, nor about the importance of the radically changed energy budget in farming to its increasing efficiency as measured in output per head or per acre.

Population growth and food supply

The final consideration which moved the classical economists to pessimism was their conviction that numbers would rise *pari passu* with food supply, or more generally overall productive capacity. It was an element in their thinking that proved to have notable stamina. In a slightly modified form it figured prominently in Marx's analysis of the reasons for mass poverty within a capitalist economic system.[57] Ironically, Malthus, with whose name the proposition is most closely associated, ultimately came to adopt a less rigid view than either Adam Smith or Ricardo. The view of the latter two was that population trends were very largely determined by the demand for labour. A rise in the demand for labour, by creating favourable employment opportunities and by raising wages, and operating through reduced mortality, enhanced nuptiality or the two jointly, would provoke a rise in population, *ceteris paribus*. A fall in the demand for labour had an opposite effect. They recognized that the absolute level of real wages might

---

[in which the farm was 'a self-sufficient productive unit'] and made the operations of the farmer much more like those of the factory owner. In fact farming moved from being an extractive industry, albeit of a model and unparalleled type which perpetually renewed what it extracted, into being a manufacturing industry.' Thompson, 'Second agricultural revolution', p. 64.

56 Grigg, *Dynamics of agricultural change*, pp. 78–80.

57 Marx was writing late enough for it to be clear that the capacity to produce was growing faster than population but, because of rapidly rising output per head, the perverse result, peculiar to a capitalist mode of production, was that competition in the labour market grew ever more acute. Marx, *Capital*, ii, p. 660.

well be culturally determined and be maintained at a level some way removed from bare subsistence, but did not expect the level to change, other than temporarily, in response to changes in the demand for labour.[58] Malthus's attitude was not greatly different but he did explicitly envisage the possibility that the labouring classes, by exercising greater restraint over reproduction, might induce a permanent upward shift in their average well-being. Malthus had in mind, of course, a fertility change brought about by later marriage rather than by controlling reproduction within marriage, and he was not sanguine about the likelihood of such a change in behaviour taking place, but he had learnt too much about the exercise of prudential restraint among west European populations since the first edition of his *Essay on population* was published to discount the possibility entirely.[59]

In the event, the expectations of the classical economists in this regard were falsified by two developments. In the short term, until the last decades of the nineteenth century, inasmuch as there was an improvement in the standard of living in the mass of the English population, it occurred because the rate of growth in output exceeded the rate of growth of population. The

58 Ricardo remarked, 'It is not to be understood that the natural price of labour, estimated even in food and necessaries, is absolutely fixed and constant. It varies at different times in the same country, and very materially differs in different countries. It essentially depends on the habits and customs of the people. An English labourer would consider his wages under their natural rate, and too scanty to support a family, if they enabled him to purchase no other food than potatoes, and to live in no better habitation than a mud cabin; yet these moderate demands of nature are often deemed sufficient in countries where "man's life is cheap".' Ricardo, *Principles*, pp. 96–7. In a characteristically complex discussion of the wages of labour, Adam Smith laid greatest emphasis on the connection between whether the economy was progressive, stationary or in decline, and rising, steady or falling real wages. But he also recognized the importance of conventional minima in consumption standards. He regarded China as in a stationary state but thought living standards abysmal. 'The subsistence which they find there [near Canton] is so scanty that they are eager to fish up the nastiest garbage thrown overboard from any European ship. Any carrion, the carcase of a dead dog or cat, for example, though half putrid and stinking, is as welcome to them as the most wholesome food to the people of other countries'. And then, using a line of thought later much extended by Malthus, he added, 'Marriage is encouraged in China, not by the profitableness of children, but by the liberty of destroying them. In all great towns several are every night exposed in the street, or drowned like puppies in the water.' Smith, *Wealth of nations*, i, p. 81.

59 He used a vivid phrase to illustrate the point he had in mind. 'If we can persuade the hare to go to sleep, the tortoise may have some chance of overtaking her.' Or, more prosaically, 'We are not, however, to relax our efforts in increasing the quantity of provisions, but to combine another effort with it; that of keeping the population, when once it had been overtaken, at such a distance behind, as to effect the relative proportion which we desire; and thus to unite the two grand *desiderata*, a great actual population, and a state of society, in which abject poverty and dependence are comparatively but little known; two objects which are far from being incompatible.' Malthus, *Essay on population* (1826), ii, p. 291. He took a similar line in his other major book. 'Yet every effort to ameliorate the lot of the poor generally, that has not this tendency [to keep the market understocked with labour], is perfectly futile and childish. It is quite obvious therefore, that the knowledge and prudence of the poor themselves, are absolutely the *only* means by which any general and permanent improvement in their condition can be affected. They are really the arbiters of their destiny.' Malthus, *Principles*, p. 279. He made it clear that he hoped they would take advantage of this possibility.

latter had accelerated to reach a peak rate of more than 1.5 per cent per annum in the second decade of the nineteenth century: thereafter it sagged slightly to a level usually close to 1.25 per cent per annum until late in the century. By the standards of the pre-industrial past this was an unprecedented rate of growth, and far in excess of the rates of growth of gross national product in earlier centuries. The economy, however, had spurted even more dramatically than had population.[60] Indeed, the rate of economic expansion had reached a point at which it was not merely growing faster than the rate at which population was actually increasing, but faster than population was capable of growing, for it must be remembered that the public health and medical circumstances of the early nineteenth century, combined with the nature of marriage as a social institution in western Europe, meant that the maximum attainable rate of population growth fell well short of 2 per cent per annum. Thus a novel situation had arisen. It was assumed by the classical economists not only, explicitly, that human populations would emulate animal populations in breeding up to a limit set principally by the supply of food, and reflected in changes in the demand for labour, but also, implicitly, that the latent powers of growth inherent in human reproductive biology would always exceed economic growth. The eye-catching contrast which Malthus made between arithmetic and geometric growth rates presented the tension in an especially vivid manner. This assumption ceased to be valid as the industrial revolution took hold, and the classical analysis therefore ceased to have a purchase upon the new situation.

In the longer term, moreover, matters were still more fundamentally altered because control of fertility within marriage rather than by marriage, from being the preserve of a tiny minority of the population before 1880, became a normal part of married life for the overwhelming bulk of the population over the next two or three generations. The assumption that fertility would tend to rise, just as mortality would tend to fall, with rising real incomes, which had seemed self-evidently true to the classical economists, not only ceased to be true but became almost the reverse of the truth for a long period of time. It became more reasonable to associate rising individual prosperity with falling fertility than the reverse. A further prop of the classical analysis of individual living standards and the limits to growth disappeared.

Conclusion

In a more extended discussion of the treatment of trends in growth and living standards by the classical economists, it would be useful to make use of other

---

60 Crafts's recent re-examination of the available data for the earlier decades of the industrial revolution led him to conclude that the annual rate of growth in national product in Britain reached 1.97 per cent per annum in 1801–31, almost three times the rate in the period 1760–80 (0.70). This permitted a modest rise in the rate of growth in national product per head in spite of the rapid acceleration of population growth rates to their peak at the beginning of the century. Rostow's data suggest that over the next 30 years, 1831–41 to 1861–71, the comparable rate

ways of conveying the characteristic qualities of their thinking. For example, both in relation to secular trends in return on capital investment and, of course, on the particular issue of marginal returns in agriculture, it is important to seize firmly on the point that classical thinking does not rest upon the assumption of a linear relationship between variables. There are indeed some relationships in their writings which take this form. For example, the response of labour supply to a particular proportionate change in the demand for labour is not affected by the absolute level of the former. Several of the most fundamental relationships, however, are not adequately captured if depicted as taking a linear form, and their collective implication is pessimistic. Most entail increasing difficulties in sustaining growth in the longer term. The return to a proportionate increase of capital invested, when expressed in the form of a percentage change in income flow, for instance, is affected by the absolute scale of the national capital stock.

Again, one might characterize the systems constructed by Adam Smith, Malthus and Ricardo as dominated by negative feedback loops. Not all the elements in their systems functioned in this way. The pinmakers whom Adam Smith described operated within a sector of the economy in which positive feedback prevailed. A larger market enabled cheaper and better pins to be produced, which in turn stimulated demand, enabling the process to move forward a stage further. But in the long run beneficial effects of this type were insufficient to offset the increasingly severe constraints to further growth imposed by the fact that elsewhere in the economy negative feedback prevailed.[61]

Each of these ways of conveying the nature of the model of reality created by the classical economists restates the same basic point. In their view there had been room for very substantial growth in the economies of European states in the seventeenth and eighteenth centuries, but the analytical principles which served best to elucidate how such growth had taken place and might be further encouraged also provided convincing reasons to conclude that it must have limits falling well short of what later generations were to learn to call an industrial revolution.

If this account of the classical economists and the industrial revolution is correct, it suggests that all analyses of the industrial revolution which treat it as a unitary, progressive phenomenon should be viewed with reserve. it has been customary in treating topics such as trends in the percentage of the gross national product invested, the balance of investment between different sectors of the economy, changes in material technology, trends in real wages, changes in the distribution or absolute size of the labour force by occupational category, problems of raw material supply and so on, to

---

of growth was 2.16 per cent per annum. The moderation in population growth by this time implies a further acceleration in the rate of growth per head. Crafts, *British economic growth*, table 2.11, p. 45: Rostow, *World economy*, table V–I, p. 378.

61 The nature of the negative feedback process in the English economy between the sixteenth and the nineteenth centuries is discussed in Wrigley and Schofield, *Population history of England*, chapter 11.

discuss developments over the industrial revolution as a whole, and to assume that it began in the later eighteenth century and came to maturity perhaps 100 years later. Perhaps it may be worth considering whether the great bulk of the changes taking place in the period down to, say, 1830 or 1840 may not be better understood within the canons of the system constructed by the classical economists as being essentially akin to developments over the preceding 200 years, whereas increasingly after the end of the first third of the nineteenth century the further changes need to be referred to a different system, in which the pace of growth, the limits to growth and the scope for the enhancement of individual welfare, were to be best understood in different terms.

The new system differed from the old above all in being able to deploy inanimate sources of energy in the production process, both manufacturing and agricultural, on a scale which dwarfed energy use in earlier periods. Lost within aggregate measures of gross national product or returns on investment which suggest relatively smooth, sequential change, there were hidden compositional changes which carry an important message. As older sources of growth gradually lost their impetus, the continued dynamism of the economy came to depend upon novel forms of impulsion. So much is hardly controversial. What may be more so is the extent and nature of the links between the old and the new. To the extent that the classical economists did justice to the world in which they lived, the closeness of such links may have been far less than is usually supposed.

3
The Process of Modernization and the Industrial Revolution in England

Modernization and industrialization are terms widely used in descriptions of the changes that have occurred in western societies over the last two or three centuries. Whether they represent concepts able to sustain adequately the explanatory and descriptive loads borne by them is disputable. Yet they enjoy very wide currency and form the most convenient point of departure for a general discussion of the industrial revolution in England.

In this essay I shall describe a view of the relationship between modernization and industrialization which seems to me to be both widespread and unfortunate when applied to the industrial revolution in England. In particular, I shall argue that the connection between the two is contingent rather than necessary. I shall begin by offering brief definitions of modernization and industrialization as a preliminary to a discussion of the way in which the assumptions which underlie the use of the terms have clouded our appreciation of the industrial revolution. The definitions will serve to introduce both a discussion of the views of percipient contemporaries, especially Adam Smith and Karl Marx, and an examination of some features of the industrial revolution itself. I have tried to present the definitions in the form in which they are most widely held – what might be called highest common factor definitions. This means a loss of rigour, but it conforms to the requirements of the essay. At times, it will be evident that the definitions of modernization and industrialization offered are used as stalking horses as much as chargers, underlining the point that they are at once convenient and yet inadequate.

The views of contemporaries are of great value in this regard. Smith and Marx stood closer to the industrial revolution than we do today. I shall argue that they identified the salient characteristics of their times in a manner from which we can still learn much – that we have been partially blinded by our knowledge of subsequent events, and so see some things less clearly than they. Finally, I shall point to some parallels and differences between English history and that of her neighbours, France and Holland, in order to throw into relief those features of English experience which set it apart from the continent and have a peculiar relevance to the question of the relationship between modernization and industrialization.

Defining the concepts

Economists and sociologists have perhaps had the most to do with attempts to define the concepts connoted by the words modernization and industrialization, but the terms are also much used by historians, political scientists, social anthropologists, geographers and others. It is not surprising, therefore, that the two words have been put to so many different uses. Often they are simply convenient umbrellas to shelter a miscellany of less ambitious ideas.

Of the two terms, industrialization is the narrower in scope and presents fewer difficulties of definition. This is because industrialization has come to be used as a synonym for sustained economic growth. It is said to occur when real incomes per head begin to rise steadily and without apparent limit, and is always associated with major and continuing changes in material technology, including the tapping of new sources of energy. The prospect of rising real incomes per head has caused industrialization to be widely and ardently pursued. To free men from the dread of periodic cold, privation, famine and disease, and from the hardship of long bouts of heavy labour in the fields or at the loom by creating the means to meet men's main wants and many of their fancies, implies a vast change from the pre-industrial past. It has placed the golden age in the future and the lure has proved universal and irresistible.

Expansion of total output alone is not a sufficient criterion of industrialization since, if population is rising more rapidly than output, it is compatible with declining real incomes per head. Nor can mere abundance of capital and land (which might give rise for a time to growing real incomes per head) produce a growth in the economy which can be described as industrialization if material technology remains unchanged. A country which retains a large, even a predominant, agricultural sector may be described as industrialized if real incomes rise and technology changes. New Zealand is an example of this possibility, although the proportion of the labour force engaged in agriculture has now fallen to a modest level. The popularity of Rostow's analogy between the behaviour of an economy during industrialization and the take-off of an airplane speaks to the same point. The crucial change is identified as a rise in the proportion of net national product invested (say from 5 to 10 per cent), but it is implicit in the selection of this criterion that population growth rates and capital–output ratios shall be such that real incomes rise, and rapid technological change is also assumed to take place.[1]

Associated with industrialization are a number of economic and social changes which follow directly from its defining characteristics. For example, as real incomes rise, the structure of aggregate demand will change, since

1 'The process of take-off may be defined as an increase in the volume and productivity of investment in a society, such that a sustained increase in *per capita* real income results.' Rostow, *Economic growth*, pp. 103–4.

the income elasticities of demand for the various goods available differ considerably. Again, and partly for the same reason, there will be a major, sustained shift of population from the countryside into the city. These, and many other related changes, are generally understood to accompany industrialization, but whereas there is room for argument about the length and make-up of any list of the concomitants of industrialization, there is near unanimity upon the central identifying characteristic: the rise in real income per head.[2]

There is also general agreement that industrialization is possible only as part of a wider set of changes which have come to be known collectively as modernization. Indeed, in discussions of the developing world today, industrialization and modernization are often used interchangeably, or the former is treated as one aspect of the latter.[3] Much the same point can be made in a different way by noting that almost everyone regards modernization as a necessary condition of industrialization, and that many writers implicitly treat it as also a sufficient condition.

If these assumptions cause difficulty in the study of the industrial revolution in England, it is not because historians have been unwary enough to transfer to past time ideas developed by economists and sociologists with only the present in mind. Adam Smith, Marx and Max Weber, prominent among the host of those who have helped to fashion the concepts now known as industrialization and modernization, had the history of western Europe chiefly in mind when they wrote. The discussion of change in Asia and Africa today is more often conducted in categories devised for the European past than vice versa. Yet, ironically, it may be that the understanding of European history has suffered the more.

It is less easy to define modernization in a way that is likely to command a wide acceptance than is the case with industrialization. There is no equivalent to the measurement of real income per head that can serve as a touchstone for

---

2 For example, Kindleberger's discussion of what he calls economic development, in which he is at pains to be authoritative without provoking controversy, runs along these lines 'Economic growth is generally thought of as unidimensional and is measured by increases in income. Economic development involves as well structural and functional changes. In the absence of effective measures of the latter, however, states of development are estimated by levels of income, and rates of development by growth of income.' Kindleberger, *Economic development*, p. 15. As Bruton remarks, 'Per capita income is chosen as the main measure of growth for two simple reasons: one, almost all writers direct attention to this variable; two, despite some obvious weaknesses in its use there does not seem to be a practical alternative.' Bruton, 'Economic growth', p. 241. See also Lewis, *Theory of economic growth*, pp. 201–303.

3 The two terms are often used almost as synonyms. Hoselitz, for example, writes: 'The use of pattern variables has had the advantage of putting some of the strategic mechanisms of social change associated with industrialization and technical progress into sharper focus. Universalistic norms need not generally replace particularistic ones. However, the transitions from allocating economic roles according to a system of ascription to assigning them on a basis of achievement, and the replacement of functionally diffuse by functionally specific norms for the definition of economic tasks, appear to have occurred in all cases of successful modernization.' Hoselitz, 'Technical change', pp. 18–19.

the extent and rate of advance of modernization. It is usually regarded as a congeries of changes which are found together and are related to each other, but the length, composition and ranking of the list of associated changes vary. The nature of the relationship between the changes is also much disputed. A cynic might say that modernization has come to be a term of convenience used by those who are aware of the profound difference between traditional and modern society, and need a word which can convey their appreciation of its importance, but which does not commit them to any one interpretation of the causes or the course of change.

In what follows, I shall do little to allay the suspicions of such a cynic. My description of modernization contains no new features. It is eclectic and is intended simply to summarize views that have often been expressed about the changes underlying the transformation of west European society between the sixteenth and nineteenth centuries. To proceed in this way cloaks issues of the greatest importance since it tends to imply that all concepts of modernization are equivalent, that the apparent differences between Adam Smith, Marx, Ferdinand Tönnies, Weber, Sigmund Freud, Talcott Parsons and others are more terminological than substantial. In a different context, this would be tendentious if not absurd. In this essay, however, my purpose is simply to provide a backcloth for a discussion of the relationship between modernization and the industrial revolution in England, and this must be my excuse for glossing over matters which would otherwise require fuller treatment.

That modernization and greater economic efficiency are closely linked is universally accepted, and the connection is usually made explicit. For this reason, the concept of rationality which underpins much of the discussion of the modernization of west European society has acquired a limited, almost technical, meaning. Given the values which obtain in a traditional society, for example, it may be perfectly 'rational' to retain in a family group, living on a small peasant holding, adult male kin who produce less than they consume. To expel them would do violence to the social system, and cause damage not offset in the eyes of members of the family by any gain in income per head for those who remained on the holding.[4] Such behaviour, however, would be counted irrational in the context of modernization because marginal labour productivity in agriculture is held down as long as attitudes like this persist. Rational behaviour has come to be defined as that which maximizes economic returns to the individual, to the nuclear family or to the state (the interests of the three do not, of course, necessarily coincide, and this has been and still is a source of difficulty with the concept). In comparison with traditional societies, the utilities to be

---

4 It is sometimes argued, following Ferdinand Tönnies, that the essential difference between modern and traditional attitudes lies less in the degree of rationality involved in decisions of this type than in the degree of consciousness on the part of the individual of the moral bases of his actions. Perhaps we overstate the uniformity of traditional societies in this respect. See the brief description of Tiwi life in this connection (below, p. 52).

maximized are concentrated in a narrower band and are pursued with a new urgency.[5]

In order to achieve this end, there must be a common measure of value, a means by which all goods and services can be related to a common yardstick, and a calculus by which alternative courses of economic action can be compared. Money provides a common measure of value and will solve the first problem if most goods and services are bought for money rather than bartered. The operation of the market in such an economy will enable goods and services to be valued on an interval scale, and so solve the second problem. And monetary accounting, if sufficiently developed, makes it feasible to estimate the costs and returns of every possible course of economic action; to balance a given present utility against some greater future utility; and to compare the potential returns from a capital sum which may be invested in several different ways, thus meeting the third requirement.

Arbitrary action and any circumstance which makes prediction difficult are held to be antipathetic to rational behaviour. The greater the accuracy with which the outcome of alternative courses of action can be foreseen, the greater the scope for rational choice and the incentive to employ rational accounting. Hence the stress first upon the importance of replacing customary arrangements by legally enforceable and specific contractual obligations, and secondly, upon the attractiveness of a sophisticated governmental bureaucracy to nascent capitalism striving to reduce the range of the incalculable. A government which is unable or unwilling to enforce the law and maintain public order, or which levies large exactions arbitrarily and without due notice, will inhibit rational calculation and is incompatible with modernization.

If rationality is defined along these lines and is regarded as central to the modernization process, it is possible to examine each aspect of social structure and function and, in many cases, define pairs of polar opposites, one of which is regarded as congruent with modernization and likely to further it, while the other is inimical to it and apt to prevent its development. Mention of three such pairs will suggest what is at issue. They are widely held both to be particularly important and also to be closely interlocked. Needless to say, no society has ever been either perfectly 'rational' or 'irrational' in regard to them. They represent limiting possibilities and each pair defines a spectrum on which, in principle, each society may be placed.

The first pair concerns the way in which men are recruited to discharge roles within a society. The rational method of selection is to consider only the fitness of the candidate to carry out the tasks associated with the role

5 This changing emphasis is well illustrated by Spengler, 'Mercantilist and physiocratic growth theory' especially in the appendix. It is, of course, the total social context which determines what is 'rational' in each society. There are no absolute touchstones: hence such charming ironies as the effect of a rise in the price of beaver fur upon the supply of pelts in French Canada. Since the Indians who caught the beaver wanted little from the French – a gun, a blanket or a knife – they were able to satisfy their wants by trapping fewer animals when prices were high, a rational if inconvenient response.

regardless of his parentage, kin, status, age, nationality, religion, race or sex. At the other extreme, recruitment to a particular role is confined to a restricted group within the whole population, which in the limiting case might contain only one member. The group may be defined by kinship, status, race or in any other way which has gained the sanction of social consent. Open, competitive examination for a governmental administrative post is an example of the first type of recruitment, while entry into a craft with preference given to sons of present members is an instance of the second. The opposite ends of the spectrum are sometimes termed achievement and ascription. The former both favours modernization and helps to define it, while the latter is the dominant form of recruitment in traditional societies.

Rationality bears not only on methods of recruitment to social and economic roles, but also on the definition of the roles themselves. The criteria for recruitment can be more exactly specified and, at the same time, greater economic efficiency achieved if roles are strongly differentiated. A jack-of-all-trades is master of none. Division of labour tends both to increase productivity and to help ensure that the men appointed to each job are well qualified to discharge it efficiently. This is one aspect of the second spectrum, that which runs between functional specificity and functional diffuseness. In traditional societies, a man may be called upon to perform a number of different roles because of his position in society. Actions and attitudes towards him will be conditioned by the consciousness of this fact. If he is a merchant, for example, men's behaviour towards him may be affected not simply by the type and price of the wares he has to offer, but by the status of merchants in the society generally, by his kinship ties, by his religion and so on. Similarly, his attitude to his customers may be influenced by considerations other than their financial means. And what is true of merchants, is true *a fortiori* of peasants or craftsmen. In economic relations, these influences are compounded by the fact that in traditional societies, the play of the market is limited and transport costs are high. Specialization of economic function cannot, therefore, be carried very far either on the peasant holding, where a substantial measure of self-sufficiency in food and simple consumer goods may be necessary, or in the craft workshop, where the size of the market and the personal predilections of customers prevent long production runs of standard products, and hence division of labour.

It is a short step from these first two polar pairs to the third, which deals with the criteria for membership of a group. At one extreme, this may be particularistic; at the other, universalistic. The latter is typified by the view that all men should be equal before the law and that the law should be the same for all men. It is at odds with this universalistic principle, for example, that a priest in holy orders should be able *qua* priest to invoke immunity from the civil courts, or that because a man is born a serf he should suffer disabilities before the law. Again, the long struggle by local communities in France to retain control of the grain supply within their areas, setting its price and limiting its export as seemed best in their interest, was particularistic in spirit. The central government moved towards the view that trade in grain should be free with the market being the sole arbiter of price and the movement of grain no longer inhibited by local regulation.[6] In this it was exemplifying the universalistic principle that all franchises, liberties and privileges which distinguished particular groups, areas or communities were to be deplored. Formal equality is mandatory.

Consideration of the several linked aspects of social and economic behaviour which change during modernization has, in turn, produced paired terms intended to connote the changes as a whole: feudal–capitalist, traditional–modern and *Gemeinschaft–Gesellschaft*. When the elements of change are analysed, and especially when their causes are discussed, major differences of interpretation appear, but the definition of modernization may be extended a little by referring to some further points which are common ground to most views of modernization.

Self-interest is the twin pillar to rationality in supporting the concept of modernization. Self-interest is held to be the guiding principle of action in a modernized society to a degree which would appear both aberrant and abhorrent in traditional communities. Like the idea of rationality, self-interest has acquired a special meaning in these discussions. It is perfectly possible to argue that a man in a traditional community who acknowledges a very wide range of kinship obligations and devotes much of his time and energy to promoting the well-being, security and status of his relatives, his dependents or his lord, is just as much actuated by self-interest as any Scrooge. The difference lies in the nature of the rewards that are sought, not in the degree of self-interest involved. It may also be argued that some traditional societies were so constituted as to put a high premium not only upon the pursuit of self-interest, but also upon a long-term calculation of advantage which in a different context might have gained the approval of Samuel Smiles. Among the Tiwi in northern Australia, for example, a man's status depended above all upon the number of his wives. No man could achieve high status in this way before his late forties, but he had to lay the foundation of his later success two decades earlier by forming links with powerful men who were willing to promise him female children born or as yet unborn as his future wives in return for present services. Twenty years is a long time to wait for an investment to mature, especially where there is a high risk that the premature death of infants, or an unfortunate run of male offspring, will make it impossible for the older man to fulfil his obligations.[7]

Whatever the justice of the prevailing stereotype of traditional societies, in the context of modernization, self-interest has come to mean the adoption

---

6 See Tilly, 'The food riot'.

7 'To become a really big man or even a minor figure among the elders, a Tiwi had to devote all his adult life to that goal. Careers were built up and influential positions gained not by executing spectacular coups at any one time, but by slow, devious manoeuvering and dealing in influence throughout adulthood. Men in their early thirties invested their very small assets in the hope of large returns twenty years later.' Wives, mothers, sisters and daughters were all 'investment funds in [a] career of influence seeking'. Hart and Pilling, *The Tiwi*, pp. 51, 52.

of a calculus of advantage. In the calculus, the unit is the individual or, at the widest, the nuclear family, and the accounting scale is pecuniary gain.

Tönnies, an early and extreme protagonist of the view that modern and traditional societies differ profoundly, wrote in *Gemeinschaft und Gesellschaft*: 'The will to enrich himself makes the merchant unscrupulous and the type of egotistic, self-willed individual to whom all human beings except his nearest friends are only means and tools to his ends or purposes; he is the embodiment of Gesellschaft.'[8] He thought the pressure toward atomistic individualism to be so acute that he added: 'The family becomes an accidental form for the satisfaction of natural needs, neighbourhood and friendship are supplanted by special interest groups and conventional society life.'[9] These attitudes eat like acid into the fabric of traditional society, destroying solidary groups. When this happens, old values and attitudes are no longer internalized by the young, and the web of rights and obligations which binds together small traditional communities weakens and, in time, dissolves.

Other attributes of modernization may be inferred from its major characteristics. Social, occupational and geographical mobility will tend to increase with the decline of ascriptive recruitment. Rights and obligations linked to kinship become less extensive and less easily enforceable, except perhaps within the nuclear family.[10] Structural differentiation at the institutional level parallels the specialization of individual roles. Again, modernization promotes the growth of towns, and in towns its attributes are more widespread, prominent and pervasive than in the countryside. Its development fosters the spread of literacy and numeracy through a population.

There remain two aspects of modernization which are widely held to be important when assessing its relationship to industrialization in western Europe. Both have received increased attention in recent years.

The first concerns the actions of the nation state. The close connection between rationality and bureaucratic method, which Weber frequently stressed, has already been remarked.[11] It is only one facet of the stimulus afforded by the state to modernizing tendencies. The state provides the sanction for the enforcement of contractual obligation and the maintenance of order. Since it encourages the growth of a bureaucracy recruited by achievement rather than by ascription, it is apt to oppose particularistic interests, and to provide an administrative framework within which rational action can flourish. The bourgeois and the nation state are congenial to each other. Impediments to commerce, to the free movement of capital, to unrestricted discretion in the use of private property and to the treatment

8 Tönnies, *Community and society*, p. 165.

9 Ibid., p. 168.

10 It may be as well to note that the prevalence of the extended family is one of several assumptions about the universal characteristics of traditional society that are disputable in the case of western Europe.

11 See, for example, Weber, *Social and economic organization*, pp. 329–41.

of labour simply as a production factor, impediments which inhibit the
growth of capitalism and which display a notable persistence in the face of
change, can all be reduced to the vanishing point by a vigorous state acting
in the bourgeois interest, which is also its own.[12]

Other forms of state action may also increase the momentum of
modernization, which is further speeded as groups whose interests lie in
accelerating change force an entry into the polity.[13] Taxation, for example,
unless payment in kind or labour is accepted, forces the peasant into the
market to raise cash. The maintenance of standing armies, like the growth
of cities, enlarges the market for foodstuffs and textiles, and encourages
specialization of economic function. Or, again, the actions of the state
may undermine alternative and older institutional frameworks. The English
poor law, for example, enshrined the view that if a man or a family fell
upon hard times, responsibility for their support ultimately devolved upon
the parish. It is evidence of the state's desire that all men who could work
should do so, but it is also an acknowledgement of the responsibility of
the state toward individuals in distress. Kinship ties and local custom were
no longer the sole basis of all help and support in bad fortune. Nor was
the lord of the manor expected to provide for his own in return for the services
owed him by his men. Instead, the state created a statutory framework
within which local communities were to make provision for the sick and
needy.

Secondly, economic and social change produce tension not only between
individuals, but also within them. For individuals to act rationally (always
in the restricted sense described above), they must achieve rational control
of affect and much greater autonomy than is needed or would be acceptable
in a traditional society. In traditional society, authority is perceived as
protective and nurturant. Hierarchical authority structures are acceptable
as long as this holds true, and the values internalized by individuals legitimate
the system. Affectual ties are strong and personal, and personal dependency
does not involve severe conscious stresses in relation to authority figures.
When, however, authority appears to be failing to fulfil its side of the bargain
upon which a hierarchical structure of authority rests, hostility towards it,
which was once successfully repressed, may surface. A competing set of
values appropriate to individual autonomy may be internalized by a part
of the population, and conflict between the old and new values will occur.[14]
Institutional (social and economic) and internal (psychic) changes both occur

12 Such at least is the 'pure type' of action by the state. It is, of course, unlikely to be paralleled
exactly in any particular case.

13 It is sometimes argued that just as formal equality before the law is mandatory, so formal
equality in political participation is ultimately inevitable, or at least that competing political
groups should stand towards the polity much as competing firms do to the market. There is
perhaps something of this in Burke's teaching about political party. The old parallel between
party in the state and schism in the church was no longer acceptable.

14 On this aspect of modernization see, for example, Hagen, *Theory of social change*; Weinstein
and Platt, *The wish to be free*.

during modernization. If they get out of step with each other, tension and violence are likely to increase.[15]

Once any considerable number of men have ceased to internalize the values upon which traditional society rests, their behaviour is certain to impede the smooth functioning of traditional authority and to call its legitimacy and its ability to protect and nurture further in question. Hence the belief that changes in the value systems of small groups of men, such as the early Calvinists, may have an importance in producing massive changes at a later date which might appear at first sight to be quite out of proportion to their number or political power. There is, of course, no reason why the later changes should necessarily follow the same pattern, for greater autonomy and control of affect may be achieved by internalizing value systems other than ascetic Protestantism. But the first successfully established alternative to the traditional ethic, if such it was, holds a special interest.

Not all analyses of modernization contain all of the elements described above. In part, this is an accident of chronology. Marx's analysis, for example, obviously could not be cast in a form which took account of the insights of Freud. Hence, psychic structural changes inevitably figure less prominently than those in social and economic structure. In part, it is a matter of terminology rather than substance. Unquestionably differences remain despite these two considerations, but there is at least tolerable unanimity that the several changes were closely interlocked and that they tended to reinforce each other. Latterly, it has also been common to assume that an adequate understanding of modernization in western Europe would entail *ipso facto* an understanding of the occurrence of the industrial revolution in England and its counterpart a little later on the continent.

In this view, the industrial revolution is a dramatic culmination in a long-gathering process of change, rather as the cylinder may be charged with a head of steam quite quickly but only if the water has long been heating. Geertz puts the matter succinctly:

In one sense, of course, increasing per capita income *is* economic growth, not a mere index of it; but in another, it is clear that such increases are but one highly visible resultant of a complex process . . . Though it may be true that, as an economic process, development is a dramatic, revolutionary change, as a broadly social process it fairly clearly is not. What looks like a quantum jump from a specifically economic point of view is, from a generally social one, merely the final expression in economic terms of a process which has been building up gradually over an extended period of time.[16]

---

15 On this argument, the attempt to impose new institutional forms by *force majeure* from the centre not only offends local interests at the conscious level, but also stirs up large anxieties which are the harder for the individual to quell precisely because they are imperfectly accessible to him at the conscious level.

16 Geertz, *Peddlers and princes*, p. 2.

The views of contemporaries

This view of the relationship between modernization and the industrial revolution is certainly plausible. The very concept of rationality as it has come to be used in the discussion of modernization is intimately related to the promotion of economic efficiency. All modernizing countries have enjoyed economic growth. The early stages of modernization produce, in Rostow's terminology, those changing propensities necessary for take-off, after which take-off itself occurs. Exponential economic growth gets under way. Real incomes rise. Material technology advances. Cities swell in size and population. Literacy becomes universal. As living standards rise, the death rate falls, presaging in its turn the control of fertility. Societies come to resemble more and more the late twentieth-century world.

It is my thesis in this essay that it is unwise to view the connection between the industrial revolution in England and the changes known as modernization in this manner. I shall argue that, although modernization may be a necessary condition for industrial revolution, it is not a sufficient condition; or, to put the same point in a different way, it is reasonable to argue that a society might become modernized without also becoming industrialized. I shall review in some detail what two major contemporary writers, Smith and Marx, had to say on this subject. It is convenient to do so because their account of the changes going on about them is a valuable corrective to some elements of the conventional wisdom about modernization and industrialization today. It is also a good base from which to explore further the evidence on which the competing explanations rest.

The *Wealth of nations* might be described as the bible of modernizing man. Rationality and self-interest are made the guiding principles of action. No one has written more trenchantly and persuasively in their favour than Smith. He caught to perfection the capitalist ethic, as well as analysing the advantages of a capitalist system in producing wealth:

> man has almost constant occasion for the help of his brethren, and it is in vain for him to expect it from their benevolence only. He will be more likely to prevail if he can interest their self-love in his favour, and show them that it is for their own advantage to do for him what he requires of them . . . It is not from the benevolence of the butcher, the brewer, or the baker that we expect our dinner, but from their regard to their own interest. We address ourselves, not to their humanity but to their self-love, and never talk of our own necessities but of their advantages. Nobody but a beggar chooses to depend chiefly upon the benevolence of his fellow-citizens.[17]

17 Smith, *Wealth of nations*, i, p. 18.

Smith used a less technical and more telling prose than those who write of modernization today, but there is little in recent discussions of the topic which does not find a parallel in the *Wealth of nations*.

Many later descriptions of the advantages of functional specificity in economic affairs and of the gains which flow from the division of labour refer to Smith's pinmakers. He was also insistent upon the importance of removing particularistic restrictions in the interest of higher overall efficiency. He advocated the abolition of the apprenticeship system. He opposed all regulations in restraint of trade, and legal incorporations. 'The pretence that corporations are necessary for the better government of the trade is without any foundation. The real and effectual discipline which is exercised over a workman is not that of his corporation but that of his customers.'[18] He favoured free trade in foodstuffs, including corn. The settlement laws were castigated: 'There is scarce a poor man in England of forty years of age, I will venture to say, who has not in some part of his life felt himself most cruelly oppressed by this ill-contrived law of settlements.'[19]

Adam Smith urged the fundamental importance of formal equality with great vigour. In a passage dealing with colonial trade, he finds its prosperity to be due above all to 'that equal and impartial administration of justice which renders the rights of the meanest British subject respectable to the greatest, and which, by securing to every man the fruits of his own industry, gives the greatest and most effectual encouragement to every sort of industry'; a splendid text.[20]

The *Wealth of nations* also makes vividly clear the close connection which Smith saw between modernization and firm, ubiquitous, reliable government. 'Thirdly, and lastly,' he remarks in a chapter entitled 'How the commerce of the towns contributed to the improvement of the country', 'commerce and manufactures gradually introduced order and good government, and with them the liberty and security of individuals, among the inhabitants of the country, who had before lived almost in a continual state of war with their neighbours and of servile dependency upon their superiors. This, though it has been the least observed, is by far the most important of all their effects.'[21] This chapter is one of the most interesting in the whole work, containing an account of the relationship between feudal law and medieval property and manners; a vignette of the redoubtable Cameron of Lochiel who in the mid-eighteenth century still exercised 'the highest criminal jurisdiction' over his people 'with great equity, though without any of the formalities of justice',[22] and an analysis of the way in which surplus income is disposed of in a country lacking commerce and manufactures – echoed more than a century later in Weber's discussion of

---

18 Ibid., i, p. 144.
19 Ibid., i, p. 158.
20 Ibid., ii, p. 125.
21 Ibid., i, p. 433.
22 Ibid., i, p. 436.

the disposal of surpluses where 'an expansion and refinement of everyday wants has not taken place'.[23] There is even a passage in which Smith's diatribes upon the iniquities of the wealthy and powerful have a Marxian sting. Both believed that their follies and greed must bring about a revolution, though they had very different revolutions in mind.

> A revolution of the greatest importance to the public happiness was in this matter brought about by two different orders of people who had not the least intention to serve the public. To gratify the most childish vanity was the sole motive of the great proprietors. The merchants and artificers, much less ridiculous, acted merely from a view to their own interest, and in pursuit of their own pedlar principle of turning a penny wherever a penny was to be got. Neither of them had either knowledge or foresight of that great revolution which the folly of the one, and the industry of the other, was gradually bringing about.[24]

The proprietors and merchants were not alone in their ignorance of an impending revolution, for Smith himself was unaware of the immense changes already in train when the *Wealth of nations* was written. Indeed, the implication of the arguments he used would rule out the possibility of rapid and sustained economic growth. The great revolution of which he wrote was an economic revolution, and was brought about by the group of changes now called modernization, but it was not an *industrial revolution* as that term has come to be used. If one were to characterize the difference between the two revolutions in a single phrase, one might say that whereas a defining characteristic of an industrial revolution is exponential economic growth, the expected outcome of modernization in Smith's view was asymptotic growth.

He believed that economic growth had been substantial during the two preceding centuries.

> Since the time of Henry VIII the wealth and revenue of the country have been continually advancing, and, in the course of their progress, their pace seems rather to have been gradually accelerated, than retarded. They seem not only to have been going on, but to have been going on faster and faster. The wages of labour have been continually increasing during the same period, and in the greater part of the different branches of trade and manufactures the profits of stock have been diminishing.[25]

This is a more optimistic picture of English economic history than would be thought orthodox today, but it did not lead Smith to an equally optimistic assessment of the future.

23 Weber, *Social and economic organization*, p. 189.
24 Smith, *Wealth of nations*, i, p. 440.
25 Ibid., i, p. 100.

His doubts sprang in part from his analysis of the limitations upon the profitable employment of capital, and in part from his views on population trends. Like many of his contemporaries, he read, in recent Dutch experience, lessons about the future of other countries. Holland he held to be a richer country than England and one in which wage rates were higher, but the rate of interest lower than in any other country. 'The government there borrow at two per cent, and private people of good credit at three.'[26] Comparable rates in England were 3 per cent and 4 per cent; in France higher still. Relative abundance of capital seeking profitable employment kept interest rates very low in Holland (and explained the large Dutch holdings in English and French funds); its relative scarcity meant much higher rates in Scotland and France. In general, he observed that high wages accompanied low interest rates, as in Holland, and vice versa as in France. Exceptionally, in colonies of recent settlement, both might be high together, although this happy state could not last long. But both might also be low, and Smith envisaged this as the most likely state towards which an economy might move. 'In a country which had acquired that full complement of riches which the nature of its soil and climate, and its situation with respect to other countries, allowed it to acquire; which could, therefore, advance no further, and which was not going backwards, both the wages of labour and the profits of stock would probably be very low.'[27]

The profits of stock would be low in this limiting case because investment opportunities had been exhausted. Wages would also tend to be low because, as Smith put it in a passage which foreshadowed in part the views of Malthus: 'Every species of animals naturally multiplies in proportion to the means of their subsistence.'[28] A country might be wealthy but no longer growing in wealth. 'If in such a country the wages of labour had ever been more than sufficient to maintain the labourer, and to enable him to bring up a family, the competition of the labourers and the interest of the masters would soon reduce them to this lowest rate which is consistent with common humanity.'[29] Labour does best during the middle stages of modernization in Smith's analysis, because for a time capital finds the opportunity for fair profit while simultaneously labour may be relatively scarce.

It is in the progressive state, while the society is advancing to the further acquisition, rather than when it has acquired its full complement of riches, that the condition of the labouring poor, of the great body of the people, seems to be the happiest and most comfortable. It is hard in the stationary, and miserable in the declining state. The progressive state is in reality the cheerful and hearty state to all the different orders of the society. The stationary is dull; the declining, melancholy.[30]

26 Ibid., i, p. 102.
27 Ibid., i, p. 106.
28 Ibid., i, p. 89.
29 Ibid., i, p. 80.
30 Ibid., i, pp. 90–1.

As modernization grew more complete, the prospects for both capital and labour would dim. The most favourable outcome that could be readily envisaged was one in which the material necessities of labouring men were set by social convention at a level well above that of bare subsistence. The least favourable might be very bleak. Both were equally consonant with what is now called modernization. Both David Ricardo, a generation later, and Marx after a further half-century, shared Smith's doubts about the prospect for the real wages of working men. The wages fund doctrine leaves little room for hope on this score. Yet, by definition, if real wages fail to rise, and *a fortiori* if they fall, industrialization is not taking place. A secular rise in real income per head is more a utopian ideal than an object for practical endeavour if economies develop during modernization in the way Smith adumbrated – and his views on the matter were echoed by most of his successors until late in the following century. Marx, for instance, was firm in his retention of Ricardo's argument on this point. 'The value of labour-power is determined by the value of the necessaries of life habitually required by the average labourer. The quantity of these necessaries is known at any given epoch of a given society, and can therefore be treated as a constant magnitude.'[31]

The course of events for many decades after the publication of the *Wealth of nations* contained little to shake the convictions of those who doubted that the lot of working men could be greatly ameliorated. It is ironic, in view of the doctrine which links industrialization to rising real income per head, that there is clearer evidence for rising real wages in England in the first half of the eighteenth century and the second half of the nineteenth than for the intervening period during which the industrial revolution is usually supposed to have occurred. To save the phenomena, if rising real incomes are to be a defining characteristic of industrialization, their appearance must be conceded to be a heavily lagged effect.

It is clear enough why it was that Smith was mistaken in ruling out any hope of industrialization (in the sense the term is used in this essay). He failed to foresee the phenomenal productive powers which the new forms of fixed investment made possible. It was inventions like the steam engine, the coke-fired blast furnace and the railway which proved him wrong in time, rather than some flaw in his logic or failure to perceive the nature of the modernization process, unless indeed this last is taken to imply the sort of technological advance which actually took place.

By Marx's time, the productive power of the new machines was already a dominant feature of the economic scene. This obliged him to treat the future prospects of man very differently from Smith, quite apart from any differences which might have sprung from their different attitudes to the modernization process in general. Factory industry appeared to Marx to be creating both greater misery and greater scope for future improvement than was conceivable without it. 'Fanatically bent on making value expand

31 Marx, *Capital*, ii, p. 527.

itself, he [the capitalist] ruthlessly forces the human race to produce for production's sake; he thus forces the development of the productive powers of society, and creates those material conditions, which alone can form the real basis of a higher form of society, a society in which the full and free development of every individual forms the ruling principle.'[32] Meanwhile, productive potential was being perverted because of the way wealth was being dissipated: 'the extraordinary productiveness of modern industry . . . allows of the unproductive employment of a larger and larger part of the working class, and the consequent reproduction, on a constantly extending scale, of the ancient domestic slaves under the name of a servant class, including men-servants, women-servants, lackeys, etc.'[33]

Marx wrote *Capital* at a time when real wages were at the start of a period of steady and substantial growth. Had he written, say, 20 years later, he might have been tempted to apply to the later nineteenth century an observation he made about the fifteenth and early eighteenth centuries: 'under special stimulus to enrichment, such as the opening of new markets, or of new spheres for the outlay of capital in consequence of newly developed social wants, etc., the scale of accumulation may be suddenly extended [and] the demand for labourers may exceed the supply, and, therefore, wages may rise.'[34] Later in the chapter in which this passage occurs, however, Marx gives reasons for supposing that such a situation must prove temporary because of the basic defects of the capitalist system.[35]

In fact, real wages have risen steadily in the century since the publication of *Capital*, with only intermittent checks, and the assumption that this may be expected to continue is deeply rooted in popular attitudes and in academic analysis (the prevailing definition of industrialization reflects this assumption). Over the same period during which real wages have been rising, mortality rates in urban areas, a measure which Marx sometimes used as a proxy for misery and degradation, have turned strongly downward; there has been a shift in the structure of aggregate demand which has combined with social preferences to reduce the numbers in domestic service drastically; the era of high mass consumption has dawned; 'mixed' economies have become common.[36]

Marx had the advantage over Smith in being able to observe very clearly that production *could* grow exponentially rather than tending to level off to some asymptote reached when the modernization process had exhausted the openings for profitable investment. He saw, in the tension between exponential

---

32 Ibid., ii, p. 603.
33 Ibid., ii, pp. 447–8.
34 Ibid., ii, p. 626.
35 Ibid., ii, pp. 634–5.
36 The possibilities latent in the last of these developments is suggested by Marx himself, although it was still too early for him to assess its longer-term significance. In discussing the effects of the Factory Acts of 1850 and 1853, he wrote: 'Their wonderful development [that of the industries affected by the Acts] from 1853 to 1860, hand-in-hand with the physical and moral regeneration of the factory workers, struck the most purblind.' Marx, *Capital*, i, p. 282.

growth in productive capacity and the absence of growth in real wages among
the vast majority of mankind, the certainty of violent, revolutionary change.
Today, as far distant in time from *Capital* as *Capital* was from the *Wealth
of nations*, we can see that the secular trend of real wages is no more bound
to be flat than that of total production, but that, on the contrary, the two
(when growth in total production is measure *per caput*) have marched closely
together across the graphs of the past century.

With the benefit of hindsight, it may be said, the link between
modernization and full-blown industrialization is evident, however it may
have seemed to Smith at the onset of the industrial revolution or to Marx
part-way through it. But hindsight is not always clear, and its benefit is
sometimes questionable. In a rather trivial sense, since modernization was
taking place in England from the sixteenth century onwards (Smith, Marx,
Weber and many lesser men are in substantial agreement here although
their descriptive vocabularies differ), and was followed by the industrial
revolution, it may be true that Smith's analysis was mistaken. But this is
to say only that what happened, happened. We know that modernization
may be followed by industrialization, but not that it *must*, or even that such
a sequence of events is likely.[37]

Marx's account of the transition from handicraft industry to large-scale
power-driven factory industry is interesting in this connection, since in his view
the crucial change came before the use of inanimate sources of power on a
large scale. He distinguished between tools and machines, the one characteristic of manufacture (handicraft industry), the other of modern industry.

> The machine proper . . . is a mechanism that, after being set in motion,
> performs with its tools the same operations that were formerly done
> by the workman with similar tools. Whether the motive power is
> derived from man, or from some other machine, makes no difference
> in this respect. From the moment that the tool proper is taken from
> man, and fitted into a mechanism, a machine takes the place of a mere
> implement. The difference strikes one at once, even in those cases
> where man himself continues to be the prime mover.[38]

Again, 'The machine, which is the starting point of the industrial revolution,
supersedes the workman, who handles a single tool, by a mechanism
operating with a number of similar tools, and set in motion by a single motive
power, whatever the form of that power may be.'[39] The distinction between

---

37 The concatenation of changes which comprise the industrial revolution are a good example
of what Hayek had in mind in writing: 'Many of the greatest things man has achieved are
not the result of consciously directed thought, and still less the product of a deliberately co-
ordinated effort of many individuals, but of a process in which the individual plays a part which
he can never fully understand'. Von Hayek, *Counter-revolution of science*, p. 84. The act of
comprehension is almost as taxing as that of creation.
38 Marx, *Capital*, ii, p. 368.
39 Ibid., ii, pp. 370–1.

animate and inanimate sources of power Marx held to be unimportant. 'The steam engine itself, such as it was at its invention, during the manufacturing period at the close of the seventeenth century, and such as it continued to be down to 1780, did not give rise to any industrial revolution. It was, on the contrary, the invention of machines that made a revolution in the form of steam engines necessary.'[40]

In a sense, the essence of the modernization/industrialization question lies in this last sentence. As rationality spreads and markets broaden, productivity in many branches of industry will increase by the division of labour and the adoption of machinery. If the 'right' invention inevitably appears to match every opportunity as it emerges, the smallest gains will tend to be cumulative. Marx's view of the introduction of the steam engine by factory industry is reminiscent of Voltaire's aphorism about God – if He had not existed, He would have had to be invented. Rostow takes a similar line.[41] Smith vividly described how this process might become institutionalized. Having noted how many machines had been designed by workers to save themselves labour, he continues: 'Many improvements have been made by the ingenuity of the makers of machines, when to make them became the business of a peculiar trade; and some by that of those who are called philosophers or men of speculation, whose trade it is not to do anything, but to observe everything; and who, upon that account, are often capable of combining together the powers of the most distant and dissimilar objects.'[42]

If, however, technological advance were a more wayward and circumstantial matter, and there were no automatic response to opportunity, it is incautious to assume that the issue can be passed over so lightly. It is interesting that Rostow takes exception to Schumpeter's discussion of innovation, quoting a passage which bears repeating:

> It might be thought that innovation can never be anything else but an effort to cope with a given economic situation. In a sense this is true. For a given innovation to become possible, there must always be some 'objective needs' to be satisfied and some 'objective conditions'; but they rarely, if ever, uniquely determine what kind of innovation will satisfy them, and as a rule they can be satisfied in many different ways. Most important of all, they may remain unsatisfied for an indefinite time, which shows that they are not in themselves sufficient to produce an innovation.[43]

Ironically, the same passage in *Capital*, from which Marx's observations about tools, machinery and the steam engine were drawn, contains an aside

40 Ibid., ii, p. 370.
41 'The appropriate general proposition concerning the composition of innovations seems to be that necessity is the mother of invention.' Rostow, *Economic growth*, p. 83.
42 Smith, *Wealth of nations*, i, p. 14
43 Schumpeter, *Business cycles*, i, p. 85n.

which might suggest a very different conclusion from that which Marx drew. He refers to the drainage of the Haarlemmermeer by steam pump in 1836–7, noting that the machinery used the same principle as an ordinary pump and differed only in that it was driven by 'cyclopean steam-engines'.[44] In a footnote he describes the earlier history of drainage in Holland.

> It was partly the want of streams with a good fall on them, and partly their battles with superabundance of water in other respects that compelled the Dutch to resort to wind as a motive power. The windmill itself they got from Germany, where its invention was the origin of a petty squabble between the nobles, the priests, and the emperor, as to which of those three the wind 'belonged'. The air makes bondage, was the cry in Germany, at the same time that the wind was making Holland free. What it reduced to bondage in this case, was not the Dutchman, but the land for the Dutchman.[45]

The perennial drainage problem which has plagued Dutch history is technically similar to the problem of evacuating water from coal mines, for which the Newcomen engine was developed in England. In both cases, a basic factor of production was in danger of destruction (or at least of becoming inaccessible) unless huge volumes of water could be pumped away. That the steam engine represents a better solution than the windmill to the drainage problem in Holland is clear from the eagerness with which it was adopted at the Haarlemmermeer and elsewhere, but that it would have been developed independently in Holland is highly doubtful, even though more was at stake for Holland than for England, and Holland was perhaps a more fully modernized country than England in the early eighteenth century.

If it is true that certain important technological innovations first introduced in the eighteenth century, such as the steam engine and the coke-fed blast furnace, were the product of special, local circumstances;[46] and if it is also true that without them, productivity, handicapped by a lack of power and precision in the available machinery, could have risen only moderately, then the connection between modernization and industrialization appears much more a matter of happy coincidence than of ineluctable necessity. It is not what was common to all modernizing countries, but what was peculiar to England which then appears important. And what is explained is not simply why the industrial revolution occurred in England earlier than elsewhere, but why it occurred at all.

Empirical evidence and historical models

The two conditions about technological innovation and productivity growth which must be satisfied if the conclusion about the nature of the connection

44 Marx, *Capital*, ii, p. 370.
45 Ibid., ii, p. 369n.
46 See chapter 4.

between modernization and industrialization is to follow are plausible but not conclusively demonstrable. It is likely on general grounds that a very large part of the total gain in productivity during the industrial revolution sprang from technological advances.[47] It is also reasonable to suppose that the relative scarcities of important raw materials in England, combined with local factor endowment, served both to produce an unusual range of problems at an early stage in industrial expansion and also to permit solutions whose long-term implications were not apparent at their first adoption. I have discussed these circumstances and their outcome elsewhere,[48] and wish in this essay to concentrate mainly on giving a context to the English experience by commenting on events elsewhere in western Europe. However, it may be useful to refer briefly to those peculiarities of English economic life which had a bearing on the development of the steam engine and a new technology of iron production.

Shortage of wood made England increasingly dependent on coal for domestic and industrial fuel from the late sixteenth century onwards and, until well into the nineteenth century, English coal production dwarfed that of continental Europe. The coal industry's growth involved severe difficulties from the start, connected above all with mine drainage as the pits went deeper. Immense pains were taken to overcome them. Three-quarters of all patents issued between 1561 and 1668 are said to have been related to the coal industry's problems in some degree, and one-seventh involved drainage. The engines of Savery and Newcomen were late entrants into the competition to find an answer to this problem. By the early eighteenth century, Newcomen engines had been developed to the point where they were reliable and necessary adjuncts to coal production, at once essential to its continued expansion and unusable without a local supply of coal. James Watt's refinement of the new machine made it the means of revolutionizing transport and transforming production in industry after industry as the nineteenth century progressed.[49]

The fuel problem also loomed large in iron production. In the first three-quarters of the eighteenth century, iron production made little progress in England due to a lack of charcoal or an acceptable substitute. In France at the same time, iron production, using traditional methods, expanded more rapidly and eventually surpassed English levels substantially. It was clear to many men that coal or coke might provide a good solution to the problem of finding a charcoal substitute, but it proved very hard to produce iron

---

47 For the class of reasons discussed, for example, by Solow, 'Technical change'.
48 See note 46 above.
49 On the question of patents, see Mason, *History of the sciences*, p. 217. Levasseur made an interesting calculation to drive home the significance of the steam engine in extending man's productive powers. He noted that, on the assumption that the amount of work done by one steam horse-power was equal to that of 21 men, France had at its disposal just over one million slaves of a new mechanical kind in 1840. By the mid-1880s, the figure had risen to 98 million, or two and one-half slaves for every inhabitant of France. Levasseur, *La population française*, iii, p. 74.

of acceptable quality in this way because of the difficulty of keeping the chemical impurities in the iron sufficiently low. Once the trick was learned, however, old limitations upon the scale of iron production disappeared. Mineral sources of heat and power, unlike the vegetable and animal alternatives which they supplanted, could be tapped in larger and larger quantities without driving up the marginal costs of production. Industry at long last escaped from the limitations under which it had laboured as long as it was dependent upon the productivity of the land. Inanimate sources of heat and power offered great advantages over animate sources for this reason.

The steam engine and the coke-fired blast furnace were the result of a long defensive struggle against intractable production difficulties. They did not occur when production was rising unusually fast. In the second case, production was barely holding its own when the crucial innovations were made. This makes a contrast with the course of change in the cotton industry, where the burst of innovations occurred at a time of rising production and bright prospects. The water frame and spinning jenny came into use in the 1770s (the patents were dated 1769 and 1770) at a time when cotton production was already growing fast. Retained imports of raw cotton had doubled in the previous quarter-century.[50] They were the result of a clear opportunity to expand rather than the wish to avoid contraction, and they presaged a period of much more hectic growth. The cotton industry during this period progressed in a manner which conforms well to Smith's view of 'the progressive state'. Considerable growth is clearly possible in this state and is linked to modernization, but for an industrial revolution to occur, there must be a switch to a new energy source.

The power requirements of the new textile machines were so modest that the steam engine was no more than a useful alternative to a waterfall for many years. The overshot wheel provided all the power that was needed to drive them. But there came a time when greater power was needed and unused waterfalls with a sufficient head were few and remote. Even in the textile industry, and still more in industrial production at large, it is reasonable to assume that the factory would not have become the predominant unit of production without the new technology of coal, steam and iron. The unprecedented and continuous growth in production per head which fascinated Marx's generation was based upon it.[51]

If it were always a case of 'Cometh the hour, cometh the engine', it would matter little how the new technology first came into being, since the need for a cheap, reliable source of energy to magnify the productive power of the new machines would have ensured its development. If, on the contrary, technological advance in a pre-scientific age is far from automatic, whatever the 'objective' possibilities of the time; if Schumpeter's view is more just

50 Deane and Cole, *British economic growth*, p. 51.

51 Jevons, in *The coal question*, published a work which reflects this interest and the new attitude to the creation of wealth very well at almost exactly the same time as *Capital*.

than Rostow's; if the development of power sources for textile machinery might have stopped short with water power as Dutch drainage did with the windmill, then the particular course of events in England will repay close attention. So, too, will the circumstances of other European countries at the same time, for they suggest other possibilities within the general framework of modernization.

Smith wrote not only of the relative abundance that was attainable in the progressive state, but also of stationary and declining states in which the lot of men was far less enviable. And it appears from the context of his remarks that he thought that a country could be modernized and yet find itself in one of the two latter states as easily as in the progressive. Europe in the eighteenth century affords examples of all three and also of more mixed conditions. Comparison with continental Europe offers some indirect warrant for thinking that England was fortunate to have remained in a progressive state.

Smith appears to have believed that Holland was in what he called a stationary state, having moved close to the asymptote which represented the full extent of growth possible in the circumstances of the day. The principal evidence for this was the prevailing rate at which money could be borrowed on good credit, and he found it necessary to remark that there was no good reason to suppose that business in Holland had actually declined, fearing that his readers would draw this inference.[52] In his view, Holland was the country with the highest real income per head of any in Europe, but was, for that reason, the more likely to be at or close to the limit of growth, rather than being poised for a continuing surge of expansion. That Holland had reached a high degree of rationality in economic affairs seems indisputable. Nor was this just an urban phenomenon, leaving the countryside largely untouched. A very telling example of the suffusion of the countryside by advanced forms of economic organization is to be found in Roessingh's analysis of a set of tax records relating to the Veluwe in 1749.[53]

The Veluwe lies in central Holland south of the Zuider Zee. It had never attained the degree of commercial or industrial development found in the west of Holland, and particularly in the province of Holland itself. It was an agricultural area with no large town, where the soils were at best of moderate quality. Yet Roessingh's study shows that even small settlements from 400 inhabitants upwards almost invariably had a village shop (at a time when shops were still rare in England in places of similar size), a tailor, a shoemaker and very often a weaver and baker as well. All were frequently found in much smaller villages too, and the hierarchical pattern of service function by settlement size was very well ordered. This was an economy in which division of labour had been pushed very far; in which money and the market entered into the lives even of small men to a degree which

52 Smith, *Wealth of nations*, i, p. 103.
53 Roessingh, 'Village and hamlet'.

supported shops in small villages and caused wives to cease baking at home. The villages of the Veluwe were far removed from the type of communities which Tönnies had in mind in describing the nature of *Gemeinschaft*, even though theirs was largely an agricultural economy in a strictly rural setting. The Veluwe was part of an economy which had been modernized but not industrialized. Such an economy does not necessarily mean steadily rising real incomes, not does it imply a move towards industrialization. When rationality prevails and men's actions are informed by self-interest, there must be gains in efficiency, but there is no certain and permanent rise in living standards for the bulk of the population.

At much the same time that the Veluwe census was taken, in another part of the Low Countries – in Belgian Flanders – the local economy was about to enter into what Smith might have called a declining state, as the work of Deprez and Mendels has shown.[54] They describe the instability of an economy, already substantially modernized, which becomes heavily dependent upon cottage industry to supplement income from agriculture. What begins as a useful addition to farming income comes to be, for many men, their prime or sole means of support. Population growth accelerates when checks upon early marriage and high fertility, which are more powerful in a landholding community, lose their force. With the labour force growing more rapidly than opportunities for profitable employment, real incomes fall and the bitterly impoverished population is pushed down towards the lowest levels of subsistence. The lives of most men in the Vieuxbourg area, where conditions were especially bad, were indeed 'melancholy', to use Smith's adjective for the declining state, by the end of the eighteenth century. In the Twente region of the province of Overijssel in east Holland, the declining, or at best stationary, state supervened about 1750. As in Flanders, the local linen industry proved unable to expand its markets as quickly as was needed to keep pace with the growth of the rural industrial population.[55] The economic history of early modern Europe contains many examples of areas at various stages along the road to modernization where change was accompanied by falling real incomes per head.[56] Eighteenth-century Holland represents as a whole a relatively happy outcome to this challenge in that real wages were maintained at a fairly high level.[57] Rationality in economic life neither led to a take-off, nor plunged the population into misery.

---

54 Deprez, 'Demographic development of Flanders'. Mendels's work is summarized briefly in Mendels, 'Industrialization and population pressure'.

55 Slicher van Bath, *Een samenleving onder spanning*. His conclusions are summarized in Faber et al., 'Population changes and economic developments in the Netherlands'.

56 Braun's study of an upland Swiss area is an example of the type of change which can easily produce this result. Braun, *Industrialisierung und Volksleben*.

57 It also illustrates a point which can hardly be made too strongly – that economic fortunes were at least as much a matter of region as of country in early modern Europe. They remained so during the early stages of the industrial revolution. I have traced one example of this in Wrigley, *Industrial growth and population change*.

Smith would not have been surprised at events in Flanders and elsewhere. Like Malthus and many later writers, including Marx, he saw dangers to living standards in rapid population growth and was inclined to regard population growth as dependent upon economic conditions. If the opportunities for employment grew, the labour supply could be relied upon to increase commensurately and was only too likely to increase more than commensurately. Marx expressed a view about what determines wage levels which is, in substance, the same as that of Smith or Malthus, although he had a special reason for taking a sombre view of their secular trend. On the former point he wrote. 'The value of labour-power is determined, as in the case of every other commodity, by the labour-time necessary for the production, and consequently also the reproduction, of this special article . . . Given the individual, the production of labour-power consists in his reproduction of himself or his maintenance . . . in other words, the value of labour-power is the value of the means of subsistence necessary for the maintenance of the labourer.'[58] Convention may, however, play a part in determining the subsistence level.

His natural wants, such as food, clothing, fuel, and housing, vary according to the climatic and other physical conditions of his country. On the other hand, the number and extent of his so-called necessary wants, as also the modes of satisfying them, are themselves the product of historical development, and depend therefore to a great extent on the degree of civilisation of a country, more particularly on the conditions under which, and consequently on the habits and degree of comfort in which, the class of free labourers has been formed. In contradistinction therefore to the case of other commodities, there enters into the determination of the value of labour-power a historical and moral element. Nevertheless, in a given country, at a given period, the average quantity of the means of subsistence necessary for the labourer is practically known.[59]

This was very much Smith's view too. He felt the disquiet to which Malthus was later to give fuller expression, although his doubts were tempered by his appreciation of the complexity of the process of growth which gave some ground for optimism. Nevertheless, if population is sensitive to economic stimuli and grows readily when conditions improve (for example, because young people marry when wheat is cheap), and if the rate at which population can grow exceeds the rate at which the economy can expand, then there is little hope of increasing subsistence wages set at some conventional standard and a pressing fear that a volatile population growth may cause the conventional standard to be eroded. There was no warrant in past experience for expecting an economy to grow steadily at, say, 3 per cent

58 Marx, *Capital*, p. 149.
59 Ibid., i, p. 150.

per annum, a rate which would ensure that production grew more rapidly than population, and so enable real incomes to rise in spite of growing numbers.

By Marx's day, it had become clear that a rapid and sustained growth in industrial production was possible, but in his analysis, labour, by one of the crucial paradoxes of the capitalist mode of production, is actually worse off as a result, both in income and in the general nature and conditions of work. His analysis depends upon his insistence that each historic mode of production has its own special population laws.[60] In a capitalist society, the industrial reserve army grows. Its relative size determines wage levels, and 'The fact that the means of production, and the productiveness of labour, increase more rapidly than the productive population, expresses itself, therefore, capitalistically in the inverse form that the labouring population always increases more rapidly than the conditions under which capital can employ this increase for its own self-expansion.'[61]

Given that over-rapid population growth may be a cause of economic distress (as it seems to have been in England in the late sixteenth and early seventeenth centuries), it is of interest that England in the second half of the eighteenth century was perhaps in greater danger than France or Holland, the two other countries in which modernization had progressed furthest.[62] The threat to wages posed by population growth had been increasing in most of Europe in the later eighteenth century. Ireland had embarked on a period of her history which brings to mind the process which Geertz calls agricultural involution, which 'resembles nothing else so much as treading water. Higher-level densities are offset by greater labour inputs into the same productive system, but output per head (or per mouth) remains more or less constant.'[63] The pool grows larger, but the numbers treading water in it increase at least as quickly.[64] Many other countries, especially in eastern and southern Europe, where population growth rates were often high, would eventually have met a fate like that which devastated Ireland, but for the safety valves afforded by industrialization in western Europe and the possibility of emigrating to countries of European settlement outside Europe. But in France, there were signs that rationality was beginning to affect reproductive behaviour.

Perhaps it is symbolically appropriate that the first group that is known to have adopted effective and conscious family limitation as part of their

60 Ibid., ii, p. 645.

61 Ibid., ii, p. 660.

62 In Holland, population increased hardly at all in the eighteenth century. In 1700, the total lay between 1.85 and 1.95 million; in 1795, 2.08 million (Faber et al., 'Population changes and economic developments in the Netherlands', p. 110). In France, the growth was faster but much less fast than that in England. The French population rose from 19.3 to 26.3 million between 1700 and 1789 (Reinhard et al., *Histoire générale de la population mondiale*, pp. 252, 683). The population of England and Wales grew from about 5.5 to 9.2 million between 1700 and 1800.

63 Geertz, *Agricultural involution*, p. 78.

64 Ibid., p. 95.

habit of life should have been the bourgeoisie of Geneva, the city of Calvin. This pattern of behaviour was firmly established by the end of the seventeenth century.[65] A century later, it was growing common throughout much of France. Characteristically, it seems to have begun in small towns before the surrounding countryside was affected, but very early in the nineteenth century there were several large areas in which family limitation was widespread among peasant populations.[66] In consequence, French population growth was much more modest in the nineteenth century than that of any other major European state. By the end of the century, this had become a matter for the keenest regret among many French writers, an attitude still evident in the work of recent French scholars.[67] If the industrial revolution had not occurred, however, France might have been the envy of Europe. French population trends were much safer than English in the economic world which Smith depicted. The principles of rationality and self-interest which inform the entire range of changes during modernization point to fertility control within marriage as surely as to the division of labour or to the principle of universalistic criteria for group membership.

The process of modernization may also have affected fertility levels in other countries earlier than in England.[68] It may prove to be the case that in parts of Holland there was restriction of family size at an early date. Van der Woude's tabulations for certain settlements in the province of Holland show that household size was unusually small in the late seventeenth and eighteenth centuries, and the number of children per family somewhat lower than in England.[69] This was an area deeply involved in commerce, with a high proportion of the population literate, perhaps the most thoroughly modernized part of that country which contemporaries regarded as the furthest advanced in modernization. Dutch church registers do not easily lend themselves to family reconstitution so that clear-cut confirmation of low marital fertility is hard to obtain, but it is at least possible that here, as in Geneva, rationality produced a lowering of fertility in marriage among

65 Henry, *Anciennes familles genevoises*, pp. 77–8, 94–110, 127–42.

66 There is an excellent brief review of early modern French demographic history in Goubert, 'Historical demography and early modern French history'. Chamoux and Dauphin, 'La contraception avant la révolution française'. Etienne van de Walle of the Office of Population Research, Princeton University, tells me that the large-scale study of nineteenth-century fertility in progress in that Office shows that by about 1830, when marital fertility was already low in parts of the south-west and Normandy, there was in those areas a very marked association between low marital fertility and early marriage – a very 'rational' pattern of behaviour in the sense that ability to limit family size within marriage removes what would otherwise be a telling 'rational' argument against early marriage. There is some discussion of this point for a later period in his article, 'Marriage and marital fertility'.

67 See, for example, Sauvy, *Théorie générale*, ii, pp. 7–20.

68 I have found some evidence of family limitation in Colyton, Devon, in the second half of the seventeenth century, but it is not yet possible to say how widespread this was. And all trace of it had disappeared in Colyton by the middle decades of the eighteenth century. See chapter 10.

69 Van der Woude, 'Huishouding in Nederland in het verleden'.

some elements of the population. There is also evidence that a substantial proportion of men and women never married. Postponement or avoidance of marriage is an equally effective 'rational' strategy (although it may also occur for other reasons). Early in the nineteenth century, a tendency towards modern patterns of marital fertility appeared among the native-born in New England.[70] It was well established there half a century before the same pattern appeared in England.

Population growth in England accelerated sharply in the mid-eighteenth century and remained at a high level until late in the nineteenth, at or a little over 1 per cent per annum. If incomes were not eventually to suffer as a result, production had to increase at least as fast as the population. To Smith, the chance of tripling the national product in a century (roughly the scale of increase needed merely to offset population growth) would have seemed slight; and time for a solution was short when growth was so rapid. Over-rapid population growth brings great dangers to a modernizing society, although in an industrializing society, population growth may even confer benefits. It was England's good fortune that the industrial revolution rescued her from what must otherwise have been a period of great stress due to the pace of population increase.

Smith regarded investment in land as the surest way of increasing national wealth.

> The capital employed in agriculture, therefore, not only puts into motion a greater quantity of productive labour than any equal capital employed in manufactures, but in proportion, too, to the quantity of productive labour which it employs, it adds a much greater value to the annual produce of the land and labour of the country, to the real wealth and revenue of its inhabitants. Of all the ways in which a capital can be employed, it is by far the most advantageous to society.[71]

The extent of the growth in industrial production was, in his view, geared to agricultural expansion. But land was virtually in fixed supply and the increases in production attainable from land in farms were limited and usually secured only over a long period. Therefore, growth in general must be limited or, in the terminology I have used in this essay, asymptotic. Modern industry based on the steam engine, a new iron technology and the organization of production in factories, came just in time to save the day. Whether the further development of the sources of increased productivity familiar to Smith could have achieved the same success is highly

---

70 See, for example, Uhlenberg, 'Cohorts of native born Massachusetts women, 1830–1920', especially tables 1 and 2'. Evidence of family limitation among small Quaker groups within the settled American population may be found in Wells, 'Family size and fertility control'. There is inconclusive but suggestive evidence that marital fertility fell at the end of the eighteenth century among high-status Dutch settlers in the Hudson valley in Kenney, 'Patricians and plebians in colonial Albany'.

71 Smith, *Wealth of nations*, i, p. 385.

doubtful. The industrial revolution represented a break which ultimately generalized and extended the scope of modernization while at the same time modifying it, but which was initially ill-matched with it.

Capital is, in a sense, a commentary on the severity of the tensions which were produced by the uneasy marriage of industrialization and modernization, a marriage in which the former proved to be the salvation of the latter in England by giving it a vastly larger economic base and freeing it from restrictions which had earlier seemed inescapable. But the price was high. Marx made an attempt to categorize the lessons to be learned from the turmoil of the first half of the nineteenth century in England, and to glean from this experience an insight into the future. His message was clear. The marriage was intolerable and must be dissolved if the benefits made possible by industrialization (but denied to the masses by the capitalist system set in a bourgeois state) were ever to be distributed equitably. The marriage proved more durable than Marx expected, and it became the object of widespread emulation. As time passed, the characters of the two partners merged into each other, and the early difficulties faded from memory. What had seemed inconceivable to Smith and intolerable to Marx developed into an acceptable commonplace. National product could rise without apparent limit, and was so divided as to assure most men of rising real incomes.

Some of the difference between the gradual development of modernization and the novel changes produced by the industrial revolution are epitomized in the contrast between old and new urban growth in England. London grew steadily throughout the period of modernization in England from the sixteenth century onwards. By the end of the eighteenth, it was already a large city with a population close to one million. London's development was relatively smooth and continuous. The city grew no faster in the nineteenth than in the seventeenth century. Already in 1700 very complex arrangements were needed to sustain it, and the London market helped to cause notable changes in areas at some distance from London – in the agriculture of Fen-edge villages in Cambridgeshire, for example, or in those Leicestershire villages which became the home of the framework knitting industry. The growth of London was made possible by the economic and social changes of modernization, which were in turn fostered by it.[72] Defoe's London at the beginning of the eighteenth century, like Dickens's London in the mid-nineteenth, might be termed modernized, but not industrialized (there was, of course, a very large employment in industry, but the production units were usually tiny, often the home itself). Literacy was higher than elsewhere in England,[73] and the economic and social functioning of the city conformed well to what would be expected from a checklist of modernization: the chief concomitants of rationality and self-interest were eminently visible, while some of the most perturbing results of sheer size became less serious

---

72 See chapter 6.
73 This is evident from the materials assembled at the Cambridge Group for the History of Population and Social Structure, and summarized in Schofield, 'Dimensions of illiteracy'.

towards the end of the eighteenth century. Mortality rates, for example, had fallen considerably from the peak reached in the early decades of the century.

In contrast to the pattern of city growth in London, the large urban sprawls which unrolled across the industrial north and midlands from the end of the eighteenth century might almost be described as industrial but not modern. In these areas, levels of literacy were often very low, as poor as in the most backward rural areas of the country, and mortality rates were frequently very high. Even the free play of the market and the universal use of money as a means of exchange were threatened by the spread of truck systems of payment and the tying of employees to the company shop. Consumption standards were low and of limited scope. Tightly knit industrial and mining villages were almost solely of one class and there were few visible 'betters' whose patterns of consumption could be aped. Rationality and self-interest had small room to flourish among men and women in the areas of working-class housing which grew up in knots round the factory or the pithead. This was a far cry from the capitalism of myriad small producers and consumers. It is not purely fanciful to see in communities of this type as many of the features which are held to go with *Gemeinschaft* as with *Gesellschaft*.[74] Industrialization brought with it major regressive features judged by the measuring rods of modernization.

In time this could be seen as a case of *reculer pour mieux sauter*, but it is hardly surprising that it was seldom seen in this way at the time. With hindsight, the magnitude of contemporary hazards and uncertainties tends to be lost to view. All one-piece theories of modernization/industrialization, such as the analogy with the take-off of an airplane, bear too heavily the marks of *ex post facto* summary to do justice to the industrial revolution. There is much to be learned from both Smith and Marx about the surprising and uncertain course taken by events. The fact that neither was right in the long run is not a good reason for ignoring their arguments. It is quite possible for a man to have, say, a one-in-fifty chance of hitting the jackpot and yet still win it. The relationship between modernization and industrialization cannot be reduced to simple odds, of course. Perhaps the analogy is misleading, but it will have served a useful purpose if it underlines the absence of any inevitability about the transition from a modernized but pre-industrial economy to the post-industrial world.

---

74 Much of this has remained and is reflected in descriptions of the life of the industrial working classes in the recent past. See, for example, Hoggart, *The uses of literacy*.

4
The Supply of Raw Materials in the Industrial Revolution

Any great increase in the output of industry, such as began in England towards the end of the eighteenth century, must have as its counterpart an equally great increase in the input of industrial raw materials at the other end of the process of production.[1] The problem of providing an adequate raw material supply had been acute in many branches of industry in earlier centuries. The removal of these constrictions is intimately connected with several important aspects of the rapid growth which occurred, and its study affords a vantage point from which they can conveniently be surveyed.

The most important change in raw material provision which took place was the substitution of inorganic for organic sources of supply, of mineral for vegetable or animal raw materials. This was a *sine qua non* of sustained industrial growth on a large scale, for when industrial growth is based upon vegetable and animal raw materials present success can usually be obtained only at the cost of future difficulties. England in the sixteenth and seventeenth centuries provides some typical examples of the dilemma which confronts industries when they use animal or vegetable raw materials. The iron industry of the Weald was able to expand without prejudice to its future prosperity only up to the point at which the annual cut of timber equalled the yearly increment of new growth. Any expansion beyond this point could take place only at the cost of contraction in the future. Expansion without prejudice to future supplies could, of course, have been secured if more land had been devoted to the production of timber, but in a country where the area of unused land was small more woodland meant less ploughland or pasture. Competition for the use of scarce land was a perennial problem in these circumstances and a permanent, radical increase of industrial raw material supply was very difficult to obtain. Those Tudor pamphleteers who complained that the sheep were eating up men were directing attention to the central problem of industrial raw material supply in an age when organic materials were essential for most industrial processes. More land devoted to the production of timber or wool meant less land available to produce food.

---

1 Except, of course, in so far as technological changes permit raw material saving.

The price of raw materials was sure to rise because of competition for the use of land and so inhibit industrial growth even where the government refrained from direct political action to guarantee the supply of food. If the government did not intervene to restrict pasture in the interest of tillage, the play of the market would ultimately produce the same result. Moreover, industrial growth not only provoked problems of this type directly by competing for the use of land, but also indirectly by encouraging a growth in population which in turn increased the demand for land upon which food could be grown. Once the spread of settlement had brought all available land into use, the only way in which the supply of food and of industrial raw materials of vegetable or animal origin could be increased simultaneously was by a general rise in the productivity of the land.[2]

The view that the productivity of the land controls the growth of industry no less than that of agriculture is a recurring theme in the *Wealth of nations*. Adam Smith wrote just before the dramatic changes in industrial raw material supply had become fully apparent and did not recognize their importance. In this chapter 'Of the natural progress of opulence' he began by defining the exchange of products manufactured in the towns for agricultural produce and raw materials as 'the great commerce of every civilized society'.[3] Later in the chapter he enlarged upon the nature of this exchange.

> It is this commerce which supplies the inhabitants of the town, both with the materials of their work, and the means of their subsistence. The quantity of the finished work which they sell to the inhabitants of the country, necessarily regulates the quantity of the materials and provisions which they buy. Neither their employment nor subsistence, therefore, can augment, but in proportion to the augmentation of the demand from the country for finished work; and this demand can augment only in proportion to the extension of improvement and cultivation. Had human institutions, therefore, never disturbed the natural course of things, the progressive wealth and increase of the towns would, in every political society, be consequential, and in proportion to the improvement and cultivation of the territory or country.[4]

If the productivity of the land in the last analysis governed the wealth of any country, it is hardly surprising that Adam Smith claimed of investment in agriculture that 'Of all the ways in which a capital can be employed, it is by far the most advantageous to the society'.[5]

---

2 Within any one national market area, of course, it was possible to expand the supply of food and raw materials without increasing pressure on the land by import from abroad. Cheap sea transport enabled England to make good some of her shortage of timber, for example, in this fashion.

3 Smith, *Wealth of nations*, i, p. 401.

4 Ibid., i, pp. 403–4.

5 Ibid., i, p. 385.

The supply of mineral raw materials forms an interesting contrast to the supply of vegetable and animal raw materials. In the very long run the mineral supply problem is insoluble in a sense which is not true of organic raw materials, since every mine is a wasting asset. It cannot be made to give a sustained yield in the way that is possible with a forest or a farm. A forest can yield indefinitely: a mine cannot. Nevertheless, in any but the very long run the difficulty of obtaining a large increase in supply is less pronounced with mineral raw materials. Given an adequate mining technique and the existence of rich deposits production can rapidly be built up to high levels. As the individual mine nears exhaustion the price of extraction must rise, of course, but as long as it is possible to sink other pits to tap equally rich deposits the price of the product need not rise, and may well fall if increasing production encourages the creation of larger and more efficient production units. Moreover, an increase in the production of mineral raw materials does not take place at the expense of the supply of food or of other industrial raw materials. There is no equivalent in the production of inorganic raw materials to the competition for land which accompanies an expansion in the production of organic raw materials.[6] In the half-century after the publication of the *Wealth of nations*, the vital importance of the new sources of industrial raw materials became clear. The passage which McCulloch in his edition found 'perhaps the most objectionable'[7] was that which concluded that capital was best employed in agriculture from the point of view of society as a whole. Adam Smith had argued that rent is created by those 'powers of nature' which give an added productivity to agriculture, but had added that in manufacture nature does nothing for man; he must do everything for himself. McCulloch objected to this definition of rent, but he also denied that the powers of nature favoured agriculture alone. His was a world in which the scale of manufacture had ceased to be regulated solely by agricultural productivity. The amount of capital which could profitably be invested in manufacture was no longer controlled by the agricultural surplus in the manner suggested by Adam Smith.[8] Mineral sources of raw material had given another dimension to the discussion. To McCulloch the 'powers of nature' revealed in the steam engine were as remarkable as any that Adam Smith had noticed in the fields.[9]

There is a second difference of great importance between mineral production on the one hand, and vegetable and animal production on the other. Production of the former is punctiform; of the latter areal. The

---

6 Open-cast mining forms a minor exception to this rule.

7 Smith, *Wealth of nations*, ed. McCulloch, p. 162n.

8 See, for example, *Wealth of nations*, i, p. 431, where his argument leads him to the conclusion that the manufactures of Leeds, Halifax, Sheffield, Birmingham and Wolverhampton are 'the offspring of agriculture'. The general argument of the chapter 'Of the different employment of capitals' is also interesting in this connection.

9 '. . . the pressure of the atmosphere and the elasticity of steam, which enable us to work the most stupendous engines, are they not the spontaneous gifts of nature?' *Wealth of nations*, ed. McCulloch, p. 162n.

transport problems involved in moving a million tons of coal from pitheads scattered over an area of only a few square miles are quite different from those involved in moving the same weight of grain or timber from an area of several thousands of square miles. The former implies heavy tonnages moving along a small number of routeways, whereas the latter implies the reverse. A heavy capital investment in improved communications is unlikely to give a good return when the raw materials of industry are organic since the traffic density along any one route is usually low. A large volume of mineral traffic, on the other hand, makes such an investment necessary to cope with physical difficulties, and financially attractive because the total possible savings are so much greater.[10]

The substitution of coal for wood

The decisive technological change which freed so many industries from dependence upon organic raw materials was the discovery of a way of using coal where once wood had been essential. The timing of the change varied a great deal between the several industries. It came earliest in industries like the boiling of salt in which the use of coal presented no problem of undesired chemical change in the product because the source of heat was separated from the object by a sheet of metal. Industries like iron smelting and hop drying in which contact was more intimate presented greater problems in a period when chemical knowledge was slight. A long period of trial and error commonly elapsed before a successful method of substitution was developed. Coal-fired salt pans were a commonplace before the end of the sixteenth century: coke-fired blast furnaces were not successfully operated until the first quarter of the eighteenth, and in some branches of the iron industry it was near to the end of the century before charcoal could be dispensed with. In spite of the rather slow spread of coal use from one industry or process to another, however, it was already an industrial raw material of the first importance by the beginning of the eighteenth century. At that time coal production in England and Wales had reached a level of about three million tons per annum, or roughly half a ton per head of population. The production of coal both absolutely and *per caput* was already of quite a different order of magnitude in England from that obtaining on the continent; and by the end of the century production had tripled. Much of the coal was used for domestic rather than industrial purposes, but all helped to relieve the pressure on timber supplies. Wherever it could successfully be substituted for wood its effect was to liberate production from the physical limits upon output imposed on industries requiring a source

10 Occasionally the older system had coped with quite heavy tonnages. The grain and timber trade, especially to the London market, was on a substantial scale and had meant large outlays on North Sea and coastal shipping and on river barges, but it was the new problems of mineral traffic on a large scale which produced the canals and the railways.

of heat in a country where the timber resources were very limited. Unlike timber, a substantial increase in coal consumption in any one period did not prejudice supplies in the next, nor did an expansion in coal use in one industry affect others adversely. Moreover, once the initial period of prejudice against coal had passed and the difficulties involved in its use had been overcome, many industries discovered that coal was better suited to their purposes than wood had been.

In the absence of coal, the timber requirements of a country whose industries were as large as those of England at the beginning of the nineteenth century would have been enormous. Much heat was needed in a wide range of industrial processes, and to have provided it with wood must have denuded the forests of England, indeed the forests of Europe, in a few decades. The classic case is perhaps that of the iron industry. Benaerts quotes an estimate, for example, that the production of 10 000 tons of charcoal iron required the felling of 40 000 hectares of forest.[11] The pig which resulted from a coal or coke melt was for many years unsatisfactory and commanded only a very low price. The prejudice against it remained for some time even after Darby had overcome the main difficulties in smelting ore with coke, yet coke pig was to prove essential to the rapid progress of industrial growth. Without it there could have been no great expansion in the scale of iron output or fall in its price, and the physical properties of iron were so essential to the age of machines that it is difficult to believe that any great changes were possible without cheap and abundant iron. Many machines which were first constructed in wood could be greatly improved when made in metal, and many of the great engineering constructions after the turn of the century could not have been made at all without cheap iron. The physical properties of iron permit great precision of working: the steam engine and the machine tool depend on this. They and the iron ships, iron rails and iron bridges of the new age required the successful supplanting of vegetable by mineral fuels.

Coal could not be used as a direct substitute for wood in the building industry where timber was used not as a fuel but as a building material, but indirectly it was important because its use in the brick industry meant that the production of bricks could be expanded without unit costs of production rising, so that brick became the prime building material of the new age. The engineering and construction industries, as producer goods industries of central importance, are points of great sensitivity in any period of rapid industrial growth. The output of producer goods must necessarily expand faster than that of consumer goods at such a time, and it is vital that it should be easily expansible, and if possible that the costs of the raw materials involved should show a secular tendency to fall as the volume of production increases. In the past these industries had been heavily dependent on wood, which tended to induce a secular rise in the costs of the raw material

11 Benaerts, *La grande industrie allemande*, p. 454. One hectare is approximately equal to 2.5 acres.

when the scale of production grew. After the changeover to mineral raw materials the possibility of a much easier and unrestricted expansion was always present.

Those consumer goods industries, such as the Staffordshire pottery industry or the glass industry, which required much heat in their manufacturing processes also benefited from growing independence of vegetable fuel. Brewing, the paper industry and some sections of the textile industry made use of coal too, though in their case the fuel was used to process organic rather than inorganic raw materials.

A part of the great increase in the productivity of industrial workers which began in the latter part of the eighteenth century and has continued down to the present day arose in the manner which Adam Smith described and analysed. Markets grew larger; production processes were subdivided; industrial skills became more specialized and workers nicer in their skills; new machinery was developed; real costs fell as productivity increased. But a part of the increase in productivity that took place, that part which became possible as a result of the rise to prominence of a class of industrial raw materials whose significance Adam Smith did not fully appreciate, that part which arose from cheaper and more abundant heat and mechanical power, could not take place as long as the land produced not merely the food of the nation but also its industrial raw materials. It is notable how frequently the industries in which expansion was marked in the years between Adam Smith and McCulloch were those which were gradually freeing themselves from dependence upon organic raw materials, especially wood. This is true of the industries making iron, non-ferrous metals, most types of machinery, glass, salt, pottery and bricks. The industry in which the most dramatic growth of all took place was, perhaps, cotton which provides an instructive contrast with most other quickly growing industries in that its raw material was vegetable. The cotton industry conformed quite closely to the picture of industrial growth envisaged by Adam Smith and will required further consideration at a later stage in this discussion.

Bulk transport

Though the large-scale use of coal offered great opportunities, it also brought problems, in the solution of which may be seen some of the most important economic and technological foundations of the industrial revolution. The prime difficulty was the great expense of transporting coal with the existing transport media. Coal could only come into general domestic and industrial use if it were cheap, and could only be cheap if it could be cheaply transported. As long as the price of coal taken overland doubled within five miles of the pithead it was not likely to be widely used. This, of course, is the reason why the first large-scale coal industry was on the Tyne, in touch by sea with the London market and the smaller markets down the east coast. Sea transport had always been the cheapest form of transport, and moreover it had long been accustomed to dealing with the range of problems raised by punctiform production on a large scale. Large ports had for centuries concentrated a great bulk of goods at a single point and forwarded them to a limited number of similar points, often far away. The biggest ships were capable of moving hundreds of tons at a time whereas on land loads measured by the hundredweight were normal. Exceptionally, much larger weights might be moved (as with large building stones), but only over short distances and by making special arrangements. Before the era of large-scale mineral production there was little incentive to try to alter the capacity of overland transport systems since the areal production of vegetable and animal products seldom calls for the movement of a great bulk of material along a single route. Improvements to overland transport which are precluded when raw material production is areal may be both necessary and economically practicable when raw material production is punctiform. Once the Newcastle–London coal trade had shown the very real advantages of coal over wood for many purposes, there was always latent the possibility that a radical improvement in overland communication might take place.

Nef has shown how important the growth of the coal trade was in developing more efficient methods of ship construction and working in this country.[12] By the end of the seventeenth century about half of the total British merchant fleet by tonnage was engaged in the coal trade. But the effect of the development of large-scale punctiform mineral production upon shipping was only to develop traits characteristic of the movement of goods by sea for a long time. Ports and pits had much in common as sources of cargo. It was otherwise with overland transport. When the production of the coal industry came to be measured in hundreds of thousands and even millions of tons annually, a new solution was necessary if the coal was to reach inland centres of consumption. However inefficient to later eyes may have been the movement of grain, wood and wool on horseback or in carts along pitted roads, it was economically inevitable since the volume of the traffic was too small to warrant the investment needed to provide good roads or canals. Areal production meant poor communications. Minerals had, of course, also been moved on horseback before the eighteenth century in spite of the punctiform nature of their production, but they had moved in quite small absolute quantities and had not afforded any opportunity for substantial improvement. For a long time coal was moved in the same way whenever it was moved overland. It moved on pack animals from the Staffordshire coalfield to the Northwich salt pans and from the Yorkshire pits to the Bradford dyers, or on small river craft on the Severn and Thames. As long as the inland consumption of coal remained small, coal moved as other raw materials had moved for centuries. Large-scale consumption provided new opportunities. The demonstration that coal could be used so successfully where wood had been used in the past created a large potential demand for it which could not be met while communications were poor, but which

12 Nef, *The British coal industry*, i, pp. 238–40, 390–4.

provided a powerful incentive to improve them. The canalization of the Weaver to Northwich after 1720 in order to provide cheaper coal than could be brought overland from Staffordshire was an early example of the improvements in transport encouraged by the use of coal; and the work done on the Douglas from Wigan to the Ribble estuary dates from the same period. As coal consumption rose, more ambitious works became possible. Waterways were not merely improved; they were created. Forty years after the work on the Weaver and the Douglas the Worsley Canal was built, to be followed by many others in the next half-century.

The art of building canals was not new to Europe. The Dutch had a long experience of making them, and several long canals were built in France in the seventeenth century, but the English canal network was constructed in response to an incentive of a new type. If mineral raw materials were to continue to grow in importance in English industry, they required such a network. Canals are well suited to the movement of goods produced at a point, but not to areal production. The truth of this is well illustrated by the history of the many canals that, in the first flush of enthusiasm for canals, were built in purely agricultural areas of the country, and were seldom successful financially.[13] The successful canals were those on which there was a heavy volume of mineral traffic, usually coal, but occasionally other minerals also: for example, the canal from the pottery district of Staffordshire to the Mersey carried a china clay traffic. Agricultural areas through which the canals passed benefited greatly from their presence, both because they made possible much cheaper movement of food to the market and because some of the essentials of good husbandry, such as lime and manure, were more easily obtainable after their construction. Agricultural traffic contributed significantly to the revenues of many canals built to cater chiefly for mineral traffic, but agricultural traffic was characteristically insufficient to sustain canal finances on its own, and canals which were built in agricultural areas in the hope that their presence would create sufficient traffic to make them profitable seldom fulfilled their promoters' expectations.

The development of railways, the other chief means of cheap internal transport created during the industrial revolution, was also closely connected with the switch to inorganic raw materials, and especially the transport of coal. From the seventeenth century there had been railways connecting pitheads with coal wharves on the Tyne, developed to deal with the problem of coal movement overland on a large scale. The laying of wooden planks along which the horse-drawn carts could move was a simple way of increasing the load which each horse could shift. When it no longer had to expend most of its energy in overcoming the mud in wet weather and the deep ruts in dry, a horse drawing a cart along planked ways was able to move two or three times as much coal. Once the volume of coal moving over the short roads to the wharves had become large, the heavy expense of improving

---

13 Clapham notes this condition, though he cast his conclusions about it in a different form. Clapham, *Economic history of modern Britain*, i, p. 82.

roads in this way proved well worth while. In time, flanged wheels were introduced and it became profitable to cover the wooden tracks with metal plates in order to increase their life under constant heavy usage. Railways were peculiarly a mining development (even down to the track gauge), and were created to overcome the problems posed by large-scale punctiform mineral production, initially as feeders to waterways, but later as an independent network. Like canals, they also proved in time of great benefit to other forms of production and made easier the movement of vegetable and animal raw materials. Moreover, they developed a great passenger traffic. Yet is is true of railways as of canals that most of those built in purely agricultural areas in England did not generate enough traffic to make them profitable.

As the eighteenth century progressed the volume of coal output rose steadily, from three million tons at the beginning to about ten million at the end. The great coalfields near Newcastle no longer grew in output as quickly as some of the inland fields because the improvement in communications, especially the development of canals, made available to industrial and domestic consumers over a steadily increasing area the advantages which during the seventeenth century had been restricted to the east coast ports and to very small areas on the inland fields. Even at the beginning of the century probably no other mineral, vegetable or animal raw material, except perhaps grain, equalled coal in weight of production: by the end it had far outdistanced any rival. It was therefore peculiarly coal which provided at once the chief stimulus to the building of traffic arteries capable of dealing with the quantities of raw materials now used by the economy, and the main goods traffic on the canals and later the railways.[14]

Or the issue may be put in different terms. The importance of the changes in raw material supply and in the transport system can be illustrated from the writings of the economists of the period, especially in their discussions of the limits of economic growth. The starkest discussion of the organization of economic life in a society bounded by the productivity of the land and the problems of transport is perhaps that of von Thünen. When von Thünen published his discussion of the pattern of land use that would be found upon a featureless plain surrounding a central city, he deliberately made a limited

14 Paradoxically, although so many of the most important changes in transport and power were connected with the mining industry and especially coal, and although it was the adoption of mineral raw materials generally in industry that alone made possible the scale of expansion that occurred, the mining industry itself did not experience any revolutionary increase in manpower productivity. Output per man-year in a large coal pit in 1700 was about 150 tons (Nef, *The British coal industry*, ii, p. 136n.), a figure already about two-fifths as large as the peak figure in the 1880s. The coal industry, indeed, is sometimes referred to as an example of the impossibility of designing machines to perform all jobs previously done by hand, and is classed with, say, agriculture, in this respect. But the central difficulty of the production of coal has never been the winning of coal at the coal-face, hard and dangerous though this has always been, but its transport within the pit, up the pit shaft and from the pithead to the point of consumption. The canal and steam engine solved the prime difficulties of the coal mines. Those at the coal-face were less pressing.

number of simple assumptions about the nature of its economic life. Upon these assumptions he was able to show that the steady rise in the cost of transporting produce as distance increased from the central market would cause the land to be divided up into a series of concentric rings each marked by a different type of land use. The innermost ring was devoted to the production of perishable commodities like milk and vegetables; the next ring to woodland to meet the city's need for fuel, charcoal, building materials, tools and furniture; and the remaining rings to agriculture of a gradually decreasing intensity, shelving off finally into pastoral activities at the point where the cost of transporting grain to the market made it unprofitable to plough and plant the land. Everything depended upon the demand in the central market, local changes in agricultural productivity and the level of transport charges. As the price of raw materials and food rose in the central market, for example, or alternatively as the cost of transport fell, the whole system of rings would expand allowing a larger area of land to be used more intensively. Von Thünen himself illustrated the dramatic effect of falling transport costs on the intensity of land use by examining the effect of a river running across the series of rings to the central city along which transport costs were only a tenth of those overland. Von Thünen's model underlined many of the characteristics of the economic life of earlier centuries. His scheme makes it clear how crippling the high cost of transport can be; how, for example, local famine might well occur in a country enjoying a general sufficiency; how, though timber was essential to such an economy, its great bulk and weight made it difficult to deliver to a market at a reasonably low cost.

When von Thünen published his book in 1826 his model still fitted the economic life of parts of Germany without excessive distortion, though by that date it was no longer appropriate to England. He acknowledged Adam Smith as his chief mentor, but his scheme embodied only a part of the world Adam Smith had studied.[15] The *Wealth of nations* describes a much more complicated world; it does not merely abstract from it some of its salient characteristics as *Der isolirte Staat* had done. Although Adam Smith maintained that a gradual rise in agricultural productivity alone made possible the development of cities and industry, and further maintained that in the last resort the size and wealth of cities must continue to be governed by the productivity of the land, he understood and entertained within his scheme of analysis the great modification and complication which arose out of the development of trade between city and city and nation and nation, not restricting himself simply to the consideration of trade between a city and its surrounding countryside. The wealth of nations could increase greatly when von Thünen's limiting assumptions were relaxed in this way, and Adam Smith showed clearly how this might come about, and discussed which policies were likely to expedite the process or to frustrate it. The wealth of nations could not, however, increase without limit upon the assumptions

15 Von Thünen, *Der isolirte Staat*, ii, p. 1.

within which Adam Smith worked since the productivity of the land set a ceiling to growth. In the following century the course of events proved beyond doubt that the assumptions might be still further relaxed. The ceiling which Adam Smith had assumed to exist generally now applied only to food and to a limited range of organic industrial raw materials. The use of mineral raw materials removed the limit for industrial production in general, both directly by making it possible for an enormous increase in the physical volume of production to take place without prejudice to future supplies of raw materials, and indirectly by demonstrating that the 'powers of nature' were present just as abundantly in the mines as in the land, so that capital invested in industry could yield at least as good a return as investment in the land from the point of view of the community as a whole.

Steam power

The importance of minerals in general and coal in particular to the development of an industrial economy at the end of the eighteenth century extends beyond the improvement in communications and the possibility of escaping the close limits set to expansion as long as organic raw materials were essential to most industrial processes, for the development of the steam engine is peculiarly a product of the problems of the mining industry.

Although the expansion of mineral production was not subject to the same limitations as the expansion of the production of vegetable and animal materials, the technological problems of increasing production were nevertheless considerable. Perhaps the most intractable was that of draining pits when they were sunk to a depth that made impossible drainage by the cutting of adits to a point on the surface below the level of the seam. Horse gins were useful when the depths were moderate, but at the depths where some of the richest seams of coal and veins of tin and copper occurred a more powerful engine was required if the inflow of water to the workings was to be held in check.[16] The urgent difficulties of the mining industry were the means of turning the Newcomen from an ingenious but unpractical machine into a reliable piece of equipment without which the deeper pits could not have been maintained in production. The early engines of Savery and Newcomen were essentially pumping machines for which the only big market was the mining industry. A few Newcomen engines were used for pumping water from rivers to help with the supply of water to towns, but the majority were used in mines. They were at once essential to the continued expansion of coal production, and virtually unusable without a supply of coal. They are a product of a coal age rather than a wood age and could only be used extensively when mines rather than woodlands were their source

16 It has been claimed that three-quarters of the patents issued in England between 1561 and 1668 were connected with the coal industry, either directly or indirectly, and that one-seventh was concerned with the drainage problem. Mason, *History of the sciences*, p. 217.

of fuel. Otherwise, they would have devastated an area of timber as quickly as the early iron industry had done, for the early engines were extremely inefficient and required very large quantities of fuel. The theoretical knowledge of the power of steam had long existed, but the coal industry's problems first provided the catalyst to convert this into workable machinery rather than engaging toys. The first use of steam engines in industries other than mining reflects their background as pumping engines in mines, for they were used initially simply to complete the cycle of water movement from tail-race to millpond and so to render waterwheels independent of ordinary stream flow and prevent those interruptions to their operation that had previously been inevitable in prolonged dry weather. Watt's improvements to the steam engine (or rather his invention of a steam in place of an atmospheric engine) and his development of methods of gearing which gave rotary rather than reciprocating motion represent radical improvements upon the earlier Newcomen engines and gave the steam engine great importance in a wide range of industries as time passed. The steam engine more than any other single development, perhaps, made possible the vast increase in individual productivity which was so striking a feature of the industrial revolution by providing a source of power which dwarfed human, animal and even hydraulic sources. Yet the machine Watt improved was already widely used in the mining industry, which had fostered its development for several decades.

The cotton industry as a paradigm case

The cotton industry has attracted more attention than any other in discussions of the industrial revolution, and since it grew vastly while continuing to use a vegetable raw material, it merits further consideration in the context of this essay. No other major industry grew as quickly as cotton in the late eighteenth century. There was a series of inventions in both spinning and weaving which led to a marked rise in output per worker. Cotton spinning was the first industrial activity to become organized in factories in the fashion which became widespread during the next century. Lancashire became the area that first acquired the full range of features characteristic of the new industrial scene: large urban manufacturing populations living a life divorced from the rhythm of the countryside about them, working in factories, caught up in a web of exchange which connected their livelihood with events throughout the world. Cotton has for long been treated as the *type par excellence* of the new manufacturing industry, the lead-off industry in the take-off into sustained industrial growth.

The cotton industry fits well into the pattern of industrial growth that Adam Smith described. The decisive importance of the size of the market is well illustrated in its history. The attempt to expand production to keep pace with demand caused new mechanical devices to be seized upon eagerly and developed rapidly into reliable manufacturing machinery. There was a steep rise in productivity as workers became more specialized and turned to cotton manufacture as a full-time employment rather than a useful subsidiary source of income. The price of the finished article fell and still further enlarged the market. Once Whitney's gin had proved its worth, the demands of the industry for raw material could be met by breaking in new land in the southern United States. There was no bottleneck in raw material supply and the price of raw cotton fell. There is nothing in the story to call in question the assumptions of Adam Smith about the part played by the growth of industry in promoting the wealth of nations. Some coal was used in the preparatory and finishing sections of the industry, but only after a generation of expansion had caused the need for power to outstrip the capabilities of the human arm and the waterwheel was the steam engine brought into use, so that the problem of raw material provision was very different in the cotton industry from those industries in which organic raw materials were replaced by inorganic. The example of the cotton industry makes it clear that industrial expansion could go far and fast in some directions without provoking difficulties in raw material supply.

For this very reason, however, the cotton industry, in spite of its importance in the industrial revolution, cannot be regarded as a microcosm of the whole process. In particular, the great changes in inland transport and in power were not closely connected with the cotton industry. The movement of cotton presented no great difficulties to the methods of goods transport that had been in use for centuries. The movement of raw cotton was measured by the million pound rather than the million ton and bore a far higher value per unit weight than, say, coal. In consequence, it was able to support relatively high transport charges without a crippling increase in price. The fact that many early mills were built in quite remote Pennine valleys close to a head of water underlines this point. Similarly, the well-tried sources of industrial power, initially the worker's arms and later the waterwheel, sufficed to move the machinery used in the cotton industry during the first two decades of rapid growth at the end of the eighteenth century. The cotton industry benefited substantially from the opening of canal communication between Manchester and Liverpool, both in that transport charges were lower than by river or on horseback and in that delivery was more reliable and quicker: but the cotton industry did not create a large enough tonnage of traffic to justify the construction of canals. The year 1800 was the first in which the import of raw cotton exceeded 50 million pounds in weight, which is only some 23 000 tons, and no more than the annual output of perhaps 150 coal miners. Even though cotton might produce a much greater revenue per ton-mile than mineral freight, it is clear that the cotton industry in itself could offer little inducement to spend capital on the scale necessary to build canals. In so far as the presence of the cotton industry in Lancashire did hasten the construction of canals it was perhaps rather as a consumer of coal and as an employer of labour which consumed coal domestically that it exerted an influence. Again, the cotton industry became an important market for Watt's new engines. Without them it might have lost impetus as the most suitable heads of water were harnessed one by one, leaving only the inaccessible or insufficient to be brought into use. But the history of the development of the steam engine lies outside the cotton industry.

It might indeed even be argued that there is a sense in which the cotton industry was exploiting old lines of development with a new intensity rather than striking out in a radically new direction. There had been periods of technological innovation in the textile industry in the past. When, for example, the spinning wheel superseded the distaff there had been a marked rise in the productivity of the individual spinner. The invention of the knitting machine and the introduction of the Dutch swivel-loom had also in their time brought about important changes in productivity and in the amount of fixed capital per worker. Water power had been used in the fulling of wool and the throwing of silk for centuries. Even the bringing together of many textile workers under one roof was not unknown before the eighteenth century. During the late eighteenth century the cotton industry brought development along old lines to a new pitch of perfection, evolving better machinery in both spinning and weaving and extending the use of water power into spinning. There was a vast increase in the quantity of cotton manufactured. It was produced more cheaply and, after early difficulties with the new machinery had been overcome, the quality of both yarn and cloth was higher than anything achieved in England in the past. In contrast with this, the range of industries in which coal replaced wood as the main source of heat might be held to have struck out along a new line of development. The change from organic to inorganic sources of raw material supply led to no sudden or dramatic change in the quantity or quality of production in the industries concerned, yet latent in this change were new possibilities for improvement in the transport of goods and the supply of power to industrial processes. To borrow a biological analogy, the raw material bottleneck produced a mutation in raw material supply which proved intensely favourable and led to changes which helped to transform industrial production and ultimately society as a whole.

The temptation to treat the cotton industry as a microcosm of the whole industrial revolution has proved difficult to resist. The signs of the new age were first readily apparent in cotton, but its history is not therefore typical of the whole. The fact that the cotton industry was singularly free from raw material supply problems marked it out from many others, at once facilitating its expansion at an early date and isolating it from a range of problems faced and solved by many other industries. Cotton benefited from the new sources of power and better transport facilities, but these were available because of the successful struggle against difficulties of raw material supply which had taken place in other sectors of the economy.

Continental comparisons

It is natural that special attention should be paid by all those interested in the industrial revolution to any aspect of English life that was different from its continental equivalent. Hence the great interest shown in such questions as social mobility and capillarity, the organization of financial affairs and the capital market in England, English agriculture and systems of land tenure, the forms of English government and law, and in exploring any differences between English and continental demographic patterns. The supply of industrial raw materials may, of course, be treated in the same way. It is not difficult to show that the continent clung longer to the traditional types of organic industrial raw material, nor is it difficult to suggest reasons for this. Wiebe's price series, for example, suggests that the supply of some types of timber was causing much less difficulty on the continent than in England in the seventeenth century.[17] Yet it is perhaps more illuminating to dwell on the occasional similarities between England and the continent than on the general dissimilarity.

The area most like the new English industrial areas was central Belgium. This was the only area on the continent in which the production of coal in the eighteenth century reached a level at all comparable with that achieved in English coalfields at the same time. Both at Liège and near Charleroi the coal seams outcropped to the surface near the good water communication afforded by the Sambre–Meuse system, and this made possible the development of a wide market for coal at an early date. The Mons coalfield was not so well endowed with natural water communication, but the same problems and opportunities which produced a burst of canal building in England led to a similar development in Mons. The Mons–Condé canal, for example, was completed in 1814, linking the coalfield area with the industries of Nord. The history of the successful search for coal in the concealed Nord field which resulted in the sinking of the famous mine at Anzin is evidence of how useful even in the middle of the eighteenth century the discovery of coal was judged to be in this part of the continent. At that time traffic along the valley of the Sambre–Meuse resembled that along the valley of the Severn in England. The metal communes of Maubeuge and Valenciennes, for example, were dependent upon primary iron imported from the *pays de Liège* in the late eighteenth century. Belgian pits were quick to adopt British devices. Already before the turn of the century Belgian pits had reached considerable depths and were using Newcomen engines extensively. Soon after the turn of the century other British developments were absorbed into Belgian practice: the use of the steam engine for winding up coal and men as well as for pumping water, the Davy safety-lamp and so on. There were independent local contributions to coal mining and other industrial problems in Belgium at this time. Joseph Chaudron, for example, discovered an improved method of protecting main shafts by using a revetment of iron (the *cuvelage en fer*). Dony succeeded in extracting zinc from calamine. Gas lighting, a Belgian invention, was in use in factories in 1810.[18]

---

17 Wiebe, *Geschichte der Preisrevolution*. See especially tables 522, 524 and 528.

18 Minckelers lighted his lecture room with gas in 1785, though it was William Murdoch who in the 1790s showed the commercial possibilities of this method of illumination.

The remarkable achievements of the Cockerill family in engineering and textiles at Seraing and Verviers during the first quarter of the nineteenth century form an industrial epic on a scale worthy of comparison with English equivalents of the period. John Cockerill constructed successful coke-fired blast furnaces at Seraing in the 1820s, and built excellent marine steam engines. The advance of central Belgium, in short, was very rapid, and it is perhaps symbolic of this that Neilson's hot blast was widely used there at a time when it was still a novelty in British iron centres outside Scotland.

The history of the rapid acceptance of British industrial advances in the valleys of the Meuse and Sambre is not vastly different from the history of their acceptance, say, in the valleys of south Wales. There was, it is true, usually a time lag, though not always longer in the case of Liège than in the case of the less active British areas. In view of the fact that Belgium during the eighteenth and early nineteenth centuries was ruled by other countries and was frequently disturbed by the passage of armies, it is striking how swiftly the areas whose problems and opportunities were similar to those of the new industrial areas of Britain followed the British lead and occasionally improved upon it.

Central Belgium was not unique among continental industrial areas. The St Etienne region, for example, showed some similar traits, but in the main it is fair to contrast the conservatism of the continent over industrial raw material supply with the rapid change in England. When von Thünen published his book the Ruhr was still an area of agriculture and marshland. The example of central Belgium, however, where change came so rapidly on the heels of developments in similar English areas, illustrates two points which are perhaps true of the industrial revolution as a whole: first, that western Europe was a single economic community within which like circumstances might give rise to similar results; and secondly, that industrial growth was essentially a local rather than a national affair. In this regard it is perhaps unnecessarily inexact to talk of England and the continent rather than, say, of Lancashire and the valley of the Sambre–Meuse. Each country was made up of a number of regional economies. Within Belgium, for example, the Flemish domestic linen industry was in great straits because of its failure to adopt English methods at just the period of brilliant advance on the Belgian coalfields.

Perhaps the chief advantage in looking at the industrial revolution from the standpoint of raw material supply is that it makes it easier to understand the nature of the gap that separates Adam Smith and his world from the world that McCulloch knew. The ordinary categories of economic analysis do not pick up the differences very well. In the world that Adam Smith described there could well exist a technically perfect capitalism, with a developed money market, extensive international trade, many intermediaries between the producer and the ultimate consumer, a divorce between the workers and the ownership of the means of production and so on. But in this world there was a ceiling to the possible size of industrial production set by the difficulty of expanding raw material supply at constant or declining prices as long as most industrial raw materials were organic. When this was no longer true, the ceiling disappeared. Adam Smith's world and that of his physiocratic predecessors was a world bounded by the fertility of the soil. This was the backcloth to any examination of industrial development. Ninety years later when Jevons published his great work on the coal industry he was prepared to assert firmly that the greatest single factor governing the industrial prospects of any nation must be its wealth in coal.[19] If McCulloch was impatient with Adam Smith it was at least in part because the world in which he lived was different. The weaknesses in his argument would not have escaped Adam Smith if he had had the benefit of being able to observe a further half-century of economic history. In that case what he would have seen would have convinced him that the use of inorganic raw materials in industry on a vast scale had revealed the existence of 'powers of nature' whose potentialities he had not suspected.

19 'Coal, in truth, stands not beside but entirely above all other commodities. It is the material energy of the country – the universal aid – the factor in everything we do. With coal almost any feat is possible or easy; without it we are thrown back into the laborious poverty of early times.' Jevons, *The coal question*, p. viii. See also the chapter 'Of the comparative coal resources of different countries'. It is interesting to note that Jevons's main concern was that supplies of coal must soon run short in Britain; that mineral raw materials, being exhaustible, were a dangerous basis of national wealth and power.

5

Some Reflections on
Corn Yields and Prices in
Pre-industrial Economies

King and Davenant

Playing with figures fascinated Gregory King. His notebooks bulge with calculations about the chief economic and demographic preoccupations of the day. Nothing King wrote was published until long after his death, but some of his estimates and speculations were published by Charles Davenant (who repeatedly made clear the extent of his debt to King).[1] Given the nature of pre-industrial society, it was to be expected that one of the topics that would attract King's attention was the scale of agricultural production and the price of the foodstuffs produced.

It had long been high in the consciousness of men and of governments that when the harvest failed the price of food was affected disproportionately and Davenant attempted to set out the relationship quantitatively. How far Davenant's discussion of this issue was directly his own work and how much it was a summary of King is unclear, but his analysis has been immensely influential and it is convenient to refer to the 'model' under Davenant's name. He specified the degree to which price was increased by harvests which were successive deciles below the average. His estimates were widely quoted and broadly confirmed by a number of later examinations of the same issue. Jevons, for example, accepted the general accuracy of the formula which Davenant published and sought an expression which would generalize the relationship between quantity and price. Having determined the general form of the function from a consideration of the behaviour of price in very extreme conditions of supply, he suggested that the price of corn would be approximated by the formula $y = 0.824/(x - 0.12)^2$ where x is the ratio of the quantity currently available to that normally available. He showed the closeness of fit between Davenant's results and those obtained by his formula in a table reproduced as table 5.1.[2] Jevons added that, 'roughly speaking, the price of corn may be said to vary inversely as the square of the supply,

---

1 Davenant, *Essay upon the balance of trade.*
2 Jevons, *Theory of political economy*, p. 182.

Table 5.1   The results of the formulas of Davenant and Jevons compared

	Price of grain	
Quantity of grain[a]	Davenant	Jevons
1.0	1.0	1.06
0.9	1.3	1.35[b]
0.8	1.8	1.78
0.7	2.6	2.45
0.6	3.8	3.58
0.5	5.5	5.71

[a]Quantity of grain in an average year = 1.0.
[b]Jevons gives a figure of 1.36 but in doing so slightly miscalculated the result obtained by his formula.

provided that this supply be not unusually small'.[3] In support of the obvious implication of the formula, he noted that Tooke had made estimates of the extent to which farmers in the bad harvest years of 1795, 1796, 1799 and 1800 had benefited from the shortfall and enjoyed incomes above the average. 'If the price of wheat', he concluded, 'varied in the simple inverse proportion of the quantity, they would neither gain nor lose, and the fact that they gained considerably agrees with our formula as given above.'[4]

Jevons's discussion of the issue occurred in the course of his general discussion of price variations and forms part of the wider thesis that 'the variation of price is much more marked in the case of necessaries of life than in the case of luxuries'.[5] He initiated his discussion by a quotation from Chalmers which includes the following passage, 'let the crop of grain be deficient by one third in its usual amount, or rather, let the supply of grain in the market, whether from home produce or by importation, be curtailed to the same extent, and this will create a much greater addition than one third to the price of it. It is not an unlikely prediction that its cost would be more than doubled by the shortcoming of one third or one fourth in the supply.'[6] Very similar observations were made by many men with practical experience of the corn trade in the eighteenth and nineteenth centuries and by those who commented upon it, notably Thomas Tooke.[7]

3 Ibid. The presence of a negative constant in the squared term of the denominator of Jevons's formula has the effect, of course, of producing a more violent increase in price when the quantity harvested falls below average by a given proportion than reduction in price when there is a harvest which exceeds the average by the same proportion.

4 Ibid., p. 183.

5 Ibid., p. 176.

6 Ibid.

7 Economic historians from Thorold Rogers to Slicher van Bath have also had resort to the ideas of Davenant (and/or King) in seeking to relate harvest quantities to price movements. Thorold Rogers, who worked so extensively on the subject, is especially warm in his praise: 'Gregory King has rarely, even in modern times, been surpassed in the special and very exceptional power of understanding what is meant by statistical figures. King discovered the law which regulates the price of the necessaries of life on the occasion of a scarcity, and formulated a geometrical proportion which experience has proved, with some minor modifications, to be

This view of the behaviour of corn prices in relation to supply is intuitively attractive as well as firmly grounded in theoretical considerations, but will bear some re-examination since it is a more complex matter than might appear at first blush. The quotation from Chalmers is instructive in this regard. In certain circumstances much hangs upon the distinction between overall yield and market supply over which he hesitated.

Davenant himself was well aware of the difference between gross yield and the quantity of grain that could be marketed. Earlier in his essay, in presenting some of King's estimates of arable production in 'years of moderate plenty', he gave a table of output exclusive of seed corn and then discussed how greatly its inclusion would have raised the output figure. But the phrasing of his introduction to the table showing the relationship between the extent of the 'defect' of the harvest and its effect in raising the price of corn 'above the common rate' is ambiguous and the rest of this passage in his essay contains no explicit clarification of the point. In commenting on his table, for example, he wrote that 'when corn rises to treble the common rate it may be presumed that we want one third of the common produce; and if we should want five tenths, or half the common produce, the price would rise to near five times the common rate.'[8] Such remarks leave his intention unclear. In referring to 'common produce', had he in mind the gross yield of corn, or what remained for consumption after setting aside seed corn and any other necessary deductions from the quantity of grain initially harvested?

The importance of the distinction between net and gross output in relation to price may be seen in table 5.2. In it farmers' incomes at varying crop yields are set out, using Bouniatian's formula for estimating price from quantity rather than that of Jevons. It is an inconvenient characteristic of Jevons's formula that in a year of average harvest, taken to be a quantity of 1.0, the implied price is not 1.0 but 1.06 (see table 5.1), which means that the price in a year of deficient harvest can only be expressed as a percentage of the price in an average year after a further calculation (thus table 5.1 shows the price of grain in a year when the harvest is only 80 per cent of normal as 1.78; this is, however, not 78 per cent above normal but only 68 per cent above ($100 \times 1.78/1.06 = 168$). Bouniatian's formula avoids this inelegance but otherwise produces results closely similar to those of Jevons.[9]

---

a rule of safe action.' Thorold Rogers, *Work and wages*, p. 465. See also Thorold Rogers, *Economic interpretation of history*, pp. 250–3 for his elaboration of King's law and the implications which flow from it. For Slicher van Bath, see below, pp. 104–6.

8 Davenant, *Essay upon the balance of trade*, p. 83.

9 Bouniatian set out his own formula after noting the difficulty with Jevons's formula. Bouniatian, *La loi des prix*, p. 64. His discussion of King's law was both well informed and judicious. He began by noting that, although normally attributed to King, it was probably due to Davenant. He was well aware that the comparative simplicity of earlier centuries had been much altered by international trade and by the development of major substitutes for grain, especially the potato. And he explained clearly how the carry-over of grain from one year to

Table 5.2 sets out two illustrative cases. In both I have assumed an average gross yield of 10 bushels per acre and that 2.5 bushels of corn were needed as seed for each acre sown, but case (b) differs from case (a) in that I have also assumed that a further bushel has to be set aside to supply 'fuel' for draught animals. The available evidence suggests that from medieval times until the nineteenth century a figure of 2.5 bushels per acre for seed must be approximately correct for wheat: it would be higher for other grains.[10] Animal fodder needs varied more widely. They were affected by the type of animal used and by local agricultural practices, and were far more likely to fluctuate from year to year according to the scale of the preceding harvest. But they could not be altered substantially without penalty in the subsequent harvest since the amount of useful work obtainable from draught animals was strongly affected by both the quantity and type of fodder given to them.[11] Animal 'fuel' was needed for many aspects of arable farming, but especially for ploughing, other forms of cultivation and carting. It could be very costly in grain. One of the most original of all writers on agricultural economics, von Thünen, provides a vivid instance of the very large requirements of draught animals for grain 'fuel' if they were to perform efficiently. He had the inestimable advantage of practical experience in running a big agricultural estate to guide him in quantifying farming operations. His estate lay at Tellow, 23 miles from the market town of Rostock. He noted that a four-horse team was used to take grain to market and that the round trip took four days. The team's normal load was 2400

---

the next could blur the impact of good or bad harvests, using French data for 1815 and 1816, and for 1819 and 1820 to illustrate the point (p. 66). Nevertheless, he argued that the relationship of price and quantity for Prussian rye in the mid-nineteenth century and for American maize between 1866 and 1911 both showed the basic soundness of King's law, and concluded by asserting, in a passage which he italicized, that King had succeeded in expressing '*la loi de formation du prix du blé lorsque la récolte de l'année représentait la quantité disponible du blé comme moyen presque unique d'alimentation de la population pour l'année à venir.*'

10 See, for example, Bowden, 'Agricultural prices', p. 652; or Slicher van Bath, *Agrarian history*, p. 173. A figure of 2.5 bushels is more appropriate for wheat than for barley. With the latter a substantially higher quantity of seed corn was used: 4 bushels was a normal figure. Beveridge also discussed this point. He gives the following average quantities of seed in bushels per acre for nine Winchester manors over the period 1200–1450, and for comparison included the comparable figures for England 1895–1914 (given in brackets): wheat 2.48 (2.72); barley 3.76 (3.04); oats 4.32 (4.80). The related yields per acre were 9.36 (31.36); 14.32 (32.96); 10.56 (40.72). Beveridge suggested that the contrast between modern and medieval yields was more pronounced even than his statistics suggested because medieval yields were for the areas actually cultivated. If they had been reckoned 'as they lie' to include various forms of wasted space, the area would have been nearly doubled whereas this consideration did not apply to nineteenth-century data. Beveridge, 'Yield and price of corn', pp. 158–9. Bairoch has summarized his findings from a large body of wheat yield data for continental Europe in the nineteenth century. He concluded that, excluding Russia, yields rose on average by just over 50 per cent between 1800 and 1910 from 11.9 to 18.3 bushels per acre (converting from quintals per hectare, and assuming 60 lb to the bushel), but that the quantity of seed sown per acre increased by only 8 per cent, from 1.84 to 1.99 bushels. Bairoch, 'Rendements agricoles', p. 9.

11 Slicher van Bath, *Agrarian history*, p. 22. Smith, *Western Europe*, pp. 204–10, especially figure 4.5, p. 206.

Table 5.2 Gross and net yields (average yield = 10 bushels)

Gross yield (bushels per acre)	Net yield		Value (Bouniatian's formula)			Value (Average year = 100)		
	(a)[a]	(b)[b]	Gross	(a)	(b)	Gross	(a)	(b)
10	7.5	6.5	10.00	7.50	6.50	100	100	100
9	6.5	5.5	11.49	8.30	7.02	115	111	108
8	5.5	4.5	13.49	9.27	7.59	135	124	117
7	4.5	3.5	16.31	10.48	8.16	163	140	126
6	3.5	2.5	20.56	11.99	8.57	206	160	132
5	2.5	1.5	27.65	13.82	8.30	277	184	128

[a] Gross yield less 2.5 bushels for seed corn.
[b] Gross yield less 2.5 bushels for seed corn and 1 bushel for fodder for draught animals.

The following table shows how the quantity of grain available affects its price using Bouniatian's formula $[y = 0.757/(x - 0.13)^2]$ where 1.0 is the quantity of an average harvest:

Quantity	Price
1.0	1.000
0.9	1.277
0.8	1.686
0.7	2.330
0.6	3.427
0.5	5.530

Hamburg pounds weight but the team needed 300 pounds of grain in fodder to perform the round trip (the Hamburg pound was slightly heavier than the English pound).[12] The assumption that one bushel of corn per acre is an appropriate allowance for animal fodder in pre-industrial agriculture is entirely arbitrary, but it may well represent a closer approach to reality than the assumption that seed corn alone need be deducted to derive a net from a gross figure. Even if animal fodder needs are treated as zero, it is still useful to consider the two alternatives. For example, the second might stand for the seed requirement of barley where the first represents wheat.

In Davenant's day average yields of both wheat and barley were probably somewhat higher than 10 bushels per acre, but 10 bushels is a reasonable, if not indeed a generous, estimate for earlier centuries or for pre-industrial western Europe as a whole.[13] In any case, the purpose of the exercise is to expose the implications of the distinction between gross and net yields under certain assumptions rather than to exemplify conditions at a particular point in time. Table 5.2 shows that if prices are obtained by applying Bouniatian's formula to gross yield as a proportion of its own average level, and it is assumed that the whole crop is sold, the value of the crop rises steeply with successively more severe harvest failure until when the crop is only half its normal level its value approaches three times that of a normal year. On this basis, the substantial farmer appears to have good reason to prefer a poor harvest to a plentiful one. If, however, price is calculated in the same way but it is assumed that only the net yield can be marketed, then the picture changes substantially. The quantity of grain which can be released into the market falls proportionately very much faster than gross output. In consequence, the total value of the crop rises more moderately and the farmer has far less reason to hope for a bad or fear a good harvest. Even on assumption (a), there is already a substantial contrast in value compared with the gross yield value figure, and the contrast is greatly accentuated

12 Von Thünen, *The isolated state*, p. 13. Unlike ploughing and cultivation, carting whether within the farm or from farm to market was not, of course, a fixed overhead but varied with the size of the harvest.

13 There is a convenient summary of estimates of wheat yields in England for the later seventeenth and eighteenth centuries in Turner, 'Agricultural productivity', table 5, p. 504. Grigg has assembled estimates of wheat yields in Europe in about 1850 which suggest that even at that date in Spain, Greece and Russia yields were about 7 bushels per acre, and that in several other countries including France, Italy and Spain they were between 7 and 10 bushels per acre. (I have taken 1 bushel of wheat to be of 60 lb weight.) Grigg, *Dynamics of agricultural change*, table 25, p. 175. Titow's work suggests that medieval English wheat yields were probably slightly less than 10 bushels per acre. Titow, *Winchester yields*, table 2b, p. 13. In converting the frequency distributions of yields given in Titow's table, I have assumed that the yields in each yield category were at the midpoint of the range except for the category 0 to 7.9 bushels where I have assumed that the average was 6 bushels. This procedure gives an overall average of 9.6 bushels. See also Bennett, 'British wheat yield', pp. 12–29; the article by Lennard, 'Statistics of corn yields'; and Jones and Healy, 'Wheat yields', table 1, p. 189. Overton's analysis of probate inventories suggests that wheat yields in East Anglia rose from about 8 to about 13 bushels per acre between the 1580s and the 1660s, and had increased still further to perhaps 15 bushels per acre by the 1720s and 1730s. Overton, 'Estimating crop yields', figure 1, p. 371.

on assumption (b). In the latter case, the value of the crop varies only modestly over the whole range of yields shown in table 5.2

If, therefore, Davenant in framing his table was relating gross output to price, it does not necessarily follow that agriculture derived a bumper income from bad years, nor suffered such a serious drop in income when harvests were exceptionally good. (Bouniatian's formula implies that a harvest 20 per cent above normal would reduce income from grain to only 79 per cent of its normal level if the marketable quantity varies with gross yield, whereas a calculation equating the marketable surplus with net yield suggests figures of 84 and 86 per cent respectively for assumptions (a) and (b) of table 5.2.)

From the farmer's point of view, the balance of advantage between good and bad harvests is further affected by any consumption of grain by his household. Because of household needs, the quantity available for sale in poor years will be even more sharply depressed than is implied by the distinction between gross and net yield in table 5.2. For example, a farmer devoting 50 acres to corn would harvest 500 bushels in an average year. On assumption (b) of table 5.2 he would need to set aside 175 bushels for seed and fodder. He might also have to reserve 75 bushels for the use of his household, making a total of 250 bushels as a fixed deduction from total production. In these circumstances, a fall of 20 per cent in gross output, from 500 to 400 bushels, would mean a fall of 40 per cent in output available for sale from 250 to 150 bushels. The resident farm family, which, together with any living-in servants, was also the prime farm workforce, took a substantial part of its 'payment' in the form of food. Grain used for this purpose falls into much the same logical category as animal 'fuel'. Maintenance of something approaching the normal level of food supply was a condition of the efficient working of the farm. If output for sale fell by 40 per cent, and if the price of corn changed in the manner set out in table 5.2, the farmer's income would be almost exactly the same in the deficit year as in an average year. Equally, he would have less to fear from a bumper harvest than might be thought at first blush since his net surplus would rise very much faster than his gross output. An increase of 20 per cent in gross output, on the same assumptions used in the previous calculation, would increase the quantity of grain for market by 40 per cent, and would reduce the farmer's income by only 7 per cent. The bigger the farmer and the higher the average output per acre, the less the force of the considerations just advanced, of course, but for many centuries and for wide tracts of territory they are relevant to the assessment of the farmer's interest in the face of fluctuating harvest fortunes.[14] The example considered is an arbitrary selection, of course. Other assumptions about farm size would lead to different relative fortunes in the wake of generous or niggardly yields, but

14 Abel provides some numerical illustrations of the importance of farm size in this connection. Abel, *Agricultural fluctuations in Europe*, pp. 9–13. Abel was also conscious of the 'leverage' exerted by low yield/seed ratios (p. 41).

to explore in full the interplay of the many factors that could affect the outcome is an enterprise beyond the scope of this essay.

The validity of the arguments used in connection with the distinction between gross and net yield retains its full force, of course, only to the degree that it is proper to assume that the absolute quantity reserved from sale was invariant, or to phrase the point differently, that the price elasticity of the farmer's demand for corn was zero. The assumption that the quantity of grain used as seed corn did not vary from year to year whatever the scale of the previous harvest is especially important since, at the levels of yield under discussion, this would be in many cases the weightiest element in deciding the matter. The issue appears to have attracted little historical attention. For many periods and places the evidence needed for empirical study is lacking,[15] and it may be thought that it is unreasonable to suppose that a constant quantity of corn was always reserved for seed (or, where seed was customarily obtained from other areas, bought through the market). Yet it is also true, that even if the price elasticity of the farmer's demand was greater than zero but much below the price elasticity of other demands, much of the effect would remain, though less starkly than under the assumptions used above. Nor should it be overlooked that a bad harvest might often result in *more* seed than usual rather than less, being sown for the next crop. For example, at a public meeting of the 'principal inhabitants' of the county of Aberdeenshire held in the December following the disastrous oats harvest of 1782, it was held to be essential, in spite of the desperate shortage of grain, to reserve 30 bolls for seed rather than the customary 25 because the seed was of poor quality.[16]

Price runs and yields

Suggestive indirect evidence exists, however, which lends plausibility to the view that usage of seed corn may not have varied significantly from year to year. Agricultural historians command far more evidence about prices in the past than about aggregate output or about yield, so that their picture of harvest fluctuation is often based principally upon a knowledge of the behaviour of prices. One of the most striking features of grain price series for earlier centuries is that they display 'runs' of years when prices were either above or below the local average. It has been common to interpret such runs as evidence that there were parallel sequences of good and bad harvests when corn was comparatively scarce or plentiful for several successive years. Sometimes the phenomenon is attributed to runs of years of favourable or unfavourable weather conditions, but it has also been

---

15 Manorial grange accounts are a promising source for the medieval period, perhaps superior to later materials before the nineteenth century.

16 Flinn (ed.), *Scottish population history*, pp. 11–12. I am grateful to John Walter for drawing my attention to this evidence.

attributed to the 'knock-on' effects of individual good or bad harvests due to seeding practice. Hoskins, for example, in two influential articles, suggested that the reason for successions of years with prices above or below the long-term moving average was to be found in the quantity of seed sown. He stressed the low level of yield/seed ratios and added:

> This means that a large part of the arable land had to be kept for growing next year's seed. It also meant that a bad harvest, by reducing the yield ratio to a dangerously low level, almost automatically ensured another bad harvest from a sheer deficiency of seed. In very bad years, the rural population must have staved off the worst of their hunger by consuming part of next year's seed corn . . . So one bad harvest tended to generate others . . . Conversely, of course, one good harvest tended automatically to produce another through the abundance of seed corn.'[17]

Hoskins's hypothesis is difficult to test effectively for the period from the late fifteenth to the mid-eighteenth century, the period whose price date he was discussing, for lack of suitable sources of information, but some light is thrown on the matter by nineteenth-century French data. From 1815 onwards information on cereal acreage, production, and therefore yields, was collected and published in France.[18] Such data for wheat, used in conjunction with a wheat price series, enable the behaviour of yield and price fluctuations to be examined, and the latter to be compared with similar English data from the medieval period onwards. These exercises are described in detail in the appendix to this essay, but the patterns they reveal lend themselves to a simple summary.

During the century 1815 to 1914 wheat yields in France varied in a random fashion. There was no tendency for years of exceptionally good or bad harvests to be followed by further years of above- or below-average yield. Nor were runs of good or bad harvests any more frequent or more prolonged than would be expected to occur by chance. Moreover, there was no relationship between the yield in one year and the area sown in the next. The die was thrown afresh each year and the result of the cast was not biased by the number produced by the throw of the previous year. If the quantity of corn retained for seed did vary with the scale of the harvest, it was not enough to influence the yield in the following year systematically, even to the limited extent of keeping it on the same side of the average yield. On the other hand, the *price* of wheat did not vary randomly from year to year, and runs of high and low prices did occur.[19] Clearly, although the quantity of the harvest varied randomly, grain prices did not follow suit.

The French data show unambiguously that it is dangerous to argue from the behaviour of a wheat price series to the pattern of annual fluctuations

17 Hoskins, 'Harvest fluctuations 1480–1619', pp. 32–3.
18 Mitchell, *European historical statistics*, tables D1 and D2.
19 Price data for harvest years were taken from Labrousse et al., *Le prix du froment*, pp. 13–14.

in the wheat harvest. Moreover, comparison with English price data reveals a striking similarity between the characteristics of wheat price fluctuations in nineteenth-century France and those of comparable wheat price series in England from medieval times onwards.

The absence of any evidence in French yield data that there were runs of good or bad years tells against the Hoskins hypothesis since he envisaged a shortage of grain in one year causing less seed than usual to be sown in the next and a smaller than average harvest to result. The proximate cause of runs in the price series, in other words, was held by him to be runs in the production series. If they are not visible, his explanation does not carry conviction. It is more plausible to assume that the scale of the carry-over from one harvest to the next was the cause of price runs. A bumper harvest in year t will mean that supplies in year $t + 1$ will also tend to be above average if yields vary randomly from year to year. Equally, a bad harvest, by restricting the carry-over, will produce an opposite effect. In this way random 'shocks' in the production series can give rise to runs in the price series, and the effect, *ceteris paribus*, need not be confined to the year next following.

The presence of very similar patterns in medieval and early modern English price series to those found in the nineteenth-century French series does not, of course, prove that an English yield series, if it existed, would display characteristics like the French, but it does suggest great caution in supposing that there were runs in the yield series in parallel with those in the price series. Moreover, there are other features of the Exeter wheat price series when the very long series (1316–1800) is broken down into sub-periods which are consonant with the hypothesis that variations in the carry-over of grain from year to year were the prime cause of the patterns in the price series.[20]

A priori one might doubt whether nineteenth-century evidence is relevant to the understanding of earlier times. For example, radical improvements in communications, and the consequent concatenation of producing areas, might be expected to have greatly reduced the pressure to trench upon seed corn after a poor harvest. Only further empirical research can adequately resolve this question, but it is worth noting that eighteenth-century French wheat price series behaved in a very similar manner to those in the nineteenth century down to at least 1860; and also that the level of wheat yields in France after the Napoleonic wars was very low by the standards of contemporary England. At about 13 bushels per acre, it was no higher than in England two centuries earlier.[21]

It is an added complication that Hoskins's assertion about variation in seed usage in response to harvest fortune might be true, but the inference which he drew might be mistaken. Bad harvests might cause seed corn to be consumed and lead to thinner sowing before the next harvest, and good harvests might be followed by an unusually liberal use of seed, without this

20 See appendix, pp. 128–30.
21 See note 56 below.

variation having a significant effect on the succeeding harvest. For example, the high price of grain after a poor harvest might encourage the employment of an abnormal amount of labour in tillage, weeding, birdscaring, gleaning etc. sufficient to offset the decline in yield per acre that might otherwise have occurred. Or again, yield may have been only very weakly responsive to seeding density even with unchanged cultivation practices. More widely spaced seeds, for example, encourage freer tillering. Against this, it is reasonable to suppose that normal seeding rates represented optimal practice in the circumstances of the day, and that any major change in the rate must have involved some penalty in output. If, however, to take an extreme position, changes in the seeding rate had little or no effect on yield, this fact, by increasing the probability that the yield series was random, would increase the likelihood that the presence of runs in the price series was attributable to the effect of carry-over.

At present, therefore, it is difficult to assemble sufficient evidence to specify unambiguous conclusions either about the invariability of the difference between gross and net yields, or about the question of the existence of runs in yield series comparable to the demonstrable runs in price series, or about the causes of such runs if they existed. But the French evidence lays the burden of proof upon those who have assumed that yield series were other than random and undermines any argument about yield runs which depends upon the existence of price runs.

Harvest yield and price

On the first point, the invariability of the quantity reserved from the market by consumption on the farm, whether for seed, self-consumption or animal fuel, Davenant's formula should be considered in relation to consumption by market purchase as well as to production requirements. If his formula were understood to mean that when the supply available in the market was reduced to half the normal level, its price rose more than fivefold, this would imply that almost three times the usual quantity of money was expended on corn. This interpretation is fraught with problems. For example, it is not easy to square with the fact that family budgets in pre-industrial times suggest that perhaps as much as three-quarters of all income were devoted to the purchase of food even in ordinary years, and that the bulk of food purchases consisted of grain. Since most families had little or no reserve of cash to call upon in hard years and were unlikely to be able to borrow, it is scarcely conceivable that they, who formed the bulk of the purchasers of corn, could raise their expenditure to the degree implied by the formula.[22] If, on the other hand, his formula for estimating price, though

22 It is often held that prices of other foodstuffs tended to move in unison with that of wheat, leaving no means of escape for most purchasers. Lee recently tested this point: 'As a first step

based on variations in gross output, should be related to the quantity available to be marketed, which was subject to much more violent fluctuations, the additional expenditure on grain even in a very bad year is relatively moderate on the assumption that the farmer's reservation from the market changed little from year to year.

The pressure towards higher prices in the wake of a bad harvest will vary not just, or even mainly, as a function of the extent of the harvest shortfall, but also as a function of the ability of purchasers to afford higher prices. For some men times of famine presented few problems. The wealthy spent relatively little of their income on food and were not greatly inconvenienced by grain price rises. Others enjoyed a sharply enhanced income in times of dearth because they had grain to sell. But many of those who depended chiefly upon wages were exposed to double jeopardy. The price of their main item of expenditure rose while at the same time employment was more difficult to find. Journeymen in the textile trades, for example, were notoriously vulnerable. Since others would always, when the pinch came, put food ahead of clothing in their domestic budgets, demand for the products of the textile industry, and hence employment within it, fell back just when it was most vital to those who made a living from it. In extreme cases, the lack of purchasing power on the part of those most in need might be so acute that famine conditions might prevail with few indications in price behaviour that a grave situation existed.[23] The scale and nature of transfer payments to those in poverty, and the sensitivity of any such payments to prevailing circumstances, played a significant part both in determining how successfully exposed members of the community could weather the storm, and in deciding how much prices rose. In bad times, high food prices may paradoxically

---

it needs to be shown that wheat prices are a good proxy for food prices in general. Numerous statistical analyses were carried out relating short-run variations in wheat prices to those of other grains, livestock, animal products such as eggs and milk, and a general food price index, using the annual price series for the period 1450 to 1650 published by Bowden. There were no systematic leads or lags, and changes in the series were closely associated with one another.' Wrigley and Schofield, *Population history of England*, p. 357. It is to be noted, however, that Bowden himself came to a rather different conclusion. Bowden, 'Agricultural prices', p. 629.

23 Sen notes that in the province of Wollo in Ethiopia during the Ethiopian famine of 1973 there were many deaths from famine even though the price of grain did not rise in that year in the main market at Dessie. Wollo peasants had no income source which could enable them to enter the market as effective purchasers. He also showed that large-scale mortality occurred during the Bengal famine in 1943 when the overall supply of rice available was little different from that of the years immediately preceding, principally because of the acute inflation in the wartime economy of Bengal which caused a very sharp increase in prices while wage labour rates increased only modestly. Thus, depending on local circumstances, it is possible for there to be heavy mortality from starvation without any shortfall in normal supply or, equally, for the level of supply to fall far below normal and to produce widespread deaths without leaving any trace in price statistics. Sen, *Poverty and famines*, pp. 63–78, 94–6, 101–2. It may be of interest to note that Malthus noticed and analysed the 'Wollo' phenomenon in a modified form, contrasting conditions in the Swedish province of Värmland with those in England, and drawing the same inference as Sen. Malthus, *The high price of provisions*, pp. 2–3, 18–20.

be a favourable sign rather than the reverse. They are evidence that additional purchasing power has been placed in the pockets of those in greatest need. It is likely that Davenant's law only applies where the worst-off members of the community can tap a wider pool of resources than that of the family.

This point was well understood by some observers in the past. Thomas Tooke, who had an exceptional familiarity with the operation of European grain markets in the late eighteenth and early nineteenth centuries, wrote 'supposing a given deficiency, the degree in which the money price may rise, will depend upon the pecuniary means of the lowest classes of the community'. Where these were very limited, as in Ireland and much of the continent, Tooke argued, 'the rise in price may not be very considerably beyond the defect of quantity', but where, as in France by the intervention of the government or in England by the operation of the poor laws, great efforts were made to alleviate the miseries of the bulk of the population, backed by public funds, 'the price would rise very considerably beyond the ratio of the deficiency'. In the former case it was likely, he argued, that some would perish and many suffer disease and malnutrition; in the latter, the effect was to 'limit the consumption and to apportion the privations resulting from scarcity over a larger part of the population; thus diminishing the severity of the pressure upon the lowest class, and preventing or tending to prevent any part of it from perishing, as it might otherwise do, from actual want of food'.[24]

Tooke's remarks represent a gloss upon a very familiar theme. The sufferings induced by famine were not spread uniformly in pre-industrial societies. Just as in animal societies one of the functions of the hierarchical ordering of individuals appears to be the identification of those who will die first when food runs short in order to safeguard the health of those higher up the pecking order,[25] so the market may perform a similar role in a monetized economy. Where little was done to assist those most exposed, more died but the spasm was reflected only in a muted form in the record of prices. Where transfer payments were substantial and well suited to need, fewer if any died but prices rose with greater apparent savagery.

The consistency with which Davenant's formula 'saves the phenomena' in pre-industrial European economies deserves much more extensive investigation than it has so far received. In pursuing the topic, it is important to be aware of the potential significance of the distinction between gross and net yield when analysing harvest information. An example may be taken from the writings of Slicher van Bath. He was in general very much alive to the importance of the distinction between gross and net yield, and provided a particularly cogent exposition of the topic in the opening section of his

24 Tooke, *History of prices*, i, pp. 13–14.
25 Wynne-Edwards has written much on this and related themes. See, e.g., his recent essay, Wynne-Edwards, 'Populations of red grouse'. For an illuminating study of a similar process at work in human populations, see Derouet, 'Une démographie différentielle'.

Agrarian history of western Europe.[26] When, however, he later turned to a discussion of Davenant's formula and those of Jevons and Bouniatian, he used an illustration which demonstrates how easily confusion can arise. The top two panels of table 5.3 reproduce the material that Slicher van Bath published. Drawing on Farmer's work on the Winchester pipe rolls, he set out the relative size of the wheat and barley crops and their prices in 1315 and 1316, which as a pair were perhaps the worst famine years in English medieval experience. In the second panel he showed the expected prices using Jevons's formula. He noted that the data were of dubious accuracy but made no comment on the poor fit between the actual price and the expected price in three of the four cases, other than to suggest that prices were kept down in 1315 by imports and by wheat stored up in previous years, and to make reference to a possible switch in demand to the cheaper grain, barley, in 1316.[27]

It appears to have escaped Slicher van Bath's notice, however, that Farmer's estimates were of *net* yield.[28] The information Farmer gave was not sufficient to convert the data back to the original gross yields, but if we assume that in an average year the gross yield exceeded the net in the ratio 4 : 3 for wheat and 3.5 : 2.5 for barley (yield ratios for barley were normally lower), then the ratio of each year's crop to the average level can be recalculated on a gross yield basis and the expected price re-estimated. If this is done, as may be seen in the bottom panel of table 5.3, the expected price and the actual price agree quite well in both years for wheat and in 1315 for barley, while the discrepancy for barley in 1316 may plausibly be attributed to the shift of demand in the second year to the cheaper grain as Slicher van Bath suggested. This evidence also strongly underwrites Tooke's view, implicit in the application of the formula to gross yields, that the total amount of money spent on grain in a year of harvest disaster could not massively exceed that of an average year unless some source were available other than their own pockets to assist the poor in their plight. For example, assuming that the top panel of table 5.3 roughly reflects the net quantity of grain available for consumption and the price paid for it, multiplying the two together gives an estimate of the total expenditure on grain. In the case of wheat, this suggests that in 1315 and 1316 total expenditure was 37 and 47 per cent above normal respectively, and in the case of barley 37 and 64 per cent – substantial, but not sensational, increases.

Intriguing as such particular illustrations are, however, only the collection of much more empirical data can clarify the question of the degree of applicability of any model of price behaviour in times of grain surplus or shortage in the past. Table 5.2 was designed to enable one extreme, though

26 Slicher van Bath, *Agrarian history*, pp. 18–23.
27 Farmer, 'Grain price movements'. Slicher van Bath, *Agrarian history*, p. 120.
28 Farmer's wheat yields were expressed as yield/seed ratios after deducting one unit for seed, 'as the resulting net yield gives a more accurate impression of the disposable harvest surplus'. Farmer, 'Grain price movements', p. 217.

Table 5.3 An illustration of the significance of the distinction between gross and net yields in calculating an implied price

	Size of wheat crop (1.00 = average)	Price (1.00 = average)	Size of barley crop (1.00 = average)	Price (1.00 = average)
Farmer's data from the Winchester pipe rolls				
1315	0.57	2.40	0.59	2.33
1316	0.62	2.37	0.77	2.13
Expected prices using Jevons's formula				
1315	0.57	4.07	0.59	3.73
1316	0.62	3.30	0.77	1.95
Expected prices after conversion to gross yield basis and using Jevons's formula (Bouniatian's formula)				
1315	0.68	2.63 (2.50)	0.71	2.37 (2.25)
1316	0.72	2.29 (2.17)	0.84	1.59 (1.50)

For details of conversion see text.
Source: For top two panels, Slicher van Bath, *Agrarian history*, p. 120.

not necessarily unlikely, possibility to be examined. At the other extreme, if the amount set aside for seed, instead of being a fixed quantity, could be shown to have been reduced in proportion to the deficiency or excess of the previous harvest, the assumptions leading to the construction of table 5.2 would be proved to be unjustified and the argument based upon it would be nugatory.[29] In connection with the pressures to reduce sowing rates for seed corn, incidentally, it may be important to note that wheat was a winter-sown grain, but barley was spring-sown. Immediately after harvest, even if the harvest were bad, the temptation to skimp on seed usage must have been less strong than after a further five months had elapsed.

Pending the assemblage of fuller information about the pre-industrial past, it may be of interest to touch upon another implication of the Bouniatian formula which is of potential importance when price data are so much more abundant than yield data. To the extent that the formula succeeds in capturing the relationship of quantity and price, it can of course be used to calculate quantity from price as easily as the reverse, though, because prices were not affected solely by the scale of the previous harvest, the estimation of harvest variations from price data must be subject to substantial margins of error. If $y = 0.757/(x - 0.13)^2$ then $x = 0.13 + 0.757/y$. An example may illustrate the use to which the reverse formula can be put, and once more suggests the value of distinguishing gross and net yields. The year 1596 is commonly held to have been the worst harvest year of the early modern period, and indeed in the Exeter wheat price series, the price of wheat rose higher relative to its own 25-year moving average than in any other year

---

29 It may be of interest to note that Robert Loder appears to have sown a relatively constant quantity of seed per unit of area on his farm in the early seventeenth century. He expressed the area he sowed each year in 'lands' and it is clear that he regarded them as of a fairly constant size. The following table shows the number of 'lands' of wheat sown over a period of nine years, the quantity harvested, the number of bushels of wheat produced per 'land', the yield/seed ratios and the quantity of seed sown per 'land' for the following year. There is no evidence here that a poor harvest tended to cause seed to be used more sparingly. Loder normally kept aside a part of his previous harvest to serve as seed, though occasionally he also bought in a little seed. He was, however, a farmer on a fairly large scale and not necessarily, therefore, typical of the majority of his contemporaries.

Year	No. of 'lands'	Production (bushels)	Production per 'land' (bushels)	Yield/seed ratio	Seed per 'land' sown for next harvest
1611	26.0	167	6.4	—	1.28
1612	23.5	238	10.1	7.9	1.41
1613	27.0	209	7.7	5.5	1.45
1614	20.0	381	19.1	13.1	1.43
1615	23.0	241	10.5	7.3	1.07
1616	20.5	444	21.7	20.2	1.19
1617	37.0	362	9.8	8.2	1.15
1618	62.0	942	15.2	13.3	1.08
1619	96.5	1054	15.2	14.1	—

Source: Fussell (ed.), *Robert Loder's farm accounts*.

The yield/seed ratios given here are in general closely similar to those given by Fussell (table 3, p. xvii), except for 1616. Fussell calculated a figure of only 7.8 for that year because he appears to have mistaken the quantity of seed sown. Loder himself referred to the 1616 wheat harvest as 'a most marveylous yeld' when the lord had made 'the cloudes to drope fatnes' (p. 110).

(though 1556 runs it fairly close).[30] In 1596 wheat stood at 2.21 times its moving average. Where y is 2.21, x is 0.72, suggesting that the gross yield of wheat in that year was 72 per cent of its normal level. This is substantially below average, of course, but if the quantity of wheat available for human consumption had fallen by only a little over a quarter it is perhaps unlikely that it would have caused the degree of distress that occurred in the wake of the harvest of 1596. However, that the net figure of food available after providing for seed corn may have fallen by a significantly larger fraction may be seen by consulting table 5.2: a gross yield of 72 per cent of an average yield of 10 bushels per acre, implies a net yield of only 63 per cent of normal on assumption (a), or 57 per cent of normal on assumption (b). It is interesting to note that these figures are not greatly dissimilar from the comparable estimates of harvest shortfall for wheat and barley on the Winchester estates in 1315 (57 and 59 per cent respectively).

Coping with risk

In order to examine various aspects of yield and price in the past, I have used figures relating to wheat and barley or more generally to corn as if all types of corn were essentially similar in their characteristics. In many contexts, this may be legitimate, but not in all. 'Corn' was not a uniform product. Wheat, rye, barley and oats were not used for the same purposes, nor did their fluctuations in yield run in parallel to one another. Whereas wheat was chiefly used for bread in England, oats were principally fodder for horses in most parts of the country. If all grains were perfectly substitutable for one another, their predominant usage in an average year would not affect an argument couched in terms of 'corn' in a year of harvest failure. But if men always ate wheat or barley and horses always ate oats, then human nutrition would be unaffected by the availability of animal fodder and vice versa. Probably the former is a better paradigm than the latter. 'Trading down' into cheaper grains was a very frequent concomitant of hard times, but different types of grain were not completely interchangeable in use.

The lack of parallelism in harvest fluctuations in the yields of different grains is worthy of emphasis. A disastrous year for a winter-sown cereal, such as wheat, for example, might be a moderate year for a spring-sown cereal, like barley, or vice versa. This may be seen either on the scale of the individual farm or on that of a whole country. The year 1619 was a good one for wheat on Robert Loder's farm. The yield/seed ratio was 14.1, 22 per cent above the average for the nine years 1612–20. Barley, in contrast, yielded only moderately well: its yield/seed ratio was 7.9, only 6 per cent above the average of the same nine years. And in 1616, an *annus mirabilis*

---

30 It is important to note that the Exeter wheat price series rose exceptionally sharply in 1596 and in other English wheat price series it does not stand out quite so strikingly.

for wheat, Loder's yield/seed ratio for that grain was 74 per cent above the average though the barley ratio was almost exactly at its average level.[31] On a national scale the contrasts could be just as striking. In France, for example, 1830 was a poor year for wheat but a very good year for barley; whereas in 1832, when there was a bumper wheat crop, barley yields were only a little above average. (Expressed as percentages of the average yields over the 11 years 1825–35, the wheat yield in 1830 was 85 when the figure for barley was 115, while in 1832 the two comparable figures were 126 and 108, when compared with the local 11-year average.)[32] The varying fortunes of different cereals at harvest time is both of interest in itself, and has related implications. For example, inasmuch as the different types of cereal were interchangeable in use, an index of 'corn' yield based on the yield of only one cereal can be a misleading guide to the availability of grain.

As an illustration of the importance of bearing such points in mind, consider the argument advanced by Appleby in one of his most stimulating articles, concerning subsistence crises in England and France. He noted that in England in the 1690s there was no longer a close correlation between price movements in wheat and the cheaper cereals, whereas in France there was still a very strong relationship as exemplified by price movements in the *mercuriales* at Pontoise. The situation in England, he argued, betokened relative sufficiency of overall grain supply and freedom from starvation: that in France meant that the poor still stood at the end of the precipice. Further, he argued that a century earlier in the 1590s the English case was more like the French.[33]

There is clearly a danger in using price data from a single market as if it were typical of the whole of France. Assuming, however, that Appleby's thesis about comparative price movements is fundamentally correct, the patterns he observed may still have been due, at least in part, to other influences. It is striking how largely wheat dominated other grains in quantity terms in the Pontoise market. Dupâquier, Lachiver and Meuvret published a large body of price data for seven markets, but information about the quantities sold only for Pontoise in the period 1752–61. For these years the quantities of wheat, maslin, rye, barley and oats are detailed separately. Over the ten years as a whole wheat formed 64 per cent of the total of *setiers* sold.[34]

Davenant's estimates suggest a very different position in England at the end of the seventeenth century. In a year of 'moderate plenty' he supposed that the national net produce (excluding seed corn), expressed in millions of bushels, was wheat 14, rye 10, barley 27 and oats 16.[35] The quantity produced and the quantity placed on the market may have been widely

---

31 See note 29 above for yield/seed ratios for wheat 1612–19. The ratio in 1620 was 14.6. The barley ratios are taken from Fussell, *Robert Loder's farm accounts*, table 3, p. xvii.

32 Mitchell, *European historical statistics*, tables D1 and D2.

33 Appleby, 'Grain prices and subsistence crises'.

34 Dupâquier et al., *Mercuriales du pays de France*, pp. 230–1.

35 Davenant, *Essay upon the balance of trade*, p. 71.

different, of course, but it is at least highly likely that, on the assumption of some interchangeability of use between the cereals, there would be a tighter correlation between wheat and other grain prices at Pontoise than in England. Shortages or gluts of wheat at Pontoise must have influenced the demand for other grains to a degree not found where wheat was much less dominant. Nor is it clear that the situation in England in the 1590s was so greatly different from that a century later. It is true that in 1596 and 1597, when wheat was so dear, the prices of other grains were also very high. But grain prices did not move in unison in all dear years. In 1600, for example, wheat was not expensive. Expressed as an indexed figure based on a 25-year centred moving average, wheat stood at exactly 100, but barley and oats were 137 and 154 respectively. On the other hand, in 1608 the comparable figures were 136, 83 and 108 (again relating each price in 1608 to the long-term average for that year). For comparison, the ratios in 1596 were 173, 172 and 196.[36] Here once more there is scope for further analysis.

Risk spreading and price behaviour might also repay increased attention. For some communities and in some periods trade links limited the effects of poor local harvests by concatenating supplies over a large area, what might be called geographical risk spreading. Price movements would then be less at the mercy of local harvest fortunes. Similarly, temporal risk spreading took place in all communities to some extent since grain might be stored for quite long periods with only limited loss or deterioration where storage conditions were good. Indeed, just as a large enough dam on a river is capable of dampening out seasonal and annual fluctuations in the volume of flow downstream from the dam, so a sufficiently large and efficient grain storage system may in principle largely offset the effects of a poor harvest or even of a run of poor seasons. Such effects were beneficial to the consumer, but could create difficulties for the small producer since they tended to exaggerate the fluctuations in his income by dampening price rises in years of poor harvest and moderating price falls when harvests were plentiful.

Contemporaries were alive to the issue as it might affect the impoverished consumer. Davenant, for example, was concerned about the small margin upon which England operated in his day. He thought that following a good harvest only five months' stock remained when the new harvest was gathered in, and in an 'indifferent' year four months' stock. This he contrasted unfavourably with the prudence of the Dutch in storing grain on a much larger scale so that 'those dearths which in their turn have afflicted most other countries, fall but lightly on their common people'. In this way the Dutch were able to sell 'us our own corn dear, which they had bought cheap'.[37] Food can, of course, be 'stored' by other means than in a granary. Animals kept for meat, for example, form a living foodstore which may be drawn upon in hard times, and in this regard England was probably relatively well provided.

36 Bowden, 'Statistical appendix', pp. 819–20.
37 Davenant, *Essay upon the balance of trade*, p. 84.

To round off the discussion of gross and net yields in relation to harvest fluctuations, two further points may be mentioned. First, it may be helpful to make explicit something which was implicit in earlier discussion. In a country which consisted exclusively of small husbandmen, each farming an area sufficient only to meet the needs of a single family in an average year, it would be impossible in a bad year to devote an unchanged quantity of corn to usage as seed, animal 'fuel' and family consumption since these between them would have comprised all types of grain usage in an average year. Since the total supply would be smaller, one or more of the usual forms of consumption would also have to be reduced. At the other extreme, where all farmers operated on a large scale and normally disposed of the bulk of their crop in the market, it would have been a relatively straightforward matter to keep the farmer's reservation of corn at a constant level in a bad year, especially as price movements were likely to be such as to enable him to enjoy an increased income even though the quantity reserved for seed and other uses on the farm was unchanged. 'Pure' cases of either extreme seldom if ever arose over wide regions of a country as a whole, but the position of individual countries varied considerably on the spectrum of possibilities. The assumption of an unchanging absolute margin between gross and net yields is probably more accurate for pre-industrial England than for other countries because of the unusual character of the farming units, and especially so in the later centuries of the early modern period. Large farms were more common; small, 'family' peasant holdings less widespread than elsewhere.

Secondly, inasmuch as the quantity of grain used for seed per acre cultivated appears to have changed very little between the middle ages and the nineteenth century, but the yield per acre increased from less than 10 to more than 20 bushels per acre for wheat, with similar gains for other cereals, the distinction between gross and net yield became less and less significant to most of the issues discussed above. At a yield of, say, 8 bushels per acre the proportion of the harvest needed for seed in the case of wheat was 31 per cent; at a yield of, say, 25 bushels per acre it was only 10 per cent. Over time, therefore, it ceased to matter greatly for most purposes which measure was employed when studying short-term changes of the relationship of quantity and price.

The significance of secular trends in yields

In other contexts, however, the distinction remains important even though, indeed because, the percentage gap between gross and net yields grew steadily less with the elapse of time and the rise in output per acre. Consider, for example, a comment made by Hoskins when reviewing the whole period covered by his survey of harvest fluctuations from 1480 to 1759. He noted that gross yield ratios appeared to have doubled between 1500 and 1650 and that population had also doubled over the same period, and added, 'Thus the remarkable advance in yields in this period brought no real improvement in basic food supplies for the mass of the population.' Yet what counted in this connection was not what happened to *gross* yields but what happened to *net* yields. If, therefore, it were the case that gross yields had risen from 4 to 8, or by 100 per cent, as he claimed, net yields must have risen by 133 per cent, that is from 3 to 7.[38]

This point has a wider relevance. Suppose that the average yield of corn per acre in England was 10 bushels in 1500 and had reached 22 bushels by 1800, and assume that there was no change in seed usage per acre. It would follow that net corn output must rise more sharply than gross. On assumption (a) of table 5.2, net yield would increase from 7.5 to 19.5 bushels. The gross yield rises by 120 per cent, the net by 160 per cent (on assumption (b) the comparable net figure is 185 per cent). It is probable that other changes between 1500 and 1800 may have further increased the difference between the percentage increases in gross and what might be termed effective net yield. Some grain is always lost between harvest and consumption because of spoilage and the depredations of rodents, insects and birds. More effective storage, say in brick or stone-built barns, would tend to reduce this loss, which may be regarded as a percentage toll rather than a fixed quantity per acre as with seed corn. Suppose that loss under this head fell from 15 to 10 per cent between 1500 and 1800, then on assumption (a) of table 5.2, the final net supply of corn per acre would rise from 6.0 to 17.3 bushels, or by 188 per cent (on assumption (b) by 226 per cent).

Viewed in this way, it is considerably less difficult to account for the success of English agriculture in keeping pace with English population growth over the early modern period. Between 1550 and 1820 the population of England roughly quadrupled, while home agriculture throughout supplied the overwhelming bulk of the corn consumed.[39] If attention is focused on gross yields the fact that population quadrupled while yields per acre rose by 120 per cent would suggest that about 80 per cent more land must have been devoted to growing corn at the end of the period compared with its start at constant consumption per head. If, on the other hand, net yield is taken as the more relevant yardstick, and if net yields did indeed rise by 188 per cent over the three centuries, then the additional land needed to cater for the increase in population is far more modest. An increase of the acreage of corn of 39 per cent will suffice. Even ignoring the supposition about reduced spoilage, an increase in cereal acreage of 54 per cent would permit a constant level of grain consumption per head to be maintained (or 23 and 40 per cent respectively under assumption (b) of table 5.2). In the light of these considerations it is reasonable to suppose that a relatively modest increase in the cultivated area may have sufficed to meet the needs of the greatly enlarged population.

38 Hoskins, 'Harvest fluctuations 1620–1759', pp. 17, 25, 27.
39 Wrigley and Schofield, *Population history of England*, table 7.8, pp. 208–9.

A further implication of any substantial rise in corn yields is that the significance of the annual fluctuations in yield is reduced. If it is safe to assume that the variations in weather and in the incidence of pests and diseases which affect crops are such as to produce the same *percentage* variations in *gross* yield on average whatever the *absolute* average level of yield, then, in contrast, the effect of weather and pests on *net* yield will not be independent of the absolute level of yield. Suppose, for example, that the mean annual percentage variation in gross yield is a constant 15 per cent irrespective of the absolute level of average yields, then with average yields at 10 bushels per acre the mean annual percentage variation in net yield will be 20 per cent on assumption (a) of table 5.2 (where gross yield is 10 bushels, net yield is 7.5 bushels, and $100 \times (1.5/7.5) = 20$). If average gross yield were to rise to 22 bushels per acre, however, the mean annual percentage variation in net yield would fall to 17 per cent ($100 \times (3.3/19.5) = 16.9$). On assumption (b), the comparable mean annual percentage variations in net yield are 23 and 18 per cent respectively. Inasmuch as short-term fluctuations in real wages in pre-industrial economies were principally a function of short-term movements in food prices and above all in the price of corn, this would mean that, *ceteris paribus*, living standards in a regime of low yields per acre would be inherently more unstable than where yields were higher. An economy which enjoyed high yields per acre would thus be in a better posture to meet the inevitable random shocks of harvest variability without as great a degree of disruption as would attend an economy which also had to cope with the effects of low yield per acre.[40]

Declining marginal returns

Another instance of the importance of distinguishing between gross and net yields may be found in considering the question of the effect of declining marginal returns to labour. An illustration is given in table 5.4. When 10 men are engaged in working the 100-acre plot, it yields on average 1000 bushels and the presence of the tenth man adds an amount equal to the average productivity of the group as a whole, or 100 bushels. At this level of activity average and marginal productivity are equal. If, however, an eleventh man is added to the labour force the gross output is assumed to increase by only 90 bushels; a twelfth would add 80 bushels to gross output, and so on until the sixteenth man adds only 40 bushels. Average labour productivity falls continuously and increasingly steeply because the marginal

40 It may be significant that the mean percentage annual variations of the real wage from its own centred 25-year moving average declined fairly steadily from 10.5 per cent in 1550–74 to 5.8 in 1750–74 before rising slightly to between 6 and 7 per cent in the first half of the nineteenth century. The real wage index used in this calculation, that of Phelps Brown and Hopkins, is heavily influenced, of course, by short-term price fluctuations, and these in turn largely reflect the behaviour of cereal prices. Wrigley and Schofield, *Population history of England*, table 8.7, p. 317.

Table 5.4 Labour inputs and output per head

Area (acres)	Men employed	Gross output (bushels)	Net output (bushels)		Last man contributes (bushels)	Average gross output per man (bushels)	Average net output per man (bushels)	
			(a)	(b)			(a)	(b)
100	10	1000	750	650	100	100	75	65
100	11	1090	840	740	90	99	76	67
100	12	1170	920	820	80	98	77	68
100	13	1240	990	890	70	96	76	68
100	14	1300	1050	950	60	93	75	68
100	15	1350	1100	1000	50	90	73	67
100	16	1390	1140	1040	40	87	71	65

Assumptions (a) and (b) as table 5.2.

product associated with each additional worker is assumed to fall away very rapidly. If we turn to net product, however, the picture is different. Once again, two cases are considered, embodying the same assumptions as were used in table 5.2. The absolute increment to net product as each additional man is employed is the same as the increment to gross product and there is also a declining marginal product per man, but for a time each additional man adds more to the total net product than the previously prevailing average and the average net output per man therefore rises. This holds true up to the point where 12 men are employed under assumption (a), or up to 14 men under assumption (b). Thereafter, with net as with gross product, the employment of further men will depress the average, but even with as many as 14 men employed the average net output per man is no lower than where 10 men are employed under assumption (a); the same point is not reached until 16 men are employed under assumption (b). Gross output per man, on the other hand, is 7 per cent lower with 14 rather than 10 men employed, and 13 per cent lower with 16 men employed. Looked at in another way, the gross output of the 100-acre plot rises only 39 per cent when 60 per cent is added to the labour force, but a part of this product is never available for food and this part is assumed to be a fixed absolute quantity for any given acreage. As a result the net product rises by 52 per cent under assumption (a) or by 60 per cent under assumption (b).

If the exercise is carried out at lower gross yields per acre, the result is, of course, even more striking. For example, if gross output with 10 men is 800 bushels, and the proportionate fall in marginal output per man is the same as in table 5.4 (i.e. the eleventh man produces 72 bushels, and the twelfth 64 and so on), then the average net product per man is only 2 per cent lower with 16 rather than 10 men under assumption (a) and 6 per cent higher under assumption (b).

The general point related to table 5.4 may be put quite simply. Any given acreage in cereal crops must first 'carry' a fixed quantity of output to be used for seed, or for seed and 'fuel', before it can begin to meet other demands for corn. The fixed element remains unaffected by the number of those at work on the land in question. As long as the addition to output achieved by introducing an extra man into the labour force exceeds the *net* productivity per man of the pre-existing labour force (their average output after the deduction of the fixed element), his presence will increase the effective (net) output per head. Similarly, a reduction of one man in an initial labour force will only increase the effective output per head if his presence contributes less than the average *net* productivity per man of the remaining workers.

The fact that, where production per acre is low, there will be a range of intensity of land use over which average output per man will be moving in opposite directions for net and gross figures may have relevance to the interpretation of long-term economic change in pre-industrial societies. For example, suppose that there was a period of falling population, such as took place during much of the fourteenth and fifteenth centuries in wide tracts of

Europe, during which the land became less densely settled and less intensively worked. The gross output of cereal agriculture is assumed to have fallen, but less steeply than population. It is tempting to draw the conclusion from such data that living standards and levels of nutrition should improve whatever the other concomitants of a contracting population. But the conclusion may be over-hasty for, whereas average *gross* output would rise, average *net* output might fall. This would be the case where the marginal gross productivity of labour lost was greater than the average net productivity at that point.

In table 5.4, for example, under assumption (b) average gross output per man rises as the number of men employed falls from 14 to 10 but average net product falls. If the marginal gross product of the ninth and eighth man were the same as the tenth (100 bushels), a further fall of two men in the labour force would leave the average gross product per man unchanged but would result in a marked further contraction in average net product per man of 13 per cent as a constant deduction for seed and animals is spread amongst fewer workers. Overall, in moving from 14 to 8 men employed on the 100-acre plot, gross output per man would rise by 8 per cent but net output per man would fall by 17 per cent. No doubt this example is over-simplified to the point of caricature, but it suggests that care is necessary in drawing inferences about living standards from gross cereal output per head.[41]

Unless labour is so plentiful that marginal gross productivity is already low, falling populations may well be associated with *falling* net agricultural output per head even when gross figures are moving upwards. Indeed, to be provocative, one might imagine the possibility of a low-density, low-living standard equilibrium trap where a population, following a fall in numbers which had led indirectly to a reduced net cereal output per head, would experience a higher mortality or a reduced nuptiality, or both, sufficient to prevent a recovery in population. It is worth repeating in this connection that a lower gross output per acre will tend to increase the mean annual percentage variation in net yield, and therefore, inasmuch as mortality may be raised by the effects of reduced food supply in the wake of bad harvests, the fall in population may indirectly be a cause of higher mortality for this reason also.

Conclusion

Until well into the nineteenth century no other aspect of economic life was consistently of such great concern to private individuals and to public

---

41 That this possibility is not entirely hypothetical is suggested by the recent work of Campbell on the manor of Martham in Norfolk. He gives details of seed sown and yields per acre in 1300–24 and 1400–24. Net yields of wheat (gross yields less seed) fell from 16.5 to 9.2 bushels, or by 44 per cent; of barley from 13.0 to 11.4 (– 12 per cent); of legumes from 7.5 to 4.0

authorities alike as the scale of the last harvest and the prospects for the next year. Jointly, they regulated the fortunes of both agriculture and industry because of the way in which they affected the price of food and the demand for goods of all types. It follows, therefore, that achieving a juster and more exact appreciation of the relationship between the quantity of the harvest and the behaviour of prices must prove of great value in gaining a better understanding of the pre-industrial economy of England.

Speculation is a poor substitute for demonstrable knowledge, yet it may prove to be its forerunner. The bulk of this essay has been speculative. When confronted by systematic empirical evidence, some of the hypotheses advanced may prove to be sustainable, but others may need to be refined or retracted. My concern, however, has not been with empirical testing so much as with showing how much uncertainty or imprecision still attaches to the treatment of a number of issues relating to the yield and price of corn in the past. In particular, I have laid stress on the importance of the distinction between gross and net yields to several topics: the relationship between yield and price, the variability of prices, the implications of good and bad harvests for the producer and the consumer, the interpretation of long-term trends in yields per acre, the returns to increasing and decreasing inputs of labour. Those with specialist knowledge may well be able to call into play evidence to clarify many of these issues forthwith. Other problems should yield to further research and reflection. The purpose of this essay will have been well served if interest in this range of questions is heightened, for any attempt to understand pre-industrial economies must be strongly coloured by the way in which the functioning of its agriculture is apprehended, and the same is equally true of the transition from an agricultural to an industrial society.

(– 47 per cent); but net yield of oats rose from 13.0 to 16.4 bushels (+ 26 per cent). Oats in the earlier period had been used as a smother crop with very dense seeding: its gross yield changed only marginally but net yields rose more substantially. Martham was an untypical manor which had used very labour-intensive methods before the Black Death, and seeding levels fell in all four crops so that gross and net yields fell about equally (apart from oats). Moreover, Campbell does not provide sufficient detail about the use of labour and the balance of crops on the demesne to make it possible to determine whether net yields per man-year fell. Nevertheless, his data do suggest that lower population densities may not necessarily connote higher output per man. The number of man-days worked by *famuli* fell by 27 per cent over the century, which seems consonant with a fall in output per man-day given the scale of the fall in yield per acre and the fact that the frequency of fallowing doubled, but Campbell notes that the fall in casual, hired labour was even steeper than the decline in *famuli* labour. Campbell, 'Agricultural progress in medieval England', pp. 38–9 and table 5, p. 38.

Appendix: The relationship between the yield and price of grain

The purpose of this appendix is to examine a single, limited issue: whether it is safe to argue from the behaviour of grain prices as they varied from year to year to certain characteristics of the grain harvest. Grain price series exist in comparative abundance for pre-industrial Europe, and in some cases a particular series may extend over many decades, even over several centuries, with only minor gaps. In contrast, evidence about the physical yield of harvest is far less abundant. Where it exists it often refers only to a particular farm or manor, and may be frequently broken by substantial gaps. Furthermore, the information may be imprecise and its use is usually complicated by the idiosyncrasies of local measures of volume, area and weight. It is therefore tempting to attempt to make inferences about fluctuations in the size of the harvest from the behaviour of prices, since an abundant supply depresses the price of grain, while a shortage causes prices to rise.

It has often been observed that grain prices display a strong tendency to develop 'runs'; a number of successive years in which prices are either above or below the longer-term average. This characteristic of the price behaviour is often supposed to be due to fluctuations in the physical yield of grain from year to year. Indeed, the connection is sometimes seen as so obvious as scarcely to warrant independent argument or empirical investigation. The reason why yields in turn should be high or low for several years in succession has also attracted some comment. Occasional runs might, of course, occur even though yields were randomly distributed through time because chance will produce them occasionally, just as several successive rolls of a die may result in the same number. But a systematic tendency for the bunching of good or bad years must have some other explanation. Environmental circumstances constitute a possible explanation but, though the weather can favour or damage the harvest and pests or diseases can each seriously affect yields, these are factors which are also broadly random in their impact.

A more promising line of attack has been to consider disturbances which, though peculiar to a particular year, might have a 'knock on' effect, boosting or depressing yields in subsequent years. Hence the attractiveness of Hoskins's argument concerning the strategic importance of seed corn.[42] If the harvest in any year is exceptionally poor due to a 'shock' of a type which may itself be random in its distribution, but the effect of a deficient supply of grain is to lure producers into eating or selling grain which in a normal year would be reserved for seed, then, even if environmental conditions revert to normal in the following year, the harvest will be below average and the price of grain will remain above the norm. This might arise either because a smaller acreage is planted or because grain is less thickly sown, or both. Conversely, presumably an unusually abundant harvest encourages a liberal

42 See above, p. 100.

use of seed with benign results to mirror the malign effects of a bad harvest. The mechanism involved seems *prima facie* less plausible as an explanation of runs of years with low prices than of runs of high prices, since there were conventional seeding densities which were unlikely to be exceeded however cheap grain might be (unless the grain was grown, as in the case of oats sometimes, as a 'smother' crop). A satisfactory explanation, however, needs to be symmetric in this respect since runs of low prices were as conspicuous and pronounced as runs of high prices.[43]

Equally attractive on general grounds, and less vulnerable in relation to the need for an explanation which implies symmetric price behaviour, is an explanation couched in terms of the carry-over of grain from one harvest year to the next. The price of grain is affected by the total supply on offer or in prospect, which at any given point in time will be influenced not only by the scale of the last harvest (and, in the later months of the harvest year, by the prospects of the next), but also by the quantity carried forward into the current year from its predecessor.[44] Here, then, there is also a mechanism that might transmit from one year to the next the price effects of good or bad harvests. Such effects might be felt not simply in the year following the 'shock', but over a more extended period.

The explanation via seed-corn usage implies that the annual output of grain, if known, would reveal runs to match those observed in prices. The explanation via the stock of corn carried forward from one year to the next, on the other hand, would hold good even if output fluctuated randomly. The discovery that price data displayed runs while output data did not would, therefore, be fatal to the former explanation, but would be congenial to the latter. As a contribution to this debate it is instructive to consider price and production data for a period when both are available and then to examine the implications of any findings for earlier data referring to price alone.

France began to collect acreage and output data from as early as 1815.[45] It is therefore possible to discover whether from this date onwards there was any tendency for good or bad harvests to be followed by others of the same type. In table 5A.1 a very simple method has been used to throw light on the subject. The yield of wheat per hectare was expressed as a ratio to its own 25-year moving average. Thus a figure of 1.10 for a particular year would indicate that in that year output per hectare was 10 per cent above the 25-year moving average centred on the year in question. If a yield in one year tended to be associated with an above-average yield in the following year, then if all years in which, say, yields were between 10 and 15 per cent above average were treated as a set, it would be expected that a set of years consisting of all years next following the years in the first set would also have above-average yields. The nature of the underlying process supposedly at work suggests that the years in the second category on average would be closer to the moving

43 See tables 5A.3 and 5A.7 below and the accompanying text.
44 For Davenant's view of the scale of the carry-over from year to year see above, p. 110.
45 Yield data are available for the UK only from 1884 onwards.

Table 5A.1   France 1828-1900: harvest yields in successive years (wheat)

Number of cases	Yield in year t	Average yield in year t + 1
10	<0.85	1.097
4	0.85-0.90	1.014
13	0.91-0.96	0.988
14	0.97-1.02	0.985
14	1.03-1.08	0.946
7	1.09-1.14	1.017
8	⩾1.15	1.015
	mean 0.999	s.d. 0.124

The figures in the second column show the harvest yield in any one year; those in the third column the yield in the following year. Both are expressed in relation to a 25-year moving average of the yield. Thus in the period 1828-1900 there were ten instances of years when the harvest yield was less than 85 per cent of the 25-year moving average for the years in question. In the ten years next following them the average yield was almost 10 per cent above average and so on. Note that the series contains two fewer cases than might be expected from the dates beginning and ending the series (70 rather than 72). This occurs because the series contained no yield figure for 1870.
Source: Annuaire Statistique de la France.

mean than those in the first category. Thus, for example, the average score of years next following years in which the yield was 10 to 15 per cent above average might be, say, 5 per cent above average and so on.

Table 5A.1 shows that there was no clear tendency for the yield in any one year to be affected by the yield in the preceding year, suggesting an absence of serial autocorrelation. The ratios in the third column of table 5A.1 are usually close to 1.00 whether following good, bad or indifferent years. Yields appear to have been randomly distributed around the long-term moving average. Any aberrant values are probably due to the small numbers of years in each category. This point can be crudely tested by considering all below-average harvests *en bloc* (the 27 cases where yields were less than 97 per cent of the long-term moving average) and comparing the value associated with them to those associated with above-average years (the 29 cases where yields were more than 103 per cent of the average). The average yield in year $t + 1$ in the former case was 1.032; in the latter, 0.982. This suggests, if anything, a weak tendency for poor harvests to be followed by good ones, and vice versa, but it is probable that the apparent pattern arises only because of the relatively small number of cases involved. A more searching and systematic test of the same point is to test the extent of the correlation between each value in the series t and its successor $t + 1$. The French yield data enable 70 paired observations to be made. The correlation coefficient $r = 0.185$. This is not a significant level and it would be unsafe to assume that the series was other than random.[46]

The same issue can be tested by another simple method. Assume once more that the yields in successive years are unrelated. If in year t the yield were above average, in year $t + 1$ there would be an equal chance that the

46 Bartlett, 'Autocorrelated time series'. The 95 per cent confidence interval would require a reading of 0.239 or greater.

yield would again be above average or that it would be below average: if the latter, a run of one year would result; if the former, a run of two or more years would have been established. By parallel reasoning, this run would have an equal chance of extending from two to three years or of ending at two, and so on. Thus, a half of all runs would be one year in length, a quarter two years in length, an eighth three years in length, and so on. In table 5A.2, using the same data as for table 5A.1, the frequency of runs of varying length in nineteenth-century French wheat yields is set out together with the 'expected' figure given the total number of runs. It is clear at a glance that this test, too, strongly suggests that yields in successive years were not related. The point can be established more formally. A one-sample runs test shows that it is highly probable that the sequence of above- and below-average yields is random.[47]

Table 5A.2   France 1828-1900: the frequency of runs of above- or below-average yields (wheat)

Length of run in years	Number of runs	'Expected' number of runs
1	17	16.5
2	7	8.3
3	5	4.1
4	2	2.1
5	0	1.0
6	1	0.5
7	1	0.3
	33	

See text for derivation of 'expected' totals.
Source: Annuaire Statistique de la France.

Price data for the same period, however, tell a different story. In table 5A.3 the same technique has been used as that employed for table 5A.1. The tabulation can either be carried out with the raw French data, or after the price ratios have been converted into yield ratios using the formula of Bouniatian.[48] Both are given in the table. The former produces a less symmetrical pattern than the latter because prices rise proportionately much higher in relation to the long-term moving average in years of low yield than they fall in bumper years.

In studying table 5A.3 it should be remembered that cases which are found at the head of the prices section will be found at the foot of the implied yield section and vice versa. This happens because Bouniatian's formula converts high prices into low implied yields and low prices into high implied yields.

47 The number of runs is only slightly smaller than the 'expected' figure (33 and 34.4), and $z = 0.3535$. With a one-tailed test $p = 0.36$ and it would clearly be unwise to reject the assumption of randomness. The way in which above- and below-average yields are defined in relation to a moving average might in certain circumstances tend to increase the length of runs. This underscores the strength of the evidence afforded by the test.

48 See above, p. 107.

Table 5A.3 France 1828–1900: wheat price ratios and implied yields in successive years

Price ratio			Implied yields		
Number of cases	Price ratio in year t	Average price ratio in year t+1	Number of cases	Yield in year t	Average yield in year t+1
5	<0.75	0.750	2	<0.85	0.955
9	0.75–0.84	0.870	6	0.85–0.90	0.983
16	0.85–0.94	0.962	14	0.91–0.96	0.971
15	0.95–1.04	1.009	24	0.97–1.02	1.004
12	1.05–1.14	1.145	13	1.03–1.08	1.020
5	1.15–1.24	1.033	9	1.09–1.14	1.087
5	1.25–1.34	1.031	2	≥1.15	1.157
3	≥1.35	1.185			
mean 1.000		s.d. 0.179	mean 1.010		s.d. 0.076

Bouniatian's formula by which the implied yield is derived from price data is given above, p. 107. The price ratios refer to harvest years (August–July). They were derived from 25-year moving averages of prices in the manner described in the notes to table 5A.1.
Source: Labrousse et al., Le prix du froment, pp. 13–14.

The general implication of table 5A.3 is clear. Allowing for the effect of small numbers in obscuring underlying patterns, it is still evident that years of high prices tended to be followed by similar years. Similarly, low prices in one year were often succeeded by further low prices. There was a drift back towards the mean, of course, but the overall association is pronounced. This effect is, of course, transmitted through to implied yields and they therefore display the same pattern.[49] It is worth noting that the implied yields tend to 'bunch' more closely around the mean than the 'true' yields (table 5A.1), though spanning the same range. This is chiefly because the variability of wheat prices declined sharply in France after the mid-century, presumably in large measure because of transport improvements. The standard deviation of physical yields actually rose slightly between 1829–59 (0.119) and 1860–1900 (0.126), but fell relatively sharply for implied yields (from 0.093 to 0.059). In the first half of the period, therefore, the variability of the two series was not greatly dissimilar. As might be expected, given the pattern visible in table 5A.3, price data also produce runs of high and low prices and implied yields which suggest that one year influences the next. In table 5A.4, and in subsequent tables, the runs in implied yields are set out. Using price data would result in a substantially similar pattern but it is convenient to concentrate on the implied yield material because the unequal distribution of prices around the long-term average means that runs of below-average prices are more common than runs of above-average prices (in table 5A.3, for example, there are 30 cases where the price ratio is below 0.95, but only 25 where the ratio is above 1.05).

Table 5A.4   France 1828-1900: the frequency of runs of above- or below-average implied yields (wheat)

Length of run in years	Number of runs	'Expected' number of runs
1	3	10.0
2	5	5.0
3	4	2.5
4	3	1.3
5	1	0.6
6	4	0.3
	20	

Source: Labrousse et al., Le prix du froment, pp. 13-14.

It is immediately obvious from table 5A.4 that one-year runs are more rare than would be expected if the scale of each successive harvest were independent of its predecessor, and that long runs occurred more often than would be expected on this assumption.[50] French nineteenth-century price and yield

49 The correlation coefficient between implied yields at t and $t + 1$ was 0.551, well above a significant level (0.237).
50 A one-sample runs test gives $z = -2.7759$. With a one-tailed test $p = 0.0028$. It is therefore highly improbable that the pattern of the 'runs' occurred because of random effects.

Table 5A.5 England (Exeter prices): implied yields of wheat in successive years

Yield in year t	1328-1519		1520-1659		1660-1789		1328-1789	
	(1)	(2)	(1)	(2)	(1)	(2)	(1)	(2)
<0.85	11	0.912	7	1.020	6	0.928	24	0.948
0.85-0.90	16	0.995	11	1.041	8	0.975	35	1.005
0.91-0.96	34	1.007	14	0.935	25	0.975	75	0.979
0.97-1.02	35	1.003	29	0.997	26	1.010	90	1.003
1.03-1.08	36	1.011	20	1.018	34	1.024	90	1.017
1.09-1.14	24	1.062	16	1.066	13	1.072	53	1.066
≥1.15	22	1.128	14	1.223	11	1.099	47	1.120
mean		1.023	mean	1.022	mean	1.017	mean	1.021
s.d.		0.109	s.d.	0.113	s.d.	0.092	s.d.	0.106

(1) Number of cases.
(2) Average yield in year t + 1.
The data refer to harvest years running October–September. See also notes to table 5A.3.
Source: Mitchell and Deane, British historical statistics, chapter 16, table 9, pp. 484-7.

data, therefore, leave no doubt that patterns may exist in the former which could be taken as suggesting that successive harvests were not independent events, even though there is no matching pattern in the yields themselves.

At this point it is natural to seek to discover whether English wheat price series display the same characteristics as those observable in French nineteenth-century data. Table 5A.5 is based on the Exeter wheat price series.[51] It shows the patterns found in implied yields over a very long period of time, from 1328 to 1789, and in three sub-periods. The first and third of these sub-periods were times of near stability in prices, but in the second sub-period there was a long-sustained rise in wheat prices, which went up more than fivefold during the 140 years in question.

If the overall English pattern is compared with that of nineteenth-century France (table 5A.3), there is a striking parallelism in the readings in the $t + 1$ column in the two cases. Extreme deviations from the average were substantially more common in England than in France, but within each yield category at time t the response in the following year was closely similar. It is easy to appreciate how a single exceptional harvest, producing unusually high or low prices, might produce a run of prices above or below the average.

In the first and last sub-periods, when there was little long-term change in the price level, the patterns in the $t + 1$ year are similar to each other though in the later period there were proportionately far fewer years of extreme prices. In the middle period the pattern is more confused. High implied yields were followed by other 'good' years as at other times, but low yields produced an irregular result. Implied yields only slightly below average appeared to have a more marked effect on succeeding years than 'worse' years. Very possibly the comparatively small number of years involved resulted in a deceptive outcome.[52] And it should be noted that the overall mean implied yield for the period was 1.022. This rather than 1.000 should be thought of as the standard by which to judge the average yield. Means greater than 1.000 are found generally with implied yields because the asymmetry of the price data from which they are derived is slightly over-compensated. Very low prices are found nearer to the mean than very high prices (table 5A.3), but although Bouniatian's conversion formula produces broadly 'correct' results, there is a tendency for the mean implied harvest size to be a little above unity.

The frequency of years of very high or low implied yields (which is, of course, a reflection of price movements) is a matter of interest in its own right. The information set out in table 5A.6 is the same as that used in tables 5A.3 and 5A.5 but the distributions are re-expressed as percentages, and in the lower panel summary statistics are used covering only the two highest

---

51 Mitchell and Deane, *British historical statistics*, chapter 16, table 9.

52 The correlation coefficients between values at t and $t + 1$ were as follows (number of observations are given in brakcets): 1328–1519, 0.430 (178); 1520–1659, 0.330 (112); 1660–1789, 0.499 (124); 1328–1789, 0.413 (414). All are significant: the related 95 per cent confidence intervals which allowed the assumption of randomness to be rejected are respectively: 0.150, 0.189, 0.180 and 0.098.

Table 5A.6 Percentage distribution of implied wheat yields

Yield	England (Exeter prices: harvest year)				France (harvest year)		
	1328-1519	1520-1659	1660-1789	1328-1789	1828-59	1860-1900	1828-1900
<0.85	6.2	6.3	4.9	5.8	6.5	0.0	2.9
0.85-0.90	9.0	9.9	6.5	8.5	9.7	7.9	8.6
0.91-0.96	19.1	12.6	20.3	18.1	22.6	18.4	20.0
0.97-1.02	19.7	26.1	21.1	21.7	25.8	42.1	34.3
1.03-1.08	20.2	18.0	27.6	21.7	9.7	23.7	18.6
1.09-1.14	13.5	14.4	10.6	12.8	19.4	7.9	12.9
≥1.15	12.4	12.6	8.9	11.3	6.5	0.0	2.9
	100	100	100	100	100	100	100
	n=178	n=111	n=123	n=414	n=31	n=38	n=70

Yield	France (calendar year)			
	1738-1827	1828-59	1860-1900	1828-1900
<0.85	2.4	0.0	0.0	0.0
0.85-0.90	8.5	12.9	0.0	5.7
0.91-0.96	20.7	32.3	28.9	30.0
0.97-1.02	24.4	22.6	39.5	31.4
1.03-1.08	25.6	6.5	26.3	17.1
1.09-1.14	15.9	19.4	2.6	11.4
≥1.15	2.4	6.5	2.6	4.3
	n=82	n=31	n=38	n=70

Table 5A.6 (continued)

	England (Exeter prices: harvest year)				France (harvest year)		
Yield	1328-1519	1520-1659	1660-1789	1328-1789	1828-59	1860-1900	1828-1900
<0.91	15.2	16.2	11.4	14.3	16.2	7.9	11.5
≥1.09	25.9	27.0	19.5	24.1	25.9	7.9	15.8

	France (calendar year)			
Yield	1738-1827	1828-59	1860-1900	1828-1900
<0.91	10.9	12.9	0.0	5.7
≥1.09	18.3	25.9	5.2	15.7

See notes to table 5A.3 and table 5A.5.
Sources: France: Labrousse et al., *Le prix du froment*, pp. 113–14. The calendar year data were taken from pp. 9–11. England: Mitchell and Deane, *British historical statistics*, chapter 16, table 9, pp. 484–7.

and two lowest categories to highlight gross changes over time. Table 5A.6 also contains additional French data. The nineteenth-century harvest year material has been split into two shorter periods, and calendar year data have been added covering both the nineteenth-century periods given for harvest year distributions and the preceding century.

In England there was no significant change in the percentage distributions before the last sub-period. The middle period was if anything slightly more given to extreme variations than the early period. Thereafter there was a very substantial reduction in extreme variations. Both the rising yield per acre and improved transport probably contributed to the new pattern after 1660.[53] Before then either these changes had yet to make a material difference, or they were offset by factors acting in the opposite sense; for example, the rapid population growth of the middle period may possibly have caused exceptional pressures on supply.

In France there was a marked contrast between the first and second halves of the nineteenth century. In the earlier period the percentage distribution of price variations was very similar to those in England before 1660, but after 1860 there was a radical reduction in extreme variations, presumably in part a result of railway construction. Rising yields no doubt also played a part. They rose 41 per cent between 1828 and 1900, but the improvement was evenly spread throughout the century.[54]

Calendar year data are available for a much longer period for France. As might be expected, price variations are somewhat less marked for calendar than for harvest years in each period for which the two series are available. It is interesting to note that the calendar year series suggest that eighteenth-century price fluctuations were rather less violent than those in the early nineteenth century, and perhaps not greatly different from those for England at much the same period. The significance of international comparisons is, however, dubious. The English series is for a single market, whereas the French is based on data drawn from all parts of the country.[55] This must tend to reduce the variability of the French series. Moreover, France in any case includes wheat-growing areas with very different climatic regimes whereas such differences are less marked in England, and this also would tend to reduce *national*, though not necessarily *local*, variation in France.

We may turn finally to the pattern of runs in English implied yield data set out in table 5A.7. In general the pattern is similar to that found in nineteenth-century France (table 5A.4). There are always more long, and fewer short, runs than would be expected on the assumption that each successive annual figure was independent of its predecessor. Overall, the picture is both straightforward and clear cut. There are only about half as

53 The effect of rising gross yields in reducing the variance of net yields is discussed above, p. 111–13.

54 The 25-year moving average of wheat yields measured in hectolitres per hectare rose from 11.85 in 1828 to 16.75 in 1900.

55 Labrousse et al., *Le prix du froment*, Introduction, gives details of the sources and methods used in constructing the French national series.

Table 5A.7 England (Exeter prices): the frequency of runs of above- or below-average implied yields

Length of run in years	1328-1519 (1)	1328-1519 (2)	1520-1659 (1)	1520-1659 (2)	1660-1789 (1)	1660-1789 (2)	1328-1789 (1)	1328-1789 (2)
1	26	33.0	5	14.5	8	19.0	39	66.5
2	14	16.5	9	7.3	11	9.5	34	33.3
3	14	8.3	9	3.6	8	4.8	31	16.6
4	6	4.1	2	1.8	4	2.4	12	8.3
5	2	2.1	2	0.9	3	1.2	7	4.2
6	4	1.0	0	0.5	3	0.6	7	2.1
7	0	0.5	2	0.2	1	0.3	3	1.0
	66		29		38		133	

(1) Observed.
(2) 'Expected'.
Source: As table 5A.5.

many one-year runs as expected, but two or three times as many five-year runs or longer. In the sub-periods there is more irregularity, perhaps associated with the relatively small number of cases involved. There is, however, some suggestion that the disparity between actual and expected was less in the first period than in the two subsequent ones. The average length of a 'run' overall was 2.60 years, and in the sub-periods 2.33, 2.83 and 2.89 respectively. The comparable French figure derived from the data in table 5A.4 is 3.30 years, while the figure to be expected if there were no tendency for the length of runs to be affected by anything other than chance is 2.00 years. It is interesting to note that runs above and below the 25-year average implied yields were equally common (66 and 67 respectively) and that they were of almost exactly the same average length (2.58 and 2.63 years respectively).

The data of table 5A.7, like those of tables 5A.2 and 5A.4, can also be examined by using a one-sample runs test to establish how probable it is that the observed patterns arose from random influences. The z scores for the three successive sub-periods and for the entire period 1328–1789 were -1.7142, -2.8744, -3.4483 and -4.4105 respectively. With a one-tailed test the corresponding p values were 0.0436, 0.0021, 0.0003 and $< = 0.00003$. The p values are suggestive in that for the earliest period, 1328–1519, the null hypothesis can only just be rejected at the 5 per cent significance level, but in the two subsequent periods it is increasingly and ultimately extremely improbable that the runs were random. If the reason for the runs were to do with trenching upon seed corn, one might have expected the effect to be most pronounced in medieval times and least in the period after 1660 when yields were much higher and supplies in general comparatively abundant. If, alternatively, the carry-over effect was the chief cause of the phenomenon, the pattern found is that to be expected. As storage capacity and effectiveness increased, and supply more commonly met or exceeded demand, the 'knock-on' effect of one year's good or bad harvest in the subsequent harvest years would become more pronounced. On this assumption, in medieval times each harvest year was, so to speak, largely self-contained, and the price of corn in one year would be comparatively little influenced by anything other than the harvest in that year. In the seventeenth and eighteenth centuries, in contrast, with a larger proportionate buffer of grain in store or accessible through better transport, harvest years were less isolated from one another.

The example of nineteenth-century France shows that runs may occur in wheat price data even though there are no runs in the physical yields per hectare; and comparison of the French data with earlier English data shows that patterns of price behaviour were closely similar. It does not follow, of course, that this similarity was due to the same cause or causes. Nor does it prove that physical yields in England were also free from serial autocorrelation. But it is clear that it is imprudent to assume that, because prices must be strongly affected by supply, they must reflect annual fluctuations in production, and that the existence of price runs necessarily implies parallel runs in yields. The French evidence suggests that fluctuations in the scale of the carry-over from one harvest year to the next is a more plausible mechanism for explaining the generation of price runs than an effect due to the consumption of seed corn. It remains an open question, however, whether the same is true of medieval or early modern England.[56]

Explanations which involve seed corn and those related to carry-over are not mutually exclusive. It is possible that a seed corn effect existed as Hoskins supposed, but the example of France should caution us against accepting his argument *tout court*. Again, the general economic circumstances of the nineteenth century were so different from those of the fourteenth, or even the sixteenth, that to proceed in the manner adopted here begs many questions. My object is simply to re-open an issue of great importance in any pre-industrial society. Much remains to be done, however, before either the general or the particular relationships involved will have been fully teased out.

---

56 It is worth stressing that French wheat yields were still quite low in the nineteenth century. The 25-year moving average in 1828 was only 11.85 hectolitres per hectare, or 13.2 bushels per acre (using the following conversion factors: 1 hectare = 2.471 acres; 1 hectolitre = 2.75 bushels), a figure similar to that found in England 200 years earlier.

Part II
Urban Growth

6

A Simple Model of London's Importance in Changing English Society and Economy, 1650–1750

'Soon London will be all England' (James I)

Towards the end of the seventeenth century London became the largest city in Europe. The population of Paris had reached about 400 000 by the beginning of the seventeenth century and was nearing 500 000 towards its end, but thereafter grew very little for a further century. At the time of the 1801 census its population was still just less than 550 000. London, on the other hand, grew rapidly throughout the seventeenth and eighteenth centuries. Its exact population at any time before the first census is a matter for argument but in round figures it appears to have grown from about 200 000 in 1600 to perhaps 400 000 in 1650, 575 000 by the end of the century, 675 000 in 1750 and 900 000 in 1800.[1] London and Paris were much larger than other cities in Europe during these two centuries and each was very much larger than any rival in the same country. The contrast between the size and rates of growth of the two cities is particularly striking

---

1 There is a very useful compilation of estimates of the size of towns and cities in western Europe chiefly for the period 1500–1800 in Hélin, *La démographie de Liège*, Annexe I, pp. 238–52. Brett-James summarizes the calculations of contemporaries and later scholars in *Stuart London*, especially pp. 496–512. He himself suggests figures of 250 000 in 1603 and 320 000 in 1625 (p. 512). John Graunt estimated the population of the capital to be 460 000 in about 1660: *Natural and political observations*, p. 371. Petty concluded that in 1682 London's population was already 670 000: *The city of London*, p. 460. Gregory King made a calculation of London's population in 1695 from the number of households, arriving at a figure of 527 560: *Two tracts*, p. 18. Creighton's estimates of London's population for 1603, 1625 and 1665 agree very closely with those of Brett-James and Graunt for the same periods: Creighton, *History of epidemics in Britain*, i, p. 660. George accepts figures of 674 500 for 1700 and 676 750 for 1750 based on the number of baptisms in the London parish registers: George, *London life*, pp. 24 and 329–30. See also Jones and Judges, 'London population'. The figures used in this text are rounded for convenience and are probably of the right order of magnitude, but nothing more can be claimed for them.

when it is borne in mind that until the last half of the eighteenth century, when the rate of growth of population in England increased sharply, the total population of France was about four times as large as that of England. In 1650 about 2.5 per cent of the population of France lived in Paris; in 1750 the figure was little changed. London, on the other hand, housed about 7 per cent of England's total population in 1650 and about 11 per cent in 1750. Only in Holland does any one city appear to have contained such a high percentage of the total national population. Amsterdam in 1650 was already a city of about 150 000 people and contained 8 per cent of the Dutch total. But Amsterdam by this time had ceased to grow quickly and a century later had increased only to about 200 000, or 9 per cent of the total.[2]

These rough facts suggest immediately that it may be valuable to look more closely at the rapid growth of London between 1650 and 1750. Anything which distinguished England from other parts of Europe during the century preceding the industrial revolution is necessarily a subject of particular interest since it may help to throw light on the origins of that extraordinary and momentous period of rapid change which has transformed country after country across the face of the globe.

The demography of London's growth

It is convenient to begin by examining first some demographic aspects of the rapid growth of population which took place in London. The implications of London's growth can be seen from a very simple model. The rates and quantities embodied in the model are at best approximations, but it would require a radical revision of the assumptions used here to upset the general argument.

We may note first that since the population of London rose by about 275 000 between 1650 and 1750 it will on average have been increasing annually by 2750. Secondly, it seems clear that the crude death rate in London was substantially higher than the crude birth rate over the period as a whole. The gap between the two rates is difficult to estimate accurately and varied considerably during the hundred years in question, being apparently much higher in the last three or four decades of the period than

2 See Hélin, *La démographie de Liège* p. 242, and Faber et al., 'Population changes and economic developments in the Netherlands', pp. 58 and 110. It should perhaps be said that only in countries like England, France and The Netherlands, if anywhere, does it make sense to relate city and national population totals. In areas like Germany, Italy or Spain, political or economic fragmentation makes this a pointless exercise. The only cities in Europe with populations of 100 000 or more around 1650, apart from London, Paris and Amsterdam, were Naples, which was a very large city (250 000–300 000), and Palermo, Venice, Rome and Lisbon (all 100 000–125 000); none of these grew much in the following century. By the mid-eighteenth century Vienna and Berlin were in this size class (around 175 000 and 110 000 respectively), and perhaps Lyon. See Hélin, *La démographie de Liège*, pp. 244, 247, 249 and 251.

earlier. The difference between them is most unlikely to have been less than 10 per 1000 per annum over the century as a whole, however, and may well have been considerable larger.[3] For the purpose of illustrating the implications of the model we may assume that this figure held throughout. Thus, at the time when the population of London was, say, 500 000 the shortfall of births each year is assumed to be 5000. At that time to make good this shortfall and to permit an annual increase of the total population of 2750, the net immigration into London must have been about 8000 per annum. Towards the end of the period, when the population of London was well above half a million and the gap between birth and death rates was at its greatest, the net figure must have been considerably larger than this. Earlier it may have been rather less.

In any population it is normally the young and single who migrate most readily. There is a growing volume of evidence that in England in the seventeenth and eighteenth centuries mobility before marriage was very high but was reduced once marriage had taken place.[4] In view of this, let us assume, as part of the demographic model of London's growth, that the mean age of those migrating into London was 20 years. Given the mortality conditions of the day, any large group of 20-year-olds coming into London would represent the survivors of a birth population at least half as large again.[5] Some 12 000 births, therefore, in the rest of England and elsewhere

3 The uncertainty arises because of the problem of under-registration. Jones and Judges underlined this heavily in their examination of London's population at the end of the seventeenth century. They were able to show wide discrepancies between totals of baptisms and burials drawn from the three available sources: the returns made under the Marriage Duty Act of 1694, the Bills of Mortality, and the counts made in parish registers at Rickman's behest in 1801. See Jones and Judges, 'London population'. Glass has made estimates of the degree of under-registration of baptisms and burials in the parish registers and the collector's returns under the 1694 Act for two city parishes: see Glass in *London inhabitants within the Walls*, pp. xxxv–xxxvii. There is a convenient summary of some of the available data in George, *London life*, App. I, pp. 405–10. Gregory King made estimates based on a notional time of peace which imply only a rather small burial surplus in the capital (about 4 per 1000); however, elsewhere he produced figures for the year 1695 which suggest a much larger shortfall of baptisms: *Two tracts*, especially pp. 27 and 43. It is worth noting that Deane and Cole suggest a rate of natural increase for London in the period 1701–50 of –10.8 per 1000 per annum and envisage an annual average net immigration into London of 10 000–12 000 (it should be added that they regard London's population as stationary in number during this half century): Deane and Cole, *British economic growth*, table 26, p. 115 and p. 111. William Farr thought the London death rate in the later seventeenth century was 80 per 1000 declining to 50 per 1000 in the eighteenth century: Farr, *Vital statistics*, p. 131. Buer estimated that between 1700 and 1750 London needed an average immigration of 10 200 a year to maintain her population, and that during this period the ratio of deaths to births was 3 : 2: Buer, *Health, wealth and population*, p. 33.

4 This appears very clearly in family reconstitution work based on parish registers. The analysis of successive nominal listings of inhabitants supports the same conclusion. See Laslett and Harrison 'Clayworth and Cogenhoe'.

5 The United Nations specimen life tables suggest that a birth population will fall to two-thirds of its original number by the age of 20 when expectation of life at birth is 40: *Methods for population projections by sex and age*, United Nations, ST/SOA/Series A, Population Studies, no. 25 (New York, 1956). If expectation of life was substantially below this at this period, then a larger birth population would be needed to produce any given number of 20-year-old immigrants into London.

were earmarked, as it were, each year to make it possible for London's population to grow as it did during this period. Once again this is a very rough figure, too high for a part of the century, too low for the later decades, but useful as a means of illustrating the nature of the general demographic relationship between London and the rest of the country. One further assumption will make the significance of this estimate clearer. If the average surplus of births over deaths in provincial England was 5 per 1000 per annum (and assuming for the moment that London grew by immigration from England alone), then it follows that London's growth was absorbing the natural increase of a population of some two-and-a-half millions.[6] The total population of England excluding London was only about five million (varying, of course, a little over the century in question), and there were some areas, especially in the west and north, in which for much of this century there was either no natural increase or even a natural decrease of population.

In view of the general demographic history of England at this time London's characteristics assume a singular importance, for the century 1650–1750 was a period marked by some surprising and distinctive features. Family reconstitution studies show that in some parts of the country at least this was a time of very late first marriage for women. And the reduced fertility which is usually associated with a rise in the average age of women at first marriage appears to have been still further diminished in places by the practice of family limitation. Moreover, there is some evidence that age-specific mortality rates, especially of young children, were higher then than either earlier or later, so that natural increase was much reduced or was replaced by a surplus of deaths over births.[7]

The preliminary results of a large-scale survey of parish register material using straightforward aggregative methods[8] suggest that these trends were least evident in the home counties and the midlands, the areas from which access to London was easiest, and it may prove to be the case that a substantial surplus of births continued to be characteristic of these counties throughout the century 1650–1750 but that instead of building up local populations the surplus was siphoned off into London to counterbalance the burial surplus there and to enable it to continue to grow quickly at a time when the rest of the country was barely holding its own.[9] The absence of any

---

6 A rate of increase of 5 per 1000 is a generous estimate for this period. Gregory King supposed that the annual number of births in England excluding London was 170 000 and of burials 148 000. Assuming the population of England without London to have been 4.9 million, this suggests a difference between the two rates of about 4.5 per 1000. But King uses different assumptions elsewhere and presents material which implies a rate of increase less than half as high. King, *Two tracts*, pp. 25 and 27.

7 On these points see chapter 10 which was based on work done on the parish registers of Colyton in Devon.

8 The survey was carried out by the Cambridge Group for the History of Population and Social Structure. More than 200 local historians were kind enough to help in this work.

9 The London apprenticeship records show that the proportion of apprentices coming from

great upward press of numbers in England as a whole meant that population growth did not frustrate a slow rise in real incomes, in contrast with the preceding hundred years. Yet this did not prevent a very marked growth in the country's largest city.

One further implication of the demography of London's growth is worth stressing. Let us assume that there was a time when the population of London was 500 000 and the population of the rest of the kingdom was 5 000 000. Let it further be assumed that the birth rate was everywhere 34 per 1000. (This is an arbitrary assumption but too little is know of the prevailing fertility characteristics of regional populations to provide substantially more accurate figures; and in any case the main line of the argument would be unaffected except by radical adjustments.) If this were so, then the number of births taking place annually in London would be 17 000 and in the rest of the country 170 000. If we assume that all the children born in London remained in London, and if to the figure of 17 000 children born each year in London is added the 12 000 born in the provinces and needed to maintain London's growth, then it is apparent that the survivors to adult years of almost one-sixth of all the births taking place in the country (29 000 out of a total of 187 000) would be living in London 20 years after the arrival of the birth cohort used as an illustration.

It does not, of course, follow from this that one-sixth of the national total of adults lived in London. The infant and child mortality rates of those born in London were far higher than elsewhere so that many fewer of these children survived to adult years. Indeed, the fact that this was so is one of the main reasons for the large inflow of migrants from outside London. The calculation assumes, moreover, that immigrants to London came only from England, whereas there was also a steady stream of young Scots, Welsh and Irish into the capital. Nor should it be forgotten that London was a great international centre with substantial Dutch, French and German communities.

On the other hand, all the calculations made above are based on figures of *net* immigration into London. The gross figures must certainly have been considerably higher since there was at all times a flow of migrants out of London as well as a heavier flow inward. If therefore one were attempting to estimate the proportion of the total adult population of England who had at some stage in their lives had direct experience of life in the great city, a sixth or an even higher fraction is as plausible a guess as any other.[10]

---

the north and west fell dramatically during the seventeenth century, while the proportion from the home counties rose. One reason for this may well have been the disappearance of a surplus of births in the north and west and its continuance nearer London. See Stone, 'Social mobility in England', pp. 31–2. Marshall noted that the great bulk of the inter-county movement from Bedfordshire was to London: 'The rural population of Bedfordshire', p. 45.

10 See George, *London life*, pp. 109–10 for an interesting discussion of the chief types of migrants into and out of London. She suggests that the settlement laws tended to encourage rather than prevent migration and that London exercised a strong attraction upon those dislodged

Some characteristics of metropolitan life

If it is fair to assume that one adult in six in England in this period had
had direct experience of London life, it is probably also fair to assume that
this must have acted as a powerful solvent of the customs, prejudices and
modes of action of traditional, rural England. The leaven of change would
have a much better chance of transforming the lump than in, say, France
even if living in Paris produced the same change of attitude and action as
living in London since there were proportionately four or five times fewer
Frenchmen caught up in Parisian life than Englishmen in London life.
Possibly there is a threshold level in a situation of this type, beneath which
the values and attitudes of a traditional, rural society are very little affected
by the existence of a large city, but above which a sufficiently large proportion
of the population is exposed to a different way of life to effect a slow
transformation in rural society. Too little is known of the sociological
differences between life in London and life in provincial England to afford
a clear perception of the impact of London's growth upon the country as
a whole. Some things, however, are already known, and other points can
be adumbrated in the hope that more research will resolve present
uncertainties.

London was so very much bigger than any other town in the country that
the lives of the inhabitants of London were inevitably very different from
the lives of men living in the middle rank of towns, such as Leicester or
Derby, where local landed society could continue to dominate many aspects
of town life and the ties with the surrounding countryside were ancient and
intimate. Family life in London, at least for the very large number who had
come to London from elsewhere, was necessarily different from the family
life of those who lived within five or ten miles of their birthplace all their
lives. Near relatives were less likely to live close at hand. Households in
the central parts of London were larger on average than those in provincial
England. And this was not because the conjugal families contained more
children but because other members of the households were more numerous.
There were many more lodgers than in the countryside, as well as servants,
apprentices and other kin in varying proportions according to the social type
of the parish.[11]

---

from their original settlement. She also quotes a contemporary, Burrington, writing in 1757,
who thought that two-thirds of London's adult population came 'from distant parts'. The records
of the Westminster General Dispensary between 1774 and 1781 reveal that only a quarter (824
out of 3236) of the married people served were London born. Of the rest, 209 were born in
Scotland, 280 in Ireland and 53 abroad, a total of 542 in the three categories or 17 per cent.
The balance was born elsewhere in England or Wales (George, *London life*, p. 111).

11 The characteristic English provincial situation has become clear from work carried out
by the Cambridge Group for the History of Population and Social Structure on listings of
inhabitants of English parishes. This work includes the analysis of London returns compiled in

Outside the household, a far higher proportion of day-to-day contacts was inevitably casual. Urban sociologists describe the characteristic tendency of modern city life to cause individuals in these circumstances to be treated not as occupying an invariable status position in the community, but in terms of the role associated with the particular transaction that gave rise to the fleeting contact. They stress the encouragement which city life gives to what Weber called 'rational' as opposed to 'traditional' patterns of action and the tendency for contract to replace custom. The '"aping" of one's betters', which often attracted unfavourable comment at the time, and which has sometimes been seen as a powerful influence in establishing new patterns of consumption, is a common product of social situations like that in which the inhabitants of London found themselves at this period. Coleman has recently suggested that in the seventeenth century there was probably a backward-sloping supply curve for labour.[12] It would be fascinating to know how far the new patterns of consumption behaviour established in London may have helped to reduce any preference for leisure rather than high earnings. There is much literary evidence of the shiftless and disorderly behaviour of many members of London's population at this time, but there were important countervailing influences at work upon the bulk of the population. The shop, a most important new influence upon consumer behaviour, was a normal feature of the London scene by the latter half of the seventeenth century.[13] Sugar, tea and tobacco had become articles of mass consumption by the early eighteenth century. Life in London probably encouraged a certain educational achievement in a wider spectrum of the population than might be expected. In 1838–9 fewer men and women were unable to sign their names on marriage than anywhere else in the country (marks were made as a substitute for signatures by only 12 per cent of grooms and 24 per cent of brides, whereas the national averages were 33 per cent and 49 per cent respectively). This differential was of long standing and suggests that the London environment put a high premium on at least a minimum degree of literacy.[14]

There were many ways in which seventeenth-century London differed from a modern city. Glass, for example, noted that in 1695 the proportion of wealthy and substantial households was highest near the centre of London and tended to fall with distance from the centre, being very low outside the city walls (apart from St Dunstan in the West). 'This kind of gradient is in contrast to that found in the modern city, in which the centrifugal movement of population has occurred particularly among the middle

---

1695 under the Marriage Duty Act. Glass's analysis of some of these London parish listings, though only a first survey of the material, provides much valuable information about the city: Glass, *London inhabitants within the Walls*.

12 Coleman, 'Labour in the English economy'.

13 See John, 'Aspects of English economic growth', p. 185.

14 Registrar General, *First Annual Report of Births, Deaths and Marriages* (London, 1839), pp. 8–9. See also Schofield, 'Dimensions of illiteracy', and Cressy, *Literacy and social order*, table 4.1, p. 73, and pp. 142–51.

classes'[15] In this respect, London was still in 1695 a pre-industrial city, but in general London was far removed from the classic type of this urban form. Sjoberg's account of the typical pre-industrial city may serve as a means of underlining the 'modernity' of London at this period. He draws illustrative material not only from the cities of Asia today, from ancient Mesopotamia and the Near East, and from the classical cultures of the Mediterranean, but also from medieval Europe.

Sjoberg's pre-industrial city is fed because the city houses the ruling elite. The elite 'induces the peasantry to increase its production and relinquish some of its harvest to the urban community'. It 'must persuade many persons subsisting, relative to industrial standards, on the very margins of existence, under conditions of near starvation or malnutrition, to surrender food and other items that they themselves could readily use'.[16] The farmer 'brings his produce to the urban centers at irregular intervals and in varying amounts'.[17] Within the city the merchants, those responsible for the organization of much of its economic life, are 'ideally excluded from membership of the elite'. A few manage to achieve high status under sufferance, but 'most are unequivocally in the lower class or outcaste groups'.[18] The chief reason for excluding merchants is that they necessarily meet all types of people, making casual contacts with men in all positions, and are therefore a menace to the stability of the existing societal arrangements.[19] Men are largely indifferent to the discipline of the clock and only half attentive to the passage of time. Almost all transactions, however trivial, are concluded only after long haggling.[20] There is little specialization of function in craft industrial production, though a good deal of product specialization.[21]

In the pre-industrial city the dominant type of family is the extended family, though necessity may prevent it developing so fully in the lower classes as in the elite.[22] Marriage takes place early, and before marriage a man does not reach full adult status.[23] On marriage the bride normally expects to move into the household of her husband's family.[24] 'However, as industrial-urbanization becomes firmly entrenched, the large extended household is no longer the ideal toward which people strive. The conjugal family system now becomes the accepted, and often the preferred norm.' This occurs because 'a fluid, flexible, small family unit is necessarily the dominant form in a social order characterized by extensive social and spatial mobility'.[25]

15 Glass, *London inhabitants within the Walls*, p. xxi.
16 Sjoberg, *The pre-industrial city*, p. 118.
17 Ibid., p. 207.
18 Ibid., pp. 120, 121.
19 Ibid., p. 136.
20 Ibid., pp. 204–5, 209–10.
21 Ibid., p. 197.
22 Ibid., pp. 157–9.
23 Ibid., pp. 145–6.
24 Ibid., p. 157.
25 Ibid., p. 162.

In his anxiety to correct naive assumptions about cities in the past and in the developing world today, Sjoberg may well have been tempted to strait-jacket his material at times in a way which does violence to history. At all events not only London but all England had moved far from his achetypal pre-industrial society by the seventeenth century. The conjugal family system was firmly established in England at that time. On marriage a man and his wife set up a new household.[26] And both sexes married late, later than in England today, and far later than in extra-European societies in which marriage, for women at least, almost invariably occurred at or even before puberty.[27] Where three generations did live together in the same household this was not usually because a son on marriage brought his wife to his parents' home, but because a grandparent came to live in the household of a married son or daughter when no longer able to look after himself or herself, for example on the death of a spouse.

London shared these sociological and demographic characteristics with the rest of the country. Three-generational households were possibly rather commoner in the wealthier parts of London than was usual elsewhere,[28] but everywhere the conjugal family appears to have been the dominant form. The status of merchants in London varied with their wealth but it would be difficult to argue that they were largely excluded from the ruling elite. The provisioning of London was secured by an elaborate and sophisticated set of economic institutions and activities, and many of the farmers who sent their produce to the London market geared their land to commodity production in a thoroughly 'modern' fashion.[29] In short, whereas pre-industrial cities in general might grow large without in any way undermining the structure of traditional society, a city like London in the later seventeenth century was so constituted sociologically, demographically and economically that it could well reinforce and accelerate incipient change.

What might be called the demonstration effect of London's wealth and growth, for instance, played an important part in engendering changes elsewhere. London contained many men of great wealth and power whose sources of income did not lie in the land and who found it possible to maintain power and status without acquiring large landed estates.[30] Indeed, inasmuch as it was the backing of London which assured the parliamentary armies of success in their struggle with the king, London could be said at the

26 See Laslett, *The world we have lost*, pp. 90–2.

27 See Hajnal, 'European marriage patterns', and, more generally, Goode, *World revolution and family patterns*.

28 See Glass, *London inhabitants within the Walls*, pp. xxxii–xxxiv.

29 See below, pp. 142–5.

30 Stone in discussing the wealth generated by the great commercial expansion of the late seventeenth century remarks: 'The closing down of the land market suggests that, however it was distributed, less of this wealth than before was being converted into social status by the purchase of an estate, and more of it was being reinvested in long-term mortgages, commerce and banking.' One reason for less money being invested in land was perhaps simply that rich Londoners no longer felt moved to use money in this way if their status did not suffer by refraining from acquiring land. See Stone, 'Social mobility in England', p. 34.

beginning of the century 1650–1750 to have shown that it possessed the power necessary to sway the rest of the country to its will. In the provinces in the later seventeenth and early eighteenth centuries there were increasingly large numbers of men of wealth and position who stood outside the traditional landed system. These were the group whom Everitt has termed the 'pseudo-gentry'. They formed 'that class of leisured and predominantly urban families who, by their manner of life, were commonly regarded as gentry, though they were not supported by a landed estate'.[31] Their links with London were close and their journeys thither frequent. They were urban in their habit of life but would have been powerless to protect their position in society if London had not existed. London both provided them with a pattern of behaviour and, because of its immense economic strength and prestige, protected them from any hostility on the part of the traditional elements in society. London was, as it were, both their normative reference group[32] and their guarantee against the withdrawal of status respect.

London as an engine of economic change

The social and economic changes of the seventeenth and eighteenth centuries reached their culmination in the industrial revolution. Although this was far more than simply an economic phenomenon, economic change was what defined it. It is natural, therefore, to consider the strictly economic effects of London's rapid growth as well as the demographic and sociological changes which accompanied it.

The importance of the London food market in promoting change in the agriculture of Kent and East Anglia from an early date has long been recognized. Fisher showed how even during the century before 1650 London was large enough to exercise a great influence upon the agriculture of the surrounding counties, causing a rapid spread of market gardening, increasing local specialization and encouraging the wholesalers to move back up the chain of production and exchange to engage directly in the production of food, or to sink capital in the improvement of productive facilities. The influence of the London food market was 'not merely in the direction of increased production but also in that of specialization, and in that direction lay agricultural progress'. 'Poulterers made loans to warreners and themselves bred poultry. Fruiterers helped to establish orchards and leased them when established. Butchers themselves became graziers.' Between 1650 and 1750 it is reasonable to suppose that the demand for food in the London market must have increased by about three-quarters since population increased roughly in that proportion. The increased demand was met from home sources rather than by import, and it follows that all those changes

---

31 Everitt, 'Social mobility in early modern England', p. 71.

32 To use the term employed by Runciman in a very lucid exposition of the concept of the reference group generally. Runciman, *Relative deprivation*, chapter 2.

which Fisher observed in the preceding century were spread over a larger area and intensified.[33]

Once more it is interesting to work initially in terms of a very crude model and review its implications, though in this case the orders of magnitude assumed are even more open to question than those embodied in the demographic model used earlier. Suppose, first, that in 1650 the population of London was 400 000 and the population of the rest of the country 5 100 000 and that in the country outside the metropolis the proportion of the male labour force engaged in agriculture was 60 per cent.[34] This would imply that 3 060 000 were dependent on agriculture (those directly employed plus their families), and that every 100 farming families supported a total of 80 families who earned their living in other ways. If in the next century the population of London rose to 675 000 and that of the whole country to 6 140 000,[35] but the proportion engaged in agriculture outside the capital remained the same, then the agricultural population in 1750 would have numbered 3 279 000 and every 100 farming families would have supported 87 other families.[36] This in turn would imply a rise in agricultural productivity per head of about 4 per cent. This figure is certainly too low, however, since this was a century of rising exports of grain, especially after 1700. By 1750 exports formed about 6 per cent of total grain production; at the beginning of the century they were only a little over 1 per cent.[37] Grain was not, of course, the only product of agriculture, but there were parallel movements in some other agricultural products. Imports of wool, for example, fell markedly in the early eighteenth century, while domestic

33 Fisher, 'The development of the London food market', pp. 56 and 63. The steady spread of the influence of London is well illustrated by the remark of a contemporary, John Houghton, who wrote apropos of meat production for the London market, 'The bigness and great consumption of London doth not only encourage the breeders of provisions and higglers thirty miles off but even to four score miles. Wherefore I think it will necessarily follow . . . that if London should consume as much again country for eighty miles around would have greater employment or else those that are further off would have some of it.' Houghton, *The improvement of husbandry*, pp. 165–6. I owe this reference to the kindness of Dr J. Thirsk.

34 This is once more rather an arbitrary figure. Different assumptions about its size produce slightly higher or lower estimates of increase in agricultural production per head. A higher percentage engaged in agriculture will result in a lower figure of increased productivity and vice versa. The Tawneys' analysis of the Gloucestershire Muster Roll of 1608 suggests that a rather lower figure might have been appropriate. Tawney and Tawney 'An occupational census', especially p. 39. Gregory King's work does not lend itself to a breakdown along these lines but is consistent with a figure of 60 per cent or slightly higher. This is true also of the analyses of listings of inhabitants carried out by P. Laslett in Cambridge. Some of the listings give details of occupations. Stone's assumption, based partly on King, that 90 per cent of the population (presumptively in the mid-seventeenth century) were manual workers on the land is very difficult to accept. Even at the peak of the harvest period when men normally engaged in other pursuits might work on the land this would be an extraordinarily high figure. See Stone, 'Social mobility in England', p. 20.

35 Brownlee's estimate, supported by Deane and Cole, *British economic growth*, pp. 5–6.

36 This assumes that farming and non-farming families were of the same average size, but could be rephrased without damaging the sense of the passage if this assumption is denied.

37 Deane and Cole, *British economic growth*, table 17, p. 65.

production rose. There was a sharp rise in the production of mutton, though not of beef, and some minor agricultural products, notably hops, were grown in greater quantities.[38] All in all, it is reasonable to suppose that these changes represent a rise of not less than 5 per cent in agricultural productivity per head. This, in combination with the rise which must have occurred in meeting London's demands, suggests an overall rise of about 10 per cent in output per head in agriculture.

A rise of 10 per cent in productivity is far from trivial. It could have released a substantial amount of purchasing power into other channels as the price of foodstuffs fell and at the same time have made it possible for a substantially higher proportion of the population to be drawn into secondary and tertiary employment. The rise, however, is almost certainly understated at 10 per cent, since the percentage of the total labour force outside the capital engaged in agriculture probably fell somewhat, implying a still steeper rise in agricultural productivity per head. It has been suggested, indeed, that the numbers engaged in agriculture actually fell in the first half of the eighteenth century.[39] This is an extreme hypothesis. Suppose, however, that the population dependent on agriculture rose only from 3 060 000 to 3 150 000 between 1650 and 1750, and not to 3 279 000 as in the first variant of the model (that is, the proportion engaged in agriculture fell over the century from 60 to 57.5 per cent of the total population outside London). If this were the case, and making the suggested allowance also for growing exports and declining imports, then the rise in agricultural productivity per head would be about 13 per cent during the century. This is not an extreme figure. Indeed, it is very probably too low. Deane and Cole suggest that the rise may have been as high as 25 per cent in the first half of the eighteenth century alone.[40] But a rise in agricultural productivity even of this magnitude is a formidable achievement and goes far to suggesting how a pre-industrial economy can slowly pull itself up by its own bootstraps to the point where a rapid growth of secondary industry can occur. The fact that income elasticity of demand for food is substantially less than unity makes it easy to understand how grain prices might sag in these circumstances and how considerable the diversion of purchasing power into the products of secondary industry may have been.

It does not follow from the above, of course, that the considerable rise in agricultural productivity per head which appears to have taken place was due to London's growth in its entirety. What can be said is that the steady growth in demand for food in London as population there increased, necessarily caused great changes in the methods used on farms over a wider and wider area, in the commercial organization of the food market and in

---

38 For wool, see Deane and Cole, *British economic growth*, p. 68; and Mitchell and Deane, *British historical statistics*, pp. 190–1. For mutton and beef, Deane and Cole, *British economic growth*, pp. 68–71. For hops, Ashton, *An economic history of England*, p. 240.

39 Deane and Cole, *British economic growth*, p. 75.

40 Ibid.

the transport of food. It must also have tended to increase the proportion of people living outside London who were not engaged directly in agriculture since tertiary employment was sure to increase in these circumstances. Drovers, carters, badgers, brokers, cattle dealers, corn chandlers, hostlers, innkeepers and the like grew more and more numerous as larger and larger fractions of the year's flocks and crops were consumed at a distance from the areas in which they were produced. As yet it is difficult to quantify the changes in employment structure satisfactorily, but a number of parish registers began regularly to record occupations from the later seventeenth or early eighteenth century onwards,[41] and it would therefore be a fairly straightforward matter to produce for these parishes a picture of changing employment structure for this period, given sufficient time and effort. Such an exercise might well reveal not only a slow fall in the proportion of men directly employed on the land, but also differences in the timing and speed of change related to the accessibility of the market.

There were other ways in which the immense demands of the London market helped to promote economic and technological changes in the structure of English production during this period. The inhabitants of London needed fuel as well as food, and before the end of the sixteenth century they were beginning to abandon wood for coal as the chief source of domestic fuel. The annual shipment of coal south along the coast from Tyneside and Wearside had reached about 650 000 tons by 1750, having doubled in the preceding hundred years.[42] This represented a very substantial fraction of the total production of coal in the north-east, and perhaps as much as a sixth of the total national production. Coal production in England was on a much larger scale during these years than in any other country in Europe, and the coal industry was the forcing house for many of the technical improvements that were to come to a fuller fruition during the classical years of the industrial revolution. Newcomen's engine was developed largely to meet the drainage problem in coal mines and found its largest sale among mine owners. And it was in the Newcastle area that the first railways were constructed to enable horses to pull much heavier loads from the pitheads to the coal staithes. The beginnings of the new technology of the steam engine and the railway lay in the eighteenth-century coal-mining industry, and one of its chief supports in turn was the large and steadily growing demand for coal afforded by the London coal market.[43]

Furthermore, the increased shipment of coal down the east coast to the Thames required a major expansion in shipping capacity. Nef estimated that during this period about half the total tonnage of the English merchant marine was engaged in the Newcastle coal trade.

---

41 In the case of marriages the occupation of the groom was given; in baptism and burial entries the occupation of the head of the household in which the birth or death had occurred. Frequently, occupations were noted in only one or two of the series rather than in all three.
42 Nef, *The British coal industry*, ii, pp. 381–2.
43 These changes are discussed from a different viewpoint and at greater length in chapter 4.

When we add, to the ships employed by the coal trade from Durham and Northumberland, the ships employed by that from Scottish and west-coast ports, it seems likely that, at the time of the Restoration, the tonnage of colliers had come to exceed the tonnage of all other British merchantmen. The coal trade from Newcastle to London was relatively no less important in the late seventeenth century than in the late eighteenth century, when Adam Smith observes, it 'Employs more shipping than all the carrying trades of England'.[44]

Apart from serving as an important reservoir of trained seamen in time of war, the growth of the coal trade played a notable part in the expansion of the English shipbuilding industry and the development of vessels which could be worked by far fewer hands per ton of cargo.[45]

The crude quantification of the importance of the London coal trade can be approached in a different way. If output per man-year of coal miners at this time was about 200 tons in favourable circumstances,[46] then by 1750 some 3500 men must have been engaged in digging London's coal. Gregory King supposed that about 50 000 men were employed in his day as common seamen[47] and it is therefore probable that at least a further 10 000 men[48] were employed on the colliers easing their way up and down the east coast (though the ships were laid up in the winter so that the employment was heavily seasonal). In addition, the movement of coal to the staithes must have been the livelihood of hundreds of carters, waggoners and coal heavers.[49] In all, the total employment afforded by the London coal trade outside London (except inasmuch as the sailors were Londoners) may well have risen from about 8000 in the mid-seventeenth century to 15 000 a century later. Including their families increases the numbers directly dependent on the coal trade to about 25 000 and 50 000 people respectively. The multiplier effect of the presence and growth of London is well illustrated by this example. Secondary and tertiary employment increased considerably at a distance as well as in London itself.[50] No doubt the flourishing state

44 Nef, *The British coal industry*, i, pp. 239–40.

45 It is interesting to remember John's comment on the growth of the export trade in corn at this time: 'Grain became a major bulk cargo and between 1730 and 1763 about 110 000–130 000 tons were, on an average, carried annually from English ports in ships which only occasionally exceeded a hundred tons burthen. This had its effect upon the more efficient use of shipping, upon investment in shipbuilding and upon the employment of dockside labour.' Coal shipments along the coast at this time were running at about five times the level of corn shipments by tonnage. John, 'Aspects of English economic growth', p. 180.

46 Nef, *The British coal industry*, ii, p. 138.

47 King, *Two tracts*, p. 31.

48 The problem of moving coal in bulk by sea brought about a substantial saving in men employed per ton of cargo moved during the seventeenth century. For this reason it is likely that fewer men were employed on colliers than might be expected in view of their large share in the tonnage of the English merchant marine. See Nef, *The British coal industry*, i, pp. 390–2.

49 Ibid, ii, p. 142.

50 This is true of a wide range of manufacturing and service industries. Fisher, for example,

of the mines around Newcastle and the consequent local demand for food produced in miniature in that area the sort of changes in agriculture which London had already produced in the home counties at an earlier date.

London's importance as a centre of consumption, which prompted Defoe in 1724 to write of the 'general dependence of the whole country upon the city of London . . . for the consumption of its produce',[51] sprang not only from its size but also from the relatively high level of wages prevailing there. Gilboy's work on eighteenth-century wage rates provides evidence of this. 'The London laborer had the highest wages of any group we have examined. In the first part of the century, at least, he had surplus income to spend and there is every indication that real wages improved as the century progressed.'[52] When George remarked that 'as early as 1751 it was said that the shoes sold in London were chiefly made in the country where labour was cheaper',[53] she was touching upon a general phenomenon. Men and women were put in work over much of the home counties and midlands because their labour was much cheaper than the labour of London artisans and journeymen. The existence of a mass of relatively well-paid labour in London played a major part in creating new levels of real wages and new standards of consumption in the century after the Restoration, when 'there was a rise in internal demand which permanently affected the level of expectation of most classes in English society'.[54]

Access to the London market was the making of many a manufacturer and a forcing house of change in methods of manufacture, in marketing techniques and in systems of distribution. Josiah Wedgwood was drawn thither, being 'quick to realize the value of a warehouse in London. For high quality goods he needed a market accustomed to "fine prices". He was not likely to find it in the annual market fairs of Staffordshire – the time-honoured *entrepôt* of their county's pots – nor among the country folk who haggled over their wares straight from the crateman's back or the hawker's basket, and to whom expense was the controlling factor in deciding their custom.'[55] But this did not isolate him from mass markets. Once having secured the custom of the London elite he was able also to sell his less expensive lines to the middle and lower classes. He studied closely the idiosyncracies of each group at home and abroad and produced goods designed to appeal peculiarly to each of them. 'By these means Wedgwood had created an enormous demand for his ware both ornamental and useful. The upper classes bought both, but mainly the expensive ornamental wares,

---

noted that London had no malting facilities and few corn mills: 'Consequently, a number of country towns found their major employment in the processing of the city's corn, and their inhabitants a regular occupation as middlemen': Fisher, 'The development of the London food market', p. 60.
51 Ibid., p. 51.
52 Gilboy, *Wages in eighteenth-century England*, p. 241. See also chapters 1 and 2.
53 George, *London life*, p. 198.
54 John, 'Aspects of English economic growth', p. 190.
55 McKendrick, 'Josiah Wedgwood', pp. 418–19.

and in imitation of their social superiors the lower classes bought the useful.'[56] Moreover, his efforts to command a countrywide market drew him into canal construction and the promotion of turnpike trusts.[57]

Wedgwood was one of the most original and successful entrepreneurs of his age. The actions of his fellows seldom show the same appreciation of the opportunities for new methods. And his product may have lent itself more than most to illustrating the sense in which a triumph in London opened up the markets of the whole country. Yet it is reasonable to quote his example, for his success hinged upon an economic and social fact of importance before Wedgwood's time: through the London market the whole country might be won. 'For a fashionable appeal in London had a vital influence even in the depths of the provinces. The woman in Newcastle upon Tyne who insisted on a dinner service of "Arabesque Border" before her local shopkeeper had even heard of it, wanted it because it was "much used in London at present", and she steadfastly "declin'd taking any till she had seen that pattern".'[58]

The London market, of course, supported many industries within the city itself. Silk weaving at Spitalfields, brewing, gin manufacture, watch and clock making, cabinet making, the manufacture of soap, glass and furniture, and a wide range of luxury industries have all received notice. They added to the economic weight of London, and furthered its growth, though few of them produced striking technological advances or were transformed into pioneering industries during the industrial revolution. They were impressive in their range but were not for the most part greatly different in kind from the industries to be found in large cities elsewhere in Europe.

London's prime economic foundation, however, had long been her trade rather than her industry. English trade expanded greatly during the century and London enjoyed the lion's share of it. It has been estimated that a quarter of the population depended directly on employment in port trades in 1700 and, allowing for the multiplier effect of this employment, 'it is clear that the greatness of London depended, before everything else, on the activity in the port of London'.[59] London's merchants, not her manufacturers, dominated her activities economically and politically, and it has long been a momentous question how best to conceive the mechanism by which the large fortunes made in London from commerce helped to transform the national economy.

Many London merchants bought land in the country. Some in doing so hastened agricultural change. The banking and general commercial facilities of London were available to men throughout England and played some part in financing the agricultural and industrial changes which occurred in many

---

56 Ibid., p. 429.
57 Ibid.
58 Ibid., p. 420.
59 Davis, *The English shipping industry*, p. 390. See also pp. 34–5 on the rapid growth of English commerce and London's predominance among English ports.

parts of the country. The success of the London merchants fostered a change of attitude towards trade. It helped to fulfil one of the necessary conditions of rapid economic growth in Leibenstein's analysis, that 'the rate of growth of the new entrepreneurial class must be sufficiently rapid and its success, power and importance sufficiently evident so that entrepreneurship, in some form or other, becomes an "honorific" mode of life in men's minds'.[60] But it is doubtful whether the prime connection between the growth of London and the great changes going forward outside London is to be sought in points of this type. London's trading pre-eminence is perhaps better conceived as acting more powerfully at one remove. It was the fact that the growth of her trading wealth enabled London herself to grow, to develop as a centre of consumption, and to dominate English society, that formed her greatest contribution to the total process of change in the country as a whole. The relationship between rising trading wealth and economic and social change outside London was primarily, as it were, indirect, springing from the changes which the steady growth of London provoked elsewhere in ways already discussed. While other large European cities during this century could do little more than maintain their population size, London almost doubled her population. Already as large as any other European city in 1650, it was much larger than any rival a century later. In order to meet the food and fuel requirements of a city of this size old methods in many cases were simply inadequate. And the new methods developed often produced those substantial increases in productivity per head which form the most promising base for a continuing beneficent spiral of economic activity.

A model of change

It is always well to be chary of accepting explanations that explain too much. The industrial revolution in England was a vastly complex congeries of changes so diverse that it would be absurd to suppose that any one development of earlier times can serve to explain more than a part of it. It will not do to pyramid everything upon changes in the supply of capital, or the burgeoning of nonconformist entrepreneurship, or an increase in upward social mobility. Complicated results had, in this case at least, complicated origins. It is therefore no part of this argument that the growth of London in the century before 1750 was the sole engine of change in the country. But London's growth is a fine vantage point from which to review much that was happening. The period between the rapid rise in population and economic activity which ended early in the seventeenth century and the onset of renewed rapid growth of population and production in the last third of the eighteenth century has remained something of an enigma in economic history. It was a period in which population grew little if at all over the country as a whole. In some areas for long periods it was probably

60 Leibenstein, *Economic backwardness and economic growth*, p. 129.

falling. Many of the chief indices of production, when estimates of them are possible, show comparatively little change and certainly grew much less spectacularly than in the succeeding period.[61] There was a slow, if cumulatively important, improvement in agricultural productivity because of the introduction of new crops like roots and clover, and because there was both a slow drift of land into enclosure and increasing flexibility of land use in the champion areas. Trade and industry expanded but in general at a modest rate.

How then should this period be understood? It was immediately followed by a period which saw the birth of a radically new economic system, the transition from the pre-industrial to the industrial world. Was England in 1750 greatly improved when compared with the England of the Commonwealth as a springboard for rapid economic and social change? Was the triggering off of the period of rapid growth connected, as it were, in great depth with the preceding period, or could it have occurred almost equally readily at a considerably earlier period? It is against a background of questions of this type that the growth of London appears so strategically important.

There were a number of developments tending to promote economic change and growth in the hundred years from 1650 to 1750. Apart from the growth of London, for example, there were the agricultural advances which improved animal husbandry and lay behind the secular tendency of grain prices to fall (thus helping real wages to rise where money wages were unchanged or improved). Or again there is the probability that because of stable numbers and a modest increase in production the national product/population ratio rose significantly. The idea of critical mass has been invoked recently as a concept of value in conveying the nature of the importance of cumulative slow change in the period immediately preceding rapid industrialization.[62] It could be used appropriately of any of these progressive changes, but is particularly telling when related to London's growth. It is not so much that London's growth was independently more important than the other major changes which modified English economy and society during the century, as that it is a most convenient point of entry into the study of the whole range of changes that took place, especially since some aspects of London's growth can be quantified fairly satisfactorily. Both the changes in agriculture that took place and the failure of national population to increase are closely intertwined with the growth of London, but not with each other. Demographically, the existence of London counterbalanced any 'natural' growth of population in much of the rest of the country, and the necessity of feeding London created market conditions

61 For the period after 1700 there is a good summary of available quantitative evidence in Deane and Cole, *British economic growth*, pp. 50–82.

62 See Landes, 'La révolution industrielle en Angleterre'. This concept is discussed also in an article by Crouzet which clearly owes much to the idea, 'Croissances comparées de l'Angleterre et de la France', especially pp. 290–1.

over great tracts of England which fostered agricultural improvement and reduced economic regionalism. The absence or slightness of population growth overall, had it not been for London's expansion, might well have inhibited agricultural change.

It is possible to write out a check-list of changes which by their occurrence in a traditional and predominantly agricultural society tend to promote social and economic change and may succeed in engendering the magic 'take-off'. On any such list the following items are likely to appear (the list is far from being exhaustive).

Economic changes

(1) The creation of a single national market (or at least very much larger regional markets) for a wide range of goods and services, so that specialization of function may be developed and economies of scale exploited.

(2) The fostering of changes in agricultural methods which increase the productivity of those engaged in agriculture so that the cost of foodstuffs will fall and real wages rise; so that a rising proportion of the workforce can find employment in secondary and tertiary activities without prejudicing the supply of food or raising its price inordinately; and possibly so that a larger export income can be derived from the sale of surplus food supplies abroad.

(3) The development of new sources of raw material supply which are not subject to the problem of rising marginal costs of production in the manner characteristic of raw materials in pre-industrial economies.[63] This occurs when mineral raw materials are substituted for animal or vegetable products (for example, coal for wood) and may well be accompanied by important technological changes contrived to overcome novel production problems (for example, the Newcomen engine or the coke-fired blast furnace).

(4) The provision of a wider range of commercial and credit facilities so that the latent strengths of the economy can be more expertly, quickly and cheaply mobilized. Under this head might fall, for example, the cluster of changes accompanying and reflected in the establishment and development of the Bank of England.

(5) The creation of a better transport network to reduce the cost of moving goods from place to place; to make it possible for goods to move freely at all seasons of the year in spite of inclement weather; to shorten the time involved and so to economize on the capital locked up in goods in transit; and more generally to foster all the changes of the type mentioned in (1) above.

(6) The securing of a steady rise in real incomes so that the volume of effective demand rises *in toto* and its composition changes with the diversion of an increased fraction of the total purchasing power into the market for the products of industry. This is closely connected with (2) above.

---

63 For a fuller discussion of the point see chapter 4.

Demographic changes

(7) The interplay between fertility, mortality and nuptiality must be such that the population does not expand too rapidly and this must hold true for some time after real incomes per head have begun to trend upwards. If this is not so, the cycle of events which is often termed Malthusian can hardly be avoided; there is a great danger that real incomes will be depressed and economic growth will peter out. This happened often enough before the industrial revolution. Leibenstein remarks with justice that 'historical evidence would seem to suggest . . . [that] it was the rate of population growth, whether or not induced by economic expansion, that ate up the fruits of expansion and resulted in expansion in the aggregate sense without much improvement per head'.[64] Too rapid population growth can, of course, be avoided by the existence of areas of surplus mortality which counterbalance those of surplus fertility as well as by the existence of a rough balance of births and deaths in each area throughout the country.

Sociological changes

(8) The steady spread of environments in which the socialization process produces individuals 'rationally' rather than 'traditionally' orientated in their values and patterns of action.

(9) The establishment of conditions in which upward social mobility need not necessarily lead to what might be called the recirculation of ability within traditional society but can also produce a steady strengthening of new groups who do not subscribe to the same priorities or use their wealth and status in the same ways as the upper levels of traditional society.

(10) The spread of the practice of 'aping one's betters'. When consumption habits become more fluid and the new styles and wants of the upper ranks are rapidly suffused throughout the lower ranks of society, men experience a stronger spur to improve their incomes, and the first steps are taken towards the era of uniform, mass consumption. To be aware that a change in one's pattern of life is possible and to consider it desirable is a vital first step to the securing of the change itself. No doubt this awareness is never wholly absent, but it may be present in widely varying intensities and its increase is an important stimulant to economic change.[65]

64 Leibenstein, 'Population growth and the take-off hypothesis', p. 173.
65 George quotes Defoe's description of the 'topping workmen' to be found in England, 'who only by their handy labour as journeymen can earn from fifteen to fifty shillings per week wages as thousands of artisans in England can . . . 'Tis plain the dearness of wages forms our people into more classes than other nations can show. These men live better in England than the masters and employers in foreign countries can, and you have a class of your topping workmen in England, who, being only journeymen under manufacturers, are yet very substantial fellows, maintain their families very well . . .': George, *London life* p. 157.

This check-list is, of course, also a catalogue of the ways in which the growth of London may have promoted social and economic change in England in the period between the dying away of the economic upthrust of Elizabethan and early Stuart times and the sharp acceleration at the end of the eighteenth century. It may also be represented diagrammatically in a form which enables the interconnection between some of the items on the list to be appreciated more concisely (figure 6.1).

Many of the changes are connected with the growth of London in two directions, at once produced or emphasized by London's growth and serving in turn to reinforce the growth process, a typical positive feedback situation, to borrow a term from communication engineering. In some cases growth was possible only because of this mutual relationship. For example, the growth of London could not have gone very far if it had not produced substantial change in agriculture over large areas and brought about sufficient improvements in the transport system to make it feasible to maintain a reliable and moderately cheap movement of food surpluses from the home counties and East Anglia into London. In other cases there is no return connection between London and one of the aspects of social and economic change promoted by its growth. For example, the continued growth of London had much to do with the slightness of population growth over the country as a whole, but it would be difficult to argue that the reverse was also true. And in still other cases, even though no arrow is shown on figure 6.1 it is obvious that some degree of connection must have existed. A link may be presumed for instance, between higher real wages (6) and improved transport (5), or between new consumption patterns (10) and agricultural change (2). Only those connections which appear more direct and more important have been shown, though of course a connection between any two boxes can be shown by moving round the network: for example, there is no direct link shown between improved transport (5) and higher real incomes (6), but an indirect link exists via agricultural change (2) and by other more circuitous routes.

Sometimes, where a connection is shown only in one direction, the absence of a return arrow may seem arbitrary: for example in the case of new forms of social mobility (9) and 'rational' not 'traditional' behaviour (8). In several of these cases there was certainly some return effect, and with equal propriety but on different assumptions a return arrow might have been drawn. The act of judgement involved here demands careful scrutiny because the relationships which are expressed by a single arrow are of particular interest. Where there are arrows in both directions this implies an interconnection so intimate that in some ways it will prove pointless to distinguish between them. They are jointly parts of a larger situation which it is convenient to record separately for clarity's sake and for some analytic purposes. Where an arrow in only one direction exists, however, a clearer distinction, a lack of interdependence and in some cases a causal sequence is implied. For example, figure 6.1 suggests that the growth of London stimulated the development of 'rational' modes of behaviour (8), but that this in turn did

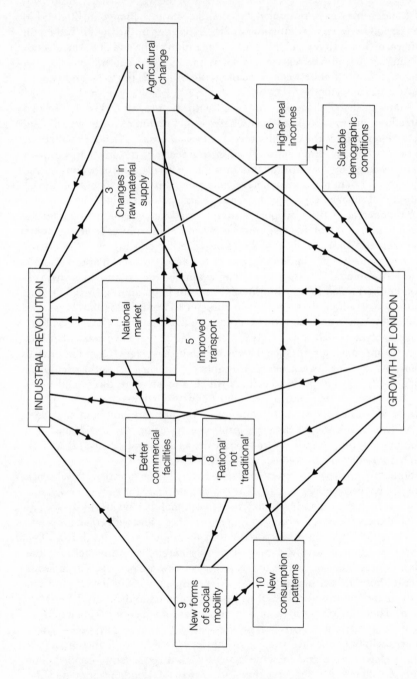

Figure 6.1 The links between London's growth and the industrial revolution in England.

The diagram shows boxes connected by lines with arrows:

- 2 Agricultural change
- 3 Changes in raw material supply
- 6 Higher real incomes
- 7 Suitable demographic conditions
- INDUSTRIAL REVOLUTION
- 1 National market
- 5 Improved transport
- 4 Better commercial facilities
- 8 'Rational' not 'traditional'
- GROWTH OF LONDON
- 9 New forms of social mobility
- 10 New consumption patterns

not have any important direct return effect on London's growth (though very soon an indirect path is opened up via (4), better commercial facilities). This is a different type of relationship from that between London and improved land and water communication (5) which is represented as facilitating the growth of London directly. The latter is shown as a chicken and egg situation, as it were; the former is not. In the one case the positive feedback is direct; in the other this is not so.

A special interest attaches to boxes (6) higher real incomes, (2) agricultural change and (8) 'rational' rather than 'traditional' behaviour. They are key nodes in the system, connected to more boxes than others, and tied into the system by single as well as double arrows. If the relationships are correctly stated, it is these aspects of the total social and economic situation which should prove most repaying to future analyses (and possibly also (5) improved transport). Unhappily the system embodies far too many subjective judgements to justify any but conditional statements about it in its present form.

Figure 6.1 underlines the poverty of our knowledge of many things that it is important to know. Sometimes the absence of an arrow betrays simple ignorance as much as an act of judgement. For example, it is impossible to feel sure as yet about the nature of the relationship between the demographic situation in the period 1650–1750 and economic and social change. Some points seem clear. It is reasonable to suppose that the relationship indicated in the figure between demographic conditions and higher real incomes is accurate. But other points are far from clear. It is very uncertain whether the reverse relationship holds good; that is to say, whether higher real incomes tended to retard population growth, and in what ways this effect, if it existed (and it would certainly be premature to rule out this possibility), was produced.

This model is, like all models, intended as an aid to further thought. It is not more than this. It may be noted, incidentally, that some lines leading to the industrial revolution box, and more particularly those leading back from the industrial revolution box, should be viewed in a different light from other connections. The industrial revolution did not get fully into its stride until after the period discussed in this essay. Arrows pointing to it, therefore, show circumstances tending to promote its occurrence. Those in the opposite direction on the other hand, cannot have existed before the event itself, if its place in time is strictly defined. In a more general sense, however, they simply underline the positive feedback elements in the situation which grew stronger as time passed but were present from an early date. In contrast with this, the period of economic growth in the sixteenth and early seventeenth centuries produced relationships between major variables which might be termed typically those of negative feedback. The very growth of industry and population, by increasing the demand for food and industrial raw materials in circumstances where they were increasing marginal costs of production, and by oversupplying the labour market, drove up food prices, forced real wages down, and increased the difficulties of industrial production, thus throttling back the growth process.

The comparative neglect of London as a potent engine working towards change in England in the century 1650–1750[66] is the more paradoxical in that the dominance of Paris within France has long been a familiar notion in political history. Yet London was larger than Paris, was growing much faster and contained a far higher fraction of the national population. All leavens do not, of course, work equally effectively in their lumps; and political dominance connotes different issues from economic and social change, but the irony remains.[67] A just appreciation of London's importance must await a fuller knowledge of many points which are still obscure. Meanwhile, this short sketch of a possible model of London's relationship with the rest of the country will have served its purpose if it helps to promote further interest in the complexities of the changes to which no doubt it does only the roughest of justice.

66 See Laslett, 'The numerical study of English society', pp.11–12 for a brief discussion of much the same point.

67 It is symptomatic of the neglect of this topic that a work as perceptive and authoritative as Deane and Cole's analysis of British economic growth from the late seventeenth century onwards passes over the growth of London almost completely. Where London is mentioned at all it is incidental to some other main line of argument.

7
Urban Growth and Agricultural Change: England and the Continent in the Early Modern Period

The complexity and contingency of any relationship between economic growth and urban growth should need no stressing.[1] It is clearly hazardous to undervalue, still more to ignore, the difficulties attending any examination of this topic. In what follows in the early part of this essay I may seem to sail close to the wind in this respect, preferring to sketch out an initial thesis rather starkly at the risk of over-simplifying 'reality'. Later, the complexity of historical experience will ensure that the discussion must be broadened and that the limitations of simple formulations will become evident.

Ceteris paribus a rising level of real income and a rising proportion of urban dwellers are likely to be linked phenomena in a pre-industrial economy. If income elasticity of demand for food is less than unity, then with rising real incomes demand for secondary and tertiary products will grow more rapidly than that for primary products and will therefore cause employment in secondary and tertiary industries to rise more rapidly than in agriculture. Such employment is likely to be disproportionately in towns, especially in the case of tertiary employment, and will result in an increase in the proportion of the total population living in towns. There may be an important 'feedback' element in this relationship since the growth of towns may help to further agricultural investment and specialization and so carry forward the rising trend in real incomes.[2] Declining real incomes will, of course, tend to have an opposite effect.

In an economy which meets its own food needs, urban growth may not only be a symptom of rising real incomes: it may also be a rough measure of the level of productivity per worker in the agricultural sector of the

---

1 The point is well illustrated in the collection of essays edited by Abrams and Wrigley, *Towns and societies*, especially in Abrams's essay in the volume.

2 Adam Smith stressed the mutual stimulus that urban growth and agricultural improvement might afford each other. Smith, *Wealth of nations*, book iii, chapter 4, 'How the commerce of the towns contributed to the improvement of the country'.

economy. If productivity per head in agriculture is sufficiently low the surplus of food available after meeting the needs of the agricultural population may be enough to sustain only a tiny urban sector. At the other extreme, if agricultural productivity is high the economy may be able to support, say, a third or a half of the population in towns without prejudicing nutritional levels elsewhere. In a closed economy, therefore, a substantial rise in the proportion of the population living in towns, is strong presumptive evidence of a significant improvement in production per head in agriculture, and may provide an indication of the scale of the change. Sufficient is now known to justify an initial application of this line of thought to early modern England.

The pace of urban growth in England

Table 7.1 sets out some estimates of the size of the populations of leading English towns in about 1520, 1600, 1670, 1700, 1750 and 1800: while table 7.2 provides estimates of the total population of England at each of these dates and of the population of London and of other urban centres with 5000 or more inhabitants.

As the notes to the tables make clear, all the estimates given are subject to a substantial measure of uncertainty. Their sources are various and, apart from those taken from the 1851 census, most have been obtained by inflating and adjusting the raw data because the latter cover only a proportion of the total population. Some figures were originally suspiciously 'rounded' and may incorporate alterations made in the light of subjective assessments of their deficiences. Moreover, it is entirely arbitrary to draw a dividing line between the urban and the non-urban at a population of 5000. This was done on the supposition that only a tiny fraction of the inhabitants of towns larger than 5000 in population would have been principally engaged in agriculture, but a plausible case might be made for a significantly lower dividing line.

To add still further to the crudity of the exercise, it is questionable whether the same dividing line should be used over a long period of time during which the population increased greatly. For example, a moderate-sized market town with a population of, say, 3000 at the start of the period serving a hinterland in which the population doubled, would itself grow in size and at some point exceed 5000 in population even though the functions it discharged did not alter. If this pattern were widely repeated, it would result in an upward drift in the overall 'urban' percentage, but this would have occurred only because the total population had risen, and it would not imply any structural change in the economy. Nevertheless, certain features of change over time are so prominent that they would remain clear cut, or might even be more pronounced, with better data.

During the sixteenth century urban growth viewed relative to national population trends was largely confined to London where the population quadrupled and the city's share of the national total rose from 2.25 to 5 per cent. The percentage of the population living in other towns, on the other hand, rose only modestly from 3 to 3.25 per cent. Even this was largely because ten towns crept over the 5000 mark (Plymouth, King's Lynn, Gloucester, Chester, Hull, Great Yarmouth, Ipswich, Cambridge, Worcester, and Oxford). Most large provincial centres were growing *less* quickly than the national population as a whole. This appears to have been true of Norwich, Bristol, Exeter, Canterbury, Coventry, Colchester and Salisbury. Indeed, of the initial list of towns above 5000 in population, excluding London, only Newcastle increased its share of the national total, and its surge in growth was no doubt partly due to London's extraordinary rise, since the coal trade down the east coast flourished as London grew and brought prosperity to Newcastle in its train.[3]

The effect of the artificial boost given to urban growth outside London by the inclusion of several new towns which had reached 5000 in population between 1520 and 1600 can be estimated, either by ignoring the new entrants on the 1600 list, or by basing the calculation on the full 1600 list. The group of nine provincial towns on the 1520 list displayed a collective growth of only about 15 per cent, sluggish growth during a period when the national total population rose by about 70 per cent. If, alternatively, the list of 19 large provincial towns in 1600 is made the basis of measurement, a rather higher percentage growth figure results. In 1520 they appear to have housed a total population of about 107 000.[4] By 1600 the total had risen to about 137 000, a rise of 28 per cent. Both calculations underline the point that the doubling of population living in provincial towns shown in table 7.2 is misleading since it was preponderantly due to the recruitment of new towns into the category, and not to growth within the individual towns.

If London's growth is ignored, the urban growth pattern elsewhere conforms to expectation quite well. In the course of the sixteenth century real incomes in England appear to have fallen quite substantially. If the Phelps Brown and Hopkins (PBH) index of real wages is used as a guide to the extent of the fall in living standards, it suggests a decline between 1520 and 1600 of over 40 per cent.[5] Even if the PBH index overstates the change, a significant deterioration is none the less probable and ought, in conformity with the model sketched earlier, to have acted as a brake on urban growth and to have tended to reduce urban population in percentage

3 The modesty of urban growth outside London may be overstated by concentrating on places with 5000 or more inhabitants. There is evidence to suggest that the smaller towns were growing more rapidly than the provincial centres. Using a total of 2000 rather than 5000 inhabitants to divide urban populations from the remainder would probably have resulted in an impression of greater buoyancy in urban population in the sixteenth century. Phythian-Adams, 'Urban decay in late medieval England', table 1, pp. 171–2.

4 Using the sources listed in the sources note to table 7.1.

5 The construction of a slightly modified version of the PBH index is described in Wrigley and Schofield, *Population history of England*, appendix 9. The 25-year centred moving average of the annual figures given in table A9.2 fell by 44 per cent between 1520 and 1600.

Table 7.1 Urban populations (thousands)

c. 1520	c. 1600	c. 1670	c. 1700	c. 1750	1801
London 55	London 200	London 475	London 575	London 675	London 959
Norwich 12	Norwich 15	Norwich 20	Norwich 30	Bristol 50	Manchester 89[a]
Bristol 10	York 12	Bristol 20	Bristol 21	Norwich 36	Liverpool 83
York 8	Bristol 12	York 12	Newcastle 16	Newcastle 29	Birmingham 74
Salisbury 8	Newcastle 10	Newcastle 12	Exeter 14	Birmingham 24	Bristol 60
Exeter 8	Exeter 9	Colchester 9	York 12	Liverpool 22	Leeds 53
Colchester 7	Plymouth 8	Exeter 9	Gt Yarmouth 10	Manchester 18	Sheffield 46
Coventry 7	Salisbury 6	Chester 8	Birmingham	Leeds 16	Plymouth 43[b]
Newcastle 5	King's Lynn 6	Ipswich 8	Chester	Exeter 16	Newcastle 42[c]
Canterbury 5	Gloucester 6	Gt Yarmouth 8	Colchester	Plymouth 15	Norwich 36
	Chester 6	Plymouth 8	Ipswich } 8–9	Chester 13	Portsmouth 33
	Coventry 6	Worcester 8	Manchester	Coventry 13	Bath 33
	Hull 6	Coventry 7	Plymouth	Nottingham 12	Hull 30
	Gt Yarmouth 5	King's Lynn 7	Worcester	Sheffield 12	Nottingham 29
	Ipswich 5	Manchester 6	Bury St Edmunds	York 11	Sunderland 26
	Cambridge 5	Canterbury 6	Cambridge	Chatham 10	Stoke 23[d]
	Worcester 5	Leeds 6	Canterbury	Gt Yarmouth 10	Chatham 23[e]
	Canterbury 5	Birmingham 6	Chatham	Portsmouth 10	Wolverhampton 21[f]
	Oxford 5	Cambridge 6	Coventry	Sunderland 10	Bolton 17
	Colchester 5	Hull 6	Gloucester	Worcester 10	Exeter 17
		Salisbury 6	Hull		Leicester 17
		Bury St Edmunds 5	King's Lynn		Gt Yarmouth 17
		Leicester 5	Leeds } 5–7		Stockport 17
		Oxford 5	Leicester		York 16
		Shrewsbury 5	Liverpool		Coventry 16
		Gloucester 5	Nottingham		Chester 16
			Oxford		Shrewsbury 15
			Portsmouth		
			Salisbury		
			Shrewsbury		
			Sunderland		
			Tiverton		

Notes to table 7.1

a Including Salford.
b Including Devonport.
c Including Gateshead.
d Stoke and Burslem.
e The Medway towns: Chatham, Rochester and Gillingham.
f Wolverhampton, Willenhall, Bilston and Wednesfield.

Sources: The following sources were used in compiling the table.
(1) Corfield, 'Urban development in England and Wales'.
(2) Corfield, *The impact of English towns*.
(3) Emery, 'England circa 1600'.
(4) Pythian-Adams, *Desolation of a city*.
(5) Patten, *English towns*.
(6) Patten, 'Population distribution in Norfolk and Suffolk'.
(7) *1851 Census*, Population tables I, Numbers of inhabitants 1801–51, vols i and ii, *Parliamentary Papers*, 1852–3, lxxxv and lxxxvi.
(8) Law, 'Urban population of England and Wales'.
(9) Finlay, *Population and metropolis*.
(10) *1801 Census*, Enumeration, Parliamentary Papers 1802, vii.

The data were abstracted as follows with the numbers given in brackets relating to the sources listed above. London 1520, 1600: (1), p. 217. London 1670: (9), table 3.4, p. 60. London 1700, 1750: (2); table 1, p. 8. Other towns 1520: (4), table 3, p. 12 and (1). p. 222. Other towns 1600: (3), pp. 294–8 and (5), figure 3, p. 115. Other towns 1670: (5). table 8, p. 106; table 9, pp. 109–10; pp. 114, 116, 120 and (1), pp. 239, 241. Other towns 1700: (1), p. 223. Other towns 1750: (8), pp. 22–6. All towns 1801: (7).

It should be noted that some of the estimates may refer to dates a dozen or more years away from the date at the head of the column, except in 1750 and 1801. Often different scholars suggest different totals, or the same scholar may present more than one estimate for the same place and period. An element of judgement and selection is therefore unavoidable in compiling a table of this type. In one instance a quoted estimate seemed improbable and has been changed (source (5), table 9, p. 109 gives a figure of 9000 for Cambridge in the 1670s which seems implausibly high in view of the estimates for 1600 and 1700), and in one or two cases (for example, Plymouth, 1670) I could find no figure for a year close to the 'target' year and the total was therefore estimated.

Table 7.2 National, London and other urban population estimates (thousands)

	c. 1520	c. 1600	c. 1670	c. 1700	c. 1750	1801
England	2400	4110	4980	5060	5770	8660
London	55	200	475	575	675	960
Other urban population in towns with 5000 or more inhabitants	70	135	205	275	540	1420
Total urban	125	335	680	850	1215	2380
Urban populations as a percentage of the national total						
London	2.25	5.0	9.5	11.5	11.5	11.0
Other urban	3.0	3.25	4.0	5.5	9.5	16.5
Total urban	5.25	8.25	13.5	17.0	21.0	27.5

The population totals and percentages have been rounded to emphasize the approximate nature of the calculations. National population totals refer to England excluding Monmouth and those for c. 1600, c. 1670, c. 1700 and c. 1750 relate to the years 1601, 1671, 1701 and 1751. All the estimates of urban populations given in this table are subject to substantial margins of error. This is true even for those for 1801 derived from the 1801 census. For example, Law's careful examination of the 1801 material in the general context of nineteenth-century censuses led him to suggest a total urban population in England and Wales of 3 009 260 (in towns of 2500 inhabitants or more) compared with Corfield's estimate of 2 725 171, using the same definition of urban. The former figure is 10 per cent larger than the latter. All earlier totals are subject to far wider margins of error. Law, 'The growth of urban population', especially table 11, p. 141. Corfield, *The impact of English towns*, table 1, p. 8.

Sources: English population totals 1600 to 1801: Wrigley and Schofield, *Population history of England*, table 7.8, pp. 208–9. The figure for 1520 is an estimate based on the discussion in ibid., pp. 565–8. London totals: see sources in table 7.1. Other urban totals: 1520, 1600, 1670, see sources in table 7.1; 1700, 1750 and 1801, Corfield, *The impact of English towns*, table 1, p. 8. The totals have been rounded and in the case of the 1801 total slightly reduced to reflect the fact that Corfield's estimates refer to England and Wales (by this date three Welsh towns exceeded 5000 in population).

terms.[6] London remains as an exception so important as to outweigh in aggregate faltering urban growth elsewhere, but its overall dominance should not be allowed to obscure the significance of trends in the provinces.

In the seventeenth century circumstances changed greatly. The national population grew by less than a quarter over the century as a whole, and was falling gently during its third quarter. The PBH index suggests that real wages bottomed out early in the century and had risen substantially by its end.[7] Urban growth went on apace whether judged in absolute or percentage terms. London continued to dominate the picture. By 1700 the capital housed perhaps 11 per cent of the total national population, more than double the percentage of a century earlier. It had become the largest city in western Europe and continued to dwarf all local rivals. But other towns also began to grow vigorously. They grew rather slowly in the first half of the century, but after 1670 their relative growth was at least as rapid as that of London. And the smaller urban centres were now increasing far faster than the country as a whole. Their population more than doubled during the century, a rate of growth more than four times that of the national aggregate. Measurement of urban growth is less bedevilled in the seventeenth century than its predecessor by the problem of 'drift' across the arbitrary 5000 dividing line between urban and rural. In the sixteenth century, as we have seen, the increase of population in towns of 5000 or more people was about 95 per cent judged crudely, but the increase in the towns represented on the 1600 list was only 28 per cent, while the increase in the towns on the 1520 list was only some 15 per cent. The comparable figures for the seventeenth century were more closely bunched at about 105, 60 and 46 per cent respectively.[8] Several major provincial centres, notably Norwich, Bristol, Newcastle and Exeter, increased by between 50 and 100 per cent. A striking portent for the future was the appearance on the list for the first time of towns never previously of much note but later to herald a new age. In 1670 Birmingham, Manchester and Leeds appear for the first time, and in 1700 Liverpool.

If the seventeenth century saw a notable acceleration of growth within an urban system still consisting largely of long-familiar names, the eighteenth brought a radical re-ordering of the urban hierarchy and further rapid urban growth. London, moreover, though still vastly larger than any other city,

6 For a recent survey of this and cognate issues see Palliser, 'Tawney's century', especially pp. 349–51. Palliser suggests reasons to suspect that the PBH index overstates the extent of the fall in real incomes.

7 The 25-year centred moving average suggests a rise of 27 per cent between 1600 and 1700. Both the extent of the rise and the timing of the end of the long fall in Tudor and early Stuart times are debatable. Bowden's index of the purchasing power of agricultural wages in southern England suggests that the beginning of a recovery may have been as late as the 1640s. From a stable plateau in the 1520s and 1530s (the index figure is 80 in both decades where 1460–9 = 100), his index falls by 35–40 per cent by the 1590s and shows no subsequent decisive trend until the series ends in 1640–9. Bowden, 'Statistical appendix', table xvi, p. 865.

8 In order to calculate the middle figure (60 per cent) some town populations had to be estimated (i.e. for some of the towns appearing on the 1700 list but not the 1600 list in table 7.1).

no longer stood out for its rate of growth. In 1801 it comprised much the same proportion of the national population as a hundred years earlier. Meanwhile, the share of other towns larger than 5000 in population increased sensationally, rising from 6 to 17 per cent of the national total, and for the first time surpassing London's share.

Growth was widely but very unevenly spread. London's old rivals fared less well than London in the main. Bristol grew rapidly, riding on the back of buoyant Atlantic trade, but several cities which had once figured prominently in the English urban hierarchy grew less quiçkly than the population overall and ended the century with smaller fractions of the national total than at the beginning, including Norwich, Exeter and York. For many centuries such towns had exchanged places in the premier urban league but the league's membership had not greatly altered. By 1801, however, only Bristol, Newcastle and Norwich of the old major regional centres remained amongst the country's ten largest towns. Manchester, Liverpool and Birmingham stood second, third and fourth after London. They ranged between 70 000 and 90 000 in population, having grown fifty-fold or more since the early sixteenth century. Lower down the list a host of new names appeared. Several were the seats of new industry – Leeds, Sheffield, Stoke, Wolverhampton, Bolton and Stockport – but others reflected changing social customs and new forms of expenditure. Bath, for example, was the twelfth largest town in England with 33 000 inhabitants, a gracious monument to the new ways in which the wealthy and well born found it convenient to make or maintain contacts with each other or to pass their hours of leisure. Ports and dockyard towns also enjoyed vigorous growth. Plymouth and Portsmouth were among the country's largest towns, and Hull, Sunderland, Chatham and Great Yarmouth all exceeded 15 000 in population at the time of the 1801 census (though in this ports category not all the towns were new names).

The simplest model connecting real income and urban growth will no longer 'save the phenomena' for the eighteenth century. The sustained momentum of urban growth, accelerating towards the century's end, would suggest a parallel rise in real incomes, but in some parts of England the long-sustained rise in real wages had ceased before the middle of the eighteenth century and it had probably halted nationally by 1780, to be succeeded by a declining trend lasting perhaps 30 years.[9] By the eighteenth century, of course, the assumption of a closed economy is even more unrealistic than for the sixteenth. External demand represented a substantial fraction of total demand in many industries, though it is easy to exaggerate the importance of overseas markets.[10] Any increase in the relative importance of overseas trade, however, would stimulate urban growth,

9 The behaviour of wages and prices, and *a fortiori* of real wages, both regionally and nationally in the period 1700–1850 has been the subject of much controversy. There have been several valuable surveys of the issues, and also some new empirical work. Flinn, 'Trends in real wages'; Von Tunzelmann, 'Trends in real wages', Lindert and Williamson, 'English workers' living standards'.

10 See, for example, Thomas and McCloskey, 'Overseas trade and empire'.

conspicuously in the case of ports like Bristol and Liverpool, but in a lesser degree also elsewhere. Equally, transport improvements within England increased the scale of internal trade. The average distance travelled by goods between producer and consumer probably also increased. Both trends must have stimulated employment in the urban foci through which goods passed.[11] The fortunes of different types of cities suggest that the deceleration in urban growth which might have been expected on the simplest possible view of the link between real incomes and urban growth affected the older centres in the expected fashion, but that the new features of the English economy imparted impetus to those towns most caught up in the new developments. London, affected by all the various and conflicting influences on urban growth, occupied an intermediate position.

The extent of the contrast between the fortunes of different types of towns in the course of the early modern period is illustrated in table 7.3. The choice of towns in each group is inevitably arbitrary, both in the sense that other sets might have been made up to represent the type in question, and in the sense that large towns are unlikely to conform to 'pure' types since size and complexity of function are closely linked. For example, the balance of market functions, craft industry, administrative services and professional employment varied considerably among the set of ten historic regional centres, and two of them, Chester and Exeter, also had important port functions. Nevertheless, the contrast between the groups is sufficiently marked to make it unlikely that other choices made with the same distinctions in mind would produce a very different result.

The historic regional centres did not keep pace with national population growth over the early modern period as a whole. In the two middle periods, when real wages were rising, they experienced a faster population growth than the national average; on the other hand, in the sixteenth and later eighteenth centuries, when real wages were probably declining, their rate of growth fell well below the national average. Thus, they exhibited what might be termed the 'classic' pattern of relative growth in terms of the model of the relationship between income and urban growth described earlier.

At the other extreme, the four towns which in 1801 were the largest manufacturing towns in England were always growing faster than any other group in the table, apart from London down to 1700. Their rate of growth accelerated steadily throughout the three centuries, becoming so hectic in the last half-century that their population almost quadrupled in 50 years.

The established ports also grew with increasing speed except in the last period, outstripping the national growth rate except in the first and last periods. The slight fall in growth rate in this group in the later eighteenth century was no doubt due in part to the extraordinarily rapid growth of Liverpool. If Liverpool were included in the group the percentage growth of population in the group would rise to 72 in 1700–50 and 82 in 1750–1801.

---

11 An excellent summary of knowledge about these topics may be found in Chartres, *Internal trade in England*, especially chapters 2 and 3.

Table 7.3 Urban growth in early modern England (thousands)

	Population total					Percentage growth			
	c. 1520	c. 1600	c. 1700	c. 1750	1801	1600/1520	1700/1600	1750/1700	1801/1750
England	2400	4110	5060	5770	8660	71	23	14	50
London	55	200	575	675	960	264	188	17	42
Ten historic regional centres[a]	62	73	107	126	153	18	47	18	21
Eight established ports[b]	38	53	81	128	190	39	53	58	48
Four 'new' manufacturing towns[c]	6	11	27	70	262	83	145	159	274

[a]Norwich, York, Salisbury, Chester, Worcester, Exeter, Cambridge, Coventry, Shrewsbury, Gloucester.
[b]Bristol, Hull, Colchester, Newcastle, Ipswich, Great Yarmouth, King's Lynn, Southampton.
[c]Birmingham, Manchester, Leeds, Sheffield.
Sources: See source notes to table 7.1.

London contrasts sharply with each of the other three groups, growing far more quickly than other groups until the end of the seventeenth century, even though it became so large that in 1700 London housed more than two-and-a-half times as many people as the other three groups combined. Thereafter, however, London was outpaced by both the ports and the 'new' manufacturing towns, and did not even quite match the national average growth rate.

The foregoing is both compressed and simplistic. Uncertainties of definition, estimation and periodization have been dealt with summarily or ignored. Nor has the nature as opposed to the quantity of urban growth been explored. It is possible, for example, that much of the growth of sixteenth-century London was a 'push' phenomenon linked to the scale and depth of rural poverty, and due to what Clark termed 'subsistence' migration; whereas later, in contrast, movement to the capital may have had a greater 'pull' element as living standards rose and 'betterment' migration came to predominate.[12]

It remains reasonable to argue, however, that there were important links between some types of urban growth and real income trends in early modern England, though equally clear that urban growth is not to be explained solely in this way. Neither the headlong growth of London in the sixteenth and early seventeenth centuries, not the acceleration of urban growth in the 'new' manufacturing towns in the later eighteenth century is explicable in terms of the behaviour of domestic real income per head, yet both were developments of massive importance.

Urban growth and agriculture

Even if the causes of urban growth are elusive, the fact of growth remains, and some of its implications can be examined. In any pre-industrial community agriculture is the dominant form of economic activity and the levels of productivity per head set in agriculture necessarily govern the growth opportunities of other industries. This was a point so well known to those living in pre-industrial economies as scarcely to warrant remark, and when political economy reached its first great statement in the *Wealth of nations* Adam Smith made the examination of this issue one of the chief concerns of the work.[13] But agricultural productivity has proved very difficult to

---

12 Clark, 'The migrant in Kentish towns'.

13 Smith's chapter, 'Of the different employment of capitals' includes a strong plea for agricultural investment as the ultimate basis of national productive capacity. 'The capital employed in agriculture, therefore, not only puts into motion a greater quantity of productive labour than any equal capital employed in manufactures, but in proportion, too, to the quantity of productive labour which it employs it adds a much greater value to the annual produce of the land and labour of the country, to the real wealth and revenue of its inhabitants. Of all the ways in which a capital can be employed, it is by far the most advantageous to the society.' Smith, *Wealth of nations*, i, p. 385.

measure directly. One way of measuring it indirectly is to consider the extent of the rise in agricultural productivity suggested by the course of urban growth in England, taking into account also changes in the occupational structure of the rural component of the population.

To simplify the calculation, I assume that consumption of food per head did not vary between 1520 and 1800 and that England was neither a net importer or a net exporter of food. The first assumption is doubtful and the second is demonstrably false, especially during the eighteenth century. In its early decades England was a substantial net exporter of grain, and towards the end of the century substantial quantities of meat and grain reached the English market from Ireland.[14] It is, however, convenient to begin with such assumptions.

In 1520 the urban percentage was 5.25: in 1801, 27.5 (table 7.2). This in itself suggests a useful gain in agricultural productivity. In 1520, 100 rural families fed 106 families in all; in 1801, 138 [$100 \times 100/(100 - 5.25) = 106$; $100 \times 100/(100 - 27.5) = 138$]. The level of productivity in 1801 is 30 per cent higher than in 1520, far from a negligible increase, if scarcely sensational. But any such exercise must understate the extent of the increase in agricultural productivity if there is also a decline in the proportion of the rural labour force engaged in agriculture.

There can be no reasonable doubt that such a decline occurred. In certain rural areas in the eighteenth century, indeed, the growth in non-agricultural employment was so great as to dwarf the remaining agricultural population. Framework knitting became the dominant source of employment in many Leicestershire villages. In parts of Warwickshire and Staffordshire there was very rapid growth in the manufacture of small metal wares: nails, chains, buckets etc. In much of Lancashire and the West Riding of Yorkshire the textile industry, whether cotton or wool, provided income for many more men and women than did agriculture. The steady growth of coal production in Northumberland and Durham produced the same result in substantial tracts of these counties. Even in more strongly agricultural counties in the south, lace-making, straw-plaiting and the like provided much employment for women.

Moreover, in areas which attracted little industry there was often a substantial growth in employment in service industries. In the rare cases where parish registers provide data on occupation over long periods of time

14 Brinley Thomas has recently estimated the relationship between the value of imports of grain, meat and butter and the income of British agriculture. In 1814–16 total imports of the three commodities represented 6.4 per cent of British agricultural income, and of these imports 70 per cent came from Ireland. See Thomas, 'Escaping from constraints', table 2, p. 743. Jones recently estimated that 90 per cent of the population of Great Britain were fed from domestic agricultural production in 1800. Jones, 'Agriculture, 1700–1780', p. 68. In contrast, in the first half of the eighteenth century English net grain exports were a substantial fraction of total production, reaching perhaps 6 per cent of gross domestic grain output about the mid-century. Deane and Cole, *British economic growth*, table 17, p. 65; also Ormrod, 'Dutch commercial and industrial decline'.

it is a commonplace to note a growth in specialist employments not previously encountered, especially during the eighteenth century. A small town like Colyton in Devon, for instance, even provided a living for a peruke-maker in the 1760s. Almost everywhere the proportion of men described as labourers, husbandmen, yeomen or farmers tended to decline as a proportion of all the occupations mentioned. It is true that many craftsmen also owned scraps of land and its produce was of crucial significance in their domestic economy. Even those who worked no land might nevertheless be drawn into the labour of harvest. However, the reverse was also often true. Those to whom an agricultural occupation was attributed might turn their hands to craftwork during the seasonal slacks on the farm. Ideally, it would be preferable to measure hours worked in different forms of employment rather than to treat each member of the workforce as uniquely engaged in a single occupation, but it is enough for the present purpose to show that there was a major fall in the proportion of the rural labour force in agricultural occupations.

By 1801 a tolerably accurate picture of rural employment structure can be drawn. Deane and Cole estimated that 35.9 per cent of the labour force in 1801 were engaged in agriculture, forestry and fishing.[15] If we assume, for simplicity's sake, that none of this occupational grouping lived in towns, then it follows that only some 50 per cent of the rural population were engaged in agriculture given that the rural population comprised 72.5 per cent of the whole ($35.9/72.5 \times 100 = 49.5$). The comparable figure at earlier periods is unfortunately difficult to establish, though useful clues may be found in the work of King and Massie. In order to make revised estimates of the changes in agricultural productivity, I have assumed that 80 per cent of the rural labour force were engaged in agriculture in 1520; that this figure declined very slowly to 70 per cent by 1670 with the bulk of the fall occurring after 1600; more quickly to 66 per cent in 1700; and then linearly in the eighteenth century to 50 per cent in 1801.[16]

These assumptions allow the population to be subdivided into three groups rather than two; the urban population, the rural population engaged in

15 Deane and Cole, *British economic growth*, table 30, p. 142. Alternative estimates of the scale of employment in early nineteenth-century agriculture may be found in Wrigley, 'Men on the land', especially table 11.10, p. 327, and accompanying text.

16 The first serious attempt to quantify the occupational and social structure of England before 1801 was that carried out by Gregory King in 1688. When Deane and Cole considered his estimates, they suggested that 'between 70 and 80 per cent of the occupied population was primarily engaged in agriculture'. Deane and Cole, *British economic growth*, p. 3. This is implausibly high. Having regard to the total national population in 1688 and 1801 (4.90 and 8.66 million) and the proportion in agriculture (say 75 per cent and 35.9 per cent), such a high proportion in 1688 would imply a fall in the absolute scale of agricultural employment of more than 15 per cent over the intervening century. Lindert has recently re-examined the changes in English occupational structure in the eighteenth century but the results, at least for agriculture, do not appear convincing. The percentage of the male labour force employed in agriculture is estimated at 22.3 in 1700, 26.1 in 1740 and 13.7 in 1811. Lindert, *English occupations*, table 6, pp. 46–7. See also note 19 below.

Table 7.4 Urban, rural agricultural and rural non-agricultural populations (millions)

	Total population (1)	Urban population (2)	Rural population (3)	Proportion of rural population in agriculture (4)	Rural agricultural population (3)×(4) (5)	Rural non-agricultural population (3)−(5) (6)	Total population per 100 rural agricultural (1)/(5) (7)	Column (7) 1520=100 (8)
1520	2.40	0.13	2.27	0.80	1.82	0.45	132	100
1600	4.11	0.34	3.77	0.76	2.87	0.90	143	108
1670	4.98	0.68	4.30	0.70	3.01	1.29	165	125
1700	5.06	0.85	4.21	0.66	2.78	1.43	182	138
1750	5.77	1.22	4.55	0.58	2.64	1.91	219	166
1801	8.66	2.38	6.28	0.50	3.14	3.14	276	209

Percentages of total population in major categories

	Urban	Rural agricultural	Rural non-agricultural	Total
1520	5.5	76.0	18.5	100
1600	8.0	70.0	22.0	100
1670	13.5	60.5	26.0	100
1700	17.0	55.0	28.0	100
1750	21.0	46.0	33.0	100
1801	27.5	36.25	36.25	100

Populations relative to 1801 total (1801 = 100)

	Urban	Rural agricultural	Rural non-agricultural
1520	5.5	58	14
1600	14	91	29
1670	29	96	41
1700	36	89	46
1750	51	84	61
1801	100	100	100

Relative population growth by period (100×total at later date/total at earlier date)

	Urban	Rural agricultural	Rural non-agricultural
1600/1520	262	158	200
1670/1600	197	105	143
1700/1670	127	92	111
1750/1700	144	95	134
1801/1750	195	119	164

Source: For population totals in top panel see table 7.3 and discussion in text.

agriculture, and the rural population dependent on employment other than in agriculture. At the same time changes in output per head in agriculture can be calculated. The results are set out in table 7.4.

Table 7.4 suggests that the rural agricultural population scarcely changed in size for a century and a half between 1600 and 1750 and that even in 1801 was only a tenth larger than 200 years earlier.[17] It is not therefore surprising that table 7.4 should show a striking rise in agricultural productivity, and indeed to the degree that the assumptions that have been made in constructing the table are justified the conclusions are inescapable.[18] The crucial assumptions are that England was not a significant net importer or exporter of food; that the growth of the percentage of the population living in towns followed the pattern set out in table 7.2; and that the proportion of the rural population engaged in non-agricultural production rose from 20 to 50 per cent between 1520 and 1801. For the second and third assumptions, the central issue is the extent of change over the period as a whole; the question of its timing, though fascinating, is of lesser importance.

Precision about any of the three basic assumptions is beyond reach. On the first it is worth noting that the fact that England was a substantial food exporter in the early eighteenth century means that agricultural productivity is probably understated at that period. Equally, by the end of the century England had become a net importer, especially from Ireland, which implies the opposite. The second set of assumptions concerning urban growth is probably sufficiently accurate to avoid significant error. The third assumption relates to the agricultural proportion of the rural population. The figure for 1801 is fairly firmly grounded in the evidence of the early censuses but earlier estimates become increasingly fallible. Any figure for the early sixteenth century must be largely guesswork. A lower figure would, of course, reduce the apparent gain in agricultural productivity, but only a radically lower figure would greatly change the general picture.[19]

17 Jones estimated that the agricultural population of England and Wales increased by 8.5 per cent in the eighteenth century. Jones, 'Agriculture, 1700–1780', p. 71.

18 Crafts's calculations produce results broadly similar to those implied by table 7.4 in relation to agricultural productivity. He estimated that agricultural output rose at the following percentage rates per annum over the periods 1710–40, 1740–80 and 1780–1800: 0.9, 0.5 and 0.6. This implies a total increase in output of almost exactly 80 per cent over the 90-year period as a whole. Assuming that the agricultural labour force grew by 13 per cent over the century, as table 7.4 suggests, the increase in output per man, at 59 per cent, is closely similar to that which may be calculated from column 7 of table 7.4 (52 per cent). Crafts, 'The eighteenth century', tables 1.1 and 1.2, pp. 2, 3.

19 It is possible to use the work of Gregory King and of Joseph Massie to test how far the estimates made by contemporaries agree with those in table 7.4. In 1760, out of a total of 1 472 000 families, Massie supposed that 210 000 were freeholders, 155 000 farmers and a further 200 000 husbandmen, making a total of 565 000 unambiguously engaged in agriculture. In addition, he estimated that there were 200 000 families of labourers outside London. Not all of these would be agricultural labourers. Massie reckoned that there were 20 000 labourers in London, only slightly short of the number to be expected on the assumption that labourers were as numerous per 1000 population inside cities as in the countryside. We may assume,

Other assumptions could, of course, be used in constructing table 7.4. For example, if one were to assume that 15 per cent of English food requirements were met by imports in 1801 and that agriculture employed 55 per cent of the rural labour force rather than 50 per cent, while other assumptions were unchanged, the estimated overall rise in agricultural productivity would be reduced from 109 to 61 per cent. Going still further, if the 1520 figure in column 4 were reduced from 0.80 to 0.70 and the modified assumptions for 1801 were retained, the figure would drop even more to 41 per cent, but this figure is improbably low.[20] On present evidence, therefore, while the particular figure given in table 7.4 is, of course, arbitrary, there is a strong likelihood that the 'true' figure lies between 60 and 100 per cent.

The phasing of changes in the proportion of the rural labour force engaged in agriculture no less than their scale is also largely a matter of judgement rather than a demonstrable pattern. The same pressures which kept urban growth outside London to such modest proportions in the sixteenth century are likely to have restricted employment opportunities outside agriculture.

----

therefore, that another 15 000–20 000 were to be found in other urban centres, and it is probable that a further group, though living in the countryside, was employed outside agriculture, especially in the building trades (which were not separately itemized by Massie). Assuming that these, too, were about 20 000 in number, then the overall total of those families engaged in agriculture would be *c*.730 000, or fractionally less than one-half of the national total. The comparable figure in table 7.4, that for 1750, is 46 per cent, a broadly similar figure.

A comparison with Gregory King (1688) is more difficult to make because of the form in which he drew up his famous table. King's totals for families of freeholders and farmers are not greatly different from Massie's (180 000 and 150 000 respectively) but he gave no separate figure for husbandmen. Instead, all other families which might be engaged in agriculture appear in two categories, labouring people and outservants (364 000) and cottagers and paupers (400 000). It is clear that most of those engaged in industrial crafts – weavers, glovers, knitters, tanners, carpenters, coopers, sawyers, thatchers, smiths, wrights, cordwainers and so on – must have been included in one of these two categories (King lists only 60 000 families of artisans or handicraft workers in the entire country), together with all labouring families living in London or other towns. If we assume that half of the cottars were what Massie would have termed husbandmen and half engaged in industrial crafts, a split similar to that found in Massie's separate tabulation of the two categories; that 15 per cent of all labourers were in towns (where at this date about 15 per cent of the population lived); and that of the remaining 309 000 labourers, 25 000 were employed outside agriculture, the total of families employed in agriculture is 814 000 or 60 per cent of the national total of 1 361 000 families. The comparable figure in table 7.4 is about 58 per cent (1670, 60.5 per cent; 1700, 55.0 per cent). There is a convenient reproduction of both King's and Massie's tables and a discussion of the difficulties in comparing them in Mathias, *The transformation of England*, pp. 171–89.

20 Sixteenth-century estimates of occupational structure are inevitably very insecurely based, and it is possible, even likely, that the dominance of agriculture is too easily overstated. The muster roll for Gloucestershire excluding Bristol taken in 1608, for example, suggests that only 46.2 per cent of the adult male population aged between 20 and 60 were engaged in agriculture. The comparable figure when the 1811 census was taken was virtually the same at 45.8 per cent. The economic history of Gloucestershire is far from typical of the country as a whole, but Gloucestershire affords an example which should caution us against assuming too readily that rural non-agricultural employment was always very limited in Tudor or early Stuart England. Tawney and Tawney, 'An occupational census'; *1811 Census*, Enumeration, Parliamentary Papers 1812, xi, p. 121.

It therefore seems appropriate to make only a small reduction in the proportion of the rural population in agriculture between 1520 and 1600. Thereafter, the pace of change probably accelerated.

One further implicit assumption deserves discussion. Individual intake of food measured in calories varies within fairly narrow limits. There is little evidence of widespread malnutrition so extreme as to cause death in early modern England. With rare and usually local exceptions, even severe harvest failure did not provoke heavy mortalities.[21] It is improbable (though also undemonstrable) that mean personal daily calorie intake varied in a manner which would significantly undermine the line of argument deployed above. Nevertheless, periods of rising real income must have been periods in which *per caput* food consumption tended to rise with the opposite happening in times of declining living standards.[22] In addition, there were changes in the composition of individual diet as incomes rose or fell. Meat was a luxury to the pauper but a commonplace to more prosperous members of society, and there were secular shifts in the relative prices of grain and meat which reflected the long-term trends of the average real income.[23] Inasmuch as food such as meat and dairy produce needed larger inputs of labour, as well as land and capital, to produce a given number of calories of food compared with grain, it might seem that an allowance should be made for the impact of secular real income trends in attempting an individual measure of agricultural productivity. This in turn would imply that agricultural productivity per head was rising faster during the seventeenth and early eighteenth century than suggested by table 7.4, but less quickly during the later eighteenth century. It also suggests that it may have been falling in the sixteenth century, a finding in keeping with common sense since rural agricultural population is estimated to have risen by almost 60 per cent between 1520 and 1600, a scale of increase very likely to involve a falling marginal productivity of labour and much concealed or overt underemployment.

Making an explicit allowance for real income changes, however, presents problems. At present, real income data are based on slender foundations and involve wide margins of uncertainty. Little is known about any changes that may have occurred over time in the income elasticity of demand for

---

21 Wrigley and Schofield, *Population history of England*, especially pp. 320–40, 370–82 and appendix 10. The principal exception to the rule that harvest failure did not provoke big mortalities was the north-west of England in the sixteenth and early seventeenth centuries. Appleby, *Famine in Tudor and Stuart England*.

22 Estimating income elasticity of demand for food in eighteenth-century England presents great difficulties for lack of relevant data. In a review of the limited evidence, Crafts concluded that the most probable figure for the late eighteenth and early nineteenth centuries was 0.7. Crafts, 'Income elasticities of demand', especially pp. 154–9.

23 Kussmaul provides a convenient graph of the relative prices of the two commodities. It bears a strong resemblance to an inverted graph of the Phelps Brown and Hopkins real wage series, though the match is by no means perfect, especially in the early seventeenth and late eighteenth centuries. Kussmaul, *Servants in husbandry*, figure 6.3, p. 104. Real wage data based on Phelps Brown and Hopkins are set out in Wrigley and Schofield, *Population history of England*, appendix 9, and shown graphically in figure 10.5, p. 414.

food. It may be noted, however, that the only existing real wage series covering the whole period, that of Phelps Brown and Hopkins, stood higher in 1800 than it had two centuries earlier.[24] The apparent gains in agricultural productivity over the seventeenth and eighteenth centuries as a whole are therefore unlikely to be overstated because of a failure to take real income explicitly into account.

Labour released from agriculture is available to increase other forms of production. The gross changes were striking. The rural agricultural population was 76 per cent of the total population in 1520 but only 36 per cent of the total in 1801 (table 7.4), and non-agricultural employment therefore grew from 24 to 64 per cent of the whole. This may overstate the extent of the change in that some of the growth of non-agricultural employment represented jobs created by increased specialization of function. A carter, for example, making his living by moving to market goods previously taken there by local farmers may be placed outside agriculture in an occupational breakdown but undertakes a task previously performed by the farmer. Yet the change was great. Adam Smith argued that a surplus of agricultural production over the food needs of the farming population might either be consumed unproductively by, say, retinues of servants, or productively if the surplus maintained an army of 'manufacturers' whose output added to the wealth of the community as a whole.[25] In early modern England the growth of employment in industry and commerce is a testimony to the predominantly 'productive' use to which the growing relative surpluses in the agricultural sector were put. Adam Smith considered that the scale of such growth was largely conditioned by the extent of the rise in agricultural productivity.[26] He did not envisage the much more radical type of change that has come to be called an industrial revolution, nor is there any compelling reason to suppose that even increases in agricultural productivity as striking as those achieved in England between 1600 and 1800 will necessarily engender an industrial revolution. Yet the scale of change in early modern England bears stressing. It stands out more clearly if comparison is made with other countries.

Urban growth on the continent

De Vries has undertaken a very informative analysis of urban growth patterns between 1500 and 1800 for Europe as a whole and for some major regional

24 The index stood at 409 on average for the 11 harvest years 1595–6 to 1605–6, compared with 507 in the period 1795–6 to 1805–6. Wrigley and Schofield, *Population history of England*, table 9.2, pp. 642–4.

25 Smith's chapter 'Of the accumulation of capital, or of productive and unproductive labour' deals with this topic in the *Wealth of nations*, book ii, chapter 3.

26 The passage leading up to the assertion that 'the manufacturers of Leeds, Halifax, Sheffield, Birmingham and Wolverhampton . . . are the offspring of agriculture' exemplifies his argument very well. Smith, *Wealth of nations*, i, p. 431.

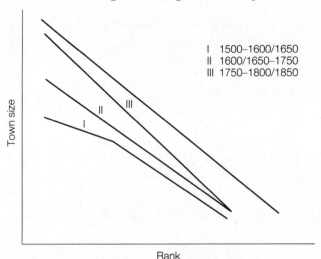

I 1500–1600/1650
II 1600/1650–1750
III 1750–1800/1850

Rank
Figure 7.1 Urbanization in Europe.
Source: De Vries, 'Patterns of urbanization', figure 3.5, p. 97.

subdivisions.[27] In it he made use of an empirical relationship between the sizes of the towns and their position in a rank ordering whereby the difference in their populations is proportional to the difference in their rank orders. Thus $p_i = p_1/i$ where p_1 is the population of the largest town and i refers to the rank order of a town after all towns have been arranged in descending order of size. The population of the fifth largest town may therefore be expected to be a fifth of that of the largest, and so on. If logarithmic scales are used to plot the population and rank coordinates of each town, the resulting distribution in the archetypal case will fall on a straight line with a slope of 45 degrees. In practice the angle of the line may vary somewhat from the 45° slope suggested by the strictly proportional relationship, and the first few points plotted are sometimes aberrant, as when the largest settlement is very much bigger than the second largest. But regularities in town size distributions are often impressive, and any anomalies within a data set, or changes in the angle of the plotted slope over time, may be illuminating.

By compiling rank-size date for European towns at intervals over a three-century period starting in 1500, de Vries was able to establish changes in the slope and shape of the urban hierarchy sufficiently pronounced and consistent to distinguish three major periods, as shown in figure 7.1. At the beginning of the sixteenth century the slope was gentle and there was a flat 'top' to the distribution. De Vries attributed the latter to the still strongly regional character of the European economy which was insufficiently articulated to produce leading urban centres of the size implied by the slope of the lower part of the distribution. During the sixteenth century the rank-size

27 De Vries, 'Patterns of urbanization'.

Table 7.5   Urbanization in England and the continent: percentage of total population in towns with 10 000 or more people

	1500	1600	1650	1700	1750	1800
England	3.2[a]	6.1	10.8[b]	13.4	17.5	24.0
North and west Europe[c]	6.0	8.1	10.7	13.0	13.8	14.7
Europe[d]	6.1	8.0	9.3	9.5	9.9	10.6

[a]*c.* 1520.
[b]*c.* 1670.
[c]Scandinavia, The Netherlands, Belgium, England, Scotland, Wales and Ireland
[d]The countries included in Europe are Germany, France, Switzerland, Italy, Spain and Portugal together with those listed as north and west Europe.
Sources: For England see source notes to tables 7.1 and 7.2. Other data are from de Vries, 'Patterns of urbanization', table 3.6, p. 88.

plot gradually straightened. The continent-wide economy was becoming more integrated, and cities such as London, Paris and Amsterdam grew very rapidly as they assumed urban functions over wide hinterlands. A second period then supervened, running from about the early seventeenth to the mid-eighteenth century. In general, in this period, the larger the town, the more rapidly it grew, so that a disproportionate part of the overall rise in urban population took place in the larger towns. The rank-size line pivoted slowly round a point close to its lowest reading and thus grew steadily steeper. After about 1750, however, urban growth changed in character again and a third period began. The rank-size line moved outwards from the origin of the graph implying a rise in the number of towns in all size categories, but there was a more rapid growth in the number of smaller towns than of larger ones. The slope became less steep once more. The sequence of changes was shared by the major subdivisions of Europe used by de Vries, though the timing of the changes varied somewhat. The pattern of change in England, however, was quite unlike that on the continent.

As table 7.5 shows, England began the period with an unusually slight proportion of her population living in large towns, but passed the European average in the mid-seventeenth century and the north-west European average by 1700. By the beginning of the nineteenth century England was relatively heavily urbanized. Events in England, however, were so different from those elsewhere as to distort patterns of change when England is included in some larger entity.

It is instructive to remove England both from the urban and the overall population totals used to generate urban percentages for continental areas. The result is shown in table 7.6. Urbanization in north and west Europe recedes rather than advancing substantially in the eighteenth century, though the scale of advance in the seventeenth century is not greatly altered. In Europe as a whole the exclusion of England slows the increase in urbanization in the seventeenth century and brings it almost to a halt in the eighteenth.[28]

28 There might be reason to suppose this finding spurious if de Vries's estimates of the population of English towns and those shown in table 7.1 were widely divergent, but a detailed comparison of his data with those of table 7.1 suggests that this is a groundless fear.

Table 7.6   Urbanization in England and the continent (revised): percentage of total population in towns with 10 000 or more people

	1600	1700	1750	1800
England	6.1	13.4	17.5	24.0
North and west Europe minus England	9.2	12.8	12.1	10.0
Europe minus England	8.1	9.2	9.4	9.5

De Vries provides estimates of population totals for north and west Europe and for Europe as a whole for 1600, 1700, 1750 and 1800 in the work listed below (though not for the other dates in table 7.5). This information and the urban percentages given in table 7.5 make it possible to calculate the size of the urban populations. The English totals can then be removed both from the urban and total populations and the percentages recalculated.
Sources: For England see source notes to tables 7.1 and 7.2. For other data see source notes to table 7.5 and de Vries, *Europe in an age of crisis*, table 1, p. 5.

Over the full 200-year period the urban percentage quadrupled in England, scarcely changed in the rest of north-west Europe and advanced rather modestly in the continent as a whole. The English experience appears to be *sui generis*.

The extent of the contrast also comes home forcibly if de Vries's estimates are reworked to permit another comparison to be made, as may be seen in table 7.7. The urban population of Europe more than doubled between 1600 and 1800, but the total population rose by almost 60 per cent so that much of the rise in urban population was caused by the rise in overall numbers rather than in increase in the proportion of the population living in towns. Column 4 shows how the urban population would have grown if the urban percentage had stayed at the level prevailing in 1600. The totals in column 5 show the 'net' gain in urban population at each later date compared with 1600, that is the number by which the urban population exceeded that which would have obtained if the urban percentage had not changed in the interim. The second panel of the table repeats the calculation for England. By combining information from the two upper panels, the proportion of total European urban growth that occurred in England can be calculated for the periods 1600–1700, 1700–50 and 1750–1800. The proportion rises steadily from 33 per cent in the seventeenth century to 70 per cent in the second half of the eighteenth. Over the two-century period as a whole the proportion exceeded one-half. Since England contained only 5.8 per cent of the population of Europe in 1600 and even in 1800 only 7.7 per cent, these proportions are an extraordinary testimony to the extent of the difference in urban growth between the island and the continent.

De Vries laid particular emphasis on the absence of growth in the smaller towns in the period 1600–1750, which he defined as the age of the rural proletariat. He argued that urban growth was almost entirely confined to very large cities, with 80 per cent of all growth taking place in towns with 40 000 inhabitants or more. These were almost all capital cities or large ports whose development was stimulated by the growth in administrative, military and legal employment in both absolutist and constitutional states, or by the

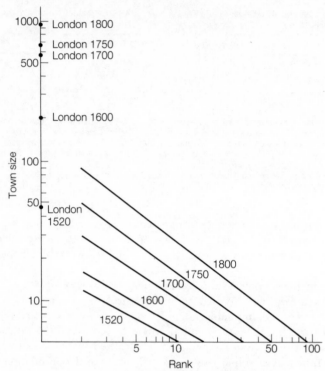

Figure 7.2 Urbanization in England

development of long-distance, often extra-European trade. Smaller towns stagnated or lost population, afflicted by loss of political autonomy and by the 'abandonment of cities as locations for many of the most labour-absorbing industries'.[29] The balance of advantage favoured proto-industrial development in the countryside.

It is unquestionably true that there was much growth of industrial employment in rural England in this period, as we have seen, nor can there be any dissent from the view that London, combining administrative, commercial and trading dominance, enjoyed an astonishing expansion.[30] But neither the development of rural industry nor the growth of London precluded an equally remarkable surge of urban growth elsewhere in England. Other towns grew by much the same absolute amount as London between 1600 and 1750 and proportionally were growing even faster than London (table 7.2). Towns with between 5000 and 10 000 inhabitants doubled in number from 15 to 31, while over the same period the number in Europe excluding England fell from 372 to 331.[31] Figure 7.2 shows rank-

29 De Vries, 'Patterns of urbanization', p. 101.
30 See chapter 6.
31 De Vries, 'Patterns of urbanization', table 3.7, p. 93. For sources of data about English towns see source notes to table 7.1.

Table 7.7 The English share of European urban growth 1600-1800 (populations in millions)

	Total population (1)	Urban proportion (2)	Urban population (1)×(2) (3)	Urban total at 1600 proportion (4)	'Net' gain on 1600 (3)−(4) (5)	'Net' gain on last date (difference between successive totals in (5)) (6)
Europe[a]						
1600	70.6	0.080	5.65	5.65	0.00	—
1700	75.0	0.095	7.13	6.00	1.13	1.13
1750	86.6	0.099	8.57	6.93	1.64	0.51
1800	111.8	0.106	11.85	8.94	2.91	1.27
England						
1600	4.11	0.061[b]	0.249	0.249	0.000	—
1700	5.06	0.134[b]	0.680	0.309	0.371	0.371
1750	5.77	0.175[b]	1.012	0.352	0.661	0.290
1800	8.66	0.240[b]	2.079	0.528	1.551	0.890

English percentage of total European 'net' urban gain

1600/1700   100(0.371/1.13) = 33
1700/1750   100(0.290/0.51) = 57
1750/1800   100(0.890/1.27) = 70
1600/1800   100(1.551/2.91) = 53

[a]For a list of the countries comprising 'Europe' see notes to table 7.5.
[b]These proportions are derived from the column (3) totals rather than vice versa as in the top panel.
Sources: For England see source notes to tables 7.1 and 7.2. For Europe see source notes to table 7.5.

size plots for England. Like figure 7.1 it is schematically drawn: empirical
data plots would show, of course, points falling on either side of the straight
lines for each date. Although the number of towns is small and the presence
of London severely distorts the top of the distribution, the lines emphasize
how different England was from the continent (compare figure 7.1).

Dr Vries's study has the admirable virtue of providing a framework of
comparison for smaller units by epitomizing the characteristics of Europe
as a whole. This helps to bring out the distinctiveness of English history,
something which may be further examined by considering some comparative
data about England's two greatest rivals, Holland and France.

Holland and France

Even in 1800 England was a less urbanized country than Holland. Already
in the early sixteenth century many Dutch people were town dwellers and
they increased in number very rapidly as the century progressed. In this
period the course of real wages in Holland was almost the reverse of the
comparable pattern in England: real wages rose to a peak about 1610, the
date when the English series approached its nadir. Urbanization proceeded
apace. The percentage of the population living in towns grew from about
21 to about 29 per cent, and since the total population of Holland was rising
moderately quickly at the time, the absolute number of town dwellers rose
very rapidly from about 260 000 to about 435 000. There followed a period
of half a century during which Dutch real wages fell back somewhat just
as a recovery was beginning in England, maintaining the inverse movement
in the two countries for a full century. After the 1650s, however, Dutch real
wages rose rapidly once more to a new, and substantially higher, peak in
the 1690s, after which they tended to fall, uncertainly at first but more quickly
and without interruption from the 1740s until the end of the century.[32] The
trend of urban percentages moved broadly in sympathy with real wage
movements, reaching a high point about 1700, when about 39 per cent of
the Dutch population comprised urban dwellers, but then slowly declining
until by 1800 it was not much higher than the English figure. Some Dutch
towns experienced very savage falls in population and, since the population
as a whole grew only very modestly in the eighteenth century, the total
number of town dwellers fell slightly.[33]

Dutch rural population trends also warrant notice. During the long period
of urban growth from 1550 to 1700 rural population grew only modestly.
It was 17 per cent larger at the latter than the former date. In the eighteenth
century, however, when there was urban decline and real wages languished,
rural population rose by 20 per cent. In England, in the eighteenth century,

32 De Vries, The pre-industrial Netherlands', pp. 671–4, and figure 2, p. 673.
33 See notes to table 7.8 for sources for these estimates. Van der Woude provides much
detail of urban fortunes in Holland between 1525 and 1795 in 'Demografische ontwikkeling',
especially pp. 134–9.

rural population grew by 49 per cent overall but rural agricultural population by only 13 per cent, even though the overall population growth in England during the century reached 71 per cent compared with a Dutch figure of only 11 per cent. If, therefore, it is safe to assume that Dutch rural agricultural population was rising as fast as rural population as a whole, a plausible supposition at a time of falling real wages, rural agricultural population in the two countries must have moved almost exactly in step in the eighteenth century even though their overall rates of population growth diverged so markedly. Conversely, in the sixteenth century while impoverishment increased in England and its rural agricultural population grew fast (by 58 per cent between 1520 and 1600), in Holland there can have been very little comparable increase, though the population of Holland was rising quite rapidly. In columns 5–7 of table 7.8, the rural population is subdivided between agricultural and other employment in confirmity with arbitrary assumptions whose basis is explained in the notes to the table. To the degree that the figures mirror reality they underline the points just made. The 'Golden Age' of the Dutch rural economy was clearly one free from increasing pressure on the land but it was succeeded by more trying times.[34]

It would be absurd to press too far any comparison of the urban sectors in England and Holland. It would make no sense, for example, to try to use estimates of urban percentages in Holland as an indirect measure of agricultural productivity since she was a large importer of agricultural products, above all Baltic grain, and was not broadly self-sufficient as England was in the early modern period. Yet the beneficial effects of urban growth on Dutch agriculture in promoting specialization and making it easier to achieve higher production per man and per farm reflect the same processes at work in Holland as London's growth produced in England. Again, the Dutch passenger canal network was the transport wonder of its age,[35] a response to urban growth and the closely associated rise in living standards, just as similar developments in eighteenth-century England promoted the investment of capital in turnpike roads and the construction of a new canal network.

Both Holland and England, therefore, vividly illustrate the beneficial interaction between urban growth, rising living standards and a surge in agricultural productivity that was possible within the context of an early modern economy. The food needs of towns were met through the operation of a commercial market in foodstuffs by farming units which benefited from specialization and avoided the subdivision and fragmentation of holdings that was commonly the bane of peasant societies when population increased. By the late eighteenth century yields per acre were substantially higher in England and The Netherlands than elsewhere in Europe, having roughly doubled over the previous two centuries.[36] Yet in neither country was the

34 De Vries, 'The pre-industrial Netherlands', figure 2, p. 673, charts the fall in real wages from a late seventeenth-century peak which, in a period of static or falling population, is eloquent testimony to Dutch difficulties.
35 De Vries, 'Barges and capitalism'.
36 Slicher van Bath, *Agrarian history*, pp. 280–2.

Table 7.8 Dutch urban and rural population estimates (thousands)

	Total population (1)	Urban proportion (2)	Urban population (1)×(2) (3)	Rural population (1)−(3) (4)	Rural agricultural proportion (5)	Rural agricultural population (4)×(5) (6)	Rural population non-agricultural (4)−(6) (7)
1550	1250	0.21	260	990	0.75	745	245
1600	1500	0.29	435	1065	0.705	750	315
1650	1875	0.37	695	1180	0.66	780	400
1700	1900	0.39	740	1160	0.66	765	395
1750	1925	0.35	675	1250	0.66	825	425
1800	2100	0.33	695	1405	0.66	930	475

Urban is defined as relating to towns of 5000 inhabitants or more.
The population totals in columns (3) and (6) have been rounded to emphasize the approximate and arbitrary nature of the calculation.
The urban proportion in column (2) was estimated from data given by de Vries. His data refer to the percentages of the population living in towns containing 2500 inhabitants or more, and in towns containing 10 000 inhabitants or more. I assumed that half of those living in towns with 2500–9999 inhabitants were living in towns of 5000–9999 inhabitants. For some dates de Vries provides data only for the urban proportion in towns of 10 000 or more inhabitants, but sufficient paired estimates are given for other dates to make it feasible to provide plausible estimates at half-century intervals.
The rural agricultural proportions (column 5) stem from the following observations and assumptions. Mitchell provides data which show that 44.1 per cent of the total Dutch labour force in 1849 were engaged in agriculture. At that date the urban proportion was the same as in 1800 (de Vries, table 1), and therefore the proportion of the *rural* labour force engaged in agriculture was 66 per cent (0.441/0.67 = 0.66). I have assumed arbitrarily that in Holland in the mid-sixteenth century the comparable figure was 75 per cent, a slightly lower figure than that used in the parallel calculation for England because Holland was far more urbanized than England in the sixteenth century and non-agricultural rural employment was probably more common. I have assumed that it fell to 0.66 linearly over the next century but did not change thereafter as the great Dutch growth spurt fell away.
Sources: Column 1: Faber et al., 'Population changes and economic developments in the Netherlands', p. 110. Column 2: de Vries, 'Population and the labour market', table 1. Column 5: Mitchell, *European historical statistics*, table C1, p. 167 (see also notes above).

agriculturally employed population very much larger in 1800 than in 1600.
The example of Holland also shows, however, that such progress is not
necessarily a passport to further success. Adam Smith, aware like so many
of his contemporaries of the exceptional economic achievements of Holland,
used it as an example of the limits to growth which must beset any country
at some stage, making it difficult to sustain the gains of the past, much less
secure further advance.[37] The tide began to ebb in eighteenth-century
Holland. Urban population fell away slightly even though numbers rose
modestly overall. Real wages sagged. Far from forming part of the vanguard
of the industrial revolution, Holland moved into the industrial era later than
most of western Europe, and even as late as 1850 was no more urbanized
than she had been in the later seventeenth century.

France makes a very different contrast to English experience. Some
relevant data are given in table 7.9. The steps leading to the estimates given
in the table are explained in the notes to the table. As with the English and
Dutch estimates, they are subject to a margin of error which may in some
cases be substantial because the empirical data base is insecure or
inconsistent, because some of the assumptions are questionable or because the
chains of reasoning used to produce some of the estimates were long and there
may be a compounding of errors. Despite such uncertainties, the contrast
between France and England stands out so strongly that no reasonable
change in the assumptions used would significantly alter the picture.

In 1500 France was not only a far more populous country than England
but also more urbanized. Within the present borders of France there were
then already 14 towns with a population of more than 20 000 and 21 with
populations between 10 000 and 20 000, while in England only London
exceeded 20 000, and probably only two other towns, Norwich and Bristol,
had 10 000 or more inhabitants. London was not only smaller than Paris
but also smaller than Lyon.[38] Overall, France was almost twice as urban
as England, though much less urban than Holland, but in the next three
centuries French towns grew very little quicker than the French population
as a whole. France closely resembled de Vries's 'Europe' both in level of
urbanization and in its change over time (table 7.5). By 1800 the degree
of urbanization reached in England was approaching three times the French
level.[39] Moreover, the proportion of English rural population employed
outside agriculture grew much faster than in France, and agricultural

37 Smith makes the general observation that, 'In a country which had acquired that full
complement of riches which the nature of its soil and climate, and its situation with respect
to other countries allowed it to acquire; which could, therefore, advance no further, and which   ✓
was not going backwards, both the wages of labour and the profits of stock would probably
be very low'. He subsequently suggested that Holland was approaching this state. Smith, *Wealth
of nations*, i, p. 106.
38 The French town population estimates are taken from de Vries, 'Patterns of urbanization',
table 3.2, pp. 82–5.
39 It should be noted, however, that the effects of revolution and war caused a sharp drop
in French city populations in the last decade of the eighteenth century in some cases. Dupâquier,
La population française, pp. 91–2.

Table 7.9 French urban and rural population estimates (thousands)

	Total population (1)	Urban population (2)	Urban percentage (3)	Rural population (1)−(2) (4)	Rural agricultural proportion (5)	Rural agricultural population (4)×(5) (6)	Rural non-agricultural population (4)−(6) (7)
1500	15 500	1410	9.1	14 090	0.80	11 270	2820
1600	19 000	1660	8.7	17 340	0.755	13 100	4240
1700	21 500	2350	10.9	19 150	0.71	13 600	5550
1750	24 500	2530	10.3	21 970	0.685	15 050	6920
1800	29 100	3220	11.1	25 880	0.66	17 080	8800

Urban is defined as relating to towns of 5000 inhabitants or more.
France was treated as if it occupied its present territory, and therefore towns such as Lille were included in urban population totals. The urban population in column (2) was estimated in several stages. Chandler and Fox provide estimates of urban populations of towns of 20 000 inhabitants or more for the dates shown. De Vries gives totals of towns in several size categories (thousands) 20–9, 30–9, 40–9, 50–99, 100 and over. Where the total for a town given by Chandler and Fox falls into the size category given by de Vries, this total was used. Otherwise de Vries was preferred and the town population was assumed to be at the centrepoint of the size range (none fell into the open-ended top category). The discrepancies between the two sources, as might be expected, were much more marked at the earlier than the later dates (the number of towns of 20 000 or more inhabitants in the two sources were as follows at the five successive dates (Chandler and Fox in brackets): 14 (20), 20 (15), 24 (26), 31 (32), 32 (36)). De Vries's totals of towns between 10 000 and 20 000 were multiplied by 13 500 to give a population total for this size range of towns. These two operations provide a figure for all towns with populations of 10 000 or more, leaving the problem of estimating a figure for towns of between 5000 and 10 000 people. De Vries provides estimates of the number of towns in this size range in Europe as a whole by extrapolating from the rank-size distributions of towns of 10 000 inhabitants and above. It can be shown that the rank-size distribution of French towns was similar to that for Europe as measured by the ratio of the number of all towns above 10 000 in population to the number in the size range between 10 000 and 20 000, and therefore the ratio of the number of towns in the size range between 5000 and 10 000 to the number of towns larger than 10 000 derived from de Vries's data was used to estimate the total of smaller towns in France (the ratios in question at the five successive dates are 2.15, 1.76, 1.60, 1.43 and 1.56; of these the third is interpolated from the second and fourth since de Vries provides no data for 1700). The total of towns in the size range between 5000 and 10 000 estimated in this fashion was multiplied by 6500 to give a population total for each date. The breakdown of the individual totals was as follows (thousands):

Table 7.9 (continued)

Population totals by town size class (thousands)

	≥20	10-19	5-9	Total
1500	637	284	488	1409
1600	866	311	481	1658
1700	1389	405	559	2353
1750	1691	324	514	2529
1800	1810	621	793	3224

The proportion of the rural population engaged in agriculture is based on the following data and assumptions. In 1851 the proportion of the population living in towns of 5000 or more inhabitants was 17.9 per cent. In 1856 the proportion of the total French labour force engaged in agriculture was 51.7 per cent. In the mid-nineteenth century, therefore, about 63 per cent of the rural labour force worked on the land (100 × (0.517/0.821) = 63). I have assumed that the comparable figure in 1800 was 66 per cent. As in the case of England I assumed that in France the comparable figure in the early sixteenth century was 80 per cent. The proportions at intermediate dates were obtained by rough linear interpolation.

Sources: Column 1: Dupâquier, *La population française*, pp. 11, 34, 81; Reinhard et al., *Histoire générale de la population mondiale*, pp. 108, 119–20; McEvedy and Jones, *Atlas of world population history*, pp. 55–60. Column 2: Chandler and Fox, *Urban growth*, pp. 15–19, 21. De Vries, 'Patterns of urbanization', especially tables 3.2, 3.4 and 3.7. Column 5: Pouthas, *La population française*, pp. 22, 76; Mitchell, *European historical statistics*, table C1, p. 163.

productivity, using the very rough measure employed *faute de mieux* in this article, progressed far more rapidly in England than in France.

Population always grew faster in England than in France, at times dramatically so (tables 7.2 and 7.9), yet because of the far faster urban growth in England and the swifter rise in the proportion of the rural population employed outside agriculture, the growth of rural agricultural employment was actually slower in England than in France apart from the sixteenth century. Between 1600 and 1800 the number of those dependent upon agriculture for a living in France grew by 30 per cent, whereas in England the comparable figure is 9 per cent (over the same period the national population growth rates were 53 and 111 per cent respectively). These apparently exact percentages should be viewed with reserve, but it is probably at least safe to assert that the rural agricultural population in England grew no faster than its counterpart in France. If the estimates given are taken to be broadly trustworthy, inferences about comparative trends in agricultural productivity in the two countries are possible.

The upper panel of table 7.10 sets out information for England and France in an indexed form to make it easier to appreciate the divergent course of development that characterized them. The value for 1600 has in each case been made equal to 100. In the sixteenth century the differences between the two countries were chiefly related to the much higher rate of growth of the English population rather than to differences in the relative proportions of the populations falling into the urban, rural agricultural and rural non-agricultural categories. After 1600 the contrasts between the two countries grew more pronounced. England continued to grow the quicker overall but the rural agricultural element in her population grew very little over the next two centuries. Indeed, it appears to have been falling for much of the time, whereas urban growth was meteoric and the rise in the rural non-agricultural component was also pronounced. Growth in France was much more balanced, and as a result, although the total population grew less than in England, the rural agricultural population grew appreciably faster.

If it were safe to assume that the level of food consumption per head was much the same in the two countries, that the estimates of rural agricultural population are accurate, and that each country may be regarded as supplying its own food needs (except that in table 7.10 imports were assumed to meet 10 per cent of English food requirements in 1800), then it is a simple matter to compare both levels of productivity in agriculture and their rates of change over time in the two countries. They are given in the lower panel of the table. The figures in columns 1 and 2 represent an absolute measure of productivity per head of the rural agricultural population while those in columns 3 and 4 index changes over time.

The extent of the contrast between England and France may well be understated by table 7.10, both because it is reasonable to suppose that consumption of food per head was somewhat higher in England than in France since English real incomes appear to have been the higher of the two, and also because a higher proportion of the output of English agriculture

Table 7.10 English and French growth patterns compared

Population relative to 1600 total (1600 = 100)

	England					France			
	Urban	Rural agricultural	Rural non-agricultural	Total		Urban	Rural agricultural	Rural non-agricultural	Total
1520	38	63	50	58	1500	85	86	67	82
1600	100	100	100	100	1600	100	100	100	100
1670	200	105	143	125	1700	142	104	131	113
1700	250	97	159	123	1750	152	115	163	129
1750	359	92	212	140	1800	194	130	208	153
1801	700	109	349	211					

Total population per 100 agricultural

	England (1)	France (2)	England (Column 1) (1500 = 100) (3)	France (Column 2) (1500 = 100) (4)
1500	132	138	100	100
1600	143	145	108	105
1700	182	158	138	114
1750	219	163	166	118
1801	248	170	188	123

See text for modification made to 1801 figure in bottom panel, columns (1) and (3). Note that in bottom panel the figures for England in the first line relate to 1520 rather than 1500.

Sources: see source notes to tables 7.4 and 7.9.

may have been used as industrial raw material rather than food. Land and labour used for the raising of sheep for wool, for example, cannot also be used to grow corn. The effect, however, is difficult to quantify since output in such cases often consisted both of food and of industrial raw materials. Producing wool for cloth or hides for the leather industry also means producing meat for human consumption. 'Pure' industrial land usage, as with flax for linen, is a rarer phenomenon.[40] The use of the land to provide 'fuel' for horses or oxen also suggests that the contrast between the two countries may be greater than appears in table 7.10 since in England by the later eighteenth century a very substantial proportion of horses were employed outside agriculture altogether on turnpike roads, on canal towpaths, but particularly in urban transport of men and goods.[41]

In England, as in Holland at an earlier date, urban growth, rising productivity in agriculture and improving real incomes were interwoven with one another, and were mutually reinforcing for long periods. The French economy was not drawn into the same pattern. On the assumptions used in constructing table 7.9, there is evidence of a significantly increased pressure on the land in the eighteenth century. In a peasant economy this will tend to provoke serious economic difficulties and increase the proportion of excessively subdivided holdings, conforming to de Vries's 'peasant' model of a rural economy while both England and Holland accord better with his 'specialization' model.[42]

Arguments couched in this manner are always too *simpliste*. It is misleading, for example, to treat pre-industrial countries as if they were homogeneous units. There were major differences between different areas even within the smallest of the three countries considered. Sometimes even intra-provincial differences in Holland were marked: inter-provincial contrasts could rival those between countries.[43] The regional variety of a country as large as France was still more notable. It could scarcely be otherwise when it is recalled that France contained more than ten times as many people as Holland and that her area was fifteen times greater.[44]

40　Thirsk presents good reasons to suppose that the value of industrial crops rose very rapidly in the later sixteenth and seventeenth centuries, and also provides abundant evidence of the enormous increase in rural employment outside agriculture. Thirsk, *Economic policy and projects*. She also makes some guarded attempts to quantify the scale of industrial crops and 'new' food crops. Ibid., pp. 177–8.

41　Thompson estimates that there were almost half a million (487 000) horses in use outside agriculture in 1811 (riding horses, carriage horses, post horses, trade horses and those in the stage coach trade). At the level of consumption of oats and hay per animal which Thompson thinks appropriate, and on reasonable assumptions about yields of oats and hay per acre, sustaining such a large horse population must have meant devoting about two million acres to their fodder. Agriculture at that date is estimated to have required about 800 000 horses. Thompson, 'Nineteenth-century horse sense', p. 78 and table 2, p. 80.

42　De Vries, *The Dutch rural economy*, chapter 1.

43　The work of the Wageningen school illustrates the point: Slicher van Bath, van der Woude, Roessingh, Faber.

44　For population totals see tables 7.8 and 7.9. The area of France today is 212 209 square miles: that of Holland 13 967. Their areas varied somewhat, of course, over the early modern period.

Furthermore, better knowledge would no doubt cause significant alterations to be made to many of the tables on whose contents the arguments advanced in this essay were based. Yet the contrasts and similarities between the three countries would probably remain even if perfect knowledge were miraculously to supervene.

Conclusion

It is not difficult to find convincing reasons why a major advance in agricultural productivity is a prerequisite of industrial growth. Only if resources can be spared from the task of ensuring an adequate supply of foodstuffs can a larger scale of industrial production be attempted. It may seem quaint that Adam Smith should have associated the prosperity of, say, Sheffield's industry with the efficiency of agriculture in the vicinity of the town, but his remark exemplifies the circumstances needed for industrial success in a pre-industrial age.[45]

England was singularly fortunate in this regard. Output per head in agriculture appears to have risen by at least three-quarters between the beginning of the seventeenth and the end of the eighteenth century. The annual gain in agricultural productivity per head was modest, about 0.3 per cent, yet it permitted a more rapid overall rate of population growth than that found in either France or Holland while simultaneously releasing into secondary and tertiary employment a far higher proportion of the active population than in any other European country. By 1800 little more than a third of the English labour force was engaged in agriculture at a time when it is improbable that the comparable figure elsewhere in Europe apart from The Netherlands was less than 55–60 per cent. In many countries it was substantially higher.[46]

The pace of English population growth in the early modern period was quite exceptional. Between the mid-sixteenth and the early nineteenth century her population grew by about 280 per cent. The population of other major European countries rose much less rapidly. Germany, France, The Netherlands, Spain and Italy all grew by between 50 and 80 per cent over the same period.[47] The demographic mechanisms by which the growth of England came about are now fairly well understood, but at one remove the

---

45 See note 26 above.

46 In Finland in 1754, 79 per cent of all economically active heads of family were engaged in agriculture, forestry or fishing: in 1805, 82 per cent. There are data for many European countries from about the middle of the nineteenth century. In the following list the percentages refer to the proportion of the total labour force (male and female) engaged in agriculture, forestry or fishing unless otherwise indicated: Belgium 1846, 51 per cent; Denmark 1850, 49 per cent (family heads); France 1856, 52 per cent; Ireland 1851, 48 per cent; The Netherlands 1849, 44 per cent; Spain 1860, 70 per cent (males only); Sweden 1860, 64 per cent; Great Britain 1851, 22 per cent. Mitchell, *European historical statistics*, table C1. Half a century earlier it is virtually certain that each of the comparable percentages would have been higher, sometimes substantially so.

47 See below, pp. 215–19.

problem of explaining the contrast remains.[48] In this connection it is important to pay heed to the probability that there was nothing unusual in the rate of growth of English *rural agricultural* population, unless it was that it grew so slowly, especially after 1600. The great bulk of the overall increase took place in that part of the population which made its living *outside* agriculture. This was what made England so distinctive.

In one sense an explanation of English agricultural improvement may be sought and perhaps found in the relatively rapid and uninterrupted growth in the urban sector of the English economy, well able to afford food but producing none itself. The extraordinary stimulus to development afforded by the growth of London, which in 1500 was not even one of the dozen largest cities in Europe but by 1700 was larger than any other, was probably the most important single factor in engendering agricultural improvement. The momentum first given by the growth of London was carried forward later by the more general urban growth of the later seventeenth and eighteenth centuries. It encouraged both change within agriculture *sensu stricto* and in a host of associated institutions and activities: transport improvement, credit facilities, capital markets, commercial exchange. The joint effect of rising productivity and increasing urbanization also fostered the great expansion in rural employment outside agriculture. The combination of a steadily rising volume of demand for goods and services other than food with a far more sophisticated market mechanism for exciting and satisfying such a demand was the basis of prosperity for the industries in the countryside.

Yet the reasons for the exceptional growth of London from the early sixteenth to the late seventeenth century remain imperfectly understood. Its rise both deserves and demands much more attention than it has received. Understanding of the phenomenon is likely to benefit especially from study of the connection between the development of the nation state under the Tudors and Stuarts and the growth of the capital city, and from considering London's fortunes within a wider framework of analysis of European commercial exchange, but the bulk of the task remains to be attempted.

Urban growth towards the end of the early modern period presents problems of interpretation no less difficult than those at its beginning. During the eighteenth century the urban hierarchy of England was turned upside down. The new industrial towns and port cities of the north and the midlands thrust their way past all rivals other than London. Only Bristol and Newcastle among the traditional regional centres matched the new challenge, and then only because they could benefit from the stimuli that had forced the pace of the growth in places like Liverpool and Sunderland. Many once-great centres were on the way to the pleasant obscurity of county rather than national fame: York, Exeter, Chester, Worcester, Salisbury.

Certainly the upsetting of the old urban hierarchy in England was at the time an event without recent precedent in European history. Elsewhere the

---

48 The secular changes in fertility and mortality which largely governed population growth rates in England are described in Wrigley and Schofield, *Population history of England*, chapter 7.

exact ranking of major cities in each country varied somewhat from time to time but it was very rare for tiny settlements to develop into major centres. The same lists of large urban centres may be found century after century slightly rearranged. Occasionally, one of the smaller centres made progress through the ranks. Atlantic and colonial trade brought Bordeaux and Nantes rapid advancement between 1500 and 1800, for example, but revolutionary changes were rare. The progress of the new centres in England was such, however, that not merely had Liverpool and Manchester outpaced all their English rivals other than London in 1800, but by 1850 they were the seventh and ninth largest cities in Europe, *and the largest anywhere in Europe other than those that were capital cities*,[49] an extraordinary tribute to their economic vitality unassisted by the employment in government, the professions and the arts associated with capital cities.

It is evident that the history of urban growth in England was quite distinctive. The contrast with the course of events elsewhere in Europe was especially notable between 1600 and 1750 since the paralysis which appears to have affected all but the largest towns on the continent was absent in England. The expansion of secondary employment in the countryside was not a bar to urban growth in England in the manner hypothesized by de Vries for Europe as a whole. In this there may be an important clue to the differences between England and her continental neighbours in real income levels or trends, in relative wage levels in town and country, in the terms of trade between the two, in urban institutions or in still other factors.

In this essay, however, I have been primarily concerned with the narrower topic of the scale and speed of urban growth and the indirect measurement of the gain in agricultural productivity per head, which probably roughly doubled in England between 1600 and 1800. By the standards of the recent past a doubling in agricultural productivity over a two-century span of time is not a startling achievement, but in terms of the pre-industrial world it is much more impressive and set England apart from the great bulk of continental Europe, conferring on her advantages denied to economies unable to release more than a tiny fraction of the labour force from work with the flock or plough.[50]

Measuring agricultural advance through urban growth, of course, falls well short of *explaining* either phenomenon. It is easy to see how these developments might reinforce one another, but the fact that similar cases were so rare, and that when they did occur they tended to lose momentum after a while, suggests that noting the logical possibility of such a link is only a first step towards understanding what took place. Perhaps the most

49 Chandler and Fox, *Urban growth*, p. 20. The first nine in order of size were London, Paris, Constantinople, Saint Petersburg, Berlin, Vienna, Liverpool, Naples and Manchester.

50 Grigg provides information about rates of growth in labour productivity in agriculture in Denmark, France, the United States and the United Kingdom in the late nineteenth and early twentieth centuries, and for all major subdivisions of the world since 1960. Grigg, *Dynamics of agricultural change*, tables 21 and 22, pp. 171–2. Rates as high as 5 per cent per annum have been commonplace in developed countries in recent years.

fundamental and intriguing question concerns the circumstances in which Ricardo's law of declining marginal returns to additional unit inputs of labour and capital may be circumvented in a land long fully settled. This law, if it had universal and invariable application, would prohibit a sustained development of the type which took place in England.

The population of England increased more than three-and-a-half times between the early sixteenth and the early nineteenth century without becoming dependent on food imports other than marginally. Some new land was taken into farming use, but the bulk of the increased output must have been obtained from land already in cultivation. Moreover, after 1600 there was little increase in the agricultural labour force. What served to neutralize the operation of declining marginal returns? The usual answer to this question is to point to innovation. If new methods of farming were introduced which significantly enhanced the productivity of labour and capital, then the operation of Ricardo's principle can be postponed, indefinitely if the flow of suitable innovations is sufficiently sustained. In a sense this must be the right answer but because it is inescapable it may be unilluminating, for though it may be logically necessary it was historically contingent. Relief from such a source was not always or even commonly forthcoming. Can anything be found in the circumstances of early modern England which provides an answer to the conundrum?

To attempt a full examination of this issue is beyond the scope of this essay, but one of its aspects may bear a slight elaboration by way of conclusion. There was a remarkably strong and regular positive relationship between the long-term rate of growth of population and the comparable rate of change in food prices in England throughout the early modern period down to 1800.[51] At first sight this suggests a uniform and inhibiting tension between population growth and the capacity to sustain rising numbers. But, although the tension was constant, it does not follow that all the demographic and economic variables involved stood in the same relationship to each other throughout. We have seen, for example, that there were major changes in national occupational structure and in agricultural productivity per head. The relationship between population growth and food prices may prove to be common to England and other countries, but the changing structure of the component variables was certainly not usually found elsewhere. The tension appears to have been beneficial and dynamic in England, when so often it was debilitating and severely inhibited growth.

---

51 Wrigley and Schofield, _Population history of England_, figure 10.2. The relationship between the rates of change of the two variables from the mid-sixteenth to the late eighteenth century was strikingly linear. This in itself may be suggestive. If there had been very tight constraints upon agricultural expansion, a curvilinear relationship might have been expected with a steeper rise in price than in population as conditions worsened. Its absence may reflect the existence of an unusual capacity to rise to the challenge of increased demand on the part of English agriculture, especially when it is remembered that the absolute rate of population growth was at times quite high, approaching 1 per cent per annum in the late sixteenth century and exceeding it in the late eighteenth. I owe this comment to Dr Schofield's reflections on the point.

Innovation may be the key to overcoming Ricardian constraints, but inasmuch as what happened in England was so rarely paralleled in other pre-industrial economies, it seems doubtful whether innovation could be counted upon to be forthcoming in response to need. When, as in England, events took a more favourable turn, it may be that the explanation is not to be found in the urgency of human need, nor in the immediate price dynamics of the market place, nor in the accident of individual inventiveness, but in the unusual structural characteristics of the prevailing situation.

If it were safe to assume that a community always exploited its knowledge of production methods to the full, it would follow that innovation meant the introduction of some element into the productive system which was previously unknown. On the other hand, if there are a range of other options capable of raising productivity which are held in reserve, so to speak, because current circumstances do not encourage or even allow of their use, the nature of the case is changed.[52] It may not be sufficient to look exclusively at changes in technology to explain a rise in productivity: new crops, altered cultivational practices, improved breeding techniques and so on; nor to turn to the gains in productivity per head arising from increasing specialization of function, the chief proximate cause of enhanced productivity in Adam Smith's analysis of the question. Other developments need to be taken into account if they encourage the exploitation of previously untapped potential and thereby transform living standards and growth prospects. It is in this context that the exceptional scale and speed of urban growth and its particular nature were probably so important.[53]

52 Some years ago Boserup made very effective use of one form of this argument, but her 'model' was one in which the changed methods of agriculture adopted to meet the challenge of rising population resulted in the broad maintenance of a given level of output per head per annum at the cost of a rise in the number of hours worked per annum. I have in mind changes which substantially increase labour productivity whether measured by the hour or by the year, though a part of the latter may be achieved because the workload becomes less markedly seasonal and therefore there are fewer periods during the year when labour is intermittent. Boserup, *Conditions of agricultural growth*, especially pp. 41–55.

53 Some further aspects of the gain in agricultural output per man and per acre are examined in chapter 5.

Part III
Population: Marriage and Reproduction

8
Fertility Strategy for the Individual and the Group

The demography of pre-industrial societies was a weighty factor in determining their welfare. It holds a special interest in the period immediately preceding the industrial revolution since the demographic posture of a society has an important bearing on its chances of breaking clear from the curbs upon sustained growth which gave pre-industrial economies some of their most distinctive features.[1] But every major aspect of pre-industrial demography was itself greatly influenced by social custom and economic circumstance so that there is difficulty in knowing how best to approach the set of relationships as a whole. In what follows I wish to examine briefly a limited number of issues to do with the effect of the size of a family upon the fortunes of its members, and more generally of the fertility levels on the fortunes of a community as a whole.

Unconscious rationality

The central issue might be called that of unconscious rationality. Ever since Darwin's day men have been intrigued by the presence of patterns of behaviour in animals which bring an apparent benefit to the species of which the individual members of the population are unaware. What is true of societies of animals may be true equally of societies of men.[2] Thus the proportions of land devoted to the several main food staples in parts of West Africa are sometimes close to the best possible mix of land use if the aim of the society were to guard itself most effectively against the danger that extremes of weather might result in starvation.[3] Trial and error may be presumed to have produced this by conferring advantages upon individuals or groups who lighted on good solutions, initially perhaps by chance. In much the same way the invisible hand working through competition in the

---

1 Wrigley, *Population and history*, chapter 4.
2 Wilkinson, *Poverty and progress*, chapter 3.
3 Gould, 'Man against his environment'.

market place is held to cause an optimal allocation of the community's resources in spite of the obtuseness of some or all the individuals concerned. Equally, it is reasonable to argue that practices such as infanticide, periods of abstinence from intercourse, conventions about the circumstances in which a couple may marry and begin a family, which may become accepted by a community for many different reasons, may survive and become rooted in the habits of the group because they serve to alleviate demographic pressures which would otherwise grow acute (and which may indeed have undermined rival groups with higher fertility). In places where high fertility was for any reason beneficial to the community, on the other hand, fertility fostering customs would have the greater value in the 'objective' circumstances of the groups in question.

Though the benefit derived from unconscious rationality is usually analysed in terms of the group, it is clear that it must influence individual behaviour if it is to operate at all. Very often, no doubt, it would be reinforced by a conscious rationality, too, as might be the case when a peasant contemplates how best to pass on his holding intact to the next generation without unfairness between his offspring. But equally the individual may be moved by traditional or religious considerations in, say, following a particular weaning custom, though the result may have important demographic results and a bearing upon the overall demographic balance of the community and may affect the interlocking of demographic, economic, social and other features of the society.

We may approach the essence of the problem more nearly by considering the general constraints within which any pre-industrial community had to work. Mean birth intervals of less than 24 months or average completed family sizes larger than 10 were very rare. Natural fertility among people, in other words, is very modest compared with that of most animals. In certain circumstances, indeed, the ceiling set by natural fertility[4] may be lower than the unavoidable minimum mortality, what might be called the basic mortality schedule. There have been many cities, for example, in which the conditions of life caused mortality rates to rise to levels at which without in-migration the population must have fallen. Equally, there were country areas, especially in low-lying marshlands, where population decline would also have been unavoidable but for the steady inflow of new residents. In the majority of pre-industrial communities, however, the level of natural fertility was such as to carry the danger that fertility might exceed the basic mortality schedule.

Neither natural fertility levels nor basic mortality schedules were the same in all communities, but the latter probably varied more than the former. The prevalence and virulence of local endemic diseases, the degree of

---

4 Natural fertility may be regarded as existing when the likelihood of a birth of rank x within a family is not directly influenced by the size of x; where, in other words, the number of children already born to a couple does not of itself affect the likelihood of a further birth. Natural fertility is thus quite compatible with a relatively low absolute level of fertility.

exposure to occasional attack from diseases which were not endemic, the annual and seasonal variations in food supply, and many other factors could all affect the basic mortality schedule (and to some extent the level of natural fertility also). In addition, mortality rates were strongly influenced by population density. Above certain levels of density the basic mortality schedule inevitably started to rise both because it tended to involve increasing difficulty in meeting food needs, and also because the risk of exposure to infectious disease appears to have been related to the density of the population. The effect of increasing density on fertility was less direct but there are several ways in which increasing density might, given the existence of an appropriate social mechanism, cause a fall in fertility (as when marriage is tied to acquiring a holding). Finally, both fertility and mortality rates in all communities were affected by a host of social customs.

Clearly, if the basic mortality schedule of a community is lower than its prevailing fertility and there is no significant socially induced mortality (through, say, war or infanticide), population will rise. Many writers of the late pre-industrial period interested in population matters, such as Adam Smith and Malthus, took the view that the normal propensity of populations was to rise unless checked by adverse circumstances. They also assumed that if a community's ability to produce expanded, population would tend to rise at least commensurately, though recognizing that the existence of conventional minima might prevent living standards falling to the lowest subsistence levels.

This is a more restrictive view than that which follows from the hypothesis of unconscious rationality since the latter may produce patterns of behaviour which ensure that the overall situation is stable and may even approach an optimum. The demonstration of the existence of such a situation, and particularly of its optimality, presents logical difficulties since it tends to be demonstrable only *ex post facto* by its power of survival, which carries dangers of circular argument. Nevertheless, it is useful to consider the question of what constituted 'rational' behaviour for the individual and the group in order to see whether this approach holds out any hope of improving our understanding of pre-industrial societies.

Heirship strategy

It is convenient to begin with what is sometimes called heirship strategy.[5] This is an interesting issue in its own right and will serve to introduce wider questions. The general problem lies in the fact (or prevalent assumption) that a man had to walk a delicate path between danger, on the one hand, that he might be without a male heir at his death and, on the other, that he might have difficulty in providing for several sons, each with a claim

---

5 See Goody, 'Strategies of heirship'; Wells, 'Demographic change'; Le Bras, 'Parents, grand-parents, bisaieux'; and Bourdieu, 'Célibat et condition paysanne'.

on his resources. Where dowries were substantial, daughters might create similar problems.

The simplest conceivable solution in a society whose resource base was static would be for each married couple to have one son and one daughter to survive and replace them. But such a solution is always unattainable. Some families have many children; others few or none. Some are depleted by death; others are luckier. Some men never marry; others marry several times. To discuss, therefore, the opportunities and handicaps produced by variations in family size can be instructive both when considered in relation to the individual family and to the larger community.

As a first step, let us consider the question of the likelihood that a man at his death will have a male heir to succeed him. In some societies this is of the greatest importance for religious reasons and because stress is laid upon the duty of maintaining the patriline, and even where such considerations are absent or of less importance, a man in possession of a holding may be anxious to have a son to succeed him.

If we make the simplifying assumption that the population in question is neither growing nor decreasing, an assumption likely to be approximately true for a substantial proportion of all pre-industrial societies, then the likelihood of having a male heir at death is little affected by the combination of fertility and mortality which produces stability in total numbers. Consider, for example, three possible situations. Each embodies assumptions which are oversimple but it is improbable that the results would be greatly modified if a more refined method of calculation had been used. I assume: (1) that the sex ratio at birth at all birth ranks is 100; (2) that the chances of any one child in a family dying are independent of the chances of death of all other children in the family; (3) that the chances of each child dying before the death of his or her father are the same without regard to the rank of the child in the family (in other words each child is treated as if it were born in the same year of life of the father rather than allowing for the fact that the births are distributed about the mean age of father at birth of child); (4) that the chances of any given child being male or female is uninfluenced by the sex of any earlier children in the family; (5) that the life table death rates for children of both sexes are the same; and (6) that every man marries.

Making use of the Princeton model life tables and appropriate assumptions about the average age of the father at the birth of the child, it seems reasonable to consider three possibilities of which the first and last are assumed to represent extremes for pre-industrial societies: (1) that a new-born child has a 1 in 3 chance of surviving to the death of his father; (2) that he has a 1 in 2 chance of surviving to the death of his father; and (3) that he has a 2 in 3 chance of surviving to the death of his father.[6]

The method used in calculating the likelihoods of each eventuality shown in tables 8.1–8.3 is explained in the appendix. It will be obvious that the relative frequencies of families of different sizes shown in the tables are

6 Coale and Demeny, *Regional model life tables*.

Table 8.1 Population 1: each child has a ⅔ chance of surviving until the death of the father

Family size	Frequency per 1000 families	No heir	At least one female, but no male heir	At least one male heir	Total number of children
0	100	100.0	0.0	0.0	0
1	200	66.7	66.7	66.7	200
2	200	22.2	66.6	111.2	400
3	150	5.6	38.9	105.6	450
4	110	1.3	20.4	88.3	440
5	85	0.3	10.9	73.8	425
6	60	0.1	5.2	54.8	360
7	40	—	2.3	37.6	280
8	25	—	1.0	24.0	200
9	20	—	0.5	19.5	180
12	10	—	0.1	9.9	120
Total	1000	196.2	212.6	591.4	3055

Table 8.2 Population 2: each child has a ½ chance of surviving until the death of the father

Family size	Frequency per 1000 families	No heir	At least one female, but no male heir	At least one male heir	Total number of children
0	85	85.0	0.0	0.0	0
1	125	62.5	31.3	31.3	125
2	125	31.3	39.1	54.6	250
3	125	15.6	37.1	72.3	375
4	125	7.9	31.8	85.4	500
5	125	3.9	25.8	95.4	625
6	90	1.4	14.6	74.0	540
7	75	0.6	9.5	65.0	525
8	60	0.2	5.8	54.0	480
9	40	0.1	2.9	37.0	360
12	25	—	0.8	24.2	300
Total	1000	208.5	198.7	593.2	4080

arbitrary sets of figures designed to produce an overall total of children born pet 1000 families sufficient to offset the mortality levels in each population. They show, however, a fair resemblance to the frequencies found in historical populations, rounded to simplify calculation. For the larger family sizes the probabilities involved are rather laborious to calculate, and therefore, in this illustrative exercise, I have considered family sizes 0 to 9, but above this size have considered only the case of the 12 child family. In a more elaborate and exact computer analysis the drastically simplified assumptions used in this essay could easily be relaxed and a wider range of possibilities examined.[7]

7 See Smith, 'Families and their property', pp. 38–62.

Table 8.3   Population 3: each child has a ⅓ chance of surviving until the death of the father

Family size	Frequency per 1000 families	No heir	At least one female, but no male heir	At least one male heir	Total number of children
0	70	70.0	0.0	0.0	0
1	70	46.7	11.7	11.6	70
2	70	31.1	17.5	21.4	140
3	70	20.7	19.7	29.5	210
4	70	13.9	20.0	36.2	280
5	70	9.2	19.1	41.7	350
6	70	6.2	17.3	46.6	420
7	70	4.1	15.5	50.4	490
8	70	2.7	13.6	53.7	560
9	280	7.3	47.0	225.7	2520
12	90	0.6	9.4	80.0	1080
Total	1000	212.5	190.8	596.8	6120

As might be expected intuitively tables 8.1–8.3 show a striking stability in the proportions of families with no heir, a female heir or heirs only, and at least one male heir, in the proportions roughly 2, 2 and 6. Thus it is immediately apparent how difficult it is likely to have been for a family to maintain a direct patriline over any considerable number of generations. The obverse of this coin is the comparative wealth of opportunity for younger sons, for what appears as a difficulty to one man who is heirless at his death or has only surviving daughters represents an opportunity for another man frustrated by the existence of a brother from obtaining access to the main holding of his own family.

The timing of marriage

Some of the assumptions used in this exercise must be examined further. For example, I have proceeded as if the expectation of life of the father at his mean age at birth of the child were not only the period of time over which a birth cohort is depleted by the stated fraction, but also the mean age of male marriage. The first point is obvious and the second should also be approximately true since, if men in the cohort of sons have already been married for some time on average when members of the older generation die, the number of marriages in the younger generation will be larger than in the older and, given the same distribution of family sizes, this will result in an increasing population. If the average age at marriage is higher than the expectation of life of the father at the mean age at birth of the child, the opposite will be the case.

It is instructive to examine the circumstances in which these assumptions are viable. Table 8.4 helps to elucidate the matter. The implicit assumption about age at marriage may be illustrated by considering population 2 (table 8.2)

Table 8.4   Expectation of life (male model West)

Age		Expectation of life	Percentage dying by
Level 1	0	18.0	0.0
	25	24.1	67.6
	30	21.6	71.0
	35	19.2	74.4
Level 6	0	30.0	0.0
	25	30.0	48.9
	30	27.0	52.3
	35	24.0	55.9
Level 12	0	44.5	0.0
	25	36.6	30.0
	30	33.0	32.7
	35	29.3	35.6
Level 15	0	51.8	0.0
	25	39.6	21.4
	30	35.7	23.6
	35	31.7	25.9

in conjunction with the level 6 expectation of life figures in table 8.4. If we assume a mean age of father at birth of child of about 31 years, his expectation of life will then be about 26 years. Since a birth cohort is depleted by one-half over a period of a little more than 26 years in level 6, the pieces fit together neatly. The interval between age at marriage and mean age at birth of child is plausible, bearing in mind that in population 2 each family has an average of four children. From level 6 to, say, level 12 the same basic relationships can be preserved, provided that, as expectation of life improves, a higher mean age at marriage is accepted. For example, at level 12 expectation of life at age 35 is about 29 years. If this were also the mean age of first marriage, about 32 per cent, or nearly one-third, of the initial birth cohort would have disappeared, and this conforms quite closely to the requirements of population 1 (table 8.1).

The range of mortality rates represented by levels 6 to 12 (expectations of life at birth between 30 and 45) fits the experience of a large proportion of early modern western European populations. Given that late marriage was normal,[8] the rule that each couple on marriage should establish themselves in a separate household could easily be maintained if there was a rough coincidence between the death of a generation of fathers and the marriage of a generation of sons. And given such a rule, mortality, fertility and marriage age could fluctuate in relation to each other in such a way as to keep a homeostatic balance in the demography of the community. If mortality improved, marriage was automatically delayed for the average son, but since a higher proportion of each generation reached the later marriage age, a lower average size of family was sufficient to maintain the population. And delay in marriage for men, if paralleled by a similar

8 Hajnal, 'European marriage patterns'.

postponement among women, would reduce fertility by approximately the required amount without additional regulation of fertility within marriage.[9] In practice, the behaviour of populations was far more complex and other variables, such as the proportion of the population never marrying, were at times of great importance, but the *possibility* of homeostatic regulation of numbers in this way is worth noting.

Mortality levels outside the range just considered produce greater problems in the context of the assumptions made earlier. Take, for example, population 3 (table 8.3) and level 1 of the model West life tables. Level 1 incorporates extremely severe mortality rates and an expectation of life at birth of only 18 years. Yet it still appears possible at first blush to maintain the implicit assumptions of population 3 (table 8.3). At age 30 for example, male expectation of life is 21.6 years, and about 65 per cent, or two-thirds, of each birth cohort have died by age 21.6. And a mean age at first marriage of 21.6 is consistent with an average age at birth of child of 30 years since family sizes in population 3 (table 8.3) are large. But there is a serious difficulty. It lies in the extremely high fertility rates which it is necessary to attain to prevent a steady decline in numbers. That they are very demanding is evident from the family size distribution of population 3 (table 8.3). Men and women even in the prime of life are subject to heavy mortality (more than a third of those living at 20 have died by the age of 40) which reduces the likelihood of having a large family. Moreover, there is very little 'play' in the system. Although the mean expectation of life of the father at birth of the child is so low, the use of a mean tends to conceal the fact that some fathers will live much longer than the average and others much less. In communities with a relatively late average age at marriage the two offset each other more effectively than in a high mortality community with early marriage, for in the former sons whose fathers die relatively young are more likely than in the latter to have reached maturity. This is so because expectation of life at mean age at birth of son is only just over 20 years in population 3 (table 8.3), whereas in population 1 (table 8.1) it is almost 30 years. The relatively early death of a father in a community with the characteristics of population 3 (table 8.3), therefore, is more likely to find his sons too young to marry. They cannot marry until they are, say, 16 while those whose fathers live relatively long will still have to wait to marry. A very early mean age at first marriage is unattainable in these circumstances.

Yet early marriage is a necessity where mortality rates are very high if families are to be sufficiently large on average to prevent a fall in population. A community in these circumstances will need to develop marriage rules which ensure that men (and still more women) marry soon after reaching sexual maturity, regardless of whether their parents are living or not. Population 3 (table 8.3) is so placed that it is almost inevitable that many men will marry before their fathers' deaths. This in turn means that many

9 Ohlin, 'Mortality, marriage and growth'.

men will, in the course of their life cycle, spend a few years soon after marriage in the household of their parents or parents-in-law. To have a rule that every couple should start married life in a house of their own would imply maintaining a stock of housing substantially larger than is necessary if spending some time in an extended family household is regarded as acceptable.

Low mortality rates, of course, produce the opposite type of difficulty, that of 'losing' fertility. Consider level 15 in table 8.4. Almost three-quarters of each birth cohort reach the age of 35 so that fertility must be modest if population growth is not to occur. Early marriage in such a population in any regime of natural fertility would mean rapid population growth, and early marriage is also inconsistent with the assumption that mean age at marriage and expectation of life of father at birth of child should be the same. The underlying assumptions used in constructing tables 8.1–8.3 can still be preserved if a mean age at marriage as late as about 31 or 32 is acceptable and provided that marital fertility is at a fairly low level. Indeed, the assumptions can be preserved at even lower mortality levels, but this will imply still higher marriage ages (or a rising proportion of men never marrying).[10] Control of fertility within marriage can solve or alleviate the problem of excessive fertility where men marry young and this alternative to late marriage will be likely to prove increasingly tempting in populations in which expectation of life has risen substantially. Most such populations are relatively wealthy and can afford the extra cost of maintaining a stock of housing large enough to enable them to do without extended family households in the period of overlap between the marriage of sons and the death of fathers.

At both extremes, therefore, sons are likely to marry before their fathers' deaths, though in the one case the reason, so far as fertility is concerned, lies in the importance of maximizing it, whereas in the other, the practice is possible over any extended period of time only because fertility can be controlled within marriage. In between there is a wide band of mortality levels where some association between the death of a father and the marriage of a son is quite a 'rational' custom. There is no reason why the marriage of a young man should be linked to the death of *his* father. The death of any father without surviving sons (which tables 8.1–8.3 suggest will happen in about four cases in ten) may create a marriage opportunity for all unmarried young men or for some class among them depending on the marriage rules of the community in question. Where a general pool of opportunities is created by the death of men without male heirs it is easy to appreciate the attraction of customs like Borough English (ultimogeniture), particularly where mortality is relatively low,[11] since older sons are likely

10 Post-famine Ireland, combining late marriage with high permanent celibacy (and much emigration), is a good illustration of this possibility.

11 For example, I assumed earlier in discussing model West level 12 mortality and population 1 that the expectation of life of a father at mean age at birth of child was 29 years. His eldest son would normally be several years older than this.

to be well on into manhood at the time of a father's death and there will be earlier opportunities of marriage for them to take up.

In what way is the symmetry between 'surplus' sons and vacant niches, apparent in stationary populations considered as a whole, reflected in the best presumptive strategy for individual families? To keep the discussion of a very complex question within bounds, I shall continue to concentrate largely on the problem of securing a reasonable certainty of a male heir while avoiding the danger of being burdened with too many sons who might cause the subdivision or overloading of the holding.

Family formation

It is easy to overlook a simple but vital preliminary point in discussing the strategy of individual families. Children are not born simultaneously but successively, except in the case of multiple births. Therefore it is misleading to argue, for example, that because (in a case like population 3) the chance of one son surviving until his father's death is only 1/3, the chance of having a son to succeed when two sons are born into the family is only 5/9.[12] This would be true only if the two were twins and the mortality of twins were like that of other children. In other cases when a second son is born either the first is still living or he has died. If the latter, the birth of the second only gives a 1/3 chance of a male heir. If the former, however, the matter is very different since the first son will by then be, say, four years old and will have survived the perils of early life. His chance of living until his father's death is now improved (about 64/100 even at level 1), and the combined chance of at least one son surviving is 75/100 at level 1. Within a year of the birth of the second son, assuming the survival of both sons, this chance improves to 84/100. The comparable figures at level 12 are 85/100 (for the first son when the second is born), 95/100 and 97/100.

In these circumstances it might seem that the 'rational' man might well pause before running the risk of having a third son whose arrival would not greatly improve his chance of a male heir, but would seriously increase the danger of having to provide for two or even three sons. For example, assuming the two earlier sons both to be living at the birth of a third, the chances of having two and three sons at death are 47/100 and 17/100 if mortality rates are those of level 1; while at level 12 the chances are 36/100 and 57/100, or a 93/100 chance of at least two surviving sons. Inasmuch as the provision of a dowry for daughters may also bring headaches for the thrifty and far-sighted, there is a parallel argument applicable to them.

The frequency distributions of completed families available from reconstitution studies show that there were a great many families in European pre-industrial village communities which had 'overinsured' against the failure

---

12 Since each has a 2/3 chance of dying before his father, the combined probability that both will die is $2/3 \times 2/3 = 4/9$, leaving a 5/9 chance that one or both will survive.

of male heirs. In most cases, it is true, the tabulated data do not deal conclusively with the issue since they show numbers ever born to a given marriage rather than the number living at a point in time, and very often they do not indicate sex combinations. More refined analysis of data of this type would be helpful in making it clear whether there is any tendency to arrest family formation when certain combinations of children *still living* are present in the family. However, the point of substance does not seem to be in much doubt. 'Over-insurance' was common. Consider, for example, the frequency distribution of family sizes given for population 2 (table 8.2). In it there are a total of 346.2 families per 1000 which have three or more sons.[13] This involves a significant danger of having to provide for more than one male heir combined with a minimal risk of having no surviving son. At level 6 in more than a third of these cases, or in about one family in eight overall, two sons will have been still living when the third was born and, of these cases in turn the chances of having two and three sons surviving to the death of the father are 47/100 and 37/100, a combined chance of 84/100. In addition, of course, many families had exactly two sons (207.2 per 1000 families). In a quarter of these cases both sons would survive the father. In population 2 as a whole the proportion of fathers having at least two sons living at their death is 276 per 1000. Thus well over a quarter of all families in population 2 would have faced such difficulties as may have been involved in providing for more than one son at the father's death.

If it were true that having more than one son to provide for created serious difficulties, therefore, it would be hard to find evidence of 'rational' control of fertility in the frequency distribution of family sizes of population 2, itself broadly similar to that of many pre-industrial European populations. This is not direct evidence of lack of desire to do so, of course, since such a desire might have been frustrated only by lack of knowledge of effective technique, but at least existing data do not generally seem to support the view that couples acted to control family size for reasons of the sort discussed, or that the same effect was brought about indirectly by the operation of social customs.

But has the problem been well conceived? For we have already seen that the imbalance between resources and claims upon those resources which is presumed to exist if a man has many sons is not mirrored in the economy as a whole if the population is stationary. The existence of families with several sons is offset by the existence of families without heirs or with daughters but no sons.

Knowledge of opportunities outside the immediate family may work through many institutional forms. The apprenticeship of a son from a large family in the household and workshop of a craftsman who is himself without a son is one possible arrangement, found in many folk tales and fairy stories.

---

13 The same method used to calculate the characteristics of populations 1, 2 and 3, described in the appendix, can be extended to yield information about the frequency of particular combinations of sons or daughters.

In complex economies the balancing out process may be indirect and multiple but knowledge of its operation embodied in the conventional wisdom may relieve parents blessed with large families from serious worry about the prospects of their children later in life.

Often there were opportunities for 'surplus' sons close at hand. The averaging out of large and small families which produces a stationary population overall will also be reflected to some extent within any group of kin larger than the nuclear family. Within such a group some redistribution of sons between the producing units may provide either temporary or permanent solutions to the problems of families with many sons and daughters and also help those with few or none. Similarly, the institution of living-in service, based on locality rather than kinship may help to redistribute young people among the productive units in a manner which eases the burdens of fertile parents while at the same time tending to keep the marginal product of labour high.

Looked at in this light it would be reasonable to argue that in a pre-industrial population in which numbers were stationary there would normally be no possibility that a rational strategy of heirship would dictate limitation of fertility even when a man had several sons. Limitation of fertility would have entailed, *ceteris paribus*, leaving ecological niches untenanted. In the simple case where each man lives on a separate holding, it would have meant leaving some holdings unoccupied. If population pressure were high, this might bring benefits for a time since the average size of holding would then creep up, but only to the level which represented one man's ability to cultivate land. Beyond that point, further contraction in numbers would bring no benefit.

It may be objected that this is special pleading since a man with many children might be poor as a result of the size of his family whatever the overall position of the economy in which he lived. He would be better off with fewer children. This is a matter which would repay much further study, both empirical and by the building of models incorporating various assumptions about age of entry into the labour force, productivity with rising age, patterns of consumption, wage rates and employment opportunities. It may well be that, provided the population is stationary and not excessive, a large family brings net economic benefit while the children are at home and that the children's longer term prospects of establishing themselves in adult life are not significantly worse if they come from a large family. In any case, the community as a whole often needed 'surplus' sons so badly that widespread family limitation would have undermined it.

Once the assumption of a stationary population is abandoned, of course, there may be penalties for excessive fertility which would be absent in a stationary population. The problem might be resolved demographically either by delaying marriage, or by restricting fertility within marriage, or by a rise in the schedule of mortality of sufficient magnitude to prevent further population growth, or by any combination of these changes or their equivalents. It could also be met by increasing production to provide the necessary opportunities for the new generation entering the labour force in larger numbers. Thus parts of Belgian Flanders in the eighteenth century attempted to meet the problem of growing population by expanding rural industry, while much of France met a similar difficulty a little later by demographic restraint rather than economic expansion.

Social control and individual choice

When the demographic transition occurred it did not take the form of a move from a situation in which fertility was uncontrolled to one in which it was reduced by the exercise of prudential restraint. Fertility is under constraint in almost all societies, as the comparison of the levels of natural fertility in pre-industrial societies clearly shows. The key change was from a system of control through social institution and custom to one in which the private choice of individual couples played a major part in governing the fertility rate. It was a change of profound importance, but the change is not best characterized as a change from lack of control to control. Even though control was not through private choice, it could be very effective none the less. Whether private choice is likely to be a solution which a society may countenance will be greatly influenced by its basic mortality schedule. At, say, level 1 model West a population could hardly allow private choice since it must mobilize maximum fertility if it is to survive at all. At level 6 (where expectation of life for women is 32.5 years and for men 30 years) a gross reproduction rate (GRR) of about 2.00 is needed if the population is to replace itself. Given the certainty that there will be many small families (from the early death of parents and from infertility), and that some men and women in every generation do not marry, there must in this case also be a substantial number of families of large size if population decline is to be avoided (in population 2 there are 290 in 1000 families with six or more children, even though it is assumed that everyone marries). A society in which death rates were at this level for reasons outside its control (that is, from the presence of endemic disease for which no effective treatment was known, and the effects of periodic failure in food supply) would run into great difficulties if any significant proportion of the population was so moved by concern for solving its immediate problems of heirship that it kept family sizes down to a level that appeared rational in the context of the immediate nuclear family. Its numbers would fall and it might well be replaced by a population which was not so inhibited. Within any given pre-industrial population of this type, of course, there might be certain socioeconomic or other groups which could practice family limitation to alleviate concern about provision for the next generation, without endangering the society as a whole, provided that the groups were small enough to leave the overall pattern of family sizes little affected.

The Genevan bourgeoisie may have been a case in point,[14] and it would not be surprising if further study brings to light similar groups in other

14 Henry, *Anciennes familles genevoises*.

western European countries at that time. Particular individuals scattered through a community might do the same without seriously affecting overall fertility. Indeed, in both cases, provided the phenomenon is not widespread, it is also in a sense self-correcting in that a high proportion of the members of the next generation will come from large families and will not have the small family system deeply implanted in their habits of life.

Since there were very many pre-industrial communities in which it is reasonable to believe that the basic mortality schedule was at least as unfavourable as level 6, it follows that there were also a large number in which what constituted the best fertility strategy for society as a whole must have prevailed over any strategy of heirship which seemed to promise benefits for individual families that restricted their fertility. Where mortality rates were substantially lower than this, however, say at level 12, the GRR necessary to ensure that numbers are maintained is more modest (about 1.45 at level 12) and the higher end of the frequency distribution of family sizes can be curtailed fairly drastically without running the risk of population decline. Expectation of life is now about 45, still not a high figure compared with the present day, though higher than in most pre-industrial communities. Such a figure appears to have been reached, however, in parts of western Europe by the eighteenth century (and even earlier in certain parishes like Colyton, Devon, which experienced comparatively low life-table death rates even in Elizabethan times),[15] and was widespread in parts of North America, such as New England, from the earliest period of settlement.

In communities such as these population will grow quite rapidly given natural fertility within marriage unless nuptiality is very low. As long as this presents few difficulties to the society in question, because economic opportunity is expanding equally fast, there is no strong stimulus to adopt a new fertility regime, but where this is not the case failure to change will bring penalties with it. For society as a whole, the problem is the familiar one that population is growing faster than productive capacity. Stability can be achieved once more only at the cost of mortality rising to match fertility. For the individual family the problem presents itself differently. Since population is rising, there will be a fall in the proportion of men dying without heirs or without male heirs. More men will have sons standing by them at their death beds and many more will have several sons rather than one to provide for. Therefore fathers in families with several living sons will face greater difficulties than in the past in assuring their future for them. The best strategy for heirs changes. There is new point to any strand in peasant wisdom about the advantage of avoiding too many sons.

The change in the outlook for 'surplus' sons can be violent when mortality improves substantially but fertility remains unchanged. In population 2 317 men in every 1000 have one son living at death, and 276 have two or more living sons. These include 427 'surplus' sons left after assuming that provision can be made for one son by each father. To set

15 Wrigley, 'Mortality in pre-industrial England'.

against this there are 407 'vacancies' created by men dying without heirs or with female heirs only. This balance between men and opportunities is implicit in the absence of growth in the population.[16]

If, however, the mortality of population 2 (table 8.2) is combined with the fertility of population 3 (table 8.3), implying a rate of growth of population of about 1 per cent per annum, there is a marked change. In this case 298 in every 1000 men have one living son at death, 384 have two or more living sons, including a total of 677 'surplus' sons, but now there are only 318 'vacancies', while if the mortality of population 1 is combined with the fertility of population 3, implying a rate of growth of population of about 3 per cent per annum, the corresponding figures are 244 (one son living), 564 (two or more sons living), 1242 ('surplus' sons) and 212 ('vacancies'). The last of these is an extreme case, though close to the situation in many developing countries today, but the second case, where the ratio of 'surplus' sons to 'vacancies' is more than two to one, was approached more and more frequently in early modern Europe. Elizabethan England saw something of this and most of Europe moved toward it in the eighteenth century. It makes for a fluid and unstable society, and demands a rapid and sustained growth in the economy if the younger generation is to find employment and to enjoy a standard of living equal to that of their fathers. In this new situation lower fertility within marriage may bring benefit both to the individual and to the community as a whole.

In 1700 there was near uniformity in Europe in maintaining natural fertility within marriage (which is not synonymous, of course, with high fertility). By 1900 there was near uniformity in converging towards the new system of private control of marital fertility, exercised in such a way that the frequency of large families fell away to negligible proportions. In between there was great variety of behaviour and trend. From late in the eighteenth century France made steady progress towards the new system which was already widely present in the regional populations of Normandy and the south-west early in the nineteenth century. In some of the new industrial areas of England and Germany, on the other hand, fertility in marriage remained high or increased, while with the transformation of society in these areas obstacles to early marriage were often much reduced, causing a rise in general fertility rates. But fertility began to fall generally in the late nineteenth century. In some measure, no doubt, the steady rise of average real incomes in the later decades of the nineteenth century and the early part of the twentieth was facilitated by the missing millions who would otherwise have pressed into the labour market.

A rational fertility strategy is much harder to define in an industrial than a pre-industrial society since the ability to expand economic production at exponential rates of growth over a long period removes one of the most

16 The small difference of 20 between 'surplus' sons and 'vacancies' is due to the nature of the fertility assumptions of population 2 (table 3.2) which result in generation $x + 1$ standing to generation x as 2040 to 2000, and of this surplus one-half is male.

significant restrictive features of the older situation. Thus at the societal level it may be a matter of less moment than in pre-industrial times to avoid population growth, at least until concern for the environment becomes a major issue. On the other hand, the individual family is relieved of whatever societal pressures are exerted in favour of natural fertility during periods of high basic mortality. Individual choice can operate freely without serious penalty and, in time, in all populations so placed, the large family has been abandoned by the great majority of couples. Perhaps in seeking an explanation for the comparative simultaneity of fertility change across much of Europe in the later nineteenth century, one should have more regard to the independent importance of falls in mortality[17] in creating a situation in which change could occur and less to measures of economic modernity: urbanization, industrialization, literacy and the like.

How far it is sensible to write of unconscious rationality exercised by individuals following the norms set for them by the society in which they live, and to contrast it with a conscious rationality characteristic of couples in industrial societies where family limitation is widespread is debatable. If the notions have value it may be more in defining polar alternatives than as descriptions of particular situations. Men's actions at all times are influenced by their appreciation of their personal interests and by their response to social norms. Nevertheless, it is interesting to examine strategies of family formation as if couples behaved in conformity with these stereotypes of thought and action. In particular, it is illuminating to try to define those demographic circumstances in which it will cease to be a matter of small consequence how large a family grows. There is a crossover point to one side of which for society as a whole, and perhaps in most cases for the individual, too, high fertility cannot bring insuperable problems because the ranks of the older generation are thinning fast enough to satisfy the needs of the younger. On the other side of this point, excess fertility ceases to be a remote problem and begins to create challenges to which some response must be made. Sometimes the challenge was met only by accepting higher mortality and reduced living standards; sometimes by economic or social changes which restored the lost balance between population and production. In Europe in the eighteenth and nineteenth centuries there was a more fundamental change – the industrial revolution – which permanently altered the terms of the problem and in so doing made possible new demographic structures within society.

17 A fall in infant mortality has received much attention as the 'trigger' which is alleged to have set off control of fertility in marriage, but the balance between 'surplus' sons and 'vacancies' is also greatly influenced by mortality in childhood and youth. This deserves equal attention. Much of the argument based on changes in infant mortality has neglected the point made earlier in this chapter about the implications of the fact that births in a family take place successively rather than simultaneously.

Appendix

The method by which the characteristics of populations 1–3 (tables 8.1, 8.2, 8.3) were derived may be illustrated by considering a single case, where five children are born to a married couple and each child has a 1/2 chance of surviving until the death of the father. There are six possible combinations of the sexes of the children in a family of five: 5 females, 4 females and 1 male, 3 females and 2 males, 2 females and 3 males, 1 female and 4 males, and 5 males. The frequency with which each combination will occur can be determined by binomial expansion

$$P(r) = \binom{N}{r} p^r q^{N-r}$$

(in this exercise I have assumed that the sex ratio at birth is 100).

Suppose that we are interested in establishing the likelihood that at least one female but no male heir will survive at the death of the father. This may be calculated for each sex combination and multiplied by the frequency with which that combination occurs. For example, if 2 female and 3 male children were born, the likelihood that at least 1 daughter will still be living at her father's death is 3/4, while the likelihood that all 3 sons will have died is 1/8, and the combined likelihood is 3/32. The likelihood of having 2 female and 3 male children in families of 5 children is 10/32 by binomial expansion. And therefore the overall likelihood of there being at least 1 female

Sex combination of children (A)	Probability of this combination occurring (B)	Probability of this combination resulting in at least one female heir but no male heir at father's death (C)	(B) × (C) (D)
5F 0M	1/32	31/32	31/1024
4F 1M	5/32	15/32	75/1024
3F 2M	10/32	7/32	70/1024
2F 3M	10/32	3/32	30/1024
1F 4M	5/32	1/32	5/1024
0F 5M	1/32	—	—
			211/1024

but no male heirs in families of 5 where 2 of the children are girls and 3 are boys is $3/32 \times 10/32 = 30/1024$. Similar calculations for each possible type of 5 child family are shown in the table above.

It will be seen from the total figure at the foot of column D that the overall probability in 5 children families of having a female but no male heir is 20.6 per cent. When the relative frequency of families of different sizes has been determined, this base figure can be adjusted accordingly. Thus in table 8.2 the cell in the row for family size 5 which expresses the probability of at least 1 female but no male heir contains the figure 25.8 $[125 \times (20.6/100)]$.

Parallel calculations are made for each possible family size and then an overall probability for each eventuality may be determined for the population as a whole.

The likelihood of, say, leaving 2 or more male heirs can be calculated similarly, and the statistics of this and other comparable eventualities were derived in the same way.

9

The Growth of Population in Eighteenth-century England: a Conundrum Resolved

England and the continent

England is a small country on the periphery of Europe. Her area is 50 333 square miles, which may be compared with 212 209 square miles in the case of France, the largest European country other than Russia. Germany, Italy and Spain are all also much larger, with areas of 137 602, 116 290 and 194 833 square miles respectively.[1] Or, to express the point slightly differently, if western Europe is taken to comprise Italy, the Iberian peninsula, France, Switzerland, Austria, Germany, the Low Countries and the British Isles, then England represents only 5.6 per cent of the land surface in question.

At the end of the middle ages England had a population which broadly matched her relative area. In 1550 her population was 3 millions: at that date the French total was about 17 million. The population of western Europe as a whole is unknown but it would be reasonable to guess that it was about 61 million. Only about 4.9 per cent of the population of western Europe in 1550, therefore, lived in England; and Germany, Italy and Spain as well as France were all much more populous than England. In 1550 France was five or six times as populous, Germany and Italy each four times, and Spain three times as populous.[2] By 1900, in contrast, England had become one of four countries which formed a leading group in western Europe in terms of population size. Her population had grown to number 30.5 million, still somewhat smaller than that of Germany (43.6 million) and France (38.5 million), but close to equality with Italy (32.5 million) and substantially ahead

1 The areas quoted are those of today. In the case of Germany the area is the sum of the Federal Republic and the German Democratic Republic. In earlier times, of course, the areas in some cases were substantially different.

2 For sources, see table 9.1 below. Western Europe was taken to comprise the countries listed in the text above.

Table 9.1   Estimated population totals and percentage growth rates

	Population totals (millions)			
	1550	*1680*	*1820*	*1900*
England	3.0	4.9	11.5	30.5
France	17.0	21.9	30.5	38.5
The Netherlands	1.2	1.9	2.0	5.1
Spain	9.0	8.5	14.0	18.6
Italy	11.0	12.0	18.4	32.5
Germany	12.0	12.0	18.1	43.6
Western Europe	61.1	71.9	116.5	201.4

	Percentage growth rates		
	1550-1680	*1680-1820*	*1820-1900*
England	64	133	166
France	29	39	26
The Netherlands	58	8	149
Spain	−6	64	33
Italy	9	53	77
Germany	0	51	142
Western Europe	18	62	73

The totals shown become progressively more accurate. Some of those for 1550 and 1680 are subject to very wide margins of error. In many cases the figures used are based on estimates for dates close to the year heading each column rather than for the year itself. For a list of countries included in western Europe, see note 2 above. The estimates refer to the present territories of the countries shown. The English data exclude Wales and Monmouth.
Sources: For 1820 and 1900 all totals are taken from or estimated from Mitchell, *European historical statistics*, table B1, except for England in 1820. Otherwise the most important sources used were the following: Wrigley and Schofield, *Population history of England*, table 7.8; Mitchell and Deane, *British historical statistics*, chapter 1, tables 2, 7; Reinhard et al., *Histoire générale de la population mondiale*; Dupâquier, *La population française*. McEvedy and Jones, *Atlas of world population history*; Flinn, *Scottish population history*; Cipolla, 'Italian demographic development'; Connell, 'Land and population in Ireland'; Faber et al., 'Population changes and economic developments in the Netherlands'.

of Spain (18.6 million).[3] England now contained about 15.1 per cent of the total population of western Europe, and the density of population in England exceeded that of any other of the west European countries not excepting Holland and Belgium.

The distinctiveness of English population history is further clarified by the data of table 9.1 and figures 9.1 and 9.2. English growth rates were much higher than those of western Europe as a whole in each of the three periods shown in the bottom panel of table 9.1, and higher also than those of the individual countries shown. But in the first period The Netherlands was growing at virtually the same pace, and in the third period both The

3 For sources, see table 9.1 above. The figure for Germany within its present boundaries was obtained by taking advantage of the fact that Mitchell provides data for the new and old areas of Germany at both occasions when large territories were lost in the wake of the two world wars. The ratios in question are 0.90027 and 0.86011. The 1900 population total for the German Empire (56.4 million) multiplied by the product of the two ratios gives the total quoted here.

Netherlands and Germany almost matched England. In the second period, the 'long' eighteenth century, the English growth rate was much the highest. Figures 9.1 and 9.2 give visual expression to the exceptional nature of English growth. Figure 9.1 shows the gradual elimination of the wide gap which once separated England from the original 'big four', France, Germany, Italy and Spain. Figure 9.2, by indexing the population of each country on its total in 1820, gives a particularly vivid impression of the scale of the difference between England and other countries over the early modern period. Many of the population estimates used are subject to wide margins of error at the two earliest dates but it is highly improbable that exact information would significantly modify the contrast apparent in figure 9.2. (It should be noted, of course, that one of the impressions suggested by the figures, that populations experienced steady growth rates between the dates shown, is very misleading: in the earlier periods especially there were wide variations in the growth rates.)[4]

The contrast has intriguing implications. For example, if output per head were invariant in all countries it would imply that the English economy was growing much more quickly than that of other European countries over the period 1550–1820 as a whole (the compound rate of growth of English population over the period was 0.5 per cent per annum compared with a figure for western Europe as a whole of 0.24 per cent). If there were good reason to suppose that output per head was growing more rapidly in England than elsewhere, the contrast in the rates of growth of national product would be even more striking than the contrast in population growth rates. Such topics are of the highest interest. In this article, however, the growth of population itself forms the chief focus of attention, and in particular the 'long' eighteenth century when the difference between English experience and that of other countries was so clear cut. In 1681 the population of England, at 4.93 million, was stationary following a period of a generation in which a combination of high mortality, heavy net emigration and moderate fertility had caused a decline of about 350 000 in the population total or 6.6 per cent. By the early decades of the nineteenth century, in contrast, population was growing faster than at any previous or subsequent period of English history and growth was faster in England than anywhere else in western Europe with the probable exception of Ireland. Between 1791 and 1831, English population rose from 7.74 to 13.28 million, at a rate of 1.36 per cent per annum, and in the peak decade 1811–21 the rate rose as high as 1.52 per cent per annum.[5]

---

4 While the contrast between England and other countries in continental western Europe is marked, it is probable that the rate of population growth in Ireland exceeded that in England between 1550 and 1800 and that Scotland came close to matching the English rate.

5 For English population totals, see Wrigley and Schofield, *Population history of England*, table 7.8, pp. 208–9.

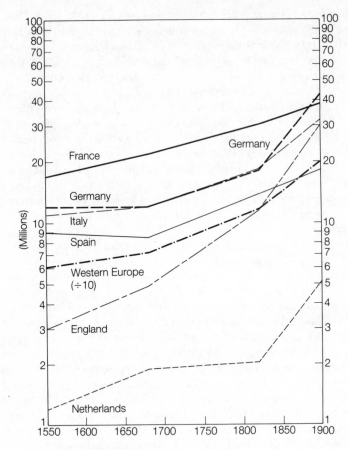

Figure 9.1 Population growth in western Europe, 1550-1900.
Sources: see source notes to table 9.1.

Changes in demographic variables

What caused such a remarkable surge in growth? The question may
conveniently be divided into two elements; the proximate causes of growth
and the wider context in which growth occurred. By proximate causes I mean
the changes in fertility and mortality which brought about growth; by the
wider context, the economic and social environment in which the
demographic changes occurred. It is in relation to the former that it seems
fair to claim that a conundrum has been resolved. This in turn gives a new
insight into the *explicandum* of the latter, though many uncertainties remain.

In the third quarter of the seventeenth century fertility and mortality in
England were roughly in balance. The crude birth rate in the period 1651–80
stood at 28.8 per 1000; the crude death rate at 28.6 per 1000. Or to use
more refined measures, the gross reproduction rate averaged 1.91 during

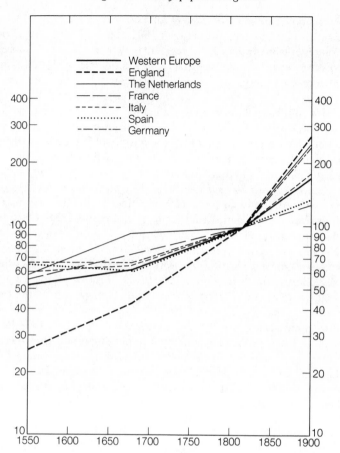

Figure 9.2 Proportionate population growth in western Europe (1820 = 100).
Sources: see source notes to table 9.1.

the 30-year period, while expectation of life at birth was 34.8 years.[6] The absolute fall in population during this period (the population in 1651 was 5.23 million; in 1681 4.93 million) was due to the high level of net emigration to the North American colonies and to Ireland. Indeed, with zero net migration the population would have risen very slightly by almost 40 000.[7] During the 'long' eighteenth century net emigration, though never

6 Annual crude birth and death rates are given in Wrigley and Schofield, *Population history of England*, table A3.3, pp. 531–5. Gross reproduction rates and expectations of life at birth in table A3.1, pp. 528–9. The quoted gross reproduction rates and expectations of life at birth represent the averages of six successive five-year periods centring on the years 1651, 1656 . . . 1676 and therefore strictly speaking refer to the period 1649–78.

7 The net migration figures needed, when combined with the national population totals, to make this calculation may be found in Wrigley and Schofield, *Population history of England*, table 7.14, p. 227.

absent, was not a major component of population change. Since the population rose by 133 per cent between 1681 and 1821, and the intrinsic growth rate increased from zero to more than 1.6 per cent per annum, it must necessarily have been the case that either mortality fell very substantially or fertility increased sharply, or both changes occurred but on a more modest scale.[8]

Discussion of this issue has been a dominant theme in English population history for many decades. That the issue can now be resolved is due to work carried out by the Cambridge Group for the History of Population and Social Structure over the past 15 years. The work involved the collection of a large body of data from over 400 parish registers. It also required the development of new methods of testing and rectifying the data and of converting the resulting estimated national totals of births and deaths into estimates of population size at quinquennial intervals from 1541 to 1871. Once these calculations had been made, it was a relatively straightforward matter to produce estimates of demographic measures such as gross reproduction rates or expectation of life at birth. The work has been described elsewhere,[9] however, and this affords me the luxury of concentrating on the particular substantive issue of the acceleration in population growth in the 'long' eighteenth century.

It is worth remarking at this juncture that contemporaries were largely ignorant of the extent of the population growth in train until Rickman carried out the first national census in 1801. Price in 1780 argued strongly for the view that there were fewer people living in England at that date than there had been at the time of the Glorious Revolution, claiming that the population had fallen by 'near a quarter' over the preceding century.[10] The balance of informed opinion at the time, represented by men such as Young, Eden and Wales, took the view that growth was taking place but there was no accurate knowledge of its extent or of the absolute size of the population.[11] Malthus, in the first edition of his *Essay on population*, writing three years before the taking of the first census in 1801, quoted a figure for the national population which proved in the event to be about 36 per cent too low.[12]

Rickman's work not only established how large the population was but provided data which enabled its pattern of growth since 1700 to be traced out with some confidence. The returns which he required from the overseers of the poor in each parish enabled the size of the population to be established,

---

8 The population in 1681 was 4.93 million; in 1821, 11.41 million. The average intrinsic growth rate in the five successive quinquennia centring on the years 1806, 1811 . . . 1826 was 1.67 per cent per annum, peaking in the quinquennium centring on 1821 at 1.76 per cent. Wrigley and Schofield, *Population history of England*, table A3.1, pp. 528–9.

9 Wrigley and Schofield, *Population history of England*.

10 Price, *Population of England*, p. 18.

11 Several of the most important essays by the leading protagonists are reproduced in Glass, *The population controversy*.

12 Malthus supposed the population of Britain to be 'about seven millions' in 1798. The 1801 census revealed that the true figure was 10.9 million. Malthus, *Essay on population* (1798), p. 23.

while the questions which he addressed to the minister of each parish yielded sufficient information about the totals of Anglican baptisms, burials and marriages at intervals during the century to make it clear that population had grown substantially between 1700 and 1800 and that the rate of growth had accelerated steadily after about 1740, having been relatively modest in the opening decades of the century. Only Cobbett thereafter possessed the self-confident obtuseness to deny the obvious, writing in 1822 after three censuses had been taken that 'I am quite convinced that the population, upon the whole, *has not increased in England one single soul since I was born*' (he was then 56 years old).[13]

Although the data published in the 1801 census established the fact of growth, they proved incapable of settling the question of how growth came about, whether because of falling mortality, rising fertility or some combination of the two. The successive efforts of those interested in the problem from the days of Rickman and Finlaison to those of Habakkuk, Ohlin, Krause, McKeown and Hollingsworth always foundered on two major problems, though there were also minor ones.[14] First, Rickman collected data about Anglican baptisms and burials, not about all births and deaths. Anglican coverage was never complete and it tended to become increasingly inadequate as the century wore on. Secondly, even if the coverage had been comprehensive and accurate there was no technique available for converting such information into reliable estimates of population totals or of fertility and mortality levels. This problem is especially taxing in any country where there is a substantial net migration flow since this prohibits the obvious expedient of calculating population totals stretching back from a known census by adding deaths and subtracting births occurring between the census and some earlier date for which a population total is to be estimated.

Rickman's data have been used by scholars possessing greater knowledge of demographic techniques than Rickman himself possessed, and their labours considerably increased knowledge of the extent of Anglican under-registration of vital events at various periods. Since different scholars took very different views of the scale and nature of the various uncertainties facing them, their calculations and debates also served the useful purpose of establishing the width of the spectrum of what was reasonably credible in respect of population size, growth rates and levels of mortality and fertility. Yet is is fair to say that the conundrum remained unresolved. At one extreme McKeown felt free to continue to argue that all or virtually all of the acceleration must have been due to mortality change, whereas Krause was confident that fertility had risen sharply towards the end of the eighteenth century and largely accounted for the more rapid rise in population taking

---

13 Cobbett, *Rural rides*, p. 67.

14 A description of earlier attempts to estimate English population trends in the eighteenth and early nineteenth centuries may be found in Wrigley and Schofield, *Population history of England*, pp. 142–52, and appendix 5.

place at the time.[15] There was unanimity about the fact of the acceleration, about its broad timing and its magnitude, but no matching agreement about its proximate cause. The more circumspect among modern scholars have tended to conclude that all Rickman-based work was built upon sand, like Flinn, or, like Glass, that the only hope of solving the conundrum lay in starting again from scratch and constructing a new data set from parish registers, rather than relying on the returns made to Rickman.[16]

Glass's view has been justified by events. A combination of newly collected parish register data and the development of a new method of analysis, termed back projection, has provided a wealth of new information and, in combination with results obtained by the slightly older technique of family reconstitution, has allowed the conundrum to be resolved.[17]

The essential changes can be described quite briefly. Expectation of life at birth, which averaged only 32.4 years in the 1670s and 1680s at the start of the 'long' eighteenth century, had risen to an average of 38.7 years in the 1810s and 1820s at its end. The increase was relatively smooth and unbroken from the early 1730s onwards. Before then the pattern was more irregular with a period of low mortality for a generation from about 1690 onwards, flanked on either side by less favourable periods. Those living in the early 1680s and the late 1720s in particular were afflicted by very severe mortality due to a succession of years in which death rates were high (1679–86 and 1727–31). Overall, therefore, expectation of life rose by about six years between the beginning and the end of the 'long' eighteenth century but the true gain is somewhat exaggerated by the periodization because the 1670s and 1680s included so many years of uncharacteristically high mortality.

15 There is a convenient summary of the views which McKeown has consistently propounded over two decades in McKeown, et al., 'The modern rise of population in Europe'. Krause believed that the birth rate rose sharply between the 1780s and 1810s but thereafter sank back to a significantly lower level, and also that fertility changes exerted a much greater influence on the growth rate than changes in mortality. Krause, 'English fertility and mortality', especially pp. 67–70.

16 'In spite of the extraordinary ingenuity of the many historians who have applied themselves to the Parish Register Abstracts material, the difficulties inherent in it only seem to become the more apparent with each successive onslaught. The P.R.A. material is coming now to be recognized as constituting an inadequate basis of study': Flinn, *British population growth*, p. 29. Glass remarked that 'any further serious attempt to investigate population growth during the eighteenth century on the basis of parish register material must break away from Rickman's series and begin with a new compilation': Glass, 'Introduction', p. 9.

17 The collection of the parish register data, their checking and amendment, and their conversion into estimates of national totals of births, deaths and marriages are described in Wrigley and Schofield, *Population history of England*, chapters 1–5. The later chapters of the book present new estimates of population totals and fertility and mortality trends derived from the data by back projection. The technique itself is briefly described on pp. 195–9, and in greater detail in appendix 15. Some reconstitution data are presented in the book and more are contained in an article with the same joint authorship, 'English population history from family reconstitution'. At a later date a volume containing detailed reconstitution material from about 20 parishes is planned.

Over the same period fertility, as measured by the gross reproduction rate, rose from 1.98 to 2.94. The rise was remarkably free from serious interruptions, though faster towards its ultimate peak in the 1810s than in the early decades of the period. In the first half of the eighteenth century, indeed, the trend was nearly flat though at a distinctly higher level than before 1700.[18]

Expectation of life at birth and the gross reproduction rate are 'pure' measures of mortality and fertility but less familiar than conventional crude birth and death rates. It may therefore be helpful to note also how these latter changed during the 'long' eighteenth century. The average crude birth rate rose from 30.7 to 39.6 between 1670–89 and 1810–29, while the crude death rate fell from 30.7 to 24.5 over the same period.[19] Clearly, the acceleration in the population growth rate owed something both to rising fertility and to falling mortality, but what was the relative importance of the two effects?

To answer this question, we may take advantage of the fact that knowledge of expectation of life and of the gross reproduction rate fixes within narrow limits the intrinsic growth rate which will be found in a particular population. The intrinsic growth rate of a population is the rate of growth which will ultimately characterize a population in which fertility and mortality are unchanging. It may differ significantly from the growth rate prevailing at a given time since this may be influenced in the short term by features of the age structure which will eventually disappear given constant fertility and mortality. Any change in fertility or mortality will, of course, affect the intrinsic growth rate. If both change, their relative contributions to any change in the intrinsic growth rate can be estimated.

The intrinsic growth rate in the 1670s and 1680s was very close to zero. Its exact level, expressed as an annual rate, was slightly negative, at − 0.0013. In the course of a century a population experiencing such an intrinsic growth rate would fall by about 12 per cent, a relatively modest change. In the 1810s and 1820s, in contrast, the rate was strongly positive, averaging 0.0167, a level sufficient to cause a population to rise by 424 per cent if maintained for a century.[20] Such was the magnitude of the change brought about by the combined effect of falling mortality and rising fertility. Which was the more important of the two? Since the effect of the changes in the gross reproduction rate and in expectation of life at birth on the intrinsic growth rate may each be calculated separately as well as jointly, an answer to the question is readily obtained. It shows that the fertility rise

18 The expectations of life at birth and gross reproduction rates quoted for the 1670s and 1680s and for the 1810s and 1820s are averages of four successive quinquennia in each case. The quinquennia are those centring on the years 1671, 1676, 1681 and 1686, and 1811, 1816, 1821 and 1826 and therefore cover the years 1669–88 and 1809–28. Wrigley and Schofield, *Population history of England*, table A3.1, pp. 528–9.

19 Ibid., table A3.3, pp. 531–5.

20 See note 18 above for details of the exact periods covered in calculating the intrinsic growth rates. The same note also gives the table from which the intrinsic growth rates were taken.

contributed about two-and-a-half times as much to the rise in growth rates as the mortality fall. Or to put it another way, if fertility had remained unchanged during the 'long' eighteenth century, but mortality had fallen in the manner just described, population instead of remaining stationary would have reached a rate of growth of about 0.5 per cent per annum. If, however, mortality had failed to improve but fertility had followed its historic course, the intrinsic growth rate would have risen from zero to about 1.25 per cent per annum.[21] The long-standing conundrum is resolved, and the answer goes against what has probably been the majority view of the matter during the lengthy debate since Rickman's day. Mortality did indeed improve but fertility accounted for the lion's share of the acceleration in population growth during the 'long' eighteenth century.

Though true, however, this statement about the dominant role of fertility may also be misleading. The great majority of all births in early modern England were borne by married women. If overall fertility rose, therefore, this could occur because marital fertility increased, that is because married women were bearing children at shorter intervals; or because nuptiality was higher, that is because women were entering marriage earlier in life or fewer were staying single all their lives; or because both marital fertility and nuptiality were rising. The relative share of marital fertility and nuptiality in producing an increase in overall fertility is also now capable of measurement, and the result is very clear cut. Marital fertility in the score of parishes which have been the subject of reconstitution studies shows no evidence of significant fluctuation throughout the parish register period (that is, from the sixteenth to the nineteenth centuries). Nuptiality, in contrast, varied substantially over time. The great acceleration in population growth during the 'long' eighteenth century was principally due to earlier and more universal marriage. Age at first marriage dropped by about three years from 26 to 23 years, while the proportion of women surviving throughout the child-bearing period who never married fell from a figure of perhaps 15 per cent at the beginning of the period to no more than half its initial level towards the end of the eighteenth century. It can be shown that these two linked changes in nuptiality, *ceteris paribus*, would serve to increase overall fertility by more than a third, and that this accounts for the bulk of the increase in the gross reproduction rate described earlier.[22] The principal cause of the dramatic surge of population growth in Georgian England, therefore, is to be found in the timing and incidence of marriage.

Some births in all periods, of course, take place outside marriage. Illegitimate births increased rapidly in the 'long' eighteenth century. They constituted only about 2 per cent of all births at its beginning but 6 per cent

21 Information concerning the measurement of the relative importance of fertility and mortality changes in altering intrinsic growth rates is fully set out in Wrigley and Schofield, *Population history of England*, pp. 236–48.

22 Age at marriage data are given in Wrigley and Schofield, *Population history of England*, table 7.26, p. 255, and proportions never marrying in table 7.28, p. 260. For a discussion of the extent of the impact of changing nuptiality on fertility, see pp. 265–9.

at its end.[23] In a formal sense illegitimate fertility and marriage are distinct phenomena, but trends in nuptiality and in illegitimate fertility were very closely interwoven in early modern England, and the increase in illegitimate fertility taking place in the eighteenth century, which accounted for that element in the overall increase in fertility not attributable directly to increased nuptiality, is best understood as a further aspect of nuptiality broadly interpreted.[24]

It might seem reasonable to expect that if what Malthus termed 'the passion between the sexes'[25] were indeed a constant, as he supposed, illegitimate births would be relatively common when marriage was long delayed but less frequent in an era of early and universal marriage. Such an expectation was justified by the course of history in some times and places. It accords well with French experience in the eighteenth century, for example, but in England matters fell out otherwise. The very low level of illegitimacy which obtained in the late seventeenth century coincided with late marriage and frequent celibacy, yet as the stock of unmarried women shrank steadily to reach a far lower level a century later, the illegitimacy ratio tripled, and it is clear that the illegitimacy rate must have increased much more sharply.[26] At the start of the 'long' eighteenth century, fewer than a tenth of all first births were illegitimate; before its end the proportion had risen to a quarter and a further quarter of all first births were prenuptially conceived. The sympathetic movements in nuptiality and illegitimate fertility which were so striking a feature of the 'long' eighteenth century, and which meant that legitimate and illegitimate fertility moved in parallel, were a feature of English population history over a much longer period of time. The phenomenon might fairly be described as a structural feature of the English demographic system. It is perhaps best interpreted as evidence of the strength and coherence of what might be termed the control system visible in English population behaviour over several centuries. When nuptiality was low and legitimate fertility therefore heavily constrained, the efficiency of the check upon growth which this represented was not undermined by a large transfer of fertility from within marriage to outside it. On the other hand, when nuptiality was high and most women entered marriage early in life the degree to which the potential fertility of the population was impeded

---

23 Laslett, *Family life and illicit love*, chapter 3, 'Long-term trends in bastardy in England'.

24 A slightly different calculation from that used here suggests that of the overall rise in the intrinsic growth rate attributable to fertility which took place in England during the 'long' eighteenth century, 52 per cent is due to the fall in age at first marriage of women, 26 per cent to the decline in proportions never marrying, 15 per cent to the increase in illegitimacy and 7 per cent to the fall in the mean age at maternity brought about by earlier marriage. Wrigley and Schofield, *Population history of England*, table 7.29, p. 267.

25 The phrase occurs in Malthus, *Essay on population* (1798), p. 11.

26 The illegitimacy ratio expresses births out of wedlock as a proportion of all births occurring. The illegitimacy rate relates the number of illegitimate births to the number of unmarried women in the fertile age groups. If the former increases at a time when fewer and fewer women were remaining unmarried among those of child-bearing age, it must be the case that the rate rises faster than the ratio.

by delay or avoidance of marriage was in any case relatively slight, and checks on fertility outside marriage would have been otiose.[27]

Thus marriage now emerges holding the centre of the stage. It has long been known that nuptiality in the short term was subject to wide variations responding above all to the fluctuating fortunes of the harvest but affected also by other influences such as epidemic mortality. And it has also been known since the pioneering work of Hajnal and Laslett that women married later in life in western Europe than in other major cultural areas and that a significant minority never married.[28] The social customs, residential rules and economic circumstances which were the correlates of late marriage have all received attention, and their operation is much more fully understood than was the case a generation ago. But it is new knowledge that there were substantial secular changes in nuptiality sustained over long periods of time and that they were of a magnitude to cause wide swings in overall fertility and in the rate of population growth.

Contemporaries knew little of this though it shaped their destiny so powerfully. Boswell reports Dr Johnson's view of these matters. Russia had been mentioned as likely to become a great empire because of its rapid population growth:

Johnson: Why, Sir, I see no prospect of their propagating more. They can have no more children than they can get. I know of no way to make them breed more than they do. It is not from reason and prudence that people marry, but from inclination. A man is poor; he thinks, 'I cannot be worse, and so I'll e'en take Peggy'.
Boswell: But have not nations been more populous at one period than another?
Johnson: Yes, Sir; but that has been owing to the people being less thinned at one period than another, whether by emigrations, war, or pestilence, not by their being more or less prolifick. Births at all times bear the same proportion to the same number of people.[29]

Later, towards the peak of the crescendo of English population growth, Robert Malthus, the greatest of all those who have reflected on population matters, gradually won through to a remarkably accurate assessment of the significance of nuptiality in controlling population trends in England, but even he, in his first formulation of his views in the 1798 *Essay on population*, had grave doubts about the prudence of the lower orders in contracting matrimony in view of the provisions of the poor law.[30]

27 The topics covered in this paragraph are discussed in greater detail and with the relevant empirical data in Wrigley, 'Marriage, fertility and population growth'.

28 Hajnal, 'European marriage patterns'. Laslett, 'Introduction'.

29 Boswell, *Life of Johnson*, p. 422.

30 Malthus believed in the possibility of prudence from the poor no less than the wealthy. 'The labourer who earns eighteen pence a day, and lives with some degree of comfort as a single man, will hestitate a little before he divides that pittance among four or five, which seems

It is in the nature of the progress of knowledge and the improvement of understanding that resolving one issue brings the next problem more clearly into focus. The disagreement about whether population was growing or declining which perplexed Price, Wales and Young in the later decades of the eighteenth century was resolved by the taking of the first census. The subsequent debate about the relative importance of fertility and mortality changes in promoting an accelerating growth of population in the 'long' eighteenth century took far longer to reach a conclusion. But new knowledge has now brought this about. Once more, however, a new conundrum has arisen to replace the old. The discovery that fertility was the dominant influence on population growth rates but that nuptiality changes account almost entirely for the great increase in fertility immediately suggests the need for a better understanding of the determinants and concomitants of nuptiality.

We are some way from a full resolution of the new conundrum. Not that it is new in the sense that it had not previously been aired. Habakkuk pointed to its possible significance a quarter of a century ago, but its central importance was not demonstrable until recently.[31] How then does the issue currently appear?

The wider setting

First, a general remark. Of the three prime demographic acts, marriage was much the most deliberate. The unpredictability of death was a constant theme of religion, poetry and practical life. The incidence of birth, affected by so many personal, social and biological circumstances, was also wayward. But matrimony, in the words of the First Prayer Book of Edward VI 'is not to be enterprised, nor taken in hand unadvisedly, lightly, or wantonly, to satisfy men's carnal lusts and appetites, like brute beasts that have no understanding: but reverently, discretely, advisedly, soberly, and in the fear of God'.[32] Whether all who heard this injunction followed it implicitly may be doubtful, but that the two principals to a marriage knew that they were taking a step of the greatest importance to the shape of their future lives, that it was not a matter to be enterprised lightly, is certain, and if any should fail to recognize the truth and relevance of the Prayer Book's advice, they

---

to be just sufficient for one . . . he must feel conscious, if he thinks at all, that, should he have a large family, and any ill luck whatever, no degree of frugality, no possible exertion of his manual strength, could preserve him from the heart rending sensation of seeing his children starve.' But the poor laws undermined prudence. Because of them, 'A poor man may marry with little or no prospect of being able to support a family in independence. They may be said therefore in some measure to create the poor which they maintain.' Malthus, *Essay on population* (1798), pp. 67, 83.

31 Habakkuk, 'English population'.

32 *The First and Second Prayer Books of Edward VI*, introduction by D. Harrison (Everyman edn, London, 1968), p. 252.

would not lack friends and relatives anxious to stress the significance of marriage to the individuals most directly concerned and to their families. Nor could the wider community fail to take a keen interest in marriage, which was the institution by which new individuals were introduced into the fully adult community, and new units of production and reproduction came into being. In early modern England *new* households were created by marriage rather than *old* households being maintained or reinforced by it as in many other cultures. And creating a viable household was an expensive business involving the investment of a substantial sum of money, feasible only when the parental generation made over a part of its wealth, or after a decade of saving while out in service. Perhaps the choice of verbs in the Prayer Book is significant. Marriage was enterprised or taken in hand: so were trading ventures or farming leases. Not all households were viable, of course, as the overseers of every parish knew well, but Dr Johnson does not appear to have captured the thought processes of his poorer fellow countrymen very well. The poor man did not take his Peggy earlier in life than his less impoverished contemporaries, nor was his Peggy a younger bride than her mistress. 'To be a servant', we have been told, 'was to be a potential farmer, but to be a labourer was to be a realized failure.'[33] To be a servant was also, of course, to be still single. Most young men, if this characterization is just, retained an ambition for success long enough to secure the country from the ill effects of a flood of marriages made for the reasons running through Dr Johnson's mind in replying to Boswell's question about the cause of rapid population growth.[34]

In the light of these general considerations about the nature of marriage in early modern England, it is not surprising to find that the timing and incidence of marriage appears to have been responsive to long-term variations in economic conditions. This topic, which is a major element in the new conundrum facing those interested in English population history before and during the industrial revolution, is difficult to pursue effectively at present because there is an imbalance between the comparative precision of our knowledge of population behaviour and the fragility of current estimates

---

33 Kussmaul, *Servants in husbandry*, p. 80.

34 Some scattered information bearing on this issue may be found in Drake, *Historical demography*, pp. 71–5. 'Prudent' marriage was not confined to the lower orders in England. For example, German reconstitution studies also show that when the age at first marriage of farmers is compared with that of labourers, the latter consistently married later than the former throughout the eighteenth and nineteenth centuries. Over the three periods 1700–99, 1800–49 and 1850–99 labourers were 29.3 years old on marriage, farmers were 28.2. Moreover, the contrast in age was much more strongly marked in the case of their brides, where the comparable average ages were 24.8 and 27.1, a striking discrepancy. Knodel, 'Demographic transitions in German villages' (paper presented at the Summary Conference on European Fertility, Princeton, 1979), table 3. His data were drawn from 13 villages in Baden, Bavaria, Hesse, Württemberg and Ostfriesland. Marriage patterns with broadly similar features are visible in Norway over the same period: Drake, *Population and society in Norway*, especially chapters 5, 6. See also the remarkable contemporary study (1855) by Sundt, *On marriage in Norway*, chapter 11.

of secular trends in basic economic indices. It is reasonable to expect that the nature of marriage would ensure that nuptiality trends would reflect changes in economic opportunity, and it is not difficult to show that nuptiality trends bore a striking resemblance to trends in the one relevant economic index which covers the whole early modern period, but how much can safely be inferred from the observed relationship is unclear. The problem lies in the unsatisfactory nature of the Phelps Brown and Hopkins indices of price and wage trends in relation to the question at issue.[35]

If we ignore the problem momentarily and treat the Phelps Brown and Hopkins indices as if they afforded an accurate measurement of real income and therefore captured the circumstance of greatest significance to young people in deciding whether or not to marry, then the general functioning of the English economic–demographic system might be described in the following terms. First, there was a tight relationship between the secular behaviour of prices and the rate of population growth from the sixteenth century until about 1800. In the absence of population growth or decline, the cost of living was stable. When population rose, the price of a basketful of consumables also rose, and the rise was faster, the faster the growth in population. Similarly, when population was falling prices also fell (figure 9.3). The general relationship between the two variables was linear. The connection between population change and price trends carries implications for real wages. Where money wages change only very slowly rising prices mean falling purchasing power for many families. The observed relationship between population growth rates and prices therefore means that population growth rates and real wages were also closely linked, though here the relationship was, of course, negative rather than positive (figure 9.4). A rapidly growing population was associated with falling standards of living: a declining population meant better times for the average family. There was, however, sufficient underlying secular growth in the capacity of the economy to produce goods and services to sustain modest rates of population growth without injury to living standards. Only when population growth rates rose to about 0.5 per cent per annum or more was the upshot a deterioration in living standards.

The relationships just described appear to have held good in a notably consistent fashion from the earliest date at which they can be measured until about 1800, but there can be few pieces of evidence which more vividly portray the reality of the sea change in economic affairs which has come to be termed the industrial revolution than the behaviour of the graphs showing the relationship between population growth rates and trends in prices and real wages. At the end of the eighteenth century there is a clean break from earlier patterns. Population growth rates were still accelerating at that period but suddenly prices no longer rose nor did real wages fall

35 Phelps Brown and Hopkins, 'Seven centuries of building wages' and 'Seven centuries of the prices of consumables'.

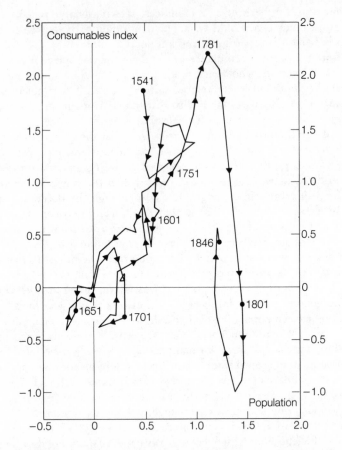

Figure 9.3 Annual percentage rates of growth of population and of a basket of consumables index.
The population growth rate was measured between any given 'census' date and the 'census' 25 years later. The rate of growth of the price of consumables was measured using the readings on a 25-year moving average of the index for the same dates as for population totals. Where a date is indicated it shows the beginning date of a 25-year period.
Source: Wrigley and Schofield, *Population history of England*, figure 10.2, p. 405.

as was to be expected from past experience. Rising numbers were no longer incompatible with rising individual prosperity.

The next element in the chain of interlinked variables which characterized early modern English society and economy is that connecting living standards and marriage. If marriage was not to be enterprised unadvisedly, then it was likely to be entered into more freely in times of rising general prosperity and to be approached more gingerly when the trend in prevailing living standards was downwards. When Roger Schofield and I tried to summarize this process, we put it as follows:

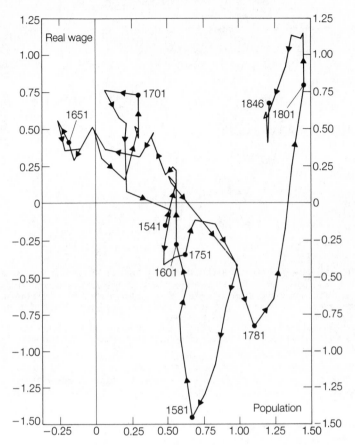

Figure 9.4 Annual percentage rates of growth of population and of a real wage index. The population growth rate was measured between each given 'census' date and the 'census' 25 years later. The rate of growth of real wages was measured using the readings on a 25-year moving average of the index for the same dates as for population totals. Where a date is indicated it shows the beginning date of a 25-year period.
Source: Wrigley and Schofield, *Population history of England*, figure 10.4, p. 410.

As each generation grew up and crossed the threshold into adult life the marriage conventions of society, reflecting its underlying economic condition, acted like a filter. At times young men and women were allowed to pass relatively freely into the married state, but at other times the mesh tightened, ponding back the flow so that many had long to wait before they passed through, while others spilled round, moving forward into middle life single and excluded from marriage.[36]

The effect of the operation of the link between economic trends and nuptiality was to encourage earlier marriage when living standards were

36 Wrigley and Schofield, *Population history of England*, p. 435.

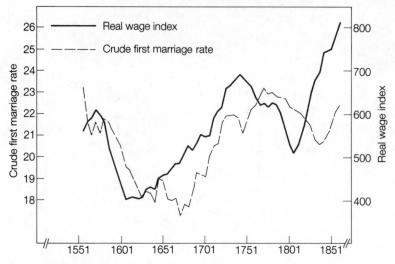

Figure 9.5 Real wage trends and crude first marriage rates (both 25-year moving averages).
The 25-year moving averages are centred on the years shown. The crude first marriage rate relates
the number of those marrying for the first time to the total population aged 15–34. It may be noted that
the prevalence of clandestine marriage in the second half of the seventeenth century substantially reduced
the number of marriages recorded in Anglican registers.
Source: Wrigley and Schofield, *Population history of England*, figure 10.9, p. 425, and figure 10.11,
p. 428 (further details of sources and methods of estimation may be found in the notes to the figures
and the accompanying text).

rising but to dissuade many brides and grooms from an early visit to the
church porch in worsening economic circumstances; and, as we have already
seen, for long periods of time, as during the 'long' eighteenth century,
nuptiality trends were so dominant an influence on secular population growth
rates as to ensure that changes in nuptiality would largely determine them.
Figure 9.5 shows the secular changes in real wages and crude first marriage
rates and demonstrates the closeness with which nuptiality trends mirrored
earlier changes in real wages.[37] This completes the circle of links, ensuring
that a population growth rate which threatened living standards would be
reduced, and that one which was low enough to allow living standards to
rise would provoke an increased population growth rate, a textbook example
of the notion of negative feedback.

It is probable that this characterization of the place of marriage in the
economy and society of early modern England does save the phenomena
adequately, but it is at best a sketch of a highly complex 'real' situation.
And it is at this point that the weaknesses of the Phelps Brown and Hopkins
indices as measures of economic circumstances begin to obtrude, making
it difficult to determine what needs to be explained.

37 The relative importance of changes in marriage age and proportions never marrying in
producing the fluctuations in the crude first marriage rate; the way in which the crude first
marriage rate was estimated; and the time lag between real wage changes and nuptiality responses
are all discussed in Wrigley and Schofield, *Population history of England*, pp. 421–35.

The proximate cause of long-term trends in nuptiality is assumed to be secular change in the ease or difficulty which young couples experienced in acquiring the means of setting up and subsequently maintaining an independent household. The Phelps Brown and Hopkins index of real wages is based upon the money wages paid to adult males in employment in a single industry and at times the data refer only to one town. The price data used are much more widely based but also present certain shortcomings. The real wage index is, therefore, evidently inadequate for our purpose. In considering the enterprise of marriage the earnings of women and children are no less relevant than those of men. Many who sought work could not find it, so that a measure based on pay when in employment is a defective guide to average earnings over, say, a period of a year. Many families derived a part or the whole of their income from sources other than wages, and trends in income derived from the ownership of land or from other productive assets did not necessarily follow trends in wage income. The list of differences between what might ideally be required and what is currently available might be further extended,[38] but it is already sufficient to show how inadequate the index is and how much this hinders interpretation. For example, although the secular trends in the Phelps Brown and Hopkins index of real wages and in nuptiality sweep up and down figure 9.5 in unison, they do so separated by a gap in time of some 30 years, with economic changes preceding those in nuptiality. It may therefore be the case that the apparent time lag between a change in the economic climate and a response by young couples contemplating matrimony is genuine and requires explanation. But the real wage estimates are sufficiently unsatisfactory to leave open the possibility that the time lag is an artefact of the defective data, or alternatively that the Phelps Brown and Hopkins index is tolerably accurate but that by excluding non-wage income it causes the nature of the problem to be perceived incorrectly.

Assuming that the problem is not spurious, there are a number of possible explanations of the time-lag problem which might serve individually or in combination to account for the observed pattern.[39] In any case, underlying the particular issue there is the larger matter of the way in which the marriage market operated in England so as to keep numbers and available resources in rough balance and to allow a relatively high standard of living. Pre-industrial England was clearly not a community in which numbers pressed close to the limits set by the necessities of bare subsistence. It was well away from what Malthus called a 'Chinese' situation,[40] and the reason for this comparatively happy state of affairs did not lie in general biological or environmental circumstances of which the community was the unconscious

38 The topic is discussed further in ibid., pp. 407–8, 411–12, 430–5, and appendix 9.
39 Some are set out briefly in ibid., p. 422.
40 'In some countries population appears to have been forced; that is people have been habituated by degrees to live almost upon the smallest possible quantity of food . . . China seems to answer this description.' Malthus, *Essay on population* (1798), p. 130.

beneficiary, but in the existence of a set of interrelated economic circumstances and social conventions which gave to marriage a degree of responsiveness to secular economic change which was probably rare outside western Europe. It is a phenomenon of great interest both in its own right, so to speak, and also as a major feature in what might be termed the ecology of the industrial revolution.

Population and the industrial revolution

In this context the 'long' eighteenth century is, of course, of special interest. At its start in 1680 the population of England was just less than 5 million and 22 per cent of the French total at that date; in 1820 the English population numbered 11.5 million and was 38 per cent of the French total. The former had grown by 133 per cent; the latter by 39 per cent. The contrast with The Netherlands was even more striking. Dutch population grew by only 8 per cent over the same period. Since France and The Netherlands were the two most prominent rivals of England for economic leadership in Europe in the late seventeenth century, the huge difference in population growth rates during the 'long' eighteenth century is very striking, and it is natural that it should have been so frequently discussed in relation to the occurrence of the industrial revolution.

The links between population change and the industrial revolution form a very broad field of investigation and ramify so widely that only a few topics can be considered here in the light of the new knowledge of English population history. The central issue is perhaps the question of how far what happened during the 'long' eighteenth century must be viewed as a novel development with features which set it apart from earlier periods.

Much has been made at times of the improvement in mortality during the eighteenth century and of its possible connection with higher living standards and better nutrition, or greater concern for public health and improved medical knowledge. As we have seen, however, the rise in expectation of life was not dramatic. Even at the end of the century it was no higher than the best levels attained in the middle decades of Elizabeth's reign.[41] In the eighteenth century, as earlier, there is scant evidence of any link between living standards and mortality levels. It is probably true that the secular tendency in standards of living as reflected in real wages was steadily upwards from the mid-seventeenth to the late eighteenth century but that thereafter there was a sharp fall for about a generation before a resumption in the upward movement in the early nineteenth century. Mortality, however, moved uncertainly between 1680 and 1730 with no decided trend in spite of rising living standards but thereafter showed a steady if not pronounced improvement, even though living standards went through a switchback period in the last decades of the eighteenth and the first decades of the nineteenth centuries.[42]

41 Wrigley and Schofield, *Population history of England*, table 7.15 and figure 7.6, pp. 230–1.
42 Ibid., figure 10.5, p. 414.

If mortality presented no new features to set apart the 'long' eighteenth century from earlier times, what of fertility and nuptiality? We have already noted that the fertility of married women does not appear to have changed other than marginally throughout the whole parish register period.[43] There is little evidence, for example, in the reconstitution studies so far carried out that the circumstances of the early decades of industrial revolution encouraged couples to increase the tempo of family formation because children represented an asset of enhanced value from the parents' point of view. Certainly there were great changes in nuptiality, and these in large measure produced the remarkable surge in population growth. Women were marrying much younger at the end of the 'long' eighteenth century than at its beginning and many fewer remained single. Teenage brides, once rare, had become quite common by 1800. But it is important to distinguish between a change in the level of a variable and a change in its relationship to other variables. The timing and incidence of marriage changed, but the response of young couples to given economic circumstances appears to have changed little. It should be remembered that the trend of real wages suggests that nuptiality should have risen steadily almost throughout the 'long' eighteenth century for real wages were probably rising from the mid-seventeenth century until about 1780 and the 'classic' response of the marriage market to such a trend was for entry into marriage to become steadily easier. Significantly, the downturn in real wages which occurred at the end of the eighteenth century is mirrored by a tightening of the marriage market. Nuptiality declined from about 1800 for a generation or so, just as real wages appear to have done a little earlier, and the recovery in real wages after the turn of the century was once again matched by a renewed rise in nuptiality after about 1840.

There are too many uncertainties about the measurement of trends in real wages or in family purchasing power more generally to press this analysis very far. There is also much still to be learnt about nuptiality changes in the later eighteenth and early nineteenth centuries. But some points stand out. For example, the view that increased nuptiality was due to proletarianization, the view in other words that those who were wage paid married young because they reached their maximum earning power earlier in life than small farmers or craftsmen and could not be disciplined into delayed marriage by a propertyless older generation, is not easy to sustain. The downturn in nuptiality in the early nineteenth century is fatal to this viewpoint since proletarianization went forward steadily during this period but nuptiality ebbed considerably. There appears to have been a substantial uniformity of reaction to changing real income trends between the sixteenth and nineteenth centuries in spite of the major changes in employment type and structure occurring over the period. It is possible that 'proto-industrialization' and proletarianization may have accentuated the rise in nuptiality during

---

43 Wrigley and Schofield, 'English population history from family reconstitution', table 6, p. 169.

the 'long' eighteenth century but older characteristics of nuptiality remained prominent, perhaps predominant, until late in the nineteenth century.

To argue in this fashion is to suggest, of course, that the acceleration in the rate of population growth in the 'long' eighteenth century was principally due to the long-sustained period during which real incomes were rising, which in turn resulted in higher fertility through encouraging earlier marriage. The population growth was due to economic circumstances. As we have seen, however, there was a two-way relationship between economic and demographic variables in early modern England, and the feedback between them was not so finely balance as to ensure that they remained in equilibrium. Further round the circle of interlinked variables, the increased pace of population growth which resulted from higher nuptiality was tending as the eighteenth century progressed to cause prices to rise faster and faster which in turn exerted increasing pressure on real incomes with money wages rising less quickly than prices.

Figure 9.6 represents an attempt to set out diagrammatically the secular linkages between the chief economic and demographic elements visible in the negative feedback system underlying so many features of life in pre-industrial England. The direction of the arrowed lines connecting the boxes in the diagram shows the nature of the causal links between the elements concerned, while the sign attached to each link shows whether the linkage was positive or negative. Thus population growth is positively linked to the price of food (*ceteris paribus* rising numbers causes rising food prices), while food prices are negatively linked to real incomes (rising food prices cause *falling* living standards). The set of relationships shown round either the inner or outer circles in the diagram constitute a system of negative feedback; that is, departure from an initial state of equilibrium tends to set in train changes within the system as a whole which restore the *status quo ante*. It is a distinguishing feature of any pre-industrial economic–demographic system that this should be so, but the means by which the negative feedback operates may vary widely. The outer circle of relationships summarizes the situation in Malthus's 'Chinese' situation where the effect of rising numbers is to cause mortality to rise and restore an equilibrium of numbers and resources. Here to balance the books nature audits with a red pencil. The inner circle represents an alternative method of resolving the same basic tension between rising numbers and individual well-being. Instead of mortality rising in the face of falling living standards (or falling when times improve), the same effect is secured by reduced (or increased) nuptiality. This 'solution' is compatible with the maintenance of substantially higher living standards and it was this system, shown enclosed by a broken line in figure 9.6, which characterized early modern England.[44]

44 The assumptions underlying figure 9.6 and the construction of variant forms of the same basic diagram in an attempt to do fuller justice to the changing character of early modern England are described in Wrigley and Schofield, *Population history of England*, chapter 11.

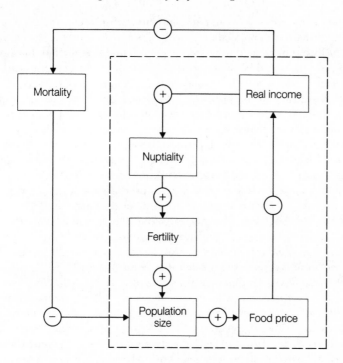

Figure 9.6 The pre-industrial demographic system.
Source: Wrigley and Schofield, *Population history of England*, figure 11.1, p. 458.

Because adjustment between some of the elements constituting the system as a whole took place quite slowly, its homeostatic character is evident only over long periods of time. In shorter periods, sometimes lasting many decades, contemporaries might be much more vividly aware of disequilibrium than of balance. The later decades of the eighteenth century formed such a period. They began to bear a strong resemblance to the later sixteenth century when prices also rose rapidly under the stress of rapid population growth and real incomes were adversely affected. It was this chain of related changes which caused Robert Malthus such great concern, and led him to criticize so severely the operation of the system of poor relief which he thought likely to aggravate an already deeply serious situation. All seemed set for a phase of sharply reduced real incomes and a matching fall in nuptiality, increased mortality associated with heightened misery or some combination of the two. Both logic and past experience seemed to justify the fear. England had enjoyed a period of striking success during which her economy had strengthened relative to those of her rivals, France and Holland. Population growth had reflected this success, just as earlier, during the sixteenth and seventeenth centuries, a comparable period of relative Dutch success had been marked by a surge in the population growth rate rivalling or exceeding those of her competitors. But there was good reason to fear that the rate of population growth had risen beyond the level at which it was balanced by matching economic growth and that the familiar reverse side of the coin would be seen again, as it had been two centuries earlier.[45]

In the event the fear that a penalty must be paid for over-rapid population growth proved not to be justified. It is clear from a consideration of the behaviour of both prices and real wages in relation to population growth rates that a radical change in the English economy must have occurred at about the end of the eighteenth century, breaking patterns which had held good for at least 250 years before 1800 (figures 9.3 and 9.4). Such evidence strongly implies a very marked and unprecedented rise in the rate of growth of the capacity of the English economy to produce goods and services and thereby to sustain both rising numbers and better standards of living. The long-sustained negative feedback between fundamental economic and demographic variables in England, which had at once made possible relatively high standards of living and yet seemed to ensure that permanently sustained improvement was not feasible, was broken.

In the period before this relatively abrupt change, however, there was little to suggest that such a change was in prospect. It was neither suspected by informed contemporaries nor visible *ex post facto* in the interplay of the variables whose behaviour we have been reviewing.[46] The most conspicuous early feature of the new situation which supervened was the disappearance of the old positive relationship between the rate of population growth and the rate at which food prices grew. With this link severed, the further, and this time negative, relationship between population growth rates and real incomes also disappeared. Other elements in the old pattern proved more durable. For two or three more generations nuptiality, and through nuptiality fertility, continued to respond to changing real incomes as in the past. Only after about 1870 did these other chief features of the earlier system disappear. Therefore, for a long time fertility remained high, though without regaining the peak reached at the end of the 'long' eighteenth century. But because of the new capacity to achieve and maintain a far higher rate of growth of production than had ever previously been attained, high rates of population growth no longer forced down living standards, nor did they

45 It is interesting to note that Harley has recently suggested that aggregate industrial production in England was at a substantially higher level by 1770 than had been suggested by Deane and Cole's calculations but that it grew much more slowly over the period 1770–1815 than had previously been supposed. Agriculture was, of course, still very much the largest industry, so that Harley's amended industrial output series would not necessarily dominate trends in an output series which also included non-industrial production. Harley, 'British industrialization before 1841', especially figure 1, p. 277.

46 Adam Smith, for example, might well have subtitled *The wealth of nations*, 'An examination of the limits to growth'. He was impressed as much by the difficulty of reaching a high plateau for incomes and then maintaining any such success as by the opportunities for growth in other circumstances. See, e.g., *Wealth of nations*, book i, chapter 9, 'Of the profits of stock'. See also chapter 3.

indirectly bring about their own moderation or reversal by delayed marriage and a throttling back of fertility.

Conclusion

The solvent of new knowledge has exposed to view a landscape with changed contours. It is now clear that, in seeking to understand the remarkable pace at which English population grew in the eighteenth century, we should look to changes in nuptiality as the principal immediate reason for the acceleration that occurred. It is highly probable that this did not reflect any major alteration in the way in which young people made their decisions to marry, to delay marriage or to remain single, but that instead over a period which lasted more than a century the inducements to marry grew steadily greater and the disincentives less as real incomes rose. In earlier periods each such episode had brought with it its own nemesis as over-rapid population growth affected standards of living adversely and by symmetry discouraged marriage and reduced or even reversed trends in population growth.

By the end of the eighteenth century, England had gained significantly on her continental neighbours in both economy and population but appeared to be on the verge of that kind of reversal of fortune which was the normal penalty of rapid growth in pre-industrial times, the *alter ego* of success which kept pace with any surge of growth like a shadow. Then, at the end of the eighteenth century, the country slipped its shadow in a manner which contemporaries such as Adam Smith, Malthus or Ricardo found hard to believe possible. The 'long' eighteenth century ended not in disaster or contraction but with the transition to a new era in which the old relationships between population and economy decayed and eventually disappeared, though some much sooner than others. By clarifying the sense in which the eighteenth century remained within the old canon as far as the interplay of population and economy is concerned, the better information now to hand about demographic behaviour has served to suggest two topics above all for further reflection and investigation. So far as the old regime is concerned, anything which throws light on the process of deciding whether and when to marry would be most welcome; and, similarly, how far this was determined consciously or unconsciously by an economic calculus; how great were the differences between different levels in society, different areas of the country, different occupations, different age groups, different marital statuses; how far children were perceived as potential props in old age, as sources of income, as ends in themselves. On all these topics and on many related matters fuller knowledge is needed.[47] Marriage was the hinge on

47 Much knowledge, of course, already exists. Hollingsworth's remarkable study of the peerage, for example, shows that there were strong similarities in secular mortality trends between the peers and the mass of the population, at least until the mid-eighteenth century, but that the peers' marriage patterns were in some respects strikingly different. The age at first marriage of peers' brides, for example, which was very low in the sixteenth century rose steadily and

which the demographic system turned, and, given the crucial importance of the tension between production and reproduction which affected all pre-industrial societies, its significance was far wider than the purely demographic. Many aspects of English social and economic life influenced and were also influenced by marriage behaviour.

The old regime can be shown to have held sway for several centuries before 1800 and was probably in being far longer than its existence can be clearly demonstrated but, unsuspected by contemporaries, it began to decay at about the end of the eighteenth century. Within the context of this discussion the first sign of its decay was the abrupt disappearance of the positive correlation between the rate of population growth and the rate of change in food prices. The breaking of this link meant the removal of a problem which had always previously dogged periods of prosperity and growth. Each present period of success had invariably provoked its own subsequent failure. If a society had briefly secured a larger output of goods and services per head and had thereby permitted a growth in numbers, that growth if long continued had always implied future impoverishment because of the rising real cost of securing a unit increase of output from the land. In their different ways, Malthus and Ricardo gave very clear expression to this seemingly inescapable dilemma.[48] Yet even as they wrote, the economy was changing in ways which secured the country from the worst implications of the logic of their

---

substantially during the next 200 years until by the end of the eighteenth century they were marrying much later than their plebeian contemporaries where once they had married much younger. Hollingsworth, 'Mortality in the British peerage families' and *The British peerage*, table 17, p. 25. Again, the examination of surviving diaries has shown how 'modern' were the expectations and worries of young men in courtship and marriage in seventeenth-century England. Such sources also suggest that children were chiefly welcomed for their own sake rather than as future contributors to family income or security (as consumer rather than producer goods in the unappealing jargon used by some economists). Wrightson, *English society*, especially chapters 3, 4. Recent work on the institution of service has also proved very helpful in furthering understanding of the calculus of marriage for young men and women, the circumstances in which they left home and the reasons why parents had little to expect from their children once this break had occurred. Kussmaul, *Servants in husbandry*, chapters 3–5. Similarly, the importance of institutional provision for the aged, widowed, sick, orphaned or out of work made under the poor laws has attracted increasing attention. Wales, 'Poverty, poor relief and the life cycle', and Newman Brown, 'The receipt of poor relief'.

48 'Were a country never to be over-run by a people more advanced in arts, but left to its own natural progress in civilization; from the time that its produce might be considered as a unit, to the time that it might be considered as a million, during the lapse of many hundred years, there would not be a single period, when the mass of the people could be said to be free from distress, either directly or indirectly from want of food. In every state of Europe, since we have first had accounts of it, millions and millions of human existences have been repressed from this simple cause; though perhaps in some of these states, an absolute famine has never been known.' Malthus, *Essay on population* (1798), pp. 138–9. Ricardo argued that the best land would be cultivated first and that unit inputs of labour or capital would yield lower returns as less productive land was taken into use. If technical advance occurred and the productiveness of labour were enhanced, higher wages would result and ultimately higher population also, thus tending to ensure that standards of living for the mass of the population were not permanently improved. Ricardo, *Principles of political economy*, chapters 2, 'On rent' and 5, 'On wages'.

arguments. Here lies a conundrum of the new regime also worthy of close attention. If both conundrums could be resolved we should be far better able both to understand the 'long' eighteenth century and also to see why the nineteenth century brought with it not a season of stagnation or contraction but the start of a period when for the first time in history poverty for the mass of mankind became not a necessary part of the lot of man but a preventable evil.

10

Family Limitation in
Pre-industrial England

M. Louis Henry of the Institut National d'Etudes Démographiques in Paris
has, by his development of the technique of family reconstitution, placed
a powerful new weapon in the hands of historical demographers in those
countries fortunate enough to possess good parish registers. By this method,
any running series of births (baptisms), deaths (burials) and marriages can
be exploited to provide a detailed picture of many aspects of the fertility,
mortality and nuptiality of a community.

Family reconstitution is in principle a simple operation.[1] Information
abstracted from the registers is transferred initially to slips, each event in
each register being recorded on a separate slip. This in turn is collated on
family reconstitution forms (FRFs) on each of which there is space to record
the dates of baptism and burial of the two principals to the marriage, the
date of the marriage itself, the names of the parents of the married couple
and, in the lower half of the form, the names and dates of baptism, marriage
and burial of all issue of the marriage. There is also space to record other
information about residence, occupation, place of baptism and burial and
so on. Only a small proportion of families can be completely reconstituted
in most parishes, but for many purposes partially reconstituted families can
also be used. From the FRFs a wide range of demographic measures can
be calculated, including such things as age at first marriage, age-specific
marital fertility, infant and child mortality, expectation of life (subject to
some margin of error), birth intervals and the percentage of pre-nuptially
conceived first births.

Only those registers in which there are few or no breaks are suitable for
family reconstitution. Nor is it always the case that a register without any
missing year is of use since for successful reconstitution the information given
at each entry must normally be sufficient to allow the individual in question
to be identified with confidence. Many English registers fall short

---

1 For a full description of the method and a discussion of the type of register to which it
can be applied see Wrigley (ed.), *English historical demography*, chapter 4. This in turn is largely
based upon the earlier French manual of Fleury and Henry, *Manuel de dépouillement et d'exploitation*.

in this respect. Nevertheless, by modifying French practice somewhat to take account of the idiosyncracies of English parish registers, it is possible to apply Henry's family reconstitution methods to some English registers. As a result it is reasonable to hope that in time the demographic history of England during the period from the mid-sixteenth to the mid-nineteenth century will be seen much more fully and in much sharper focus.

Although in general it may be true that French parish registers lend themselves more easily to family reconstitution than English because the French *curés* were in the habit of recording much more detail in their registers than the English vicars in theirs,[2] in one respect England is very fortunate. A few hundred English registers go right back to 1538 and a much larger number is still extant from the early seventeenth century though, of course, it often happens that there are gaps, especially for the Civil War years.[3] In France, in contrast, the registers are seldom of use for family reconstitution purposes before the last quarter of the seventeenth century. The early years of the seventeenth century both in England and on the continent were often a turning-point in demographic history when a period of rapid population growth came to an end and a different pattern of slower growth, stagnation or decline set in. This occurred before most French registers are suitable for reconstitution, but some English parishes maintained good registers from a much earlier date. In them a complete cycle of demographic experience can be examined, beginning with a period of rapid growth in the sixteenth century, followed by a check and decline, which in turn gave way to renewed growth during the eighteenth century.

The aggregative picture

The parish of Colyton in the Axe valley in east Devon possesses an exceptionally complete register. The record of baptisms, burials and marriages is uninterrupted from 1538 to 1837 (the date of the beginning of civil registration) and beyond. Moreover, the degree of detail given at each entry varies considerably in different periods of the register. These two characteristics in combination made the Colyton register particularly suitable for a pilot study of family reconstitution using English parish registers. The second is important because it makes it possible to determine the threshold level of information necessary for successful reconstitution below which the identification of the people named (especially in the burial register, the most sensitive of the three in this respect) becomes in many cases impossible.[4] In

---

2 The second chapter of Gautier and Henry, *Crulai* gives an account of the type of information to be found in a good French register. See also Wrigley, 'Some problems of family reconstitution'.

3 No good general inventory of parish registers exists, though the Society of Genealogists hopes shortly to publish a revised edition of the *National index of parish registers* which will cover both originals and transcripts. The inventory which Rickman published in the 1831 Census is still the best starting point for work in many counties.

4 This question is dealt with in Wrigley, 'Some problems of family reconstitution'.

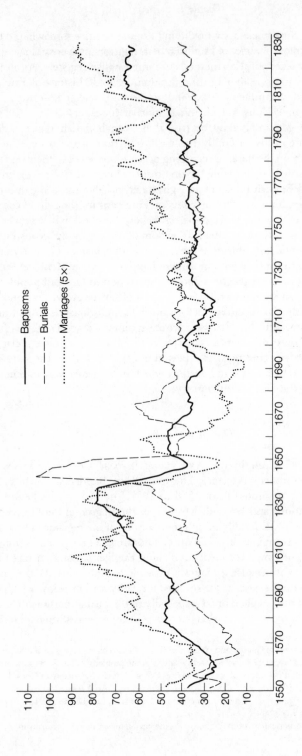

Figure 10.1 Baptism, burial and marriage totals (nine-year moving averages).

the event Colyton proved to be a parish of the greatest interest from a general, as well as a technical, point of view, for Colyton's population history was very varied during these three centuries. The changes in fertility which occurred are especially striking. The bulk of this article is devoted to this topic. Other aspects of the parish's demographic history are touched on only *en passant*.

Figure 10.1 shows the totals of baptisms, burials and marriages in Colyton plotted as nine-year moving averages. From them it appears that the population history of the parish fell into three phases: a first in which there was usually a substantial surplus of baptisms over burials and the total population rose sharply; a second during which burials usually exceeded baptisms and the population as a whole appears to have fallen somewhat; and a third beginning only in the 1780s when large surpluses of baptisms over burials again appear and the population rose sharply once more. The second period may be subdivided about 1730, since after that date there was near balance between baptisms and burials, whereas before it there was usually a surplus of burials. The abruptness of the division between the first and second periods is masked by the moving averages but is clearly revealed by annual figures. Between the beginning of November 1645 and the end of October 1646, 392 names are recorded in the Colyton burial register, in all probability as a result of a last and virulent outbreak of bubonic plague. This was perhaps a fifth of the total population. After this drastic mortality the number of baptisms fell to a much lower level. The average annual figure 1635–44 was 72.8, higher than in any subsequent period in the Colyton register. In the decade 1647–56 the annual average fell to 40.0. Apart from the first decade after the catastrophe, the moving averages show that there were normally more burials than baptisms for two generations. The boundary between the second and third major periods is also quite sharp. In the decade 1776–85 the average annual surplus of baptisms over burials was only 0.5, a figure typical of the preceding half century. In the next ten years the average surplus rose to 7.8 and increased considerably thereafter.

Table 10.1   Age at first marriage

	No.	Mean	Median	Mode
Men				
1560–1646	258	27.2	25.8	23.0
1647–1719	109	27.7	26.4	23.8
1720–69	90	25.7	25.1	23.9
1770–1837	219	26.5	25.8	24.4
Women				
1560–1646	371	27.0	25.9	23.7
1647–1719	136	29.6	27.5	23.3
1720–69	104	26.8	25.7	23.5
1770–1837	275	25.1	24.0	21.8

The total numbers of marriages in the four periods were 854, 379, 424 and 888 respectively.
The mode was calculated from the mean and median using Tippett's formula, mean – mode = 3(mean – median). See Tippett, *Statistics*, p. 35.

The changes in the balance between births and deaths revealed in the annual totals of baptisms and burials show that great changes took place in Colyton in the three centuries between Thomas Cromwell's injunction and the inception of civil registration. But although the crude figures may arouse curiosity about the changes in fertility, mortality, nuptiality and migration which could produce such big swings in the relative numbers of baptisms and burials, they cannot go far towards satisfying that curiosity. To penetrate more deeply into the matter it is essential to dispose of more refined measures of demographic conditions. For example, a fall in the number of baptisms might be the result of a rise in the average age at first marriage, or a rise in the average interval between births (perhaps as a result of changes in suckling customs, perhaps through the practice of abortion or the employment of a contraceptive technique), or even in some communities a reduction in the number of illegitimate births.[5] On the other hand, it might simply be the result of heavy emigration without any significant changes in general or marital fertility of the type just mentioned. And still other changes, for example in the age and sex structure of the population, might produce similar fluctuations in the relative number of births and deaths. To be able to decide between the many possibilities and to measure the changes accurately family reconstitution is necessary.

Marriage and marital fertility

It is convenient to begin the discussion of fertility changes in Colyton by considering the fluctuations in age at first marriage of the two sexes. In societies in which there is little control of conception within marriage this is one of the most important influences upon reproduction rates. Indeed, it is sometimes asserted that a lowering of the age of first marriage for women largely accounted for the rapid rise of population in England in the second half of the eighteenth century. The mean age at which women bore their last child in European communities with little or no control of conception was usually about 40,[6] and for some years before this their fecundity declined rapidly. It is clear, therefore, that a mean age at first marriage of 22 in these circumstances will give rise to twice as many births in completed families as a mean age of, say, 29 or 30. Table 10.1 shows that in Colyton there were remarkable changes in the mean age at first marriage of women, though the mean age of men did not greatly vary. The strangest period to modern eyes was the period 1647–1719.[7] Immediately after the terrible

5 Registered bastard baptisms might reach quite a high percentage level even as early as the sixteenth century. For example, 135 out of the total of 876 children baptized at Prestbury in Cheshire 1581–1600 (16 per cent) were bastards. I am indebted to Dr Stella Davies for this information.

6 See, for example, Henry, *Anciennes familles genevoises*, p. 88; Ganiage, *Trois villages d'Ile de France*, pp. 71–2; Gautier and Henry, *Crulai*, p. 157.

7 The time divisions used here and in subsequent tables were chosen to maximize the difference between the main periods of Colyton's demographic history.

Table 10.2   Mean age at first marriage

	Men		Women	
	No.	Mean	No.	Mean
1560-99	73	28.1	126	27.0
1600-29	124	27.4	162	27.3
1630-46	61	25.8	83	26.5
1647-59	38	26.9	48	30.0
1660-99	36	27.6	61	28.8
1700-19	35	28.1	27	30.7
1720-49	55	26.2	58	27.2
1750-69	35	25.0	46	26.3
1770-99	93	27.6	107	26.4
1800-24	67	25.6	100	24.9
1825-37	59	25.9	68	23.3

Table 10.3   Age of women at first marriage

	Under 20		30 and over		40 and over	
	No.	%	No.	%	No.	%
1560-1646	24	6.5	95	25.6	18	4.9
1647-1719	6	4.4	54	39.7	14	10.3
1825-37	17	25.0	5	7.4	1	1.5

mortality of 1646 the average age at first marriage of women shot up to almost 30 and was maintained at this very advanced age for some 70 years.[8] During this period, moreover, the mean age of women at first marriage was two years higher than that of men.[9] Table 10.2 shows the means for shorter periods. It is noteworthy that the new pattern established itself very quickly after 1647 in Colyton. The change was abrupt and decisive. Before this middle period and again for a time after it, the mean age for men and women differed very little, being in each case 26–27, while in the latest sub-period and possibly also in the earliest the more familiar pattern of men marrying women younger than themselves is found. By the period 1825–37 the mean age at first marriage for women had fallen to only 23 while that for men was 26, figures which appear to modern eyes much more 'normal'.

   Changes in the median age at first marriage for women were much less violent than the changes in the mean while the modal age did not change at all until the end of the eighteenth century, being unaffected in the middle period, 1647–1719. The commonest age at first marriage at that time

   8 The difference between the two means 1560–1646 and 1647–1719 is 2.61 years. The standard error of the difference is 0.69 years. The difference of the means is therefore 3.8 times the standard error of the difference, and we may properly conclude that women in the second period were really marrying later than in the first.

   9 See Wrigley, 'Some problems of family reconstitution', for a full discussion of the accuracy of the figures of age at marriage. See Drake, *Population and society in Norway*, especially pp. 121–49, for a very interesting examination of the factors which might induce men to take brides older than themselves in Norway in the late eighteenth and early nineteenth centuries.

remained about 23, but there was a much longer 'tail' to the right of the distribution. The contrast between different periods is well brought out by table 10.3, showing the percentage of old and young brides at different periods of Colyton's history. By the last decade of the three centuries a quarter of the brides were teenagers, in the period 1647–1719 only 4 per cent; while on the other hand 40 per cent were above 30 when they married for the first time in the earlier period compared with only 7 per cent in the later.

The male means, medians and modes were notably 'sticky'.[10] Men entered married life at much the same time for almost 300 years (only in the last few decades of the period was there a slight fall in the male mean), but they proved remarkably flexible in their judgement of what constituted an acceptable age in their brides. A higher proportion of men married women older than themselves in the period 1647–1719 than either before or later. In the period 1560–1646 in 48 per cent of the first marriages in which the age of both parties is known the man was older than the woman, in 47 per cent the woman was older than the man, and in 5 per cent their ages were equal. In the period 1647–1719 the percentages were 40, 55 and 5, while by the period 1800–37 the figures were 59, 29 and 12.

The figures of age at first marriage demonstrate immediately the great range of general fertility levels that might be found in pre-industrial communities. Other things being equal, the changes in mean age of marriage alone provided scope for a very wide range of rates of increase (or decrease) of population. In marriages not prematurely interrupted by death, an average age at first marriage for women of, say, 24 might well produce two more children than marriages contracted at an average age of, say, 29. The most extreme female mean ages at first marriage found at Colyton (30.7 in 1700–1 and 23.3 in 1825–37) could easily result in average completed family sizes differing from each other by a factor of 2.

The details of age at first marriage in themselves go far towards explaining the changes in numbers of children baptized that are apparent in the moving averages of crude totals of baptisms. However, any changes on the fertility side of the population history of Colyton which arose from changes in the mean age of first marriage were considerably amplified by changes in fertility within marriage as table 10.4 and figure 10.2 make clear.

In the first period 1560–1629 the age-specific marital fertility rates in Colyton were high, being distinctly higher than those found at Crulai in the late seventeenth and early eighteenth centuries.[11] There was a marked decline of fertility in the last 15 years before the plague of 1645–6 and this

10 This may well be a very common feature of European demography in many centuries. See, for example, *Report of the Royal Commission on Population*, Cmd. 7695, p. 249, para. 25, for England in recent decades. See also Wrigley, *Industrial growth and population change*, pp. 155–7, for nineteenth-century France and Germany.

11 The Crulai figures reveal in a very striking way the phenomenon of teenage sub-fecundity. This is absent in the Colyton figures, but its absence is not significant because a very high proportion of first births in Colyton were pre-nuptially conceived (about a third until the nineteenth century when the figure rose to about half). A large proportion of these in turn

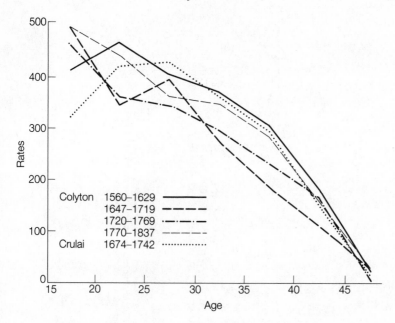

Figure 10.2 Age-specific marital fertility (rates per 1000 woman-years lived).
The period 1630-46 has been omitted to avoid over-crowding the graph.

became more pronounced after 1646. Fertility remained low throughout the period marked also by an exceptionally high average age at first marriage for women.[12] During the period 1720–69 there was some recovery in the rates, while during the final period 1770–1837 the rates were much higher though still not quite at the level attained in the sixteenth and early seventeenth centuries. Both the transition from the initial high level to a lower level of marital fertility and the subsequent recovery in fertility levels are of the greatest interest, but in this essay I shall concentrate chiefly on the change from high to low levels of fertility in the mid-seventeenth century. Comparison of the periods 1560–1629 and 1647–1719 reveals the fact that the relative difference between the five-year age-groups becomes more and more marked with rising age. With 1560–1629 as 100 in each case the figures for 1647–1719 are 74, 98, 74, 61 and 60 for the age-groups 20–4, 25–9, 30–4, 35–9 and 40–4 respectively. The anomalous figure for the 20–4 age-group may be explained perhaps by the small number of years in marriage

were born shortly after marriage (22 per cent of all first births were baptized within six months of marriage 1538–1799, 36 per cent 1800–37). Teenage brides, like others, were often pregnant at marriage and since most births to teenage mothers were first births, the 15–19 rate is inflated as a result and no valid comparison with Crulai can be made. The same is true to a lesser degree of the age-group 20–4.

12 It is unfortunately not possible to estimate what changes took place in the proportions of women ever married at, say, 45.

Table 10.4 Age-specific marital fertility (rates per 1000 woman-years lived)

	15–19	20–4	25–9	30–4	35–9	40–4	45–9
Colyton							
1560–1629	412 (17.0)	467 (205.5)	403 (473.5)	369 (561.5)	302 (517.0)	174 (443.0)	18 (383.5)
1630–46	500 (4.0)	378 (63.5)	382 (120.5)	298 (107.5)	234 (55.5)	128 (23.5)	0 (16.0)
1647–1719	500 (4.0)	346 (52.0)	395 (187.5)	272 (253.5)	182 (258.5)	104 (249.5)	20 (200.5)
1720–69	462 (19.5)	362 (69.0)	342 (164.0)	292 (216.0)	227 (203.0)	160 (156.0)	0 (138.0)
1770–1837	500 (34.0)	441 (279.0)	361 (498.0)	347 (504.5)	270 (430.0)	152 (224.0)	22 (186.0)
Crulai							
1674–1742	320(65.5)	419(305.5)	429(599.0)	355(633.0)	292(588.5)	142(505.5)	10(205.5)

The number of woman-years on which the rate is based is given in brackets. The Crulai figures are taken from Gautier and Henry, *Crulai*, pp. 102 and 105, and table vii, pp. 249–54. The Colyton rates are derived from marriages formed during the years specified, except that marriages which bridge the period 1630–46 to 1647–1719 are divided at the end of 1646, data from before that date being allocated to the earlier period, beyond it to 1647–1719. The reason for this appears in the text below, pp. 252–3.

Table 10.5 Number of children born to married women by five-year age-group

No. of children	Age-groups						
	20-4	25-9	30-4	35-9	40-4	45-9	Total
1560-1629[a] 0	1	2	6	16	34	61	120
1	1	16	19	24	32	6	98
2	6	31	49	35	9	0	130
3	2	9	14	9	4	0	38
4	0	2	0	3	1	0	6
5	1	0	1	0	0	0	2
Total	11	60	89	87	80	67	394
Average	2.18	1.88	1.84	1.53	0.83	0.09	
1647-1719[b] 0		1	8	17	23	32	81
1		6	11	15	14	2	48
2		4	16	9	3	0	32
3		4	3	0	0	0	7
4		2	0	0	0	0	2
5		0	0	0	0	0	0
Total		17	38	41	40	34	170
Average		2.00	1.37	0.80	0.50	0.06	

[a]In this table and subsequently in tables 10.11 and 10.12 the period 1560-1629 is used rather than 1560-1646 both because fertility was somewhat lower in 1630-46 and because of the problem of the 'bridging' families (see pp. 252-3 below).
[b]The absence of figures from the first column for the period 1647-1719 reflects the rarity of young brides in this period.

from which it was derived, but apart from this the progressively greater gap is well marked. When represented graphically the curve of the period 1560–1629 is convex to the upper side, while the curve of the later period is slightly concave to the upper side in the later years of the fertile period.[13] Since the latter is often taken as an indication of the restriction of fertility within the family it is important to look further into the fertility characteristics of women in the period 1647–1719. The reason why a concavity to the upper side of a curve representing age-specific marital fertility often indicates family limitation is, of course, that most married couples want some children but not as large a number as might be born to them without any limitation of fertility. They concentrate their reproductive effort into the earlier part of the wife's fertile period. Age-specific fertility in the younger age-groups in these circumstances may remain high, but in the later age-groups there will be a progressively greater shortfall from the full fertility potential of the women in question, producing the characteristic concavity in the curve.

Table 10.5 shows the frequency with which women bore 0, 1, 2, 3, 4, or 5 children when living throughout a specified five-year age-group. At the foot of each column the average number of children born in the five-

13 The changes which took place at Colyton are very similar to those which took place at the same period in the Genevan bourgeoisie. See Henry, *Anciennes familles genevoises*, especially pp. 75–81. The family limitation which began amongst the Genevan bourgeoisie in the second half of the seventeenth century, however, became accentuated in the eighteenth, whereas in Colyton there was a reversion to the earlier fertility patterns.

Table 10.6   Age-specific marital fertility, 1647–1719 (rates per 1000 woman-years lived)

	30-4	35-9	40-4	45-9
Women marrying				
Under 30	265 (215.5)	146 (191.5)	96 (146.0)	0 (108.5)
30 and over	316 (38.0)	284 (67.0)	116 (103.5)	43 (92.0)

The number of woman-years on which the rate is based is given in brackets.

year period is shown. The figures when converted approximate closely to the rates shown in table 10.4 as is to be expected. (Where they are a little lower it is because they largely eliminate the influence of the very short interval between marriage and first baptism; see note 11 above.) It is possible to make an analysis of variance on the four age-groups over 30 in the two periods, with the following result.

	Sum of squares	Degrees of freedom	Estimate of variance	F
Total	490.00	475		
Age-groups	168.92	3	56.31	88.2
Periods	20.38	1	20.38	31.9
Error	300.70	471	0.6384	

A test for interaction produces an F which is not significant and the assumption of additivity can be retained. The difference between the two periods is very highly significant (beyond the 0.1 per cent level) and we may therefore say with confidence that there was a fall in fertility above the age of 30 between the two periods.

The possibility of the existence of some form of family limitation immediately suggests a comparison of the fertility rates in the age-groups 30–44 of those women marrying below the age of 30 with the rates for those marrying in their thirties. Since the former will already in most cases have borne children before entering their thirties, it is to be expected that their fertility rates will be lower than those of women marrying after 30 who will have less reason to seek to restrict the number of their children. Table 10.6 shows that the expected pattern is present, though it should not be forgotten that rather higher rates amongst those marrying at 30 or over are to be expected anyway because fertility is lower among higher parity women than amongst lower parity women of the same age, *ceteris paribus*, since each successive birth carries with it a risk of sterility or impaired fecundity from the accidents of parturition. The differences, however, are much too large to be accounted for on this ground.

It is of interest also to follow the short-term experience of the couples who had married before the plague visitation of 1645–6 and who survived the terrible year. It has sometimes been supposed that the 'instinctive' reaction of a population after a heavy loss of life is to increase fertility to fill the gaps created by death. Table 10.7 shows the age-specific fertility rates of women in families which bridged the plague year and where the age of the wife is

Table 10.7 Age-specific marital fertility (rates per 1000 woman-years lived)

	15-19	20-4	25-9	30-4	35-9	40-4	45-9
Up to 1646	572 (3.5)	429 (28.0)	412 (51.0)	370 (40.5)	194 (15.5)	0 (4.0)	
1647 and after			174 (11.5)	247 (36.5)	154 (52.0)	127 (55.0)	0 (43.5)

The number of woman-years on which the rate is based is given in brackets.

Table 10.8 Mean birth intervals (in months)

	0-1	n	1-2	n	2-3	n	3-4	n	Last	n
1560-1646	11.3	87	25.2	87	27.4	84	30.1	77	37.5	76
1647-1719	10.3	23	29.1	23	32.6	26	32.1	18	50.7	34
1720-69	11.9	24	25.1	24	29.8	24	32.9	22	40.6	24

Birth intervals 1-4 combined

	Mean	n
1560-1646	27.5	248
1647-1719	31.4	67
1720-69	29.1	70

The smaller number of intervals 3-4 arises because when the interval 3-4 was also the last interval it is not included in the 3-4 totals. The large number of last birth intervals 1647-1719 and the reduced number 1560-1646 is a result of splitting families which bridged the year 1646 in the way described above. A difference of means test may be applied to the means of the last birth intervals 1560-1646 and 1647-1719. The difference in the two means is 13.2 months. The standard error of the difference is 4.62 months. The difference of means is therefore 2.88 times the standard error of the difference, and the difference is significant at the 1 per cent level. The same test applied to the means of all birth intervals 1-4 shows the mean of 1560-1646 to be significantly different from the mean of 1647-1719 at the 5 per cent level (difference of means 2.15 times the standard error of the difference).

known. Some were at the beginning of their child-bearing period when the plague struck, others were near the end, which explains how there are rates on both sides of the temporal division for most age-groups. The numbers involved were, of course, small, but the picture which emerges is none the less suggestive. Fertility rates dropped sharply and immediately to the levels which were to be characteristic of Colyton for the next two or three generations even though the women in question had displayed a fertility well above the average in the period before the swingeing losses of 1646.[14] The change from a high to a low level of fertility within these families was abrupt and complete, just as was the change to a later age at first marriage for women.

The examination of mean birth intervals can also throw much light on the question of family limitation. Table 10.8 shows the mean birth intervals 0-1, 1-2, 2-3, 3-4 and penultimate to last of completed families of four or more children in the three periods 1560-1646, 1647-1719 and 1720-69.[15] A completed family is one in which the woman reached the age of 45 in marriage and would therefore in almost all cases have completed her

14 It may be of interest to note that Creighton, in discussing the aftermath of the Black Death, quotes a passage from the *Eulogium Historiarum* that 'the women who survived remained for the most part barren during several years'. Creighton, *History of epidemics in Britain*, i, p. 200. Creighton also quotes Piers the Plowman to much the same effect.

15 The period 1770-1837 yields too few completed families to be worth including.

child-bearing. Only those women who married under 30 are included in the table, since if family limitation was to be found in the period 1647–1719 it is in such families that it would be most clearly apparent for reasons touched on above. To those in each group of whom the exact age at marriage is known have been added completed families[16] in which the age of the wife is not known when there are six or more children born to the marriage in the periods 1560–1646 and 1720–69 and where there were four or more children in the period 1647–1719, since in the vast majority of these cases the wife was under 30 at marriage. Including such marriages increases substantially the number of cases which can be studied (by almost three-quarters). The most striking feature of table 10.8 is the contrast between the middle period and the other two in the mean interval between the penultimate and last births. A marked rise in this interval is typical of a community beginning to practise family limitation.[17] It rises in these circumstances because even after reaching an intended final family size additions are nevertheless occasionally made either from accident (failure of whatever system of restriction is in use), from a reversal of an earlier decision not to increase family size or from a desire to replace a child which has died.

Figure 10.3 shows the distribution of final birth intervals of the two periods 1560–1646 and 1647–1719 in the form of a histogram. In the earlier period the distribution is unimodal with a fairly clear peak about the 30–5 month interval. In the later period this peak is again apparent but there is also a suspicion of a second peak in the 54–65 month intervals, suggesting that while the 'natural' distribution continued to occur in some cases, there was superimposed upon it a different pattern which might be the result of family limitation.

Table 10.8 contains other points of interest. The mean interval between marriage and first baptism did not change materially over the two centuries covered by the table. The later birth intervals, 1–2, 2–3 and 3–4, were always higher in 1647–1719 than in 1560–1646, though, rather surprisingly perhaps, the difference showed no tendency to grow greater as the rank of birth increased. It is also surprising to find the higher mean present as early as the 1–2 birth interval. One might have expected in the light of experience elsewhere that the early stages of family formation would have been as rapid in the middle period as either earlier or later, but this appears not to have been the case. The frequency distribution of all birth intervals 1–2, 2–3 and 3–4 (taken together since the numbers involved are small and the pattern much the same at each birth interval) (figure 10.4) shows that the reason for the higher mean in the period 1647–1719 does not lie in a shift of the peak frequency but in the greater skewness of the distribution to the right. The figures for the median and mode underline this point (table 10.9). The frequency distribution pattern is compatible with the view that family

16 Completed families here comprise any in which at least 27 years is known to have elapsed between the beginning and end of the marriage.
17 See Henry, *Anciennes familles genevoises*, especially pp. 93–110.

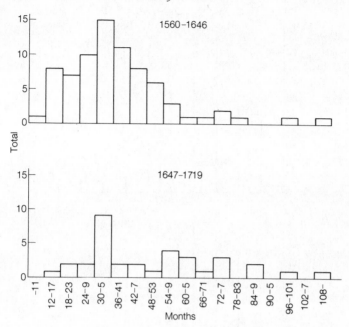

Figure 10.3 Final birth intervals (months).

Table 10.9 Means, medians and modes of all birth intervals 1-4

	Mean	Median	Mode
1560-1646	27.5	26.6	24.8
1647-1719	31.4	29.0	24.1

limitation was being practised. Some other changes in frequency distributions which might have occurred and which would have produced a higher mean would have shown a different pattern. For example, if there had been a general increase in the customary suckling period which would have increased the mean birth intervals by prolonging the period of lowered fecundity in the mother, there would probably have been a shift in the peak frequency to the right.[18]

Another tell-tale sign of family limitation is a fall in the age at which women bear their last child in families in which they are at risk to the end of the child-bearing period (45 years of age). This is likely to arise for the same reasons which tend to produce a very long final birth interval and will be most evident among women who marry young and have had several children well before the end of their fertile period. Table 10.10 shows the mean ages at the birth of the last child of women marrying above and below the age

18 See the searching discussion of this question and the data presented in Henry, *Anciennes familles genevoises*, chapters 4 and 5.

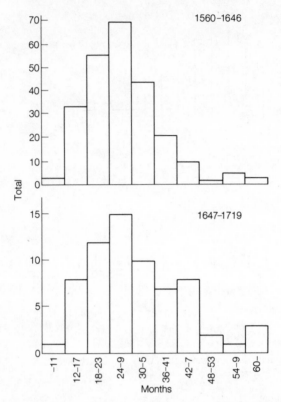

Figure 10.4   Birth intervals 1-2, 2-3 and 3-4 combined (months).

of 30. In the first of the three periods the mean age at birth of the last child was much the same for women marrying under 30 as for those marrying over 30, in each case about 40, and the same is true of the period 1720–69. But in the middle period the mean age at birth of the last child for women marrying under 30 was lower than for those marrying over 30 and lower than for women in the same age-group in the other two periods. Both these features are to be expected if family limitation were taking place.[19] The fall between 1560–1646 and 1647–1719 in the mean for women marrying under 30 was 2.25 years. This, in combination with a steep rise in the mean interval between the penultimate and last births, underlies, of course, the very low age-specific fertility figures found in the age-groups 30-4, 35-9 and 40-4 for women marrying under 30 (table 10.6). The eighteenth century shows a reversion to the earlier pattern in age at birth of last child as in the other fertility characteristics considered.

19 The difference in mean age at birth of last child of women marrying under 30 between 1560–1646 and 1647–1719 is 2.25 years. The standard error of the difference of the two means is 1.24. The difference between the two means is therefore not significant at the 5 per cent level (the former is only 1.81 times the latter).

Table 10.10   Age at birth of last child (completed families only)

	Under 30	n	30 and over	n
1560-1646	39.8	50	40.5	25
1647-1719	37.6	22	42.7	14
1720-69	40.4	14	41.4	5

A convenient measure which reflects the combined effects of the changes already discussed is the mean size of completed families. Table 10.11 sets out the chief statistics.

The extent of the decline between the first and second halves of the seventeenth century is underscored by the figures of completed family size.[20] Figure 10.5 gives more detail of the distribution of family sizes in the form of a series of histograms.

Perhaps the most striking single feature of the detailed distribution is that only 18 per cent of women marrying under 30 between 1647 and 1719 and living right through the fertile period had families of six children or more (3 in 17), compared with 55 per cent (29 in 53) in 1560-1629, 48 per cent (10 in 21) in 1720-69 and 60 per cent (12 in 20) in 1770-1837. Very large families, on the other hand, were rare at any time in Colyton, the largest during the full three centuries being only 13. Childless marriages were also rare in the period of high fertility before 1646. Of all marriages formed when the bride was under 35 and lasting till she was 45 or more, only 5 out of 70 were childless (table 10.12). Since a small number of marriages prove

Table 10.11   Mean completed family size

	Age at marriage		
	Under 25	25-29	30-9
1560-1629	7.3±1.3	5.7±1.1	2.7±0.8
1646-1719	5.0±2.0	3.3±1.7	1.7±0.9
1720-69	5.8±2.5	3.8±1.7	2.4±1.7
1770-1837	7.3±1.6	4.5±2.3	3.2±0.9

The figures after the means are the 95 per cent confidence intervals.

Table 10.12   Childless completed marriages (wife marrying under 35)

	Childless	Total	%
Colyton			
1560-1629	5	70	7
1647-1719	4	22	18
1720-69	6	29	21
1770-1837	2	26	8
Crulai			
1674-1742	5	77	6

The Crulai figure is calculated from Gautier and Henry, *Crulai*, table vii, pp. 249-54.

20 The fall occurred at a time when age-specific death rates, especially of young children, were rising so that the net reproduction rate fell even more sharply than the gross rate. It is doubtful whether the net reproduction rate of the population of Colyton reached unity during the period when fertility rates were at their lowest.

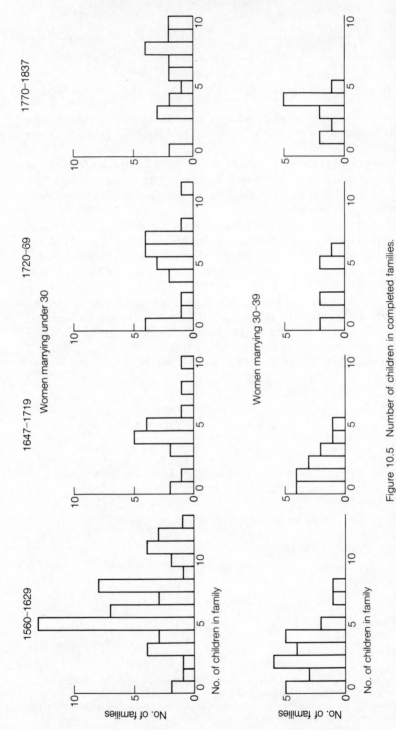

Figure 10.5   Number of children in completed families.

Women marrying under 25 and 25–9 are brought together in the upper set of histograms. Since the number of women marrying under 25 and 25–9 was much the same in each period (24 and 29 in 1560–1629, 9 and 8 in 1647–1719, 9 and 12 in 1720–69, and 10 and 10 in 1770–1837), this does not introduce much relative distortion and allows a clearer pattern to emerge.

infertile for physiological reasons, the position in the earliest period may well represent a figure close to the minimum which can be expected.[21] It is notably similar to the Crulai figure, and is found also in the latest period 1770–1837 when marital fertility was again high at Colyton. In the other two periods, 1647–1719 and 1720–69, the proportion of childless families was much higher. It is interesting that the period 1720–69, an intermediate period in most other respects, had such a high proportion of childless marriages, though the absolute numbers involved are not large and are subject to wide margins of error. The difference between the first period, 1560–1629, and the two succeeding periods, 1647–1719 and 1720–69, is, however, not significant at the 5 per cent level even if the latter two periods are grouped together (χ^2 test).

The mean size of completed families substantially exceeded average family size, of course, since many marriages were interrupted by the death of one of the partners before the wife had passed through her child-bearing period. Table 10.11 shows, for example, that in 1560–1629 the mean sizes of completed families born to women marrying under 25, 25–9 and 30–9 were 7.3, 5.7 and 2.7 respectively. But if to these families are added all those cut short before the wife reached 45, the mean sizes fall to 5.2, 4.9 and 2.4 respectively. Marriages contracted in early life are, of course, more likely to be affected and the proportionate fall in family size is greater in their case. In all the tables expressing family size the importance of age at marriage is clear. At all periods, the contrast between marriages contracted in the early twenties and those which took place when the bride was in her thirties is marked. The immense social and economic import of the fall of seven years in the average age at first marriage for women which took place between the beginning of the eighteenth and the early nineteenth centuries, therefore, is firmly driven home.

Before turning to the more general issues raised by the history of family formation in Colyton during the three centuries when the parish registers are the prime source of information about demographic changes, it is appropriate to touch upon the question of the completeness of registration. This is too large a topic to be treated here in its entirety, but one issue must be mentioned. It is evident that when the figures err they will err by understating rather than over-stating the levels of fertility reached. For example, although the families used for the calculation of age-specific fertility are subjected to a fairly rigorous test of presence in the parish,[22] there must be a small proportion of baptisms recorded in the registers of other parishes which should ideally have been included in the fertility data for Colyton families. In addition to small 'leakages' of this sort, there is a major source of 'leakage' which deserves attention. In some periods in English parishes many children who died soon after birth were never baptized[23] and some of these were buried without benefit of church

---

21 See, for example, the tables of Glass and Grebenik, 'World population, 1801–1950', p. 114.

22 For details see Wrigley (ed.), *English historical demography*, chapter 4.

23 It would be more accurate to say that they never appeared in the baptism register. In some parishes it was the custom to baptize privately in the home if the child were in danger of death,

service. No system of correction can overcome the difficulties arising from under-registration entirely, but some idea of the order of magnitude of correction which seems appropriate can be gained from a consideration of infant mortality and especially the frequency distribution of the apparent age at death of children dying under the age of one year.

Table 10.13   Age at death

	1st day	1-6 days	1-4 wk	1 mth	2 mth	3-5 mth	6-11 mth	Total
A	33	28	21	9	8	20	21	140
B	35	19	27	16	9	15	24	145
C	19	18	20	26	7	24	24	138

A, St Michael le Belfrey, York, 1571-86.
B, Colyton, 1538-99.
C, Colyton, 1600-49.

Table 10.13 shows the age at death of children dying under one year for the parish of St Michael le Belfrey in York and for Colyton at two different periods. The register of St Michael le Belfrey during the years 1571–86 is very remarkable in that an exact age at burial is given (even down to an age in hours if the child died during its first day of life) and every care appears to have been taken to secure a complete coverage of vital events. The baptism register contains many entries of baptism by the midwife in the house and the burial of unbaptized children is also scrupulously set down. In Colyton in the same period only an apparent age at death can be calculated by comparing the dates of baptism and burial. Comparison of the A and B lines in table 10.13 does nothing to undermine the view that in the sixteenth century children in Colyton were normally baptized very soon after birth and that consequently the 'leakage' was very slight. The comparatively high proportion of children buried on the day they were baptized is difficult to reconcile with any other view.[24] Line C in table 10.13, however, presents a very different picture. In the period 1600–49 the proportion apparently dying in the first week of life was much lower and this proportion fell further in later periods. There are several ways in which estimates may be made of the correction necessary to offset the effects of delayed baptism on the assumption that the true distribution by age of deaths under one year was unchanging.

These several exercises suggest that the fertility rates quoted in table 10.4 understate the true position by between 2 and 6 per cent, with a low figure appropriate for the first period, 1560–1629, and figures in the upper part of the range more likely in the later periods. It appears most unlikely that differences in the degree of under-registration at different periods can serve

but only to record it in the register after a subsequent public ceremony if the child survived its first dangers.

24 It is interesting to note that at Crulai in the late seventeenth and early eighteenth centuries, where baptism is known to have taken place almost invariably on the first day of life, 30 per cent of all deaths under one year were on the first day (99 in 331), compared with 24 per cent at Colyton, 1538–99. Gautier and Henry remark, however, that a proportion of these may well in fact have been born dead. Gautier and Henry, *Crulai*, p. 170.

to explain any of the major changes which appear in tables in the earlier sections of this article.

Was there family limitation?

I have so far written of the striking changes in marital fertility which took place in Colyton between the first and second halves of the seventeenth century as if they were the result of a system of family limitation deliberate in the sense that social or individual action caused fewer children to be born, or at all events to survive long enough to be baptized, than would have been the case without such restraints. But is this a correct assumption? And if so, what were the means employed to reduce fertility so drastically?

Any explanation other than family limitation must take account of the fact that fertility fell much more steeply in the later years of the fertile period than the earlier, of the remarkable change in the mean age at first marriage for women and, if possible, of the later reversion to a position not unlike that of the late sixteenth and early seventeenth centuries. Some of the explanations which might be entertained on one score are unacceptable on other grounds. For example, a fall in marital fertility might simply reflect a change in suckling habits, but this would not explain the much more drastic fall in fertility in the higher age-groups. Perhaps the only explanation other than family limitation which might cover the known facts is an economic reverse of such severity that the physiological condition of women of child-bearing age was affected by it (either from simple undernourishment, or from the absence in their diet of elements necessary for high fertility). This might plausibly be argued to be likely to affect the older age-groups more than the younger. Such an explanation has the additional attraction that it is fully consonant with the steep rise in child mortality which took place at that time.[25] This alternative explanation deserves further careful study, but suffers from several defects.

The first difficulty is that fertility in the higher age-groups was much higher among women who married late in life than among those who married early. This might be explained on the ground that those who had already borne several children were exhausted by this and that their physical condition deteriorated seriously as a result. But it is doubtful whether child-bearing would have had this effect on the mass of women. Gautier and Henry remark

---

25 The late seventeenth century was much more unhealthy for young children at Colyton than the preceding century, as is shown by the following life-table mortality rates. (The figures in brackets for 1600–49 are the rates which result from eliminating the deaths from plague in 1645–6. Rates are per thousand.)

Age	1538–99	1600–49	1650–99
1–4	88	97 (85)	162
5–9	30	54 (30)	45
10–14	16	41 (19)	37

that this did not occur at Crulai, and that it is not apparent in modern Indian rural populations.[26] Again, the abrupt change to much lower fertility levels among the families which spanned the great mortality of 1645–6 creates a problem. It is difficult to imagine a change in economic conditions effecting such a swift and complete change in the absence of family limitation. It is possible, of course, that this fall in fertility was due to the after-effects of plague infection on the women who survived, but against this it must be noted that their fertility after 1647 was closely similar to the general pattern over the next two generations. But perhaps the most important difficulty is that although death rates at all ages rose in the second half of the seventeenth century, and expectation of life fell by several years to the mid-30s,[27] it was still as high in Colyton at this period as it was in Crulai at much the same time. Yet fertility rates at Crulai were almost as high as in Colyton in the sixteenth century, and moreover the pattern of age-specific rates in Crulai shows no sudden dip in the thirties. This undermines a main base of the argument from a general worsening of economic conditions, unless indeed it is held that diet and other conditions of life in Colyton, though generally no worse than in Crulai, were nevertheless more deficient in certain vital constituents necessary for high fertility in women.

There are, however, difficulties also with the view that family limitation lay behind the change in fertility in Colyton. These difficulties fall under two main heads: the explanation of the rise in child mortality which accompanied the fall in fertility, and the question of the means which it is reasonable to envisage having been employed to secure a lower fertility. The first is a problem because it might seem natural to suppose that if a population began to limit its fertility drastically it would take the better care of those children who were born. If child mortality changed it would fall rather than rise. The second is a problem for the reason that Malthus expressed succinctly when he referred to the 'passion between the sexes' as a potent and unchanging feature of behaviour. Yet if the passion between the sexes is given free rein within marriage, how can one explain a sudden fall in marital fertility in a period long before modern mechanical and chemical methods of birth control were practised? Both these are objections of weight and any answer to them is bound to be tentative. I am more concerned in this section of the article to set an argument in train than to suggest that a full answer can as yet be given.

It may be that the problem of the fall in fertility coinciding with a rise in child mortality is only a problem if viewed, anachronistically, in modern terms. If the reason for limiting family size had been prudential in the modern sense, then a concomitant rise in child mortality would be very surprising.[28]

26 See Gautier and Henry, *Crulai*, pp. 98–100.
27 Wrigley, 'Mortality in pre-industrial England', pp. 572–5.
28 Unless indeed the change in economic conditions had been so catastrophic that not even a fall in marital fertility as steep as that which took place in Colyton could ensure as good a life for the children of the small families of the late seventeenth century as their parents and grandparents had enjoyed in the much larger families of their childhood. There is, unfortunately,

But the change may well have been of a very different type. It must be borne in mind that the view that pre-industrial societies normally did little or nothing to restrict the level of fertility within marriage is an extreme hypothesis. Societies at a low level of material culture frequently developed taboos upon intercourse during long periods of married life, and practised abortion or infanticide.[29] There is a very large literature about the connection between the social activities of animals and the maintenance of population size at a level substantially below the maximum number which their habitat could support.[30] Both in primitive human groups and in an enormous range of insect, fish, bird and mammal species it is clear that methods developed within the group through social activity to prevent numbers from pressing too hard upon the food base confer a notable selective advantage. If numbers are allowed to grow too great the ecological balance of the area may be upset and the ability of the area to provide food for the population impaired. Moreover, the group as a whole is more likely to be successful if its members are well fed and in good health than if the constant pressure of numbers makes it hard to keep adults vigorous. A tribe of Australian aborigines having only a limited food base on which to support itself behaves much as bird and animal communities do in similar circumstances. It throws up social controls which prevent so large a number of new mouths coming into existence as to prejudice the well-being of those already living. This may be done in animal populations either by preventing some adults from breeding in a given season, or by delaying the entry of adolescents into the breeding population, or by restricting the number of viable offspring, or by causing the early death of many which are born, or indeed by many combinations and modifications of these methods. But in all cases the effect is to keep population numbers fluctuating some way beneath the maximum, that is, at a level which neither prejudices the flow of food by creating too great a pressure on the available food base (over-fishing in Wynne-Edwards terminology; encroaching on capital rather than living off dividend in more familiar jargon), nor stunts the development of the adult members of the community, but yet does not restrict numbers much below the level imposed by these desiderata. It is important to note that when a population has risen substantially above this level and a contraction of numbers is necessary it is normally secured, in part at least, by reducing

---

very little evidence as yet about the state of the Colyton economy in the late seventeenth century. Study of the Exeter wheat price series suggests that living was dear in this region at the beginning of the period of low fertility, though prices had fallen to low levels well before its end. (In 1647 wheat was 62.72 shillings per quarter at Exeter, a level not surpassed until 1795, and prices stayed high for much of the 1650s and 1660s, but they had been very high before this, reaching 62.94 shillings in 1596.) The state of affairs in Colyton may, of course, have been either better or worse than in the county or country as a whole.

29 See, for example, Himes, *Medical history of contraception*; and Lorimer et al., *Culture and human fertility*

30 This subject is brilliantly reviewed in Wynne-Edwards, *Animal dispersion in relation to social behaviour*. Carr-Saunders has also used this argument in *The population problem*.

the flow of new members into the community, and it is to be expected both that the number of births will fall and that the infant death rate will rise. Conversely, if numbers fall below the optimum range it is probable that there will be both a rise in fertility and a fall in the wastage of life among the very young members of the population. If, therefore, a model drawn from the study of animal populations were made the basis of expectation, it would occasion no surprise that fertility and child mortality should change in Colyton in the way that they did in the later seventeenth century.[31] Such a model, incidentally, also makes the changes in mean age at first marriage of women (particularly the reversal of the usual age gap between the sexes at marriage) easier to understand.

Populations whose economy was based upon hunting and the collection of food appear to have conformed closely in their methods of population control to the general model of animal communities. Pre-industrial populations whose economies were based upon the cultivation of the land were differently placed. In their case, the food base might be substantially broadened from time to time by technological advance (for example by the development of a more effective plough or the introduction of a new type of food crop). Their population control problems were much less simple, since in periods following technological or organizational advance and an expansion of the food base populations could rise for several centuries with only intermittent checks from epidemics and bad harvests, but they were brought up against the same problem once more when the possibilities of any given advance in material culture had been exhausted. The Malthusian model under which populations tended to approach a maximum rather than to fluctuate well below it was perhaps an aberration in the history of populations from the more general model to which many animal societies conform, rather as the classical model of full employment is a limiting case of Keynesian employment theory. In the absence of much more empirical work much of this discussion is inevitably speculative, but it may well explain why populations in the late fourteenth and fifteenth centuries remained at a lower level than before the Black Death in spite of the rise in real incomes which apparently took place among the peasants. Upon Malthusian assumptions this should have produced a fall in the age of marriage and a rise in population.[32]

All the foregoing, of course, does not imply that the individual man or woman was conscious of this range of issues in the least, any more than the individual robin or rook is conscious of the problems of avoiding too large a population, but like robins and rooks people respond sensitively to

---

31 The argument here is, of course, very general. Several other possible causes of higher child mortality can be envisaged. It may be, for example, that smallpox at this period was both more virulent and more widespread than earlier.

32 Bean argues that recurrences of plague in the fifteenth century were not sufficiently severe to keep population down to post-Black Death levels and that therefore it is reasonable to suppose that numbers were increasing. This view is advanced with proper caution, but is interesting as an illustration of the tendency to expect populations to rise unless some exogenous agency keeps them down. See Bean, 'Plague, population and economic decline', pp. 431–6.

social pressures. It would be surprising if in pre-industrial European populations there were not latent a range of patterns of social behaviour which could secure a stabilization of numbers well short of the maximum attainable. Such patterns might not merely result in alterations in socially acceptable patterns of age at marriage, but also in normal levels of fertility within marriage (perhaps in ways which bore more heavily upon the lower sections of the social pyramid), and might even produce changes in social custom likely to produce higher child mortality.[33]

There remains the second general problem in accepting at its face value the evidence for control of fertility within marriage at Colyton, the problem of the methods used to produce this result. Once more one can plausibly argue that this is a problem only if approached with preconceived ideas, or more properly, since this is to some extent inevitable, with a particular set of preconceived ideas. It is quite clear that European pre-industrial populations could severely restrict their family sizes, not merely in the wealthy and leisured families, but throughout a whole community. When in the late eighteenth century rural populations in France, still set in traditional economic ways, began to limit the size of their families they did not have at their disposal any of the modern chemical or mechanical means of contraception.[34] They limited their families, so far as is yet known, by practising *coitus interruptus* or *reservatus*, no doubt by procuring many abortions and possibly also by infanticide. Any means which may have been available to French peasants of the Ile de France or Normandy at the end of the eighteenth century were also available to English communities a century and a half earlier, and indeed to European communities for many centuries before that.[35] Such means may perhaps be regarded as being permanently at the disposal of European pre-industrial populations, requiring only the right sort of 'trigger' to bring them forth. Circumstances in Colyton in the middle of the seventeenth century appear to have been such as to produce this change. The parish register of Colyton carries no clues to the methods of family limitation used. These may never be known with certainty, but it is likely that there was scope for the quiet disposal of abortions, and indeed of the victims of infanticide if this was practised. The early hours of a child's life provide many occasions when it is easy to follow the maxim that 'thou shalt not kill but needst not strive officiously to keep alive'. In the nature

33 This possibility must have been in Krause's mind when he wrote: 'The usually cited infant death rates greatly exaggerate pre-industrial European infant mortality, especially among infants born to families which wanted to keep them alive.' Krause, 'Recent work in historical demography', p. 77.

34 See Gautier and Henry, *Crulai*; and Ganiage, *Trois villages d'Ile de France*.

35 Helleiner concluded that contraception and abortion may have been more widely practised in pre-industrial Europe than has usually been supposed. He takes issue with Mols on this question quoting literary evidence of *coitus interruptus* from Germany in the sixteenth and eighteenth centuries. In commenting on the large fall in births recorded during many French *crises* he writes, 'But when all is said, the magnitude of the decline in births is such as to suggest to most students of the phenomenon that people during crises had recourse on a considerable scale to birth control or abortion.' Helleiner 'History of urban populations', pp. 60–1.

of things' there cannot be much evidence about the frequency of *coitus interruptus* and similar methods of avoiding conception in the absence of literary evidence on the subject. There is, however, a good deal of evidence from more recent times of the large scale upon which *coitus interruptus* may be practised and that it is an effective means of controlling conception.[36] *Coitus interruptus* may well have been the most important method of family limitation in use in Colyton in the seventeenth and early eighteenth centuries.[37] It was probably widely employed by French populations to secure a lower marital fertility a century later.

Population characteristics and their economic setting

Colyton's population history shows that in pre-industrial English society a very flexible response to economic and social conditions was possible. This may well have important implications for the general course of social and particularly economic change in England in the seventeenth and eighteenth centuries. It is now often asserted that during the early decades of the industrial revolution it was largely rising home demand which sustained the increasing output of industrial goods.[38] It is arguable that the growing home demand occurred because of rising real incomes spread broadly through large sections of the community.[39] The changes in real incomes and in the level of production were not very dramatic or abrupt, but continued over many decades. If the Malthusian picture of demographic behaviour were correct, this type of slow sea change coming over an economy is very difficult to credit since one would expect precarious gains in real incomes however achieved to be wiped out quickly in a flood of additional babies produced by earlier marriages (and possibly by increased fertility within marriage). If, on the other hand, populations might behave in a manner more likely to secure optimum than maximum numbers, the establishment and holding of gains in real income are much easier to

36 See, for example, Glass and Grebenik, 'World population, 1800–1950', pp. 113–18, especially note 1 on p. 118.

37 Sutter remarks that *coitus interruptus* is a technique which has sprung up independently in many places and at many times. He writes 'Chaque couple pourrait l'inventer. Il ne nécessite, d'autre part, l'intervention d'aucun corps étranger, ni d'aucune manœuvre féminine particulière.' It is a technique 'capable d'auto-apparition et pouvant se diffuser sans propagande. Ce n'est pas une manifestation culturelle comme les autres méthodes, il est propre à l'espèce humaine et n'est pas une charactéristique ethnologique spécifique.' Bergues et al., *La prévention des naissances*, p. 345. It may be of some importance that *coitus interruptus* is essentially a male act since in animal populations in general the social activities which serve to maintain populations near an optimum are normally a male preserve.

38 Deane and Cole, for example, remark 'it seems that the explanation of the higher average rate of growth in the second half of the century should be sought at home rather than abroad.' Deane and Cole, *British economic growth*, p. 85.

39 This is the tenor of the argument used by Landes in his review of the industrial revolution in Britain. See Landes, 'Technological change and industrial development', pp. 280–5.

understand. The course of events in Colyton shows this to be a possibility. The balance between fertility and mortality was probably at all times delicate and unstable under stress. Colyton itself shows that the very restrictive adaptation which appeared in the middle of the seventeenth century was beginning to give way after 1720 and that in the 1770s or 1780s demographic behaviour reverted to the sixteenth-century type. Nevertheless, for three-quarters of a century in an extreme form and for well over a century altogether, Colyton behaved demographically in such a way as to make possible an increase and even a steady growth in real incomes.[40] If changes in the economy and technology of the period made possible rising production and real incomes, demographic behaviour was not such as to prejudice them immediately.

This forms an instructive contrast with the course of events in the sixteenth and early seventeenth centuries which do seem to fit what might be called a Malthusian model quite well. There is much evidence that over the country as a whole population in the sixteenth century was rising faster than production and that real incomes became depressed. One of the reasons why the 'industrial revolution of the sixteenth century' which Nef has documented had no chance of fructifying into a steady expansion in production and real incomes was that population behaved much in the way Malthus supposed to be almost inevitable. The sixteenth-century English economy and population was 'over-fishing'[41] and paid the penalty, just as the Irish population of the late eighteenth and early nineteenth centuries was 'over-fishing'. As with animal populations in similar circumstances a sharp adjustment was inevitable. It is possible that at times in the late eighteenth and early nineteenth centuries the same cycle of events came close to being repeated for the great surge of population increase towards the end of the eighteenth century caused serious difficulties of which contemporaries were keenly aware. But if the new pattern of behaviour which can be seen in Colyton in the intervening period proved fragile and eventually gave way to a reversion to the older pattern, it may have helped to win a vital breathing space in the interim. Contemporary French population behaviour appears to have been very different and much more Malthusian (in the sense in which I have used the adjective in this article). Sauvy has estimated that towards the end of the eighteenth century French population was 100 per cent above

---

40 In this connection it is important to note that a decline of fertility as great as that which occurred in Colyton in the seventeenth century must have had a marked effect on the age structure of the population. The proportion of the population of working age must rise and the burden of unproductive mouths be reduced. For example, the United Nations study, *The aging of populations and its economic and social implications*, Department of Economic and Social Affairs, Population Studies no. 26 (New York, 1956), table 15, p. 26, gives 52.5 as the percentage of a stable population in the age-group 15–59 when the gross reproduction rate is 3.0 and expectation of life at birth is 40 years, compared with 60.9 per cent in the same age-group when the gross reproduction rate is 2.0 and expectation of life at birth is 30. The ratio of productive to non-productive people in the first case is 1.11 : 1.00. in the second 1.56 : 1.00.

41 See pp. 75–6.

the optimum level.[42] In consequence, any adventitious increase in real incomes in the short term was not likely to be used to swell demand in the industrial sector but simply to secure a slightly better level of nutrition.

Conclusion

In this essay I have been unable to deal extensively with more than a small fraction of the interesting topics which spring to mind in studying the family reconstitution data of Colyton. Mortality remains largely untouched, and on the fertility side such factors as pre-nuptial pregnancy rates, the interval between being widowed and remarrying, and bastardy rates. Moreover, though much has been written of the remarkable fall in fertility in the mid-seventeenth century, the equally remarkable recovery in the eighteenth century has not been fully analysed; not have the implications of the high level of fertility during the reigns of Elizabeth and James I been sufficiently discussed. While the middle period is perhaps the most fascinating because it is the most unexpected, the significance of the earlier and later periods is also great. Each period is the more interesting and intelligible because a knowledge of the others provides a perspective in which to view it.[43]

The life of men in societies is a subtle and complex thing which can and does influence behaviour at marriage and within marriage. Since the disadvantages to society and to the individual of the unrestrained flow of births which it is within the physiological capacity of women to sustain are very great, societies take care at all times not to expose themselves to such strains. In comparing the sixteenth and the late seventeenth centuries in Colyton, the contrast is not between a society producing children at a maximum rate and a society imposing maximum restrictions but rather between two points on a spectrum of possibilities, each some way from the furthest extremes. In the earlier period the control appears to have lain largely in conventional ages at first marriage which were even then so late for women as to cause them to spend on an average at least a third of their fertile life unmarried. But once marriage had taken place restraints upon fertility appear to have been slight. In the later period, the restraint through age at marriage became more pronounced and was compounded by new restraints within marriage. These in combination lowered fertility to the point where increase stopped.

It is likely that among the circumstances which produce large changes in fertility economic conditions often bulk large, but it also seems probable

42 Sauvy, *Théorie générale*, i, pp. 186–7. Sauvy sets the optimum between 10 and 12 million at most in 1790 against an actual population of 24 million.

43 Colyton shows not only that it was within the power of pre-industrial communities to halt population growth, but also that their powers of growth were very remarkable. Over a period of about 90 years (1538–1629) when fertility was high and mortality comparatively low (expectation of life was about 40) baptisms stood to burials in the ratio of 1.61 : 1.00, a ratio as high as this was common in other parishes at this period. Rates of increase well above 1 per cent per annum were clearly possible: equivalent, say, to a doubling of population within about half a century.

that the relationship is not direct and simple but indirect and flexible. The buffer provided by a society's sociodemographic organization to cushion the shock of harvest fluctuation and economic débâcle may be either thin or thick, may be as inadequate as in parts of south-east Asia today or parts of the Beauvaisis in the seventeenth century, or so ample that the society has scope for further economic advance and is free from the periodic *crises démographiques* which are sometimes thought typical of all pre-industrial societies. The *mercuriale* may be a reliable guide to demographic fluctuations in parts of France in the seventeenth century, but other pre-industrial societies were much better buffered against the hazards of the weather and harvest. In the absence of a continuing advance in material culture a population will always find in time a rough equilibrium level of numbers, but the living standards which result from this will not be the same in all cases. The adjective Malthusian has come to be associated with one limiting case, that in which living standards are minimized but numbers maximized. Other equilibria are also possible and will vary with the extent of the restrictions upon fertility characterizing the society in question. If the restrictions are widespread and effective, the equilibrium may occur at a point substantially beneath the maximum level of population, with all that this implies for the likelihood of success in establishing a beneficent spiral of economic activity rather than becoming locked into that other condition which keeps the masses miserably short of food and prevents economic growth.

11

The Fall of Marital Fertility in Nineteenth-century France: Exemplar or Exception?

The study of the onset of family limitation in Europe owes a great deal to the Princeton fertility project which has collected, analysed and published a huge mass of data in a standard form during the past two decades. Two of the most distinguished participants in this project have attempted to distil the essence from the plethora of empirical historical data which it has produced in order to discuss their policy implications for countries in which fertility has started recently to fall.[1] They present their conclusions firmly while agreeing that the evidence does not preclude other interpretations, suggesting *inter alia* that 'increases in the practice of family limitation and the decline of marital fertility were essentially irreversible processes once under way'.[2] This conclusion is closely related to their view that ignorance of an effective method of limiting family size was a main reason for the absence of an earlier fall in marital fertility. They take, in other words, a strongly 'innovation' rather than an 'adjustment' view of the fertility transition, and argue that developments in the Third World today are following a similar pattern. The only figure in the article is introduced to show how similar the patterns of fertility decline in Sweden and Taiwan have been, though changes which took six decades in the former were compressed into only two in the latter.[3]

One of the two authors of the article, van de Walle, has done more than any other living scholar to describe and explain the fertility history of France in the nineteenth century, and it is therefore interesting that he and Knodel do not regard France as out of conformity with their view of the nature of the European fertility decline. They note that the early start of the fertility decline in France sets it apart from the rest of Europe and that it occurred when France 'could hardly be considered very advanced . . . in terms of any

---

1 Knodel and van de Walle, 'Lessons from the past'.
2 Ibid., p. 219.
3 Ibid., p. 223.

standard definition of development', but show no inclination to treat it as an exception to their generalized picture.[4]

In this essay I shall present an alternative interpretation of French population history during the nineteenth century. Instead of treating the period from the earliest decline about 1800 to the ultimate 'bottoming out' in fertility about 1930 as one variant of the normal European pattern, differing from other countries only in being unusually long drawn out, I shall argue that it is better regarded as falling into two halves sufficiently dissimilar to be treated as distinct, the earlier having much in common with the 'traditional' European systems of population control, the later indistinguishable in character from the changes taking place in most of the rest of Europe. What follows is intended only as a *ballon d'essai*. It contains no new empirical data but may help to define some of the issues to which future research might be addressed.

France and her neighbours

As a background to a more detailed consideration of French population history, it is convenient to compare French population history with that of other European countries in order to drive home the remarkable extent and the immense general importance of the contrasts between France and her neighbours. Table 11.1 gives the population totals of France, England, Sweden and Germany for 1700, 1800 and 1900.

Even in the eighteenth century, the rate of growth in France was somewhat lower than in the other three countries, though the differences were not large. In France population increased by 35 per cent, while in England, Sweden and Germany the comparable figures were 71, 72 and 43 per cent respectively. But, during the nineteenth century, the contrast became much more strongly marked for in France the rate of growth rose only fractionally to 38 per cent, whereas in the other three countries there was a marked acceleration in growth rates to 252, 119 and 172 per cent respectively. In all three countries, moreover, unlike France, there was net emigration. In Sweden it was particularly heavy, a fact which further underlines the strength of the contrast between France and other west European countries.

The extent of the divergence of French population history from that of other countries can also be pictured in other ways. From the 1740s onwards the annual totals of births occurring in France are known with only a small margin of error. In figure 11.1 the decadal averages from 1740–9 to 1900–9 are plotted together with those for England. In the 1740s the English total was only 19 per cent of the French but thereafter it rose so swiftly that by the first decade of the twentieth century it was slightly the large of the two. The French total indeed scarcely varied between the 1740s and the 1870s, declining slowly thereafter. Such growth of population as occurred in France

---

4 Ibid., p. 224.

Table 11.1   Population totals in France, England, Sweden and Germany (millions)

				Percentage increase	
	1700	*1800*	*1900*	*1700–1800*	*1800–1900*
France	21.50	29.10	40.17	35	38
England	5.06	8.66	30.52	71	252
Sweden	1.37	2.35	5.14	72	119
Germany	c.14.50	c.20.70	56.37	43	172

The French total for 1900 refers to 1901. The English totals for 1700, 1800 and 1900 refer to 1701, 1801 and 1901. The French totals relate to the territory of 1861. The German totals relate to the territory of the German Empire in 1900. The total for 1800 was obtained by inflating the 1816 total given by Mitchell (see source note below) in the ratio of the addition to the German population resulting from the cession of territory by Denmark, Austria and France between 1864 and 1871 (1.042), and then assuming that population grew between 1800 and 1816 at the rate of 0.75 per cent per annum. The estimated total for 1700 was obtained by assuming that Germany as defined here grew at approximately the same rate as the population of the Holy Roman Empire in the eighteenth century. The English totals relate to England less Monmouth.

Sources: France 1700 and 1800: Dupâquier, *La population française*, pp. 34, 81. France 1900: Mitchell, *European historical statistics*, tables B1, B3. England 1700 and 1800: Wrigley and Schofield, *Population history of England*, table 7.8, pp. 208-9. England 1900: Mitchell and Deane, *British historical statistics*, pp. 6, 22. Sweden: Hofsten and Lundström, *Swedish population history*, table 1.1, p. 13. Germany 1700: McEvedy and Jones, *Atlas of world population history*, pp. 67-72. Germany 1800 and 1900: Mitchell, *European historical statistics*, table B1.

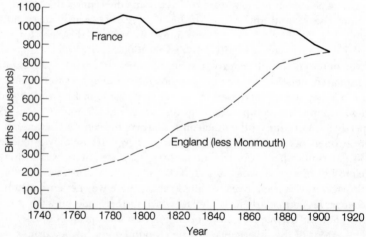

Figure 11.1   Mean annual totals of births in France and England by decade, 1740-9 to 1900-9.

The French totals relate to France within the boundaries of 1954 (virtually identical to those of 1861). The English totals relate to England without Monmouth. For 1870-9 onwards they were estimated by reducing the totals for England and Wales on the assumption that the crude birth rate in Wales and Monmouth was the same as in England and Wales as a whole (the proportion of the total population of England and Wales living in Wales and Monmouth in the successive decades 1870-9 to 1900-9 was 6.15, 6.08, 6.15 and 6.45 per cent respectively: the percentages are averages of the percentages found in the two censuses at either end of each decade).

Sources: France 1740-9 to 1820-9: Blayo, 'Mouvement naturel de la population française', pp. 52-3. France 1830-9 to 1900-9: data kindly supplied by J. Dupâquier which he had adjusted to conform to the basis of the earlier data. England 1740-9 to 1860-9: Wrigley and Schofield, *Population history of England*, table A2.1, p. 494. England 1870-9 to 1900-9: Mitchell and Deane, *British historical statistics*, pp. 6, 20, 22, 29-30.

in the later eighteenth and nineteenth centuries, therefore, was due to declining mortality. The base of the population pyramid did not vary in breadth but, with falling death rates, it supported a greater weight of numbers above it.

French mortality history has received much less attention than her fertility history, but it might repay greater study since it was also quite distinctive. The trends for France, England and Sweden are set out in table 11.2 and figure 11.2. The latter has a logarithmic vertical scale so that *proportional* changes in expectation of life can be more readily appreciated. Table 11.2 and figure 11.2 show that expectation of life in France did not differ greatly from that in England from about 1820 onwards. Before that date there was a marked difference for in the middle of the eighteenth century e_0 in France was by far the lower of the two. The average level of e_0 in France over the five decades 1740–9 to 1780–9 was only 27.4 years, while in England the comparable figure was 36.3 years, but by 1830–9 the French figure had risen to 39.9 years, a gain of 12.5 years, whereas improvement in England was far more modest; in 1830–9 the English figure stood at 40.2 years, representing a gain of only 3.9 years. It is ironic that the improvement in mortality in England in the later eighteenth century, which has often been cited as the chief reason for the rising rate of population increase, should prove to have been relatively slight, whereas in France the extent of the improvement was much greater even though the population growth rate remained so modest. The course of mortality change in Sweden closely resembled that in England until the 1830s, but thereafter expectation of life in Sweden consistently exceeded the comparable figures in the other two countries.

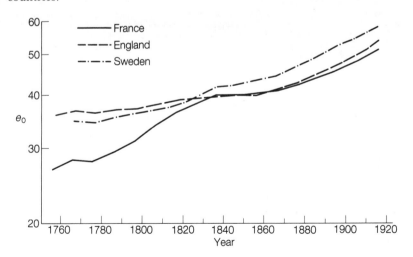

Figure 11.2   Expectation of life at birth in France, England and Sweden (sexes combined) in 30-year periods 1740–69 to 1900–29.
The points plotted are the central years of each 30-year period. For the sources used and other details of the data shown, see the notes to table 11.2.

Table 11.2 Expectation of life at birth in France, England and Sweden (sexes combined)

	France	England	Sweden
1740-9	24.7	35.3	—
1750-9	27.9	37.3	36.0
1760-9	27.7	35.0	35.0
1770-9	28.9	38.2	33.3
1780-9	27.8	35.9	35.2
1790-9	31.3	36.8	37.9
1800-9	34.1	38.7	35.8
1810-19	36.7	37.9	37.0
1820-9	38.8	39.9	40.8
1830-9	39.9	40.2	41.0
1840-9	41.3	39.6	43.8
1850-9	38.9	40.4	42.4
1860-9	41.0	40.3	44.6
1870-9	43.1	42.8	46.9
1880-9	43.3	45.2	50.0
1890-9	46.1	46.4	52.3
1900-9	48.2	50.1	55.7
1910-19	51.5	53.1	57.0
1920-9	54.8	58.8	62.0

Except for England 1740-9 to 1860-9, the expectations of life were calculated by combining data for males and females. In doing so, it was assumed that the sex ratio at birth was 105 males to 100 females. The French data refer to the decades shown for 1740-9 to 1820-9. Thereafter, they refer to 1835-7, 1845-7 etc., except that the figure shown for 1910-19 is the average of two figures for 1910-12 and 1920-2. The English data for the periods 1740-9 to 1860-9 refer to five-year periods centring on the years 1746, 1756 etc. Thereafter, they refer to the averages of paired five-year periods 1871-5 and 1876-80, 1881-5 and 1886-90 etc. From 1870-9 onwards, they relate to England and Wales; before then to England less Monmouth. The Swedish data for 1750-9 to 1830-9 were read off from the figure referred to in the source notes below and relate to the averages of the paired five-year periods 1751-5 and 1756-60, 1761-5 and 1766-70 etc. The data for 1840-9 and 1850-9 are similarly averages of the five-year periods 1841-5 and 1846-50, and 1851-5 and 1856-60. Thereafter, the data are for the decennia 1861-70, 1871-80 etc.

Sources: France 1740-9 to 1820-9: Blayo, 'La mortalité en France', tables 15 and 16, p. 141. France 1830-9 to 1910-19: Bourgeois-Pichat, 'The population of France', table 2, pp. 504-5. England 1740-9 to 1860-9: Wrigley and Schofield, *Population history of England*, table A3.1, p. 529. England 1870-9 to 1910-19: Case et al., *Serial abridged life tables*, pp. 45-56 and 69-80. Sweden 1750-9 to 1830-9: Hofsten and Lundström, *Swedish population history*, figure 3.8, p. 54. Sweden 1840-9 to 1910-19: *Historisk statistik för Sverige*, Del 1. Bevolkning 1720-1967 (Stockholm, 1969), table 42, p. 118.

The explanation of the absence of any acceleration in the French population growth rate with the fall in mortality lies, of course, in a matching fall in fertility. In figure 11.3 and table 11.3 the changing levels of the gross reproduction rate are set out for the same three countries whose mortality history is described in figure 11.2. The gross reproduction rate (GRR) fell uninterruptedly in France from the mid-eighteenth century onwards, except for a hesitation about 1860. In England, on the other hand, the GRR rose strikingly between the 1740s and the 1810s, fell away substantially to the 1840s, stagnated for a generation, and then sagged rapidly thereafter. Sweden contrasts with both countries. Her history conforms more closely to the conventional stereotype of pre-transitional fertility behaviour. The GRR moved irregularly but within a fairly narrow range and without clear trend until the 1870s and then fell with increasing steepness. By the 1920s fertility in all three countries had converged to a common level below that necessary for replacement.

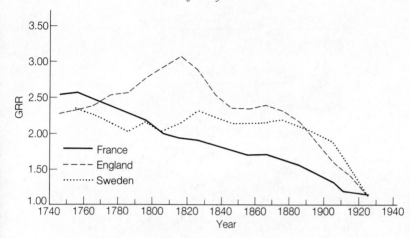

Figure 11.3 Gross reproduction rates in France, England and Sweden.
For the sources and other details of the data used, see the notes to table 11.3.

Table 11.3 Gross reproduction rates in France, England and Sweden

	France	England	Sweden
1740-9	2.53	2.27	
1750-9	2.56	2.32	2.33
1760-9	2.48	2.39	2.26
1770-9	2.38	2.53	2.15
1780-9	2.28	2.62	2.02
1790-9	2.19	2.76	2.16
1800-9	2.00	2.93	2.04
1810-19	1.94	3.06	2.14
1820-9	1.91	2.86	2.31
1830-9	1.84	2.53	2.22
1840-9	1.77	2.35	2.14
1850-9	1.70	2.34	2.15
1860-9	1.71	2.39	2.15
1870-9	1.65	2.31	2.19
1880-9	1.56	2.16	2.10
1890-9	1.43	1.88	1.99
1900-9	1.32	1.60	1.87
1910-19	1.20	1.41	1.52
1920-9	1.15	1.14	1.14

The French data from 1770 onwards are averages of paired five-year periods 1771-5 and 1776-80 etc., except that the figure for 1910-19 relates to 1911-13. For the decades before 1770 the GRRs were estimated from the crude birth rates (CBR) of the decades in question. The CBR for 1770-9 was equated with the GRR for the decade and earlier GRRs assumed to bear the same ratio to that of 1770-9 as the CBRs of earlier decades bore to that of 1770-9. The English data for 1740-9 to 1860-9 refer to five-year periods centring on the years 1746, 1756 etc. The later figures are averages of paired three-year periods 1870-2 and 1880-2, 1880-2 and 1890-2 etc. The figures for 1840-9, 1850-9 and 1860-9 are slightly modified from the originals to allow for the sex distribution in the age group 15-49 (Wrigley and Schofield, *Population history of England*, table 7.16, p. 232). The Swedish data are averages of paired five-year periods 1751-5 and 1756-60 etc.
Sources: France 1740-9 to 1760-9: Henry and Blayo, 'La population de la France', table 22, p. 109. France 1770-9 to 1920-9: Bourgeois-Pichat, 'The population of France', table 3, p. 506. England 1740-9 to 1860-9: Wrigley and Schofield, *Population history of England*, table A3.1, p. 529; England 1870-9 to 1920-9: Glass, 'Changes of fertility in England and Wales', table 2, p. 168. Sweden: *Historisk statistik för Sverige*, Del. 1. Bevolkning 1720-1967 (Stockholm, 1969), table 34, p. 105.

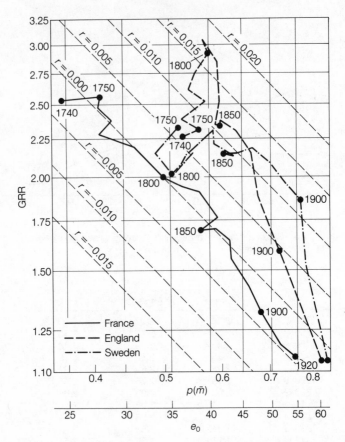

Figure 11.4 Intrinsic growth rates in France, England and Sweden.
For the sources used and other details of the data shown, see the notes to tables 11.2 and 11.3.

Every combination of levels of fertility and mortality, if sustained sufficiently long to ensure that a stable age structure supervenes, will result in a particular growth rate intrinsic to that combination. Figure 11.4 sets out the changes in fertility and mortality and the resulting vicissitudes in the intrinsic growth rate, r, in France, England and Sweden. The vertical axis represents fertility (expressed as log GRR); the horizontal axis mortality (expressed as log $p(\overline{m})$, here shown with the associated e_0).[5] Figure 11.4 possesses by construction the property that all combinations of fertility and mortality which give rise to a particular level of r will lie on a diagonal line running at 45° to the two axes of the graph, and also that the ratio of the vertical to the horizontal distance between any two points expresses the

5 For a full description of this method of presenting data and its limitations, see Wrigley and Schofield, *Population history of England*, pp. 236–48.

relative importance of any changes in fertility and mortality in altering the intrinsic growth rate.

It is easy to appreciate when the data are displayed in this fashion that the intrinsic growth rate in France was never far from zero between 1740 and 1880, and that changes in fertility and mortality offset one another, causing the set of points relating to France to be strung out along the diagonal representing the zero intrinsic growth rate. Figure 11.4 underlines the distinctiveness of French population history during the eighteenth and nineteenth centuries.

The behaviour of a measure of general fertility such as the GRR is not necessarily a good guide to changes in marital fertility. Changes in the timing and prevalence of marriage may have a powerful influence on general fertility even though the level of marital fertility is constant. For societies in which marriage is early and virtually universal for women, this point has little relevance since marriage will largely be determined by a biological event, the onset of menarche; but the marriage system of early modern western Europe was highly flexible. Age at marriage and proportions never marrying varied substantially both between populations and in the same population over time. The English GRR, for example, was only about 2.30 in the middle of the eighteenth century but rose to more than 3.00 at its peak about 1815, yet there was no significant change in marital fertility between the two periods.[6] The fall in general fertility in France after 1750, therefore, does not demonstrate *ipso facto* that the change was due to a fall in fertility within marriage.

That such a fall occurred, however, is not in doubt. Reconstitution studies have shown that marital fertility fell substantially in the early decades of the nineteenth century in many parishes. In some cases the fall was under way before the nineteenth century began.[7] From 1831 onwards van de Walle's work has provided both national and departmental estimates of marital fertility.[8] His national series starts too late to capture the beginnings of the fall but it documents its subsequent behaviour and shows that after 1831 the fall in marital fertility dominates fertility trends and was so

---

6 For English GRRs see Wrigley and Schofield, *Population history of England*, table A3.1, pp. 528–9. For a discussion of the notable stability of marital fertility levels in England before about 1870, see table 7.25, p. 254, and also Wrigley and Schofield, 'English population history from family reconstitution', pp. 168–72.

7 The number of French reconstitution studies covering the eighteenth and early nineteenth centuries has become very large. The most authoritative single source of information on the subject of changing marital fertility during the period is the INED study based on a random sample of 1 in 1000 of the 40 000 French parishes. The resulting data have been published in four articles by Henry and Houdaille covering the four quarters of France (north-west, north-east, south-east and south-west). The articles are listed in the source notes to table 11.4. The data have also been published in a convenient, consolidated form by Dupâquier, *La population française*, tables 1 and 2, pp. 52–3 and 108–9. There is an extensive bibliography of individual studies and a very useful table of empirical results in Flinn, *The European demographic system*, table 1, pp. 104–7 and pp. 152–60. Weir, re-analysing INED national sample data, has recently presented strong evidence that the onset of fertility is first unambiguously evident at the national level in the 1790s. Weir, *Fertility control in rural France*, especially pp. 113–16.

8 Van de Walle, *Female population of France*.

substantial as to drive general fertility downwards in spite of the rise in nuptiality taking place at the same time.

Since van de Walle's study formed a part of the Princeton European fertility project, he expressed his findings in the demographic measures devised by Coale to ensure comparability between the data relating to different countries. In table 11.4 and figure 11.5 the Princeton measure of marital fertility, I_g, is used to show the extent of the difference between France and other west European countries in the course of the nineteenth century. In the late eighteenth century I_g was about 0.75, or 75 per cent of that observed among the Hutterites (an I_g equal to 1.00 represents the Hutterite level: this standard was chosen for the Princeton fertility measures as representing the maximum known for any population).[9] It was distinctly higher than that found in England before the transition (about 0.67); somewhat higher than the pre-transition level in Sweden where the average level of I_g was about 0.70; and closely similar to that found in Germany immediately before the transition. (The term transition is used as a shorthand method of referring to the steep fall in marital fertility that occurred with the adoption of family limitation by more and more married couples.)

Her level of marital fertility before the onset of family limitation, therefore, did not set France apart from other west European countries but, whereas elsewhere marital fertility showed no tendency to fall until about 1880, in France it fell very sharply in the early decades of the nineteenth century. By 1840 it had already fallen to two-thirds of its level before 1800 and by 1900 to only about one-half of that level. The very much slower rate of population growth occurring in France is principally due to the differences in marital fertility history summarized in figure 11.5.

Figure 11.5 also shows why it is difficult to treat France as conforming to the model of the fertility transition described by Knodel and van de Walle. The lack of conformity lies in the interruption to the smooth decline in marital fertility which took place in the middle decades of the century. The fall in marital fertility decelerated sharply after 1830 and was even replaced by a slight rise between 1850 and 1870. After 1870 the fall was resumed and continued until the 1930s, though by then the precipitous fall in fertility elsewhere in western Europe meant that France was no longer significantly different from her neighbours. The view that France differed from other countries only in starting earlier and taking longer to pass through the fertility transition is therefore difficult to sustain. The problem does not lie in the length of time taken but in the cessation of fall in I_g at a point where experience elsewhere suggests that it should have been falling most rapidly. Knodel and van de Walle showed that the recent decline of fertility in Taiwan

---

9 The Princeton measures I_g, I_f, I_m and I_h (measuring marital fertility, general fertility, nuptiality and illegitimate fertility respectively) are well described by Knodel, *The decline of fertility in Germany*, pp. 33–5.

Table 11.4 Marital fertility (I_g) in France, England, Sweden and Germany

France		England and Wales		Sweden		Germany	
1740-69	0.775[a]	1851	0.675	1801-10	0.688	1866-8	0.761
1770-89	0.742[a]	1861	0.670	1811-20	0.705	1869-73	0.760
1790-1819	0.658[a]	1871	0.686	1821-30	0.721	1874-7	0.791
1831	0.537	1881	0.674	1831-40	0.695	1878-82	0.735
1836	0.518	1891	0.621	1841-50	0.708	1883-7	0.726
1841	0.515	1901	0.553	1851-60	0.733	1888-92	0.706
1846	0.498	1911	0.467	1861-70	0.726	1898-1902	0.664
1851	0.478	1921	0.375	1871-80	0.751	1908-12	0.542
1856	0.478	1931	0.292	1881-90	0.716	1923-7	0.334
1861	0.478			1891-1900	0.695	1931-5	0.264
1866	0.481			1901-10	0.649		
1871	0.494			1911-20	0.535		
1876	0.471			1921-30	0.406		
1881	0.460			1931-40	0.306		
1886	0.435						
1891	0.410						
1896	0.396						
1901	0.383						
1911	0.315						
1921	0.321						
1931	0.273						

[a]The data refer to women married between the dates shown.
The French figures for 1740-1819 were obtained by using age-specific marital fertility rates to calculate a total marital fertility rate for the age-group 20-49 and then expressing the result as a ratio to the comparable rate for the Hutterites (10.94). Hutterite rates, as the highest reliably observed, were used as a standard by Coale in the Princeton fertility project. Coale, 'Factors associated with the development of low fertility'. The French national figures for 1740-1819 are unweighted averages of the figures for each quarter of France. The French figures for 1831-1931 each refer to ten-year periods centred on the dates shown. The English figures refer to ten-year periods centred on the dates shown. There is strong evidence that the level of I_g prevailing in England immediately before the start of the fertility fall had also obtained for the preceding 250 years. Wrigley and Schofield, 'English population history from family reconstitution', table 8, p. 172. The Swedish figures, like the early French figures, were obtained from age-specific marital fertility rates as described above. Before 1870 they should be regarded with some reserve since the censuses before 1870 did not provide breakdowns of the population by marital status as well as sex and age, and vital registration birth data did not include age of mother as well as legitimacy. The rates before 1870 depend upon estimates made by Sundbärg.
Sources: France 1740-1819: Henry, 'Fécondité des mariages dans le quart sud-ouest (suite)', table 1, p. 979; Henry and Houdaille, 'Fécondité des mariages dans le quart nord-ouest', table 9 bis, p. 889; Houdaille, 'La fécondité des mariages dans le quart nord-est', table 9, p. 353; Henry, 'Fécondité des mariages dans le quart sud-est', table 8, p. 866. France 1831 to 1901: van de Walle, *Female population of France*, table 5.5, p. 127. France 1911 to 1931: data supplied by Prof. A. J. Coale to whom I should like to record my grateful acknowledgement. England and Wales: data from a preliminary draft of M. Teitelbaum's forthcoming book on the British Isles in the Princeton fertility series. I gratefully acknowledge his kindness in making the data available. Sweden: Hofsten and Lundström, *Swedish population history*, table 2.3, p. 30. Germany: Knodel, *The decline of fertility in Germany*, appendix table 2.1, p. 272.

'maps across' onto the earlier fall in Sweden with only minor discrepancies if the time-scales are adjusted to give a common span to the two transitions. They treat the two as broadly representative of European countries in the late nineteenth and early twentieth centuries on the one hand, and of Third World countries in the recent past on the other. The 'learning curve' of family limitation is treated as broadly invariant in shape but with different

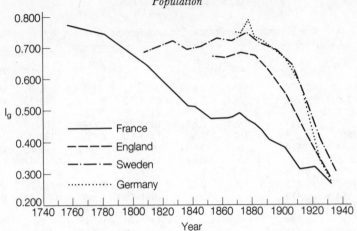

Figure 11.5   Marital fertility (I_g) in France, England, Sweden and Germany.
For the sources and other details of the data used, see the notes to table 11.4. Because the first three French readings refer to marriage cohorts, it might have been more appropriate to displace the plotting points, say, seven years or so to the right to make their positioning more directly comparable with the later I_gs calculated on a current basis.

time-spans in different countries.[10] In figure 11.6 France and Sweden are treated similarly. The transition in Sweden lasted for 60 years from 1875 to 1935. The comparable period in France, on the supposition that the period of fertility fall was unitary, lasted 180 years from about 1750 to 1930. The horizontal scales in the figure are adjusted to facilitate comparison of the 'shape' of the phenomenon in the two countries from start to finish.

It is immediately clear that the differences between France and Sweden, or other west European countries, already visible in figure 11.5, are not changed by bringing the two sets of data onto the same relative time-scale as in figure 11.6. France appears to be an exception to the rule suggested by Knodel and van de Walle that 'increases in the practice of family limitation and the decline in marital fertility were largely coincident and, once under way, were largely irreversible and gained momentum'.[11] In France, after a long period of steady and rapid fall, and at just the period when experience in other countries suggests that the fall should have been at its most pronounced, it slowed down sharply, and there was even a recovery lasting for about a generation before the fall was resumed after 1870. This is the phenomenon which van de Walle christened the 'ski-jump' effect.[12] Was it simply an aberration, or is it to be regarded as symptomatic

10 Knodel and van de Walle, 'Lessons from the past', pp. 232–5. They remark that 'examination of the changes in the age pattern of marital fertility in European populations over time . . . indicates that throughout Europe once the practice of family limitation rose above minimal levels, it continued to increase in a virtually uninterrupted fashion until much higher levels of control prevailed'.

11 Ibid., p. 232.

12 Van de Walle, *Female population of France*, p. 179. In discussing the phenomenon elsewhere he remarks that 'it is possible that the diffusion of contraception that had widely started by 1830, stopped and even lost ground in some regions during this era of prosperity.' Van de Walle, 'France', p. 130.

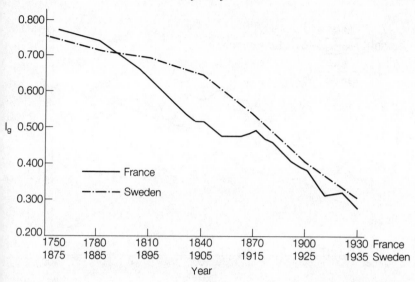

Figure 11.6 A comparison of the pattern of the fall in marital fertility (I_g) in France and Sweden.

of a situation which should cause France before 1870 to be regarded not as an early entrant into a process of change later to be found throughout Europe, but rather as experiencing a development *sui generis*?

The pattern in France as a whole

Van de Walle's work has made available a substantial body of detailed demographic data covering France as a whole and most of its constituent departments from 1831 until the end of the century. Complementing this work, the scholars at INED have published much national and regional data for an earlier but overlapping period usually running from the early eighteenth to the mid-nineteenth century. Their work culminated in a special issue of *Population*, but may also be found in a wide scatter of specialist articles and monographs.[13] Their findings are of great value in this context since they make it possible to see more clearly the background to the fall in marital fertility that began in the late eighteenth century.

The classic regulatory mechanism among west European populations of the early modern period was marriage.[14] Substantial differences in

13 *Population*, numéro spécial, Démographie historique, xxx (November 1975).

14 The classic paper setting out the uniqueness of west European marriage characteristics and reintroducing into modern discussion several of the considerations originally examined by Malthus is Hajnal, 'European marriage patterns'. There is also an excellent survey of cognate issues in Smith, 'Fertility, economy and household formation'.

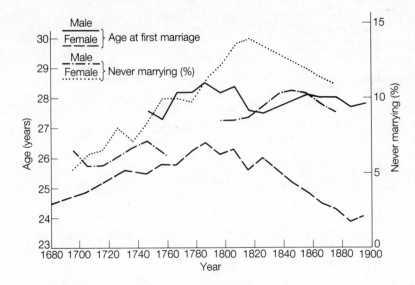

Figure 11.7   Nuptiality in France.
The original data on proportions never marrying referred to birth cohorts. In this figure they have been brought forward by 25 years to make them more easily comparable with the age at marriage data. Thus, for example, those born between 1695 and 1704 are plotted at 1725. The original data referred to five-year birth cohorts (e.g. 1695-9 and 1700-4): these were converted into ten-year cohorts by averaging successive quinquennial pairs. The estimates were based on the percentages of all those dying above the age of 50 who had never married. The age at marriage data were based on several different types of sources: family reconstitution, stated ages at marriage drawn from parish registers and civil registration. The figures for the 1830s and 1840s are not drawn from empirical data but are interpolations.
Sources: Henry and Houdaille, 'Célibat et âge au mariage. I', tables 5 and 6, p. 50 and tables 11 and 12, p. 57; and 'Célibat et âge au mariage. II', table 9, p. 413.

nuptiality existed, and whether such differences are found in studies relating to several communities at the same period, or in studies of the same place over a long period of time, the relative levels of nuptiality found often lend themselves to a homeostatic interpretation of the function of marriage in the general demography of the communities under study.[15] Where mortality was unusually high or marital fertility unusually low, nuptiality tended to be high, and vice versa, resulting in intrinsic growth rates close to zero (or at a level in close adjustment to local economic circumstances). In view of this it is intriguing to note that nuptiality declined substantially in France during the eighteenth century as may be seen in figure 11.7.

Both age at first marriage and the proportion never marrying rose throughout the eighteenth century. The effect of the changes in female nuptiality on fertility was substantial. If we assume constant age-specific marital fertility at the level obtaining in France among the marriage cohort of 1740–69 (see sources and notes to table 11.4 above), a woman marrying at

15 See, for example, Scott Smith, 'A homeostatic demographic regime'; Dupâquier, 'De l'animal à l'homme'; Schofield, 'Demographic structure and environment'; and Ohlin, 'Mortality, marriage and growth'.

the mean age of first marriage prevailing about 1680, 24.5 years, would have borne 6.48 children by the age of 50, assuming that the marriage was not prematurely ended by the death of one of the spouses. The rise in marriage age that had occurred by about 1780, to 26.5 years, would have cut this total to 5.63 children. This is already a significant fall but it was compounded by a rise in the proportion of women never marrying. Allowing for the fact that 5 per cent of all women never married in the earlier period but as many as 13 per cent by the later date, the two figures fall to 6.15 and 4.89 children respectively.[16] Nuptiality changes in the eighteenth century therefore had the effect of reducing fertility by 20 per cent, *ceteris paribus*.

The reduction in fertility brought about by nuptiality changes in eighteenth-century France was substantial and would have sufficed to offset a considerable improvement in mortality without provoking an increase in the population growth rate. For example, assuming that female expectation of life at birth had been 24 years in the late seventeenth century, it would have offset an improvement of about six years in the expectation of life.[17]

In the later eighteenth century, however, there were both some indications of 'strain' associated with the new nuptiality patterns and rapid improvements in mortality. The latter would have caused a rapid acceleration in the rate of population growth in the absence of additional restraints on fertility.

Nuptiality and illegitimacy

In order to appreciate the nature of the evidence of an increasing tension generated by nuptiality change in eighteenth-century France, a comparison with England is illuminating. As may be seen in figure 11.8, there was a remarkable consistency and coherence in English fertility behaviour throughout the early modern period. In periods of falling nuptiality, and therefore of declining overall fertility, illegitimacy was also less prevalent and pre-nuptial pregnancy was comparatively rare. Conversely, when marriage took place earlier in life and few women remained permanently single, illegitimate births were much more common and pre-nuptial pregnancy was rife. The social regulation of fertility through marriage was not frustrated by the behaviour of fertility outside marriage or on the fringe of marriage. On the contrary, the reproductive careers of women whatever their marital status moved in parallel in an apparently consistent response to prevailing circumstances.[18]

Matters fell out differently in eighteenth-century France. As nuptiality declined, producing a fall in the GRR, the illegitimacy ratio rose and the proportion of brides who were pregnant increased, as may be seen in figure 11.9. The changes were comparatively slight until the middle of the

16 In making these estimates I have ignored the question of the effect on overall fertility of changing age at marriage, that is duration effects on fertility.

17 Using model North of the Princeton family of life tables.

18 Wrigley, 'Marriage, fertility and population growth'.

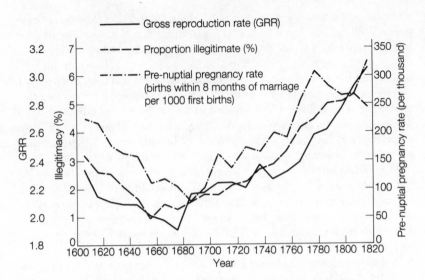

Figure 11.8   Fertility, illegitimacy and pre-nuptial pregnancy in England 1600-9 to 1810-19.
The GRRs refer to five-year periods centred on the dates shown (1606, 1616 etc.). The illegitimacy ratios
refer to ten-year periods (1600-9, 1610-19 etc.) and based on pooled data drawn from 98 parishes
during the period 1660-1809, but on smaller numbers in other decades, though never fewer than 71
parishes. The pre-nuptial pregnancy rates are based on 12 reconstitutions (Alcester, Aldenham, Banbury,
Campton with Shefford and Southill, Colyton, Gainsborough, Gedling, Hartland, Methley, Shepshed,
Terling, Willingham). The rates are unweighted averages of the rates in the individual parishes. The rates
refer to ten-year periods (1600-9, 1610-19 etc.). Down to the decade 1660-9, the rates are based on
a sub-set of all marriages with a recorded baptism but the sub-set was not selected on a basis likely
to bias the result and there is a close agreement between the two series during a 50-year overlap period.
It should be noted that the data refer to all *baptisms* within eight months of marriage as a proportion
of all first baptisms rather than to *births*.
Sources: Gross reproduction rate: Wrigley and Schofield, *Population history of England*, table A3.1,
pp. 528-9. Illegitimacy ratio: Laslett, 'Introduction: comparing illegitimacy', table 1.1(a), pp. 14-15. Pre-
nuptial pregnancy rate: Cambridge Group reconstitutions.

eighteenth century, but then accelerated sharply. It is notable also that the
proportion of older brides who were pregnant was higher than among
younger brides in France, whereas the reverse was true of England (table
11.5). The trends in illegitimacy and pre-nuptial pregnancy in France suggest
that a rising marriage age and more widespread celibacy made extramarital
liaisons increasingly hard to resist, and the rise in pre-nuptial pregnancy
with age of bride suggests women in their later twenties felt the tension more
acutely than younger women.[19] It is especially significant in this connection

19 Fairchilds came to a similar conclusion in studying the rising trend of illegitimacy in
eighteenth-century France. She writes, 'After 1740, the population began to rise, leading to
increased competition for land and work while the notorious price rise of the last years of the
Old Regime drastically raised the cost of living for the poor. These trends made it much harder
to a young couple to save enough to rent or own land of their own. Many couples may have
started what they took to be legitimate courtships, only to discover in the end that they could
not afford to marry.' Fairchilds, 'Female sexual attitudes', p. 652. It is also interesting to note
that Dupâquier considered that the work of Reinhard and Armengaud suggested that in the
Napoleonic period there was a close relationship between population density and the proportion

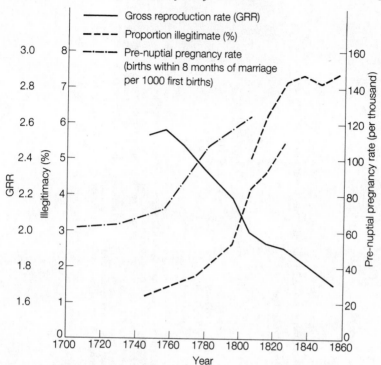

Gross reproduction rate (GRR)
Proportion illegitimate (%)
Pre-nuptial pregnancy rate
(births within 8 months of marriage
per 1000 first births)

Figure 11.9   Fertility, illegitimacy and pre-nuptial pregnancy in France.
The GRRs refer to ten-year periods, 1740-9, 1750-9 etc. The parochial illegitimacy ratios also refer to similar ten-year periods, but the ratios derived from civil registration data to periods running 1801-10, 1811-20 etc. The pre-nuptial pregnancy rates refer to five periods, 1690-1719, 1720-39, 1740-69, 1770-89 and 1790-1819.
Sources: Gross reproduction rate: table 11.3. Illegitimacy ratio (parochial registration): Blayo, 'Naissances illégitimes', table 4, p. 68 (première hypothèse). Illegitimacy ratio (civil registration): van de Walle, 'Illegitimacy in France', table 10.1, p. 270. Pre-nuptial pregnancy rate: see notes to table 11.5.

that van de Walle and Lesthaeghe found a strong negative correlation between I_g and I_m in their analyses of the course of departmental population change in nineteenth-century France and noted that it was strongest when I_m was lagged on I_g:[20] that is to say that women appeared to enter marriage more freely following the inception of the control of fertility within marriage. They were handicapped in their analysis by their inability to

---

of all births that were illegitimate. In part, this was due to the proportion of the population that was urban, but he regarded it as true more generally. Dupâquier, 'Problèmes démographiques de la France napoléonienne', p. 352. On a similar theme, Flandrin considered that there was a connection between falling real wages and the rising number of foundlings in eighteenth-century France. Some of the foundlings were, he remarked, legitimate children, 'abandoned by parents who considered themselves to be incapable of feeding them'. They were the offspring of those who married 'with lack of foresight'. Flandrin, *Families in former times*, p. 186.

20   I_m is the Princeton measure of nuptiality. It attempts to capture the proportional loss in fertility occasioned by celibacy and widowhood. See also note 9 above.

Table 11.5 Pre-nuptial pregnancy in France and England (children born/baptized within 0–7 elapsed months after marriage: rate per 1000)

	France			Age at marriage	England		
	Under 25	25 and over	All		Under 25	25 and over	All
1690–1719	44	74	62	1650–99	82	114	95
1720–39	52	75	64	1700–49	212	148	178
1740–69	70	78	72	1750–99	303	250	283
1770–89	93	123	107	1800–49	342	244	314
1790–1819	116	136	124				

The French rates are unweighted averages of the four quarters of France used by INED. It should be noted that for south-west France only the rates for the under- and over-25s were published. It was assumed that the overall rate in this instance was the mean of the two sub-categories. No data were published for south-west France for 1690–1719. It was assumed that the rates for this quarter in 1690–1719 bore the same relation to the average of the other three quarters in this period as was the case in 1720–39. The English rates are unweighted averages of the same 12 parishes listed in the notes to figure 11.8. Note that the rates given for 1800–49 are based principally on data for the first two decades of the nineteenth century since several reconstitutions finished early in the nineteenth century and almost all by 1841.
Sources: France: Henry, 'Fécondité des mariages dans le quart sud-ouest (suite)', p. 998. Henry and Houdaille, 'Fécondité des mariages dans le quart nord-ouest', p. 918. Houdaille, 'La fécondité des mariages dans le quart sud-est', p. 385. Henry, 'Fécondité des mariages dans le quart sud-est', p. 881. England: Cambridge Group reconstitutions.

calculate the standard Princeton measures for any period earlier than 1831, by which date the fall in fertility had been under way for a generation or more in many departments, but they concluded by remarking that 'As early as 1831, the control of fertility made possible the abandonment of the restrictive nuptiality of the *ancien régime*.'[21] A rise in nuptiality following closely on the heels of the beginning of fertility control within marriage suggests an unsatisfied demand for higher nuptiality which found expression in rising illegitimacy and pre-nuptial pregnancy before the control of fertility in marriage, but thereafter in earlier and more universal marriage for women.[22]

Mortality changes

Because of the countervailing movements in illegitimacy and pre-nuptial pregnancy, the institution of marriage in eighteenth-century France was less well attuned than its equivalent in seventeenth-century England to securing a substantial lowering in overall fertility. But if marriage may have been a less effective means of influencing growth rates in France than in England, it is also true that France faced an exceptionally severe test towards the end of the eighteenth century in the form of an improvement in mortality on a scale probably without parallel in earlier French history or in the contemporary experience of other European states. Between the 1780s and the 1820s, as we have seen, expectation of life rose from 28 to 39 years, an enormous improvement. This was a very large absolute gain, but it is more to the point to note that it was a huge *proportional* rise. As may be seen in figure 11.4, the effect of any given absolute gain in expectation of life at birth on the intrinsic growth rate decreases as expectation of life itself rises: it is proportional rather than absolute gain that determines the magnitude of its impact. The *proportional* gain in e_0 between the 1780s and 1820s was as great as the subsequent gain over the next hundred years (about 40 per cent). The change taking place in France over the 40 years from the 1780s to the 1820s would have raised the intrinsic growth rate by fully 1 per cent per annum if fertility had not altered.[23]

21 Van de Walle and Lesthaeghe, 'Facteurs économiques', table 1, p. 354 and p. 357. Also van de Walle, 'Alone in Europe'.

22 The rise in illegitimacy, which was so marked in the later eighteenth and early nineteenth centuries, ceased about 1820. Thereafter, there was very little change during the remainder of the nineteenth century. Van de Walle, 'Illegitimacy in France', tables 10.1 and 10.2, p. 270.

23 In 1780 age at first marriage for women was about 26.5 years and about 10 per cent of women never married (figure 11.7). To have offset the improvement in mortality between 1780 and 1820, which would have increased the proportion of women surviving to the mean age of child-bearing by about 36 per cent (see below p. 290), it would have been necessary for age at first marriage to have risen to just over 30 years, while the proportion never marrying

Although a change in mortality on this scale would have had a momentous impact on growth rates with unchanged fertility, it is not immediately obvious why it should have constituted a 'problem'. Had the fertility level in the 1820s remained at its 1780s height, the intrinsic growth rate in France would still have been well below the English level and about equal to that found in Sweden (figure 11.4). Possible answers to this question are at present little more than speculation. Two may warrant further consideration. First, it may prove important to distinguish between changes in the growth rate brought about by developments within the socioeconomic circumstances of society and those engendered by exogenous forces. An example of the former might be a rise or fall in the intrinsic growth rate brought about by nuptiality changes which might themselves be regarded as reflecting altered economic conditions.[24] They are evidence of the ability of demographic characteristics to keep in step with economic change rather than a reason for further demographic change. But an exogenously determined change, such as that brought about by the appearance of new infectious diseases, or a change in the virulence of existing diseases, is another matter. In this case an offsetting change in some other element in the community's demography may be needed to preserve an unchanging relationship between a population and its economic environment. A mortality change endogenous to the economic system, such as might arise from a major improvement in diet, would fall into the same logical category as the nuptiality changes used in the first example, and would not imply any need for offsetting change. Until more is known about the causes of the fall in mortality in France which began in the 1780s, however, it is not clear whether this line of argument can have any relevance to the problem of explaining the onset of family limitation in France.

A second consideration which may also have point in this context lies in the possible differences between a peasant economy and one in which most workers are wage-paid. In the former the number of 'niches' may be either static or capable only of very slow expansion, whereas in the latter there may be greater flexibility. Conceivably, therefore, a sharp fall in mortality in a peasant country like France may engender pressures to reduce fertility commensurately that may have no parallel in a country like England in the early decades of the industrial revolution.[25]

---

simultaneously increased from 10 to 20 per cent, using the assumptions about marital fertility referred to on p. 278 above and set out in the sources and notes to table 11.4.

24 This appears to have happened in England. Wrigley and Schofield, *Population history of England*, especially chapter 10.

25 Henry and Houdaille made a comparison of rising trends in definitive celibacy in Norway, Sweden and France in the eighteenth and nineteenth centuries, and remarked that 'in the three cases, the growth of population in an agrarian economy without new land for settlement gave rise to problems in setting up children in life which were first reflected in reduced nuptiality; family limitation followed at a later date, in contrast to what is found among the Genevan patriciate where reduced nuptiality and family limitation appeared almost simultaneously. In support of this interpretation, it is significant that in France, where family limitation occurred very early, the increase in definitive celibacy stopped earlier than in the Scandinavian countries.' Henry and Houdaille, 'Célibat et âge au mariage. I', p. 61.

The question of whether the early adoption of family limitation in France took place in areas experiencing exceptionally large or unusually early falls in mortality would repay further investigation. At a slightly later period, the data published by van de Walle are consonant with such a pattern but his series begin too late to be more than suggestive in this regard.[26]

Preserving intrinsic growth rates close to zero

It will be clear from the foregoing that I envisage the growing adoption of family limitation in France about 1800 as a variant form of the classic prudential system of maintaining an equilibrium between population and resources to which Malthus drew attention. Marriage was the linchpin of the Malthusian preventive check system. The level of fertility was altered *through* marriage rather than *within* marriage. Where successful, this sytem made it possible to avoid population growth on a scale that would bring the positive check into operation, with mortality rising as misery deepened. That nuptiality could operate very effectively in this role seems evident from the example of England, but the same object could, of course, be realized by controlling fertility directly and within marriage. This alternative was already practised by small populations, both elite and peasant, before the end of the eighteenth century but was first widely visible in France.[27]

The data already presented in figure 11.4 imply that the net reproduction rate (NRR) in France from the late eighteenth to the late nineteenth century was always close to 1.00. The NRRs for the period 1740–1880 are set out in table 11.6. They vary only between a minimum of 0.95 and a maximum of 1.08, averaging 1.04, equivalent to an intrinsic growth rate of only just over 1 per 1000 per annum.

The tendency of changes in French nuptiality, fertility and mortality to interact in such a way as to keep the NRR very close to unity (and hence the intrinsic growth rate close to zero) is of especial interest given the history of mortality in France as the nineteenth century progressed. After the exceptionally rapid improvement in mortality which took place between the 1780s and the 1820s, further progress for the next 60 years was much more

---

26 Van de Walle published estimates of e_0 from 1801 onwards. He was therefore only able to provide data from about half-way through the period of exceptionally rapid mortality fall. Van de Walle, *Female population of France*, table 8.1, pp. 191–5.

27 The following studies may be noted as suggesting that family limitation came early in certain populations. Andorka, 'La prévention des naissances en Hongrie'; 'Un exemple de faible fécondité légitime'; and 'Birth control'. Henry, *Anciennes familles genevoises*. Gaunt, 'Family planning and the pre-industrial society'. Dupâquier and Lachiver, 'Sur les débuts de la contraception'. Wrigley, 'Family limitation in pre-industrial England'; and 'Marital fertility in seventeenth-century Colyton'. Imhof, 'Die Familien von Giessen'. Scott Smith, 'Colonial New England'. See also Rogers, 'The study of family planning in pre-industrial societies'.

Table 11.6   French net reproduction rates

1740-9	0.97	1810-19	1.06
1750-9	1.07	1820-9	1.08
1760-9	1.06	1830-9	1.07
1770-9	1.03	1840-9	1.06
1780-9	0.95	1850-9	1.02
1790-9	1.03	1860-9	1.04
1800-9	1.04	1870-9	1.03

The net reproduction rates (NRR) were calculated using the approximation NRR = GRR × $p(\bar{m})$ where $p(\bar{m})$ is the proportion of women reaching the mean age at maternity. This was taken to be 31 years. In the earliest decades this figure is probably too low having regard to the average age at marriage and the age-specific marital fertility rates. Equally by the 1870s the true figure was probably somewhat lower. Festy, *La fécondité des pays occidentaux*, p. 268. A mean age of 31 years may be taken as a plausible average figure over the period as a whole but no more. In consequence, the NRRs are probably slightly exaggerated in the early decades and understated towards the end of the period. (Bourgeois-Pichat's assumption of a mean age at maternity of 28 years for a similar calculation seems unrealistic before about 1930. Bourgeois-Pichat, 'The population of France', table 3, p. 506.) The $p(\bar{m})$s down to 1820-9 were calculated from data relating to each decade as a whole; thereafter, they were calculated as the averages in each case of data drawn from three life tables; 1830-2, 1835-7, 1840-2; and 1840-2, 1845-7, 1850-2 etc. *Sources*: gross reproduction rates: see source notes to table 11.3. Female life tables: see source notes to table 11.2.

gradual (table 11.2). Expectation of life at birth advanced by an average of 2.75 years per decade between the 1780s and the 1820s, but by only 0.75 years per decade between the 1820s and the 1880s, and since the NRR is affected by proportional rather than absolute changes, the contrast between the two periods is even more striking so far as the impact of mortality change on growth rates is concerned. The NRR is the product of the GRR and the proportion of women reaching the mean age at maternity, $p(\bar{m})$. The latter may be estimated to have risen by 36 per cent between the 1780s and the 1820s but by only a further 13 per cent in the next 60 years.[28]

If rough homeostasis was to continue, therefore, with the NRR close to 1.00, a reduction in the rate of decline in marital fertility to match the deceleration in mortality improvement was indicated, *ceteris paribus*. But nuptiality, the third factor affecting measures such as the NRR or the intrinsic growth rate, was rising during this period. This necessarily increased the scope for further falls in marital fertility to preserve an unchanging NRR. The nuptiality changes shown in figure 11.7 would have increased fertility by about 13 per cent between the 1820s and the 1870s, but even when this effect is added to that deriving from the improvement in mortality, it still implies that an unchanging NRR close to unity could be maintained only by a slackening in the rate of fall in marital fertility.[29] An alteration of this

28   Assuming a mean age at maternity of 31 years and using the female life tables listed in the source notes to table 11.2.

29   The fall in age at first marriage was taken to be from 25.7 to 24.2 years, and the decline in the proportion of women never marrying was assumed to be from 13 to 11 per cent. The marital fertility assumptions were those referred to on pp. 282-3 above. It is worth noting that van de Walle's estimates of the singulate mean age at marriage suggest virtually no change between 1831 and 1871. Van de Walle, *Female population of France*, table 5.5, p. 127. It is also interesting that his general measure of nuptiality rises by only 3 per cent between the same two dates (table 5.5, p. 127), or by 6 per cent in the France of 77 departments described in some

kind is very clear in table 11.4. I_g fell by about 28 per cent between 1780 and 1831, but only by a further 14 per cent in the following half-century, and for part of this period was rising slightly.

At the national level, therefore, the behaviour of marital fertility down to the 1870s is consistent with the view that it was a part of a system of the social regulation of overall fertility, differing only from the 'classic' European pattern in that it operated not only through the timing and incidence of marriage but also through the level of fertility within marriage. As long as the improvement in mortality was comparatively slow and hesitant, it was broadly matched by nuptiality changes. This seems to have held true until the 1780s. Thereafter, for about 40 years, there was a precipitate fall in mortality. Nuptiality fell still further in the early part of this second period, but with the increasingly widespread adoption of fertility control within marriage, the fall in nuptiality flattened out and was reversed. After 1820 mortality rates fell much less swiftly for the next half-century. In this third period nuptiality continued to rise moderately, and marital fertility moved downwards fast enough to offset the mortality and nuptiality changes, but less quickly than in the second period. Indeed, for part of the third period marital fertility was rising. Throughout all three periods, from the early eighteenth century to 1870, the intrinsic growth was always close to zero.

The 'model' just proposed is vulnerable to the danger of a compositional fallacy. An intrinsic growth rate close to zero for the country as a whole might be found only because large regional differences in intrinsic growth rates cancelled out in the broader frame. Inferences about the existence of a homeostatic process drawn from national data can only be provisional until the same topic has been examined for subdivisions of the larger whole. If there were large regional contrasts between the course of change in mortality, nuptiality and marital fertility within France, and yet in each region intrinsic growth rates were close to zero, the persuasiveness of the thesis is enhanced. If, for example, there were parts of France in which mortality improved dramatically but where marital fertility fell unusually quickly, and other areas where mortality showed little change but fertility and nuptiality changes were equally muted, it is difficult to regard the overall pattern as the product of coincidence, without wider significance. On the other hand, if there were marked variations in regional intrinsic growth rates, the national pattern might more convincingly be dismissed as intriguing but meaningless. Accordingly, I now turn to the examination of regional patterns using the departmental data published by van de Walle.

---

detail in the next section (see table 11.8 below). The measure in question, I_m, should capture the increase in fertility arising as a result of nuptiality changes by the nature of its construction (see van de Walle, *Female population of France*, p. 128 for definition). The discrepancy is the more intriguing since, *ceteris paribus*, I_m will rise when mortality improves because fewer marriages will be broken by death during the child-bearing age-groups. To the degree that van de Walle's estimates are to be preferred, of course, the scope for marital fertility fall with an unchanged NRR is reduced.

French regional population history

Van de Walle's data refer to a total of 77 departments. He was obliged to omit from his study several departments containing great cities and their environs: Seine and Seine-et-Oise (Paris), Rhône (Lyon), and Bouches-du-Rhône (Marseilles). The boundary changes resulting from the Franco-Prussian war enforced the omission of four other departments whose series were interrupted by the war (Moselle, Meurthe, Bas-Rhin and Haut-Rhin); and for the purposes of the present study Corsica was also omitted. Using departmental data does not, of course, overcome entirely the danger of being misled by the compositional fallacy. It is greatly to be desired that the same issue should be taken up using still smaller units of analysis. To do so is outside the scope of this essay, but not to have done so means that any conclusions (and still more any explanations) remain provisional.[30]

The regions are shown in figure 11.10. Any exercise of regional subdivision is likely to be both arbitrary and unsatisfactory to some extent, and the scheme shown in figure 11.10 is no exception. It was arrived at by experiment and reflection rather than in a more systematic procedure. France was divided into 11 regions. Ideally, one might wish to see regions in which fertility, mortality and nuptiality were each at closely similar levels in the constituent departments within each region, and where trends were also alike in each case. But the facts are too refractory to permit this. For example, similarity in level in a particular demographic variable among a group of neighbouring departments at a particular date does not guarantee that trends over time will be similar, or vice versa. And 'boundary' departments inevitably tend to blur matters by reducing the distinctiveness and homogeneity of the 'core' areas of a region. In general greater weight was given to similarity of trend rather than level in deciding to which region a particular department was to be allocated, but as far as possible homogeneity in both respects was sought.

In framing a strategy for regional subdivision, I had in mind the object of examining changes in the NRR in each region, both because the NRR is a useful summary measure of the population growth rate, and because its calculation affords an opportunity to consider variations in all three major aspects of demographic behaviour: fertility, mortality and nuptiality. We have already noted that $NRR = GRR \times p(\bar{m})$, and that there is a close relationship between NRR and r, the intrinsic growth rate. Since the GRR is largely a function of marital fertility and nuptiality, the two Princeton

---

30 Chaunu has long emphasized the extraordinary particularity of the local demographies of France, what he termed 'la structure moléculaire des comportements démographiques', and has produced some telling illustrations of his thesis for Normandy. Chaunu, *Histoire, science sociale*, pp. 347–52. For the department of Nord, Spagnoli's work provides ample illustration of the extent of local variation in the nineteenth century. Spagnoli, 'Population history from parish monographs'; see also his 'High fertility in mid-nineteenth century France'.

Figure 11.10 A regional subdivision of France.
The shaded areas are excluded for reasons referred to in the text.

measures, I_g and I_m, which van de Walle has calculated for each department, can be simply converted into an estimate of the GRR. The GRR is the sum of general fertility rates experienced over the full fertile age range 15–49. I_g is a summary measure of the same phenomenon in married women, expressed as a fraction of the level found among Hutterite women. The total fertility rate over the age range 15–49 at Hutterite levels of marital fertility is 12.44. Dividing by 2.05 to restrict the measure to female births, yields a figure of 6.068.[31] Thus an I_g of, say, 0.600 implies that the marital fertility rates in the population in question are such that 3.64 female

31 The individual age-specific marital fertility rates per 1000 married women for the seven successive five-year age-groups 15–19 to 45–49 are as follows: 300, 550, 502, 447, 406, 222, 61. The data for all except the first age-group were first set out in Henry, 'Some data on natural fertility'. They are reproduced by Knodel, who proposed the rate for the earliest age-group in *The decline of fertility in Germany*, pp. 33–5. A sex ratio at birth of 105 : 100 was assumed.

Table 11.7 Levels of marital fertility, nuptiality and mortality in nineteenth-century France, and the associated coefficients of variation (per cent)

	I_g			I_m			$p(m)$		
	Level	C	1831 = 100	Level	C	1831 = 100	Level	C	1831 = 100
1831	0.557	20	100	0.519	13	100	0.567	9	100
1871	0.488	25	88	0.549	13	106	0.614	8	108
1901	0.398	27	71	0.566	12	109	0.703	6	124

The data relate to 77 departments (see table 11.8 below). The levels shown are unweighted averages of the departmental figures.
Source: see table 11.8 below.

births (0.6 × 6.068) would result from the cumulated rates over the age range 15–49. Since I_m measures the degree to which potential fertility is restricted by celibacy and late marriage, $I_g \times I_m \times 6.068$ yields an estimate of the GRR, except that it ignores illegitimate births.[32] These were a ·substantial element in total fertility in nineteenth-century France, usually accounting for between 7 and 9 per cent of total births between 1830 and 1900, but in what follows they are ignored.[33] The estimated GRRs are therefore always below the true level by about 8 per cent, but with some regional variation.

The final element needed to estimate the NRR is the proportion of women reaching the mean age at maternity, $p(\overline{m})$. Van de Walle made estimates of female e_0s. From these $p(\overline{m})$ was calculated assuming a mean age at maternity of 31 years and using Princeton model North life tables. This, too, over-simplifies reality, of course. Van de Walle showed that some departments were closer to model West than to model North in their mortality characteristics. Model North was used in this exercise because it gives a substantially better agreement than model West with the l_{30}s calculated by Bourgeois-Pichat.[34] Using model North results in slightly lower $p(\overline{m})$s than would have resulted from using model West, but the difference is minor.

Since the product of I_g, I_m and $p(\overline{m})$ multiplied by a constant yields an estimate of the NRR, it is possible to identify the relative importance of any changes in marital fertility, nuptiality and mortality in influencing the NRR, and to discover whether there was mutual accommodation between the three to keep the NRR close to 1.00 (or the intrinsic growth rate close to zero). It may be seen from table 11.7 that I_g and $p(\overline{m})$ changed more substantially than I_m during the nineteenth century. Accordingly, in deciding upon the boundaries of the regions, greater attention was given to I_g and $p(\overline{m})$ than to I_m.

It may prove a little wearisome to review the characteristics of each region in turn, but it also seems a necessary preliminary to a discussion of what was common to them all, or distinctive about individual areas.

In table 11.8 I_g, I_m, $p(\overline{m})$ and e_0 are set out for the 11 regions in 1831, 1871 and 1901. Two mortality measures are given since e_0 is a much more familiar measure than $p(\overline{m})$: the proportional changes over time, or their relative level in different regions at the same date are, however, closely similar. The choice of the first and last of the three dates simply reflects the fact that these were the earliest and latest dates in van de Walle's study (except that e_0 was calculated from 1801 onwards). The year 1871 was chosen as the third date because it marks the end of the quarter-century

32 I_m is also affected by the indirect effects of changing adult mortality. See note 29 above.

33 Van de Walle, 'Illegitimacy in France', table 10.1, p. 270.

34 His data are set out in Bourgeois-Pichat, 'The population of France', table 2, pp. 504–5.

in which marital fertility paused in its long descent, the putative dividing line between a period when the control of fertility within marriage may be regarded as a variant solution to the classic west European search for low-pressure homeostasis and a period when the control of marital fertility in France conformed to a pattern found almost throughout western Europe.

Table 11.8 also gives the relative changes in each demographic measure between the several dates and, by showing the coefficient of variation of the level of each variable among the departments in each region, and of the changes in level among the departments in each region over each time period, enables the presence or absence of homogeneity in level and change in each variable to be assessed.

Region 9

In view of the theme of this article, it is natural to begin by considering first the areas of France in which marital fertility was already low in 1831. In region 9, which bears a broad resemblance to the ancient province of Guyenne, I_g was already as low as 0.415 in 1831, the lowest figure of any amongst the 11 regions, reflecting a level of marital fertility not found nationally in Germany, Sweden or England until about 1920. It is reasonable to suppose that there had been a big fall in marital fertility in the preceding half-century. In the south-west quarter of France as a whole Henry's work suggests that I_g was 0.705 in 1740–69 and 0.663 in 1770–89, though as it happened only one of the nine parishes comprising his sample lay in the five departments of region 9, and that the smallest (Samouillan, Haute-Garonne, with a population of 389 in 1821).[35] It is possible, therefore, that by 1831 I_g in region 9 had already fallen by about 40 per cent from the level prevailing in the mid-eighteenth century. Marital fertility was not uniformly low, however, as is immediately apparent from the relatively high C associated with the average I_g figure. Haute-Garonne at this date had a much higher level of marital fertility than the other four departments in the region. Fertility in this department fell rapidly, however, faster indeed than elsewhere in the region, or than in neighbouring departments of other regions. The homogeneity of the region in respect of marital fertility increased substantially after 1831 as Haute-Garonne came to resemble the other departments more closely. The individual departments were very similar to one another in their mortality characteristics throughout the century, while there was an average degree of homogeneity in nuptiality. Here, too, Haute-Garonne was something of an outlier, with consistently lower nuptiality than elsewhere in the region. No doubt if data were available for smaller areas, Haute-Garonne would subdivide into an area strongly resembling the rest of region 9, and an area with a greater similarity to region 8.

35 Henry, 'Fécondité des mariages dans le quart sud-ouest. I', p. 613. The I_gs for 1740–69 and 1770–89 may be found in the article listed in the source notes to table 11.4.

Table 11.8 The regional pattern of change in marital fertility, nuptiality and mortality in nineteenth-century France, and the associated coefficients of variation (C) (per cent)

	Marital fertility						Changes in I_g				
	I_g			C			(100 × later date/earlier date)			C	
	Level										
Region	1831	1871	1901	1831	1871	1901	1871/1831	1901/1871	1901/1831	1871/1831	1901/1871
1	0.471	0.380	0.324	10	11	7	81	86	70	6	9
2	0.547	0.433	0.360	16	16	17	79	84	66	5	7
3	0.766	0.735	0.619	8	12	16	96	84	80	6	6
4	0.451	0.424	0.397	22	24	19	94	95	89	4	6
5	0.620	0.653	0.526	6	7	9	105	81	86	1	16
6	0.464	0.396	0.363	4	3	7	86	92	78	2	7
7	0.618	0.506	0.445	6	11	11	82	88	72	6	6
8	0.549	0.455	0.341	10	8	9	83	75	63	7	5
9	0.415	0.327	0.255	13	9	8	79	78	62	6	6
10	0.674	0.616	0.499	6	9	16	92	81	74	8	11
11	0.547	0.528	0.392	13	15	20	96	74	71	4	10
France	0.557	0.488	0.398	20	25	27	87	82	71	10	11

(continued)

Table 11.8 (continued)

Nuptiality

	I_m Level			I_m C			Changes in I_m (100 × later date/earlier date)			C	
Region	1831	1871	1901	1831	1871	1901	1871/1831	1901/1871	1901/1831	1871/1831	1901/1871
1	0.582	0.617	0.618	7	5	5	105	100	106	4	3
2	0.497	0.554	0.581	10	8	7	112	105	117	4	2
3	0.430	0.415	0.439	7	6	6	97	106	102	4	2
4	0.513	0.559	0.567	17	17	12	109	102	111	3	6
5	0.473	0.502	0.520	1	2	2	106	104	110	3	0
6	0.581	0.596	0.604	5	4	3	103	102	104	3	2
7	0.466	0.498	0.514	8	7	7	107	103	110	6	2
8	0.547	0.586	0.611	7	7	4	107	105	112	4	5
9	0.571	0.627	0.640	8	8	8	110	102	112	6	3
10	0.447	0.478	0.493	9	7	10	107	103	110	5	5
11	0.557	0.549	0.565	7	6	6	99	103	101	5	4
France	0.519	0.549	0.566	13	13	12	106	103	109	6	4

Mortality

	$p(\bar{m})$ Level				$p(\bar{m})$ C				Changes in $p(\bar{m})$ (100 × later date/earlier date)				C			
Region	1806	1831	1871	1901	1806	1831	1871	1901	1831/1806	1871/1831	1901/1871	1901/1831	1831/1806	1871/1831	1901/1871	1901T/1871
1	0.447	0.545	0.663	0.720	12	6	4	4	123	122	109	132	10	5	5	5
2	0.555	0.609	0.643	0.740	9	6	4	4	110	106	115	122	9	4	5	5
3	0.500	0.517	0.574	0.681	10	7	10	5	104	111	119	132	5	8	8	7
4	0.619	0.612	0.623	0.677	9	6	7	5	99	102	109	111	5	7	7	3
5	0.547	0.527	0.600	0.686	2	5	7	1	97	114	115	130	3	3	7	3
6	0.558	0.580	0.646	0.709	6	6	4	3	104	112	110	122	6	6	3	0
7	0.542	0.569	0.599	0.679	6	5	2	1	105	105	114	119	5	5	3	1
8	0.491	0.544	0.618	0.739	9	8	6	4	111	114	120	136	8	7	2	2
9	0.573	0.614	0.658	0.728	4	3	1	3	107	107	111	119	2	3	5	5
10	0.610	0.601	0.595	0.692	8	8	7	5	99	99	117	115	6	4	3	4
11	0.530	0.522	0.550	0.643	6	7	5	3	99	106	117	123	6	7	4	6

Table 11.8 (continued)

	e_0			
1	30.0	37.0	46.4	51.1
2	38.0	42.1	44.7	52.7
3	33.9	35.0	39.4	47.7
4	42.9	42.3	43.1	47.5
5	37.2	35.7	41.4	48.3
6	38.2	40.2	44.9	50.1
7	36.8	38.9	41.2	47.7
8	33.1	37.1	42.8	52.6
9	39.2	42.4	45.9	51.8
10	42.2	41.4	41.0	48.7
11	36.0	35.4	37.5	44.8
France	36.6	38.8	42.5	49.7

The mortality data refer to ten-year periods centring approximately on the dates shown: 1801-10, 1826-35, 1866-75, 1896-1905: those for marital fertility and nuptiality refer to ten-year periods centring on the dates shown. The data for France relate to the 77 departments listed below, treated as an aggregate (i.e. not unweighted averages of the 77 individual departments). The composition of the regions is as follows:

Region 1   Eure-et-Loir, Loir-et-Cher, Loiret, Seine-et-Marne, Yonne, Aube, Haute-Marne, Côte-d'Or.
Region 2   Orne, Mayenne, Sarthe, Maine-et-Loire, Indre-et-Loire, Vendée, Deux-Sèvres, Vienne.
Region 3   Finistère, Côtes-du-Nord, Morbihan, Ille-et-Vilaine, Loire-Inférieure.
Region 4   Manche, Calvados, Eure, Seine-Inférieure, Oise.
Region 5   Pas-de-Calais, Nord.
Region 6   Somme, Aisne, Ardennes, Marne, Meuse.
Region 7   Vosges, Haute-Saône, Doubs, Jura, Ain, Isère.
Region 8   Charente-Inférieure, Charente, Dordogne, Lot, Tarn, Landes, Haute-Vienne, Creuse, Indre, Cher, Allier, Puy-de-Dôme, Nièvre, Saône-et-Loire.
Region 9   Gironde, Lot-et-Garonne, Gers, Tarn-et-Garonne, Haute-Garonne.
Region 10 Loire, Haute-Loire, Ardèche, Lozère, Cantal, Corrèze, Aveyron, Ariège, Hautes-Pyrénées, Basses-Pyrénées.
Region 11 Pyrénées-Orientales, Aude, Hérault, Gard, Vaucluse, Drôme, Hautes-Alpes, Basses-Alpes, Var.
Source: Van de Walle, Female population of France, part ii; 2, the data by department.

Table11.9 The rankings of the French regions and their relationship to the national average

Region	I_g 1831	I_g 1871	I_g 1901	I_m 1831	I_m 1871	I_m 1901	$p(\overline{m})$ 1806	$p(\overline{m})$ 1831	$p(\overline{m})$ 1871	$p(\overline{m})$ 1901
1	4	2	2	1	2	2	11	7	1	4
2	5	5	4	7	6	5	5	3	4	1
3	11	11	11	11	11	11	9	11	10	8
4	2	4	7	6	5	6	1	2	5	10
5	9	10	10	8	8	8	6	9	7	7
6	3	3	5	2	3	4	4	5	3	5
7	8	7	8	9	9	9	7	6	8	9
8	7	6	3	5	4	3	10	8	6	2
9	1	1	1	3	1	1	3	1	2	3
10	10	9	9	10	10	10	2	4	9	6
11	5	8	6	4	7	7	8	10	11	11

Relative levels of I_g, I_m and $p(\overline{m})$ to national average (100 = arithmetic average of 77 departments)

	I_g 1831	I_g 1871	I_g 1901	I_m 1831	I_m 1871	I_m 1901	$p(\overline{m})$ 1806	$p(\overline{m})$ 1831	$p(\overline{m})$ 1871	$p(\overline{m})$ 1901
1	85	78	81	112	112	109	83	96	108	102
2	98	89	90	96	101	103	103	107	105	105
3	138	151	156	83	76	78	93	91	93	97
4	81	87	100	99	102	100	115	108	101	96
5	111	134	132	91	91	92	102	93	98	98
6	83	81	96	112	109	107	104	102	105	101
7	111	104	112	90	91	91	101	100	98	97
8	99	93	86	105	107	108	91	96	101	105
9	75	67	64	110	114	113	107	108	107	104
10	121	126	125	86	87	87	114	106	97	98
11	98	108	98	107	100	100	99	92	90	91

Source: as table 11.8.

The characteristics of region 9 relative to those of other regions are most easily picked out by looking at table 11.9. This table shows, in the upper panel, the rankings of the 11 regions. In the case of I_m and $p(\overline{m})$ the highest figure secures the ranking '1', the lowest the ranking '11'. For I_g the lowest figure is given the ranking '1'. This procedure is adopted because it enables any unusual association of characteristics to be picked out immediately. Low marital fertility and high nuptiality were normally found together, and both in association with low mortality (i.e. high $p(\overline{m})$). The lower panel of the table shows the level of the variable in the individual regions relative to the average of the 77 departments. Thus, in 1831 I_g in region 9 was only 75 per cent of the average, and in 1901 only 64 per cent of the average. The distinctive nature of region 9 is immediately visible. It always had the lowest marital fertility of any of the regions, and usually the highest nuptiality, while mortality was always very low.

Region 4

Normandy, region 4, had the second lowest level of I_g in 1831, at 0.451, but there was very marked variation in I_g from department to department, so that C in 1831 and 1871 was the highest of any region. Calvados, Eure and Oise had very low marital fertility. In Eure it was lower than in any other department in 1831, at 0.348. In Manche and Seine-Inférieure, on the other hand, I_g was quite high, at 0.567 and 0.580 respectively in 1831. If, however, the level of I_g varied within the region, the trend was markedly similar in all five departments (note the *C* of the changes in the final group of columns in the top panel of table 11.8), and it was also most unusual. In 1901 the level of I_g was only 11 per cent lower than it had been 70 years earlier. Over the same period, I_g fell by 38 per cent in region 9. In spite of the differing levels of marital fertility in the Norman departments, therefore, it makes good sense to keep them together in a single group.

If marital fertility fell less in Normandy than anywhere else in France, this was matched by an equal sluggishness in the improvement in mortality. Expectation of life at birth was higher than anywhere else in France when the century began, but did not change significantly for the next 70 years, and only rose modestly in the last three decades of the century.[36] Both in level and trend, the region displayed considerable homogeneity of mortality experience. Nuptiality, like marital fertility, varied widely from department to department, with the lowest levels being found where marital fertility was relatively high.

Normandy stands out in table 11.9 because of the major changes in its rank order compared with other regions, both in I_g and $p(\bar{m})$. Early in the century it was a low fertility area. By 1900 it had the fifth highest fertility, and the level of I_g exactly equalled the average of all 77 departments. The relative rise in fertility, however, was offset by a relative deterioration in mortality. The change might fairly be called sensational since in 1806 Normandy was the healthiest region in France; in 1901 the second least healthy. In contrast, nuptiality was always close to the average.

Normandy contained several departments in which marital fertility was already at a very low level in 1831, with I_g below 0.400. However, fertility in the region as a whole was only fractionally lower than in two other regions, 1 and 6, though thereafter there was quite a wide interval to the region with the fifth lowest level of I_g (region 2). Regions 1 and 6, together with Normandy, form a huge swathe of territory round Paris, and they may conveniently be considered next.

Regions 1 and 6

Region 1, roughly the old province of Champagne and parts of Orléans and Burgundy, lies to the south and east of the capital, and had perhaps the most strikingly distinctive demographic history of any region of France in

---

36 In Calvados e_0 in the first decade of the nineteenth century already stood at the remarkably high figure of 47.8 years (at the same period the comparable figure for region 1 was only 30 years), but for the ten-year period centring on 1871, expectation of life at birth had fallen back more than three years to 44.3 years.

Table 11.10　Female population totals and densities in the regions of France

| Region | Population (thousands) | | | Population (1831 = 100) | |
	1831	1871	1901	1871	1901
1	1224	1270	1208	104	99
2	1504	1584	1530	105	102
3	1335	1519	1636	114	123
4	1380	1320	1269	96	92
5	841	1094	1417	130	168
6	1034	1076	1051	104	102
7	1129	1123	1078	99	95
8	2490	2700	2636	108	106
9	963	1023	1008	106	105
10	1511	1648	1609	109	106
11	1162	1214	1236	104	106
France	14 573	15 571	15 678	107	108

| Region | Area (1000 km²) | Density (female population per km²) | | | Density relative to national average (France = 100) | | |
		1831	1871	1901	1831	1871	1901
1	53.3	23.0	23.8	22.7	77	74	70
2	50.5	29.8	31.4	30.3	99	102	94
3	34.0	39.2	44.6	48.1	131	139	149
4	29.7	46.5	44.4	42.8	155	138	133
5	12.4	67.7	88.1	114.1	226	274	353
6	33.1	31.2	32.5	31.7	104	101	98
7	34.7	32.6	32.4	31.1	109	101	96
8	97.9	25.4	27.6	26.9	85	86	83
9	31.6	30.4	32.3	31.9	101	101	99
10	57.8	26.2	28.5	27.9	87	89	86
11	50.8	22.9	23.9	24.4	76	74	76
France	485.8	30.0	32.1	32.3	100	100	100

The data for France refer to the 77 departments listed in the notes to table 11.8.
Sources: Population totals: van de Walle, Female population of France, part ii, 2, the data by department.
Areas: Population et sociétés, no. 168 (April, 1983).

the nineteenth century. As may be seen in table 11.10, it was very sparsely peopled. Except in 1831 when the population density in region 11 was marginally lower, there were fewer women per square kilometre than anywhere else in France, and it was one of only three regions to have fewer women in 1901 than in 1831. In spite of its low population density, however, mortality was cripplingly high in the first decade of the century. Expectation of life at birth was only 30 years, the worst in France, more than six years below the average of the 77 departments, and almost 13 years lower than in Normandy immediately to the north. Yet by 1871 it had become the healthiest region in the country (tables 11.8 and 11.9), with an e_0 four years above the national average and more than three years higher than in Normandy. Expectation of life improved by more than 16 years between 1831 and 1871 while in Normandy it did not change at all. A better understanding of the regional mortality history of France in the nineteenth century appears an urgent necessity for an adequate account of its demographic development in the period. Other neighbouring regions also displayed notably different trends. Regions 8 and 10 are almost as odd a pair as regions 1 and 4.

Like region 9 in the south-west, the low marital fertility in region 1 was offset by high nuptiality. In 1831 it stood first in this respect, and at the two later dates it stood second. The tendency for marital fertility and nuptiality to be linked in this fashion with the one high where the other was low was a very consistent feature of French regional demography (table 11.9). Almost always the rankings of the two variables are similar for any given region. The absolute level of nuptiality in region 1 was high by the general standards of western Europe. It was higher, for example, than that found in any province of Belgium or Holland or than in any *Regierungsbezirk* in Germany.[37] In the main, nuptiality rankings were very stable in nineteenth-century France. Mortality rankings might fluctuate wildly and marital fertility rankings sometimes changed significantly (regions 4 and 8) but, though most regions experienced a moderate rise in nuptiality, their relative station changed little. A simple test of this point may be made by summing the maximum differences in rankings for each region over the period 1831 to 1901 found in table 11.9. Thus, for region 1 the maximum difference in nuptiality ranking is 1 (the rankings being 1, 2 and 2); for region 2, 2; for region 3, 0; and so on. The sum of such scores for nuptiality is 13, for marital fertility 19, and for mortality 41.

Region 6, like region 1, had relatively low marital fertility in 1831. This region, which might be called Picardy, though it includes parts of Champagne, had an I_g of 0.464 in that year, fractionally below that of region 1. Unlike region 1, however, the subsequent fall in I_g was less rapid than the national average, and its ranking dropped from 3 to 5 between 1831 and 1901. It formed part of a long belt of territory, beginning in Brittany and running along the northern shore of France and then east in parallel with the Belgian border, where the proportionate fall in marital fertility was less than anywhere else in France in the period 1831 to 1901 (regions 3, 4, 5 and 6; see table 11.9). Broadly in parallel with the relatively slow fall in marital fertility, there was a relatively slow rise in nuptiality, at least in the sense that the region slipped from second to fourth in this respect between 1831 and 1901. There was nothing especially worthy of note in Picardy's mortality history. Expectation of life at birth was always a little better than in the country as a whole, but the region's ranking showed no marked trend. Inspection of the coefficients of variation both of level and change shows that in all three series Picardy was a homogenous region.

Regions 3 and 10

Brittany and the Auvergne, regions 3 and 10, were the two regions in which marital fertility was highest in 1831, and there are sufficient similarities

37 Lesthaeghe, *Belgian fertility*, table 3.4, p. 55.

between them to make it reasonable to consider them in juxtaposition. Brittany may be taken as the polar opposite to region 9, Guyenne. Marital fertility in 1831 was very high, and not merely by comparison with other parts of France in the nineteenth century. It was at much the same level as in France a century earlier, or as in Germany before the fall began after 1880. In 1831 I_g stood at 0.766. It was still 0.735 40 years later and even rose slightly in the following decade to 0.753 in 1881 before falling quite sharply in the last 20 years of the century. The inclusion of Loire-Inférieure in the region, indeed, causes the exceptionally high level of marital fertility to be somewhat understated. It seems very probable that parts of the department were more akin to region 2 than to Brittany proper.[38] Without Loire-Inférieure I_g in the other four departments in 1831 was almost 0.800.

The nuptiality history of Brittany was just as distinctive as its fertility history. Once again the data are not only exceptional by French standards, but would have placed Brittany towards the bottom of a comparable list for Germany.[39] Moreover, nuptiality actually fell between 1831 and 1871, and even in 1901 was scarcely above the level found 70 years earlier. The transitional nature of the demographic history of Loire-Inférieure is visible here also. In Loire-Inférieure nuptiality rose a little between 1831 and 1871. Without it, I_m in the other four departments would have fallen from 0.432 to 0.409 over the 40-year period, quite a sharp drop, especially in view of the substantial rise found in most other areas of France at the time.

Brittany experienced high mortality rates in the nineteenth century. In 1831 e_0 was the lowest of any region. Thereafter, however, there was fairly rapid improvement, so that the level of $p(\bar{m})$, which in 1831 had been only 91 per cent of the general average, had reached 97 per cent by 1901 (table 11.9). It is perhaps worthy of note that, apart from region 5, with its large industrial population, and Normandy in 1831, Brittany had the highest population density of any of the French regions and, again with the exception of region 5, it was the only region to end the century with a substantially bigger population than that of 1831. Three regions (1, 4 and 7) actually lost population between the two dates. None of the others grew by more than 8 per cent, but Brittany grew 23 per cent (table 11.10).

Region 10, including much of the southern Massif Central and some Pyrenean departments, was also a region of high fertility in 1831. At that date I_g in the region as a whole was at about the same level as in pre-transition England,[40] and there is therefore no a priori reason to suppose that family limitation was widely practised. Thereafter, its fertility history was a little less unusual than that of Brittany. Marital fertility fell moderately between 1831 and 1871 with some increase in inter-departmental variability.

38 It makes sense to place Loire-Inférieure in region 3 rather than region 2, however, because the trend in marital fertility in the department conformed to the Breton pattern. See also note 46 below.

39 Knodel, *The decline of fertility in Germany*, appendix table 2.1, p. 274.

40 See table 11.4 above; also Wrigley and Schofield, 'English population history from family reconstitution', table 8, p. 172.

In two departments, Aveyron and Lozère, I_g actually rose in the period. After 1871 marital fertility began to fall quite rapidly and the coefficient of variability rose sharply. Some departments had reached low levels of I_g by 1901 (Ariège, Hautes-Pyrénées, Loire, Corrèze), but in others change was much slower, notably in Basses-Pyrénées, Ardèche, Haute-Loire and especially Lozère.

Just as Brittany consistently experienced the lowest nuptiality in France, so region 10 always came second in this respect, with I_m always about 13 per cent lower than in France as a whole. Region 10 differed from Brittany, however, in that nuptiality rose between 1831 and 1871 instead of falling as in Brittany.

No region had a more striking mortality history than this part of France. It affords a mirror image of events in region 1 over the first 70 years of the century. Region 1 passed from being the least to being the most healthy region between 1806 and 1871. Region 10 began the century with the second highest expectation of life at birth found anywhere, only slightly behind Normandy but, like Normandy, found it impossible to achieve any advance in e_0 until the last 30 years of the century. In 1806 e_0 stood at 42.2 years: in 1871 it had fallen to 41.0. By the latter date it stood ninth among the regions, with only Brittany and its neighbour, region 11, below it.

Region 5

Region 5, Artois and Flandre, was quite unlike any other French region because it was not an area of agriculture, market towns and administrative centres, but one of the tracts of Europe in the van of the industrial revolution. Lille, Roubaix and Tourcoing were among the leading textile centres on the continent. Valenciennes, Anzin and Denain formed an area of iron manufacture and coal mining. These towns were all in Nord. The other department in this small region, Pas-de-Calais, was initially largely agricultural but, from the 1850s onwards, coal mining spread westward into the Pas-de-Calais to exploit what proved to be by far the most productive coalfield in France. In consequence, the density of population was more than twice the average of the 77 departments in 1831 and approaching four times the average in 1901. The female population rose by more than two-thirds in 70 years in the region, and far more rapidly in the industrial areas. Between 1846 and 1901 about 86 per cent of the total growth of population in Nord (male and female combined) took place in the industrializing cantons; the comparable figure for Pas-de-Calais was 73 per cent.[41]

41 The total population of Nord in 1846 (in thousands) was taken to be 1122 (averaging the populations of 1841 and 1851). The comparable figure for Pas-de-Calais was 689, while in 1901 their populations were 1867 and 955 respectively. The population of the industrial cantons of Nord in 1846 was 532; in 1901, 1172. In Pas-de-Calais the comparable totals were 123 and 317. Hence the overall increase and the industrial increase were 745 and 640 respectively in Nord, and 266 and 194 in Pas-de-Calais. Mitchell, *European historical statistics*, table B3, p. 69. Wrigley, *Industrial growth and population change*, table 15, p. 67.

In 1831 marital fertility was much higher than in the adjacent area of France, region 6, though somewhat below the level across the border in Belgium. Hainaut, the neighbouring Belgian province, had an I_g of 0.717 in 1846, for example, compared to 0.620 in region 5 in 1831.[42] But in Nord, which was much more heavily industrialized at this date than Pas-de-Calais, I_g in 1831 was 0.658, a level fairly close to that in Hainaut.[43] Marital fertility then rose over the next 40 years to place the region behind only Brittany in this respect. It was the only French region in which I_g increased. Thereafter there was a fall, broadly comparable proportionately to the national average, but the two departments diverged in this period. The very rapid growth of coal mining in Pas-de-Calais ensured that I_g fell only slightly, for coal miners had large families, but in the predominantly textile-manufacturing Nord the fall was exceptionally steep, for I_g fell by 32 per cent between 1871 and 1901.[44] Only four other departments among the 77 recorded a steeper proportionate fall (Gard, Vaucluse and Pyrénées-Orientales in region 11 and Allier in region 8).

Nuptiality in this heavily industrialized area was consistently 8 or 9 per cent below the average, as measured by I_m, and it was ranked eighth throughout. In view of the assertions sometimes made about proto-industrialization or wage-paid work in factories and early universal marriage,[45] the low nuptiality in region 5 deserves note. (There had been a very heavy involvement in handicraft textile industry before the advent of steam power and factories.) Nuptiality was always far lower in this region than in the neighbouring region 6, though somewhat higher than in Hainaut across the frontier with Belgium.

In 1831 region 5 was an area of fairly high mortality, being the third worst of the regions in this respect, but thereafter it improved relative to the national average. In both 1871 and 1901 it lay in seventh place with an e_0 a little more than one year less than the general average. Over the last 70 years of the century it made substantially faster progress than the neighbouring

42 Lesthaeghe, *Belgian fertility*, table 4.3, p. 103.

43 There is good reason to think that fertility was much higher in the industrial areas of Nord and Pas-de-Calais than elsewhere in the two departments or than in neighbouring departments. For example, in 1872 the crude birth rate in the urban communes of Nord (those with a *population agglomérée* of 2000 or more) was 41.4 per 1000 at a time when in the two neighbouring departments of Aisne and Somme the comparable urban birth rates were 28.2 and 25.9 respectively. Yet the rates in the rural communes of the three departments were far less dissimilar: Nord, 24.8; Aisne, 21.2; Somme, 23.6. Nor is it likely that the high crude birth rates in the industrial Nord were due to unusually high nuptiality. In 1871, for example, I_m in region 5 was 0.502 (Nord 0.491; Pas-de-Calais 0.512), while in Aisne and Somme the rates were 0.637 and 0.571. Wrigley, *Industrial growth and population change*, table 36, p. 135. See also, however, the analyses of Spagnoli, 'Population history from parish monographs', and 'High fertility in mid-nineteenth century France'.

44 On the special demographic characteristics of coal-mining populations, see Ariès, 'La population minière du Pas-de-Calais'; and Haines, *Fertility and occupation*.

45 See, e.g., Medick, 'The structures and function of population development'.

region 6. In 1831 there was a gap of 4.5 years in expectation of life at birth between the two regions, but by 1901 this had shrunk to 1.8 years. Rapid urban growth and industrialization does not appear to have disadvantaged the women of the region in ways that were reflected in its mortality statistics.

Regions 2, 7, 8 and 11

The four remaining regions can be dealt with more summarily. Region 11, comprising Provence and Languedoc, is perhaps the most interesting. It was one of three regions in which mortality scarcely improved between 1806 and 1871, but unlike the other two, regions 10 and 4, it began the century with very high prevailing mortality rates. In 1871 e_0 in region 11 was still only a little better than the average of all departments in 1806. In view of the near absence of change in mortality until late in the century, it will come as little surprise that marital fertility fell only slightly, by about 4 per cent between 1831 and 1871. In 1831 I_g was relatively low, indeed slightly less than the overall average, but its fall over the next 40 years was so slight that the region's ranking increased from 5 to 8 over the period. But in the last 30 years of the century, there was a particularly rapid fall, proportionately greater than in any other region.

Region 10 makes an interesting comparison with region 11, its neighbour. In both, mortality changed little over the first 70 years of the century, but mortality was considerably more severe in the latter. In both, marital fertility fell only slightly between 1831 and 1871 but was much higher in the former. In the case of nuptiality, however, there was both a difference of level and of trend between 1831 and 1871. Languedoc and Provence were close to the overall average in nuptiality, whereas region 10 was an area of markedly low nuptiality. In addition, region 11 was one of only two regions (the other being Brittany) in which nuptiality declined between 1831 and 1871. The fall was very slight but may be found in six of the nine departments in the region.

Region 8 covers a large area comprising broadly the ancient provinces of Limousin, Berry and part of Burgundy. Its population was much larger than that of any other region, about 17 per cent of the total population of the 77 departments. Although so heterogeneous geographically, including two 'outliers', Landes and Tarn, its demographic history was both distinctive and homogeneous. Perhaps its most striking trait was an improvement in mortality comparable in scale to that of its northern neighbour, region 1, though differing in timing. At the century's beginning only one region had a lower expectation of life at birth: by its end only one was above it. Once again, changes in ranking in mortality were offset by matching changes in marital fertility. Between 1831 and 1901 the region's mortality ranking rose from eighth to second, but over the same period its fertility ranking rose from seventh to third. In other words, marital fertility was falling unusually fast while mortality did the same. Characteristically, nuptiality was less volatile. The region had relatively high nuptiality even in 1831 and this tendency became rather more pronounced as the century wore on.

Region 2, consisting of Maine and Poitou, was a less volatile area. It was always fortunate in having low mortality and, showing particularly rapid improvement late in the century, it headed the ranking list in 1901. Throughout the period during which I_g can be measured it was an area of below-average marital fertility, but this characteristic became more pronounced with the passage of time.[46] Nuptiality in the region was always at a moderate level, rising from just below to just above the overall mean.

Region 7, Franche Comté with some additions, the last of the eleven, was one of only two regions (the other was Normandy) in which the female population fell steadily. In 1901 it was 5 per cent less than in 1831 but, in spite of the fact that it included much high land in the Vosges and the Jura, it was fairly densely peopled. Indeed, in 1831 only three other regions had a higher population per square kilometre. It was a stable area demographically and moderately homogeneous in all three demographic variables. Marital fertility was always somewhat above the general average. Nuptiality was consistently low, the third lowest in the country at each date; while mortality, though showing a very slight gain relative to the general average throughout the century (table 11.9), was always very close to the average.

Intrinsic growth rates

The rehearsal of the characteristics of each region suggests the nature of the general conclusions to be drawn from French demographic history for at least the first three-quarters of the nineteenth century. The pattern visible in the top panel of table 11.9 provides a clue. In general, the ranking numbers found for each separate demographic characteristic tend to be repeated across the board. Low marital fertility, low mortality and high nuptiality tend to be found in association as, similarly, do high marital fertility, high mortality and low nuptiality. Furthermore, several instances have come to light of changes in one ranking list over time visible, say, in marital fertility, being paralleled by similar relative changes in one or both of the other two.

To complete the picture we may consider the behaviour of the net reproduction rate in the regions, treating it as I_g, I_m and $p(\bar{m})$ were treated in table 11.8. The results are set out in table 11.11. The change in the NRR in France as a whole was slight, especially between 1831 and 1871. (It will

46 The level of I_g varied widely in region 2 (table 11.8). This stems from the inclusion of Mayenne and Vendée. In both, I_g was very high in 1831 (0.677 and 0.685 respectively). In this they resembled Loire-Inférieure on the other side of the border with Brittany, but the *trend* as opposed to the level of marital fertility links them with region 2 rather than region 3 for in both it fell substantially between 1831 and 1871, in contrast with the Breton pattern.

be recalled that this method of estimating NRR is based on legitimate births only, so that the true figure would be a little above 1.00 rather than a little below it.)[47] Marital fertility, nuptiality and mortality all changed substantially but the combined effect of the changes upon the intrinsic growth rate of the population was negligibly small. Moreover, the coefficient of variation of the 77 departments was relatively modest, demonstrating that the national picture did not arise because of the averaging out of marked departmental variations. The coefficient was far lower in the case of the NRR than with I_g and, at the first two dates, also lower than with I_m. A strong 'cancelling out' effect was evidently at work.

What was true of France as a whole tended to be true of its constituent regions. The most conspicuous exception was region 5, the industrial north of France. There the rise in marital fertility between 1831 and 1871 was accompanied by lower mortality and a modest increase in nuptiality. The combined effect was a sharp rise in NRR to a level not rivalled elsewhere in France. In other regions, the level of NRR did not usually stray far from the national level, especially at the two earlier dates. It was always rather high in Brittany but, in view of the fact that I_g was 40 or 50 per cent above the national average (table 11.9), the comparatively modest percentage differences in NRR are an eloquent testimony to the way in which the three key demographic variables combined to produce a net reproduction rate close to unity. The least 'successful' case was region 9, Guyenne. Marital fertility, it will be recalled, was very low in this part of France, though not as far removed from the national average as Brittany, but high nuptiality and low mortality only partially offset the low prevailing fertility. The NRR was 10 per cent below the national average in 1831, 16 per cent below in 1871 and 23 per cent below in 1901, whereas Brittany was above the national average by 6, 9 and 19 per cent respectively at the three dates. In general, the regional discrepancies from the national average grew greater with time, and became much more pronounced in 1901 than earlier.

Table 11.8 shows that there were some instances of large intra-regional variation in one or more of the three variables covered in the table. The coefficient of variation was particularly high in Normandy (region 4), for example, both in I_g and in I_m. Once more, however, this did not carry through into the C for the net reproduction rate, which was close to the average for the 11 regions (table 11.11).

Apart from region 5, therefore, the evidence of table 11.11 is consonant with the view that during the first three-quarters of the nineteenth century the demographic regime in France preserved an intrinsic growth rate close to zero not merely at the national level but at the regional and the departmental level also. There were very marked differences from region to region both in the level and in the rate of change of marital fertility, mortality and nuptiality, but the mutual accommodation between the three was such as to leave the net reproduction rate broadly unchanged. The

47 See above, p. 295.

Table 11.11 The regional pattern of change in the net reproduction rate (NRR) in nineteenth-century France, and associated coefficients of variation (C) (per cent)

Region	NRR Level 1831	Level 1871	Level 1901	C 1831	C 1871	C 1901	Changes in NRR (100 × later date/earlier date) 1871/1831	1901/1871	1901/1831	C 1871/1831	C 1901/1871
1	0.899	0.939	0.872	5	8	8	104	93	97	7	5
2	0.989	0.922	0.931	10	9	11	93	101	94	5	6
3	1.030	1.047	1.112	10	3	13	102	106	108	7	10
4	0.829	0.858	0.902	9	7	7	104	105	109	6	5
5	0.934	1.187	1.141	2	3	12	127	97	122	1	16
6	0.948	0.926	0.942	7	7	7	98	102	99	5	6
7	0.988	0.909	0.935	6	7	7	92	103	95	8	6
8	0.984	0.995	0.935	7	8	9	101	94	95	8	8
9	0.874	0.812	0.718	7	3	6	93	89	82	8	5
10	1.091	1.057	1.021	6	8	12	97	97	94	11	10
11	0.955	0.955	0.853	8	4	12	100	89	89	7	10
France	0.969	0.961	0.931	10	11	14	100	97	96	10	10

NRR was calculated using the approximation $I_g \times I_m \times p(\overline{m}) \times 6.068 = NRR$. For discussion, see text above, pp. 292-5.
Source: as table 11.8.

history of region 5 before 1870 is particularly suggestive. In Nord and Pas-de-Calais, intrinsic growth rates were broadly similar to those found elsewhere in Europe and marital fertility did not start to fall until about the date normal elsewhere in Europe. Homeostatic forces were perhaps weak in this region because its economy was so radically different from that of the vast tracts of rural France in which traditional constraints remained powerful.

Social regulation and individual control

In describing and commenting upon the change from control of fertility *by* marriage in the period before 1780 to the control of fertility *within* marriage thereafter, I have drawn attention to the remarkable absence of change in the intrinsic growth rate in spite of the striking changes in mortality, marital fertility and nuptiality which occurred in France, but have largely ignored all but the demographic mechanics of the change. The notion of population homeostasis by the social regulation of marriage is a comparatively well-explored topic.[48] But is it plausible to suppose that the notion is also applicable to a situation in which a similar result arises through fertility control within marriage? When individual couples begin to assume responsibility for the number of their offspring, what might lead them to act in such a way as to produce a similar result to that arising 'automatically' from, say, the link between the stock of marriages and the total of suitable economic niches?

It is clearly premature to attempt to answer such questions fully. Their nature and relevance are only just becoming clear with the accumulation of evidence about the regularity and precision with which French regional populations under widely varying demographic regimes succeeded in maintaining intrinsic growth rates so close to zero over long periods of time apparently irrespective of the extent and speed of their adoption of fertility control within marriage. Yet some discussion seems in order, if only to clarify the nature of the issues involved.

First, it would not be perverse to argue that the prime question is how rather than whether. The timing of the onset of fertility control within marriage and the pace of its subsequent spread varied so greatly in different parts of France, and yet the intrinsic growth rate varied so little before the last decades of the nineteenth century, that it is difficult to resist the view that changes in nuptiality and marital fertility must have been sensitive, so to speak, to each other's trends, and jointly sensitive to mortality change. It is stretching credulity very far to suppose that individual control of fertility within marriage was not capable of acting homeostatically in the same way as nuptiality appears to have done.

The difficulty in accepting this supposition lies in identifying an element in the decision-making of married couples which might produce the same

48 See note 15 above.

result as that which may flow from the constraints on entering into marriage in the first place. Either demographic feedback mechanisms, such as that linking a marriage in the current generation of young people to the death of a niche-holder in the previous generation; or similar relationships involving economic variables also, as where the timing and extent of marriage is conditioned by real wage trends, might serve to produce homeostasis where marriage is the key.[49] But if marriage itself ceases to play this regulatory role, why should the decisions of individual couples in 'spacing' or 'stopping' the haphazard flow of children give rise to a similar result? Control of fertility by marriage may perhaps betray 'unconscious rationality', but why should control of fertility within marriage do the same?[50]

Clearly, the effect will be visible only in a large number of couples rather than in each separate case. Family size variance declines with family limitation but it does not disappear. Methods of contraception were not infallible, and infant child mortality levels remained sufficiently high to make 'targets' for individual couples hard to hit, or even to define. Equally, conscious and effective planning of family size was not unknown well before its widespread appearance in nineteenth-century France.[51] The Genevan bourgeoisie makes an especially clear-cut example of this point. When rising marriage age, sharply increased female celibacy and high rates of emigration among young men during the seventeenth century failed to resolve the tensions produced by over-rapid population growth within this select group, they rapidly adopted methods of birth control which resulted in small families and an end of child-bearing at a low average age.[52] Suggestive statistical evidence of family limitation has come to light in a number of other studies of small communities,[53] and there is no lack of anthropological evidence of the apparently universal interest in marital fertility and of a wish to control it (in both an upwards and a downwards direction), sometimes coupled with the employment of practices likely to be effective in restricting the number of births.[54]

49 Ohlin, 'Mortality, marriage and growth'. Schofield, 'Demographic structure and environment'. Wrigley and Schofield, *Population history of England*, chapter 11.

50 The concept of 'unconscious rationality' is used in Wrigley, 'Fertility strategy'. Its limitations are discussed in Lesthaeghe, 'On the social control of human reproduction'.

51 Even a balance between boy and girl children within individual families, as well as overall control of family size, appears to have been actively pursued by certain Japanese village populations in the eighteenth century, using a mixture of infanticide and adoption. Smith, *Nakahara*, chapter 5.

52 Henry, *Anciennes familles genevoises*, figures 3, 4 and 6, pp. 53, 56 and 67; and chapter 4.

53 See note 27 above.

54 There is a vast literature on this topic. Some of it is surveyed, and its implications related to the special case of early modern England, in Macfarlane, 'Modes of reproduction'. Flandrin has discussed at length the cultural, economic and religious pressures influencing both the married and the unmarried in France between the sixteenth and nineteenth centuries which may have created both upward and downward pressures on fertility. He throws much light on the aims and effectiveness of church discipline, and his analysis is enhanced by his willingness to contrast English with French experience. He does not, however, advance explanations directly relevant to the main theme of this essay, the close adhesion to zero rates of intrinsic growth visible through

Until more is known about the characteristics of marital fertility behaviour in France before 1870 – whether in regions like Normandy and Guyenne control was practised more widely by certain groups within the local populations than by others and, if so, by which groups; what mixture of 'stopping' and 'spacing' strategies was employed, and whether it varied from region to region; whether the cessation of the fall in marital fertility in the mid-nineteenth century was to be found in all socioeconomic groups, or not; and so on – it is perhaps unprofitable to spend a great deal of time in speculating about the circumstances which may have triggered the falls that took place. But on the general issue, the following points may be made. First, a major fall in infant and child mortality both increases the total of surviving children and reduces the average interval between them, *ceteris paribus*. The former may result in a stronger incentive to call a halt to the continued flow of births within a family, for example from concern about the subdivision of the patrimony. The latter may enhance the attractiveness of action to lengthen the interval between births if the increased 'density' of surviving children too young to earn their own keep has a major impact on the living standards of the family. Any tendency towards 'stopping' behaviour will also be especially responsive to a move towards an earlier age at marriage for women.

Secondly, the relevant unit of analysis may remain a local community and economy rather than the individual family after as well as before a switch from control by marriage to control within marriage. The variance of family size under conditions of natural fertility is so large that a high proportion of families will have 'surplus' offspring or be in deficit in relation to their particular, individual needs.[55] The movement of young people between families overcomes this difficulty without inducing overall pressure when the rate of growth of the local population and the local economy are in harmony. There is, so to speak, a very high rate of immigration and emigration between individual family enterprises, and this may be supplemented by migration between the local community and the larger world. Where the brake upon excessive population growth depends principally upon the timing and incidence of marriage, any pressure may be mediated in part through direct economic problems, such as finding a vacant holding or workshop, or saving sufficient out of current income to enter the 'market' for niches suitable for a married couple. But in part it is also likely to be mediated indirectly through community norms about the conventional age at which to begin courtship, or about the family circumstances that justify such an initiative. Similarly, with the advent of a statistically visible level and type of family limitation, individual couples may be directly conscious of a need to restrict the number of their children or to optimize their spacing in relation to perceived economic problems or

---

the many demographic vicissitudes of eighteenth- and nineteenth-century France. Flandrin, *Families in former times*, section 4, 'Reproduction and sexual life'.

55 See above, pp. 206–12.

opportunities, but others may be carried along by changed behavioural norms which cause them to wish to avoid being conspicuously different from friends and neighbours who have adopted new patterns of reproductive behaviour.

If there has long been homeostasis in the circle of relationships between economic opportunity and demographic behaviour, and if a change in some aspect of demographic behaviour supervenes, as when fertility within marriage is manipulated in new ways, it is perhaps rather to be expected that homeostasis will continue to be preserved by accommodating adjustments within the system than that the system as a whole should immediately fall into disrepair. Only after a further three-quarters of a century had elapsed did a fundamentally different set of relationships emerge in the last decades of the nineteenth century, but by then the French economy was greatly changed from its state in the revolutionary period.

Marital fertility before 1831 and after 1871

There remains the question of the periods before 1831 and after 1871, the former stretching back to the time in the later eighteenth century when marital fertility was relatively high throughout France, the latter stretching forward to the inter-war period when the demographic character of France ceased to set her apart from her neighbours.

The period before 1831 has already been covered in outline for France as a whole. Stress was laid upon the exceptionally rapid fall in mortality in the late eighteenth and early nineteenth centuries, and its possible connection with the contemporaneous fall in marital fertility. Unfortunately, it is not possible as yet to discover whether regional trends conformed to this pattern. Van de Walle was able to construct estimated crude birth rates and also e_0s for each department from 1801 onwards, but lacked the data necessary to calculate more refined measures.[56] By 1831, of course, the first phase of rapid change in marital fertility and mortality was over, but at that date the regional data are suggestive. The two regions with the lowest level of marital fertility were also the two in which mortality was lowest (regions 4 and 10, Normandy and Guyenne). If it were the case that in these two regions mortality was not only the lowest in France, but had fallen more sharply than elsewhere, it would be difficult to resist the conclusion that the two phenomena were connected. In Normandy this was probably the case. Although, as we have seen, expectation of life at birth changed so little in the nineteenth century, in the eighteenth Chaunu remarks that it increased by ten years.[57] It may also be significant that the region in which there was by far the greatest relative improvement in mortality in the first half of the

---

56 They are set out together with other departmental measures in part ii of *Female population of France*. Departmental e_0s are given in table 8.1, pp. 191–5.

57 Chaunu, *Histoire, science sociale*, p. 349.

nineteenth century (region 1) was one in which marital fertility showed a greater than average decline, between 1831 and 1871. Nor should it escape notice that where, as in regions 4 and 10, mortality showed virtually no change until late in the century, marital fertility also scarcely altered (though the *absolute* levels of I_g were very different in the two regions: the low rate in Normandy being offset by a much higher level of I_m than in the Auvergne).

The period after 1871 forms a substantial contrast to the preceding century. Now at last mortality improved substantially throughout France with a clear fall both in regional mortality differences and in the extent of the variation of the rate of improvement between different regions (table 11.8). For the first time, also, marital fertility was falling everywhere, at least after 1881.[58] Regional differences in level were still marked, but all were now moving towards a more homogeneous pattern and by 1931, as may be seen in table 11.12, the differences were much reduced. In 1831, I_g in region 9 was only 54 per cent of that in region 3, in 1871 only 44 per cent, in 1901 only 41 per cent, but by 1931 the comparable figure had risen to 62 per cent. The first decade of the new century was a period of particularly rapid change. In France as a whole I_g fell by 17 per cent, but there was marked regional variation in the extent of the fall. It was much steeper in the high than in the low fertility regions. In 1901 the four regions with the highest marital fertility in order were regions 3, 5, 10 and 7, while the four with the lowest were regions 9, 1, 8 and 2. In the former the percentage falls were 21, 26, 22 and 19 per cent respectively, whereas in the latter the comparable figures were 12, 10, 18 and 10.

There was a marked tendency, beginning after 1871, for areas of high and low I_g to converge towards a more uniform pattern. In 1871 the four regions with the lowest marital fertility had an average I_g of 0.382, while the four regions with the highest marital fertility averaged 0.633. In the former group, the average I_g fell by 24 per cent between 1871 and 1931 to 0.292; in the latter, the comparable fall was 49 per cent and the average I_g in 1931 was 0.323. At the beginning of the period marital fertility in the 'high' group was 66 per cent higher than in the 'low' group; by its end only 11 per cent higher. The changes in the coefficients of variation also show the existence of a general trend both regionally and nationally towards greater homogeneity.

In view of the stress laid upon the relationship between a fall in I_g and an associated rise in I_m during the earlier decades of the century, it is notable how muted any such pattern became towards the end of the century. This is a point of much potential significance. The implicit argument had been that a pent-up demand for marriage was released when family limitation became widely practised, causing a sharp rise in nuptiality. The evidence for such a relationship is persuasive in the close correspondence at the departmental level between a fall in I_g and a lagged rise in I_m, though as may be seen in table 11.8 the scale of the rise in I_m was not as striking as the contemporary changes in either I_g or $p(\overline{m})$.

58 See appendix to this chapter.

Table 11.12 Regional marital fertility in France in the early twentieth century, and associated coefficients of variation (C) (per cent)

Region	Ig Level				C				Changes in Ig (100 × later date/earlier date)				C	
	1901	1911	1921	1931	1901	1911	1921	1931	1911/1901	1921/1911	1931/1921	1931/1901	1931/1901	1931/1871
1	0.324	0.292	0.313	0.284	7	8	7	9	90	107	91	88	88	75
2	0.360	0.324	0.350	0.328	17	13	13	11	90	108	94	91	91	76
3	0.619	0.486	0.466	0.391	16	18	15	12	79	96	84	63	63	53
4	0.397	0.347	0.361	0.327	19	13	11	11	87	104	91	82	82	77
5	0.526	0.391	0.379	0.313	9	12	10	10	74	97	83	60	60	48
6	0.363	0.321	0.346	0.309	7	7	6	7	88	108	89	85	85	78
7	0.445	0.362	0.365	0.314	11	11	8	9	81	101	86	71	71	62
8	0.341	0.280	0.291	0.259	9	6	5	6	82	104	89	76	76	57
9	0.255	0.255	0.258	0.243	8	7	5	7	88	115	94	95	95	74
10	0.499	0.389	0.372	0.328	16	17	15	15	78	96	88	66	66	53
11	0.392	0.323	0.325	0.259	20	18	16	14	82	101	80	66	66	49
France	0.398	0.331	0.340	0.299	27	23	18	17	83	103	88	75	75	61

The data for France refer to the 77 departments listed in the notes to table 11.8.

Source: Data for 1911, 1921 and 1931 supplied by Professor A. J. Coale to whom I should like to record my grateful acknowledgement. All data refer to ten-year periods centring on the dates shown.

After 1871, this pattern of relationships appears to have changed. Marital fertility, as measured by I_g, fell in the 77 departments by 12 per cent between 1831 and 1871, and by a further 18 per cent in the following 30 years but nuptiality, as measured by I_m, having risen by 6 per cent in the earlier period, rose by only a further 3 per cent in the later period. Moreover, almost all of the rise in I_m between 1871 and 1901 occurred in the first decade of the period: between 1881 and 1901 the rise was under 1 per cent nationally. After allowing for the effect of improved mortality in preserving marriages which might otherwise have been interrupted by the death of one or other partner, 'true' nuptiality may even have fallen. As may be seen in table 11.13, there was a significant rise in I_m in only two regions, Brittany and the industrial north, regions 3 and 5. The former had had by far the lowest level of nuptiality of any part of France and nuptiality had also been well below average in Nord and Pas-de-Calais. In Brittany no doubt something of the pressure that had existed earlier elsewhere, and which had been relieved following the adoption of family limitation, still existed, since marital fertility had remained high and unaltered in the region until after 1871. The industrial north was also an area of high fertility, the next highest after Brittany in 1871, but it was so different from other regions in socioeconomic character that it may be unwise to press a direct comparison. Elsewhere, nuptiality showed virtually no change. In three regions I_m actually fell slightly. Two of the three, Normandy and Guyenne, regions 4 and 9, were the areas in which marital fertility had first fallen to very low levels. In the latter, marital fertility was still falling rapidly in the last few decades of the century but nuptiality, though very high, no longer rose. It was as if the 'appropriate' level of nuptiality had been reached, leaving no further unmet need.

After the long pause in marital fertility fall in the middle decades of the century, in other words, the renewed fall towards the end of century displayed

Table 11.13   The regional pattern of change in nuptiality in late nineteenth-century France

Region	I_m 1881	I_m 1901	Changes in I_m (100 × later date/earlier date) $\dfrac{1901}{1881}$
1	0.618	0.618	100
2	0.576	0.581	101
3	0.417	0.439	105
4	0.575	0.567	99
5	0.502	0.520	104
6	0.602	0.604	100
7	0.508	0.514	101
8	0.606	0.611	101
9	0.641	0.640	100
10	0.495	0.493	100
11	0.562	0.565	101
France	0.562	0.566	101

Source: as table 11.8.

novel features. There was still a simultaneous improvement in mortality but earlier links with nuptiality change had all but vanished, and the net reproduction rate, which for so very long had hovered close to unity, whether viewed at the level of the nation, the region or the department, now sank steadily to fall well below unity in the early part of the twentieth century (table 11.11 and figure 11.4). France was converging rapidly towards the pattern visible throughout western Europe instead of following a distinctive path of her own as during the earlier period of falling fertility.

Conclusion

The case has been stated. It is scarcely conclusive.[59] To make it so, much more must be learnt about the fertility behaviour of much smaller units, communes and individual families rather than departments or regions; and how such behaviour differed during the early period of precipitate fall, the subsequent long generation of near stability and the final move to the modern small family. Influences of profound importance locally, above all migration, have been completely ignored in this sketch. Perhaps the data themselves may prove not to be beyond reproach. Certainly, the Princeton measures used almost exclusively to describe the later changes are less than ideal. The measure of nuptiality, I_m, in particular, both confounds the effects of marriage age and proportions never marrying, is influenced by mortality change and, being fertility weighted, involves difficulties of comparison with more conventional measures. Yet, with the exception of the industrial north, and in spite of the extraordinary range of regional patterns within France, there is also a notable unity in French experience down to about 1870 if it is viewed principally in terms of the intrinsic growth rate, the summation of fertility, mortality and nuptiality rates. Understanding the population history of France may still present great difficulties, but achieving a clearer insight into what requires explanation is a first step towards a solution. Perhaps it may prove helpful to suggest that the issue as a whole is best tackled by distinguishing the period down to about 1870 from that which came later, and seeking different explanations for the characteristics of two periods whose apparent continuity and similarity are deceptive.

---

59 Nor is it new. McInnis, for example, in reviewing the fertility transition in Europe and America, wrote 'There are some indications that the fertility decline in France, as in America, may have involved two distinct phases . . . '; and 'This seems to be consistent with the view that there was in France a pre-industrial adaptation of fertility to local circumstances that was certainly greater in degree but not necessarily different in its fundamental nature from what was happening in many other areas of Europe. Later, France may have participated in the international fertility transition of the late nineteenth century, but in many areas of France the earlier phase of fertility decline left relatively little further change to be accomplished late in the century.' McInnis, 'The fertility transition in Europe and America', pp. 12–13.

The recovery in the level of marital fertility in France in the 1850s and 1860s was a widespread phenomenon. The 'ski-jump' shape of the curve representing I_g, visible in figures 11.5 and 11.6, was not produced by widely divergent

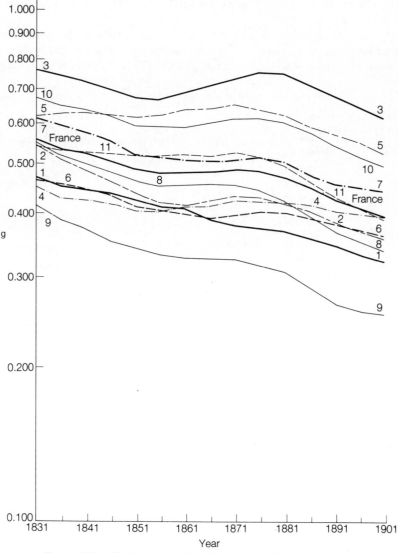

Figure 11A.1   Regional marital fertility in nineteenth-century France.
For the source used and other details of the data shown, see the notes to table 11.8.

regional patterns. Indeed, as may be seen in figure 11A.1 there was only
one region in which marital fertility fell uninterruptedly from 1831 to 1901.
This was region 1 where mortality improvement was the greatest of all until
the last decades of the nineteenth century. Region 9 might also be regarded
as a virtual exception since I_g remained unchanged there for three
successive 'readings' between 1861 and 1871. Marital fertility fell more
proportionately in region 9 than in any other region between 1831 and 1901,
however, so that in relation to the general trend in I_g in the region the
pause in the 1860s may be regarded as analogous to the modest rises found
in most other regions.

Figure 11A.1 and table 11A.1 bring out points of interest other than
demonstrating the widespread tendency for the fall in marital fertility to be
reversed in the middle decades of the century. Perhaps the most intriguing

Table 11A.1   Marital fertility in nineteenth-century France

Region	*The mid-century rise in I_g* Period of fall in I_g	I_g at earlier and later date[a]	*Rise from earlier to later date* (%)	*Period when I_g below its later 19th-century peak* (years)
1	none	—	—	—
2	1856-71	420 : 433	3	15
3	1856-76	669 : 756	13	40
4	1856-71	403 : 424	5	25
5	1851-71	616 : 653	6	unknown
6	1866-76	391 : 403	3	15
7	1866-76	503 : 515	2	15
8	1856-66	454 : 456	0	10
9	1861-71	327 : 327	0	10
10	1856-76	591 : 617	4	25
11	1856-71	517 : 528	2	25
France	1856-71	480 : 488	2	20

The renewed fall in I_g 1881-1901

Region	Level 1881	1901	Percentage fall 1881/1901
1	0.370	0.324	12
2	0.420	0.360	14
3	0.753	0.619	18
4	0.420	0.397	5
5	0.626	0.526	16
6	0.401	0.363	9
7	0.503	0.445	12
8	0.424	0.341	20
9	0.308	0.255	17
10	0.608	0.499	18
11	0.499	0.391	22
France	0.474	0.398	16

France consists of the 77 departments listed in the notes to table 11.8.
[a]For ease of representation the I_gs have been multiplied by 1000.
Source: as table 11.8.

issue is the pronounced and prolonged rise to be found in region 3, Brittany. Marital fertility in region 3 rose by 13 per cent between 1856 and 1876, from an I_g of 0.669 to 0.756. By 1876 it was at virtually the same level as it had been half a century earlier in 1831. Either, therefore, a rather modest initial move towards family limitation was abandoned for a time, or there were other influences at work in a population characterized by 'natural' fertility throughout, perhaps analogous to those recently discussed by Knodel and Wilson in their study of German village populations at a similar period. A very similar pattern is visible in the marital fertility history of region 10, where also fertility was high and family limitation must either have been absent or practised only on a limited scale until the last decades of the century.

Elsewhere rises were modest in scale. The highest proportionate rises are found in region 5, where in any case fertility was high and buoyant, but where the industrialized economy complicates comparison with other regions; and in region 4. The latter, Normandy, experienced remarkably little change over the whole period 1831–71: I_m fell by only 12 per cent in this period, and between 1841 and 1901 by only 7 per cent. With such a flat overall trend, a small departure from it was more likely to produce a relatively sharp rise in an index of absolute level than where the prevailing trend was more sharply downwards.

The contrast between the high and low fertility regions before and after the Second Empire fertility recovery is also instructive. There were five regions with I_g above the average of the 77 departments in 1881 (3, 5, 7, 10 and 11). Between 1881 and 1901 marital fertility fell by 17.2 per cent in these regions, compared with a rather more modest fall of 12.8 per cent in the six remaining regions. Between 1831 and 1871, on the other hand, I_g fell by only 5.2 per cent on average in the former group, but by 16.5 per cent in the latter. Regional experience was too particular for too much to be read into this contrast (and it should be noted that one region, region 11, changed category from below to above average during the earlier period), but the last two decades of the century were already witnessing the start of the convergence upon a new and more homogeneous regional pattern, which was different from earlier times when homeostasis rather than homogeneity was the watchword.

60 Knodel and Wilson, 'The secular increase in fecundity'.

References

The following abbreviations are used in this reference list.

A. A. G. Bijdragen	Afdeling Agrarische Geschiedenis Bijdragen
Ag. Hist. Rev.	Agricultural History Review
Annales de dém. hist.	Annales de démographie historique
Annales, E. S. C.	Annales. Economies, sociétés, civilisations
Annals Assoc. Am. Geog.	Annals of the Association of American Geographers
Beds. Hist. Rec. Soc.	Bedfordshire Historical Record Society
Comp. Stud. Soc. & Hist.	Comparative Studies in Society and History
Econ. Hist. Rev.	Economic History Review
Econ. J.	Economic Journal
Eugenics Qu.	Eugenics Quarterly
J. Dev. Stud.	Journal of Development Studies
J. Econ. Hist.	Journal of Economic History
J. Econ. Lit.	Journal of Economic Literature
J. Eur. Econ. Hist.	Journal of European Economic History
J. Fam. Hist.	Journal of Family History
J. Interdisc. Hist.	Journal of Interdisciplinary History
J. Jap. Stud	Journal of Japanese Studies
J. R. S. S.	Journal of the Royal Statistical Society
Local Pop. Stud.	Local Population Studies
London Rec. Soc. Pub.	London Record Society Publications
Pop.	Population
Pop. Dev. Rev.	Population and Development Review
Pop. Stud.	Population Studies
Qu. J. Soc. Affairs	Quarterly Journal of Social Affairs
Research Econ. Hist.	Research in Economic History
Rev. Econ. & Stat.	Review of Economics and Statistics
Rev. d'hist. mod. et contemp.	Revue d'histoire moderne et contemporaine
Trans. I. B. G.	Transactions, Institute of British Geographers

Abel, W., *Agricultural fluctuations in Europe from the thirteenth to the twentieth centuries*, trans. of 3rd German ed. (London, 1980).

Abrams, P. and Wrigley, E. A. (eds), *Towns and societies. Essays in economic history and historical sociology* (Cambridge, 1978).

Anderson, M., 'The relevance of family history', in C. Harris (ed.), *The sociology of the family: new direction for Britain* (Keele, 1979), pp. 49-73.

Anderson, M., *Approaches to the history of the western family 1500-1914* (London, 1980).

Andorka, R., 'La prévention des naissances en Hongrie dans la région "Ormansag" depuis la fin du XVIIIᵉ siècle', *Pop.*, xxvi (1971), pp. 63-78.

Andorka, R., 'Un exemple de faible fécondité légitime dans une région de la Hongrie', *Annales de dém. hist.*, 1972, pp. 25-53.

Andorka, R., 'Birth control in the eighteenth and nineteenth centuries in some Hungarian villages', *Local Pop. Stud.*, xxii (1979), pp. 38-43.

Appleby, A. B., *Famine in Tudor and Stuart England* (Stanford, 1978).

Appleby, A. B., 'Grain prices and subsistence crises in England and France, 1590-1740', *J. Econ. Hist.*, xxxix (1979), pp. 865-87.

Ariès, P., 'Au pays noir. La population minière du Pas-de-Calais', in P. Ariès, *Histoire des populations françaises et de leurs attitudes devant la vie depuis le XVIIIᵉ siècle* (Editions du seuil, 1971), pp. 69-118.

Armstrong, J. and Bagwell, P. S., 'Coastal shipping', in D. H. Aldcroft and M. J. Freeman (eds), *Transport in the industrial revolution* (Manchester, 1983), pp. 142-76.

Ashton, T. S., *An economic history of England: the eighteenth century* (London, 1955).

Bairoch, P., 'Impact des rendements agricoles, de la productivité agricole et des coûts des transports sur la croissance urbaine de 1800 à 1900', paper presented to seminar on Urbanization and Population Dynamics in History, IUSSP Committee on Historical Demography, Tokyo, January 1986.

Bartlett, M. S., 'On the theoretical specification and sampling properties of autocorrelated time series', *J.R.S.S.*, series B, xxvii (1946), pp. 27-41.

Bean, J. M. W., 'Plague, population and economic decline in England in the later middle ages', *Econ. Hist. Rev.*, 2nd series, xv (1963), pp. 423-37.

Benaerts, P., *Les origines de la grande industrie allemande* (Paris, 1933).

Bennett, M. K., 'British wheat yield per acre for seven centuries', *Economic History* (supplement to *Econ. J.*), iii (1935), pp. 12-29.

Bergues, H., Ariès, P., Hélin, E., Henry, L., Riquet, R. P., Sauvy, A. and Sutter, J., *La prévention des naissances dans la famille. Ses origines dans les temps modernes* (Paris, 1959).

Beveridge, W., 'The yield and price of corn in the middle ages', *Economic History* (supplement to *Econ. J.*), i (1927), pp. 155-67.

Blayo, Y., 'La mortalité en France de 1740 à 1829', *Pop.*, xxx, numéro spécial, Démographie historique (1975), pp. 123-42.

Blayo, Y., 'Mouvement naturel de la population française de 1740 à 1829', *Pop.*, xxx, numéro spécial, Démographie historique (1975), pp. 15-64.

Blayo, Y., 'La proportion des naissances illégitimes en France de 1740 à 1829', *Pop.*, xxx, numéro spécial, Démographie historique (1975), pp. 67-70.

Boserup, E., *The conditions of agricultural growth* (London, 1965).

Boswell, J., *Life of Johnson*, ed. R. W. Chapman (Oxford, 1980).

Bouniatian, M., *La loi de la variation de la valeur et les mouvements généraux des prix* (Paris, 1927).

Bourdieu, P., 'Célibat et condition paysanne', *Etudes Rurales*, v–vi (1962), pp. 32–135.

Bourgeois-Pichat, J., 'The general development of the population of France since the eighteenth century', in D. V. Glass and D. E. C. Eversley (eds), *Population in history: essays in historical demography* (London, 1965), pp. 475–506.

Bowden, P., 'Agricultural prices, farm profits and rents', in J. Thirsk (ed.), *The agrarian history of England and Wales. 1500–1640*, vol. iv (Cambridge, 1967), pp. 593–695.

Bowden, P., 'Statistical appendix', in J. Thirsk (ed.), *The agrarian history of England and Wales, 1500–1640*, vol. iv (Cambridge, 1967), pp. 814–70.

Braun, R., *Industrialisierung und Volksleben: die Veränderung der Lebensformen in einem ländlichen Industriegebiet vor 1800* (Zürich, 1960).

Brett-James, N. G., *The growth of Stuart London* (London, 1935).

Bruton, H. J., 'Contemporary theorizing on economic growth', in B. F. Hoselitz, J. J. Spengler, J. M. Letiche, E. McKinley, J. Buttrick and H. J. Bruton (eds), *Theories of economic growth* (Glencoe, 1960), pp. 239–98.

Buer, M. C., *Health, wealth and population in the early days of the industrial revolution* (London, 1926).

Campbell, B. M. S., 'Agricultural progress in medieval England: some evidence from eastern Norfolk', *Econ. Hist. Rev.*, 2nd series, xxxvi (1983), pp. 26–46.

Cannadine, D., 'The present and the past in the English industrial revolution 1880–1980', *Past and Present*, ciii (1984), pp. 131–72.

Carr-Saunders, A. M., *The population problem* (Oxford, 1922).

Case, R. A. M., Coghill, C., Harley, J. L. and Pearson, J. T., *The Chester Beatty Research Institute serial abridged life tables. England and Wales 1841–1960*, part i (London, 1962).

Chamoux, A. and Dauphin, C., 'La contraception avant la révolution française. L'exemple de Chatillon-sur-Seine', *Annales, E.S.C.*, xxiv (1969), pp. 662–84.

Chandler, T. and Fox, G., *3000 years of urban growth* (New York, 1974).

Chartres, J. A., *Internal trade in England 1500–1700* (London, 1977).

Chaunu, P., *Histoire, science sociale. La durée, l'espace et l'homme à l'époque moderne* (Paris, 1974).

Cipolla, C. M., 'Four centuries of Italian demographic development', in D. V. Glass and D. E. C. Eversley (eds), *Population in history: essays in historical demography* (London, 1965), pp. 570–87.

Clapham, J. H., *An economic history of modern Britain*, 2nd ed., reprinted, 3 vols (Cambridge, 1950–2).

Clark, P., 'The migrant in Kentish towns 1580–1640', in P. Clark and P. Slack (eds), *Crisis and order in English towns 1500–1700* (London, 1972), pp. 117–63.

Coale, A. J., 'Factors associated with the development of low fertility: an historic summary', World Population Conference, Belgrade, Yugoslavia, WPC/WP/194 (1965), pp. 1–8.

Coale, A. J. and Demeny, P., *Regional model life tables and stable populations* (Princeton, 1966).

Cobbett, W., *Rural rides*, first published 1830, edited with introduction by G. Woodcock (Harmondsworth, 1967).

Coleman, D. C., 'Labour in the English economy of the seventeenth century', *Econ. Hist. Rev.*, 2nd series, viii (1956), pp. 280–95.

Connell, K. H., 'Land and population in Ireland, 1780–1845', in D. V. Glass and D. E. C. Eversley (eds), *Population in history: essays in historical demography* (London, 1965), pp. 423–33.

Corfield, P. J., 'Urban development in England and Wales in the sixteenth and seventeenth centuries', in D. C. Coleman and A. H. John (eds), *Trade, government and economy in pre-industrial England* (London, 1976), pp. 214–47.

Corfield, P. J., *The impact of English towns 1700–1800* (Oxford, 1982).

Crafts, N. F. R., 'Income elasticities of demand and the release of labour by agriculture during the industrial revolution', *J. Eur. Econ. Hist.*, ix (1980), pp. 153–68.

Crafts, N. F. R., 'The eighteenth century, a survey', in R. Floud and D. N. McCloskey (eds), *The economic history of Britain since 1700*, 2 vols (Cambridge, 1981), i, pp. 1–16.

Crafts, N. F. R., *British economic growth during the industrial revolution* (Oxford, 1985).

Crafts, N. F. R. and Ireland, N. J., 'Family limitation and the English demographic revolution: a simulation approach', *J. Econ. Hist.*, xxxvi (1976), pp. 598–623.

Creighton, C., *History of epidemics in Britain*, 2 vols (Cambridge, 1891–4).

Cressy, D., *Literacy and the social order. Reading and writing in Tudor and Stuart England* (Cambridge, 1980).

Crouzet, F., 'Croissances comparées de l'Angletere et de la France au XVIIIᵉ siècle', *Annales, E.S.C.*, xxi (1966), pp. 254–91.

Davenant, C., *An essay upon the probable methods of making a people gainers in the balance of trade* (London, 1699). |ν

Davis, R., *The rise of the English shipping industry* (London, 1962).

Deane, P. and Cole, W. A., *British economic growth, 1688–1959: trends and structure* (Cambridge, 1962).

Deprez, P., 'The demographic development of Flanders in the eighteenth century', in D. V. Glass and D. E. C. Eversley (eds), *Population in history: essays in historical demography* (London, 1965), pp. 608–30.

Derouet, B., 'Une démographie différentielle: clés pour un système auto-régulateur des populations rurales d'Ancien Régime', *Annales, E.S.C.*, xxxv (1980), pp. 3–41.

De Vries, J., *The Dutch rural economy in the Golden Age, 1500–1700* (New Haven, 1974).

De Vries, J., *The economy of Europe in an age of crisis* (Cambridge, 1976).

De Vries, J., 'Barges and capitalism. Passenger transportation in the Dutch economy, 1632–1839', *A. A. G. Bijdragen*, xxi (1978), pp. 33–398.

De Vries, J., 'Patterns of urbanization in pre-industrial Europe 1500–1800', in H. Schmal (ed.), *Patterns of European urbanization since 1500* (London, 1981), pp. 77–109.

De Vries, J., 'Population and the labour market in the Netherlands, 1500–1850', papers given at the Conference on British Demographic History, Asilomar, California, 1982.

De Vries, J., 'The population and economy of the pre-industrial Netherlands', *J. Interdisc. Hist.*, xv (1985), pp. 661–82.

De Zeeuw, J. W., 'Peat and the Dutch Golden Age. The historical meaning of energy attainability', *A. A. G. Bijdragen*, xxi (1978), pp. 3–31.

Drake, M., *Population and society in Norway 1735–1865* (Cambridge, 1969).

Drake, M., *Historical demography: problems and projects* (Milton Keynes, 1974).

Duckham, B. F., 'Canals and river navigations', in D. H. Aldcroft and M. J. Freeman (eds), *Transport in the industrial revolution* (Manchester, 1983), pp. 100–41.

Dupâquier, J., 'Problèmes démographiques de la France napoléonienne', *Rev. d'hist. mod. et contemp.*, xvii (1970), pp. 339–58.

Dupâquier, J., 'De l'animal à l'homme: le mécanisme autorégulateur des populations traditionelles', *Revue de l'Institut de Sociologie*, xlv (1972), pp. 177–211.

Dupâquier, J., *La population française aux XVIIe et XVIIIe siècles* (Paris, 1979).

Dupâquier, J. and Lachiver, M., 'Sur les débuts de la contraception en France ou les deux malthusianismes', *Annales, E.S.C.*, xxiv (1969), pp. 1391–406.

Dupâquier, J., Lachiver, M. and Meuvret, J., *Mercuriales du pays de France et du Vexin français (1640–1792)* (Paris, 1968).

Emery, F. V., 'England circa 1600', in H. C. Darby (ed.), *A new historical geography of England before 1600* (Cambridge, 1976), pp. 248–301.

Everitt, A., 'Social mobility in early modern England', *Past and Present*, xxxiii (1966), pp. 16–55.

Faber, J. A., Roessingh, H. K., Slicher van Bath, B. H., van der Woude, A. M. and Xanten, H. J., 'Population changes and economic developments in the Netherlands: a historical survey', *A. A. G. Bijdragen*, xii (1965), pp. 47–113.

Fairchilds, C., 'Female sexual attitudes and the rise of illegitimacy: a case study', *J. Interdisc. Hist.*, viii (1978), pp. 627–67.

Farmer, D. L., 'Some grain price movements in thirteenth-century England', *Econ. Hist. Rev.*, 2nd series, x (1957), pp. 207–20.

Farr, W., *Vital statistics* (London, 1885).

Festy, P., *La fécondité des pays occidentaux de 1870 à 1970* (Paris, 1979).

Finlay, R., *Population and metropolis. The demography of London 1580–1650* (Cambridge, 1981).

Fisher, F. J., 'The development of the London food market, 1540–1640', *Econ. Hist. Rev.*, v (1935), pp. 46–64.

Flandrin, J.-L., *Families in former times. Kinship, household and sexuality* (Cambridge, 1979).

Fleury, M. and Henry, L., *Des registres paroissiaux à l'histoire de la population. Manuel de dépouillement et d'exploitation de l'état civil ancien* (Paris, 1956).

Flinn, M. W., *British population growth, 1700–1850* (London, 1970).

Flinn, M. W., 'Trends in real wages, 1750–1850', *Econ. Hist. Rev.*, 2nd series, xxvii (1974), pp. 395–411.

Flinn, M. W. (ed.), *Scottish population history from the 17th century to the 1930s* (Cambridge, 1977).

Flinn, M. W., *The European demographic system 1500–1820* (Brighton, 1981).

Flinn, M. W., *The history of the British coal industry*, vol. 2, *1700–1830: The industrial revolution* (Oxford, 1984).

Freeman, M. J., 'Introduction', in D. H. Aldcroft and M. J. Freeman (eds), *Transport in the industrial revolution* (Manchester, 1983), pp. 1–30.

Fussell, G. E. (ed.), *Robert Loder's farm accounts 1610–1620*, Camden Third Series, liii (London, 1936).

Ganiage, J., *Trois villages d'Ile de France au XVIIe siécle* (Paris, 1963).

Gaunt, D., 'Family planning and the pre-industrial society: some Swedish evidence', in K. Ågren, D. Gaunt, I. Eriksson, J. Rogers, A. Norberg and S. Åkerman, *Aristocrats, farmers, proletarians. Essays in Swedish demographic history* (Uppsala, 1973), pp. 28–59.

Gautier, E. and Henry, L., *La population de Crulai* (Paris, 1958).

Geertz, C., *Agricultural involution: the process of ecological change in Indonesia* (Berkeley, 1963).

Geertz, C., *Peddlers and princes: social change and economic modernization in two Indonesian towns* (Chicago, 1968).

George, M. D., *London life in the eighteenth century* (London, 1930).

Gilboy, E. W., *Wages in eighteenth-century England* (Cambridge, Mass., 1934).

Glass, D. V., 'Changes of fertility in England and Wales, 1851 to 1931', in L. Hogben (ed.), *Political arithmetic* (London, 1938), pp. 161–212.

Glass, D. V., 'Introduction', in D. V. Glass and D. E. C. Eversley (eds), *Population in history: essays in historical demography* (London, 1965), pp. 1–22.

Glass, D. V., 'Introduction', in *London inhabitants within the Walls, 1695*, London Rec. Soc. Pub., ii (1966), pp. ix–xxxviii.

Glass, D. V. (comp.) *The population controversy* (Farnborough, 1973).

Glass D. V. and Grebenik, E., 'World population, 1800–1950', in *The Cambridge Economic History of Europe*, vi, part I (Cambridge, 1965), pp. 56–138.

Goldstone, J. A., 'The demographic revolution in England: a re-examination', *Pop. Stud.*, xl (1986), pp. 5–33.

Goode, W. J., *World revolution and family patterns* (New York, 1963).

Goody, J., 'Strategies of heirship', *Comp. Stud. Soc. & Hist.*, xv (1973), pp. 3–20.

Goubert, P., 'Historical demography and the reinterpretation of early modern French history: a research review', *J. Interdisc. Hist.*, i (1970), pp. 37–48.

Gould, P. R., 'Man against his environment: a game theoretic framework', *Annals Assoc. Am. Geog.*, liii (1963), pp. 290–7.

Graunt, J., *Natural and political observations*, reprinted in C. H. Hull (ed.), *The economic writings of Sir William Petty*, 2 vols (New York, 1963–4), ii, pp. 314–435.

Grigg, D., *The dynamics of agricultural change* (London, 1982).

Habakkuk, H. J., 'English population in the eighteenth century', *Econ. Hist. Rev.*, 2nd series, vi (1953), pp. 117–53.

Hagen, E. E., *On the theory of social change: how economic growth begins* (Homewood, Ill., 1964).

Haines, M., *Fertility and occupation. Population patterns in industrialization* (New York, 1979).

Hajnal, H. J., 'European marriage patterns in perspective', in D. V. Glass and D. E. C. Eversley (eds), *Population in history: essays in historical demography* (London, 1965), pp. 101–43.

Harley, C. K., 'British industrialization before 1841: evidence of slower growth during the industrial revolution', *J. Econ. Hist.*, xlii (1982), pp. 267–89.

Hart, C. W. M. and Pilling, A. R., *The Tiwi of north Australia* (New York, 1960).

Hélin, E., *La démographie de Liège aux XVIIe et XVIIIe siècles* (Brussels, 1963).

Helleiner, K. F., 'New light on the history of urban populations', *J. Econ. Hist.*, xviii (1958), pp. 56–61.

Henry, L., *Anciennes familles genevoises: étude démographique, XVIe-XXe siècle* (Paris, 1956).

Henry, L., 'Some data on natural fertility', *Eugenics Qu.*, viii (1961), pp. 81–91.

Henry, L., 'Fécondité des mariages dans le quart sud-ouest de la France de 1720 à 1869. I', *Annales, E.S.C.*, xxvii (1972), pp. 612–40.

Henry, L., 'Fécondité des mariages dans le quart sud-ouest de la France de 1720 à 1869 (suite)', *Annales, E.S.C.*, xxvii (1972), pp. 977–1023.

Henry, L., 'Fécondité des mariages dans le quart sud-est de la France de 1670 à 1829', *Pop.*, xxxiii (1978), pp. 855–83.

Henry, L. and Blayo, Y., 'La population de la France de 1740 à 1860', *Pop.*, xxx, numéro spécial, Démographie historique (1975), pp. 71–122.

Henry, L. and Houdaille, J., 'Fécondité des mariages dans le quart nord-ouest de la France de 1670 à 1829', *Pop.*, xxviii (1973), pp. 873-924.

Henry, L. and Houdaille, J., 'Célibat et âge au mariage aux XVIIIᵉ et XIXᵉ siècles en France. I. Célibat définitif', *Pop.*, xxxiii (1978), pp. 43-84.

Henry, L. and Houdaille, J., 'Célibat et âge au mariage aux XVIIIᵉ et XIXᵉ siècles en France. II. Age au premier mariage', *Pop.*, xxxiv (1979), pp. 403-42.

Himes, N. E., *Medical history of contraception* (Baltimore, 1936).

Hofsten, E. and Lundström, H., *Swedish population history. Main trends from 1750 to 1970*, Urval no. 8 (Stockholm, 1976).

Hoggart, R., *The uses of literacy. Aspects of working class life, with special reference to publications and entertainments* (London, 1967).

Hollingsworth, T. H., *The demography of the British peerage*, supplement to *Pop. Stud.*, xviii, no. 2 (London, 1964).

Hollingsworth, T. H., 'Mortality in the British peerage families since 1600', *Pop.*, xxxii, numéro spécial, La mesure des phénomènes démographiques (1977), pp. 323-53.

Hoselitz, B. F., 'Main concepts in the analysis of the social implications of technical change', in B. F. Hoselitz and W. E. Moore (eds), *Industrialization and society* (Paris, 1963), pp. 11-31.

Hoskins, W. G., 'Harvest fluctuations and English economic history, 1480-1619', *Ag. Hist. Rev.*, xii (1964), pp. 28-46.

Hoskins, W. G., 'Harvest fluctuations and English economic history, 1620-1759', *Ag. Hist. Rev.*, xvi (1968), pp. 15-31.

Houdaille, J., 'La fécondité des mariages de 1670 à 1829 dans le quart nord-est de la France', *Annales de dém. hist.*, 1976, pp. 341-91.

Houghton, J., *A collection of letters for the improvement of husbandry* (London, 1681).

Imhof, A., 'Die namentliche Auswertung der Kirchenbucher, die Familien von Giessen, 1631-1730 und Heuchelheim, 1691-1900', in A. Imhof (ed.), *Historische Demographie als Sozialgeschichte: Giessen und Umgebung vom 17. zum 19. Jehrhundert*, 2 vols (Darmstadt, 1975), i, pp. 279-516.

Jevons, W. S., *The coal question: an inquiry concerning the progress of the nation, and the probable exhaustion of our coal mines* (London, 1865).

Jevons, W. S., *The theory of political economy*, ed. R. D. Collison Black (Harmondsworth, 1970).

John, A. H., 'Aspects of English economic growth in the first half of the eighteenth century', *Economica*, new series, xxviii (1961), pp. 176-90.

Jones, E. L., 'Agriculture, 1700-1780', in R. Floud and D. N. McCloskey (eds), *The economic history of Britain since 1700*, 2 vols (Cambridge, 1981), i, pp. 66-86.

Jones, E. L. and Healy, M. J. R., 'Wheat yields in England 1815-59', in E. L. Jones (ed.), *Agriculture and the industrial revolution* (Oxford, 1974), pp. 184-90.

Jones, P. E. and Judges, A. V., 'London population in the late seventeenth century', *Econ. Hist. Rev*, vi (1935), pp. 45-63.

Kenney, A. P., 'Patricians and plebians in colonial Albany', *Halve Maen. Quarterly Magazine of the Dutch Colonial Period in America*, xlv (1970-1), 1, pp. 7-8, 14; 2, pp. 9-11, 13; 3, pp. 9-11; 4, pp. 13-14; xlvi (1971), 1, pp. 13-15.

Kindleberger, C. P., *Economic development*, 2nd ed. (New York, 1965).

King, G., *Two tracts by Gregory King*, ed. G. E. Barnett (Baltimore, 1936).

Knodel, J. E., *The decline of fertility in Germany, 1871-1939* (Princeton, 1974).

Knodel, J. and van de Walle, E., 'Lessons from the past: policy implications of historical fertility studies', *Pop. Dev. Rev.*, v (1979), pp. 217-45.

Knodel, J. and Wilson, C., 'The secular increase in fecundity in German village populations: an analysis of reproductive histories of couples married 1750–1899', *Pop. Stud.*, xxxv (1981), pp. 53–84.

Krause, J. T., Changes in English fertility and mortality, 1781–1850', *Econ. Hist. Rev.*, 2nd series, xi (1958), pp. 52–70.

Krause, J. T., 'Some implications of recent work in historical demography', *Comp. Stud. Soc. & Hist.*, i (1959), pp. 164–88.

Kussmaul, A., *Servants in husbandry in early modern England* (Cambridge, 1981).

Labrousse, E., Romano, R. and Dreyfus, F. -G., *Le prix du froment en France au temps de la monnaie stable (1726–1913)* (Paris, 1970).

Landes, D. S., 'Encore le problème de la révolution industrielle en Angleterre', *Bulletin de la société d'histoire moderne*, 12th series, no. 18 (1961).

Landes, D. S., 'Technological change and industrial development in western Europe, 1750–1914', in *The Cambridge Economic History of Europe*, vi, part I (Cambridge, 1965), pp. 274–601.

Laslett, P., *The world we have lost* (London, 1965).

Laslett, P., 'Introduction: the numerical study of English society', in E. A. Wrigley (ed.), *An introduction to English historical demography* (London, 1966) pp. 1–13.

Laslett, P., 'Introduction: the history of the family', in P. Laslett and R. Wall (eds), *Household and family in past time* (Cambridge, 1972), pp. 1–89.

Laslett, P., *Family life and illicit love in earlier generations* (Cambridge, 1977).

Laslett, P., 'Introduction: comparing illegitimacy over time and between cultures', in P. Laslett, K. Oosterveen and R. M. Smith (eds), *Bastardy and its comparative history* (London, 1980), pp. 1–68.

Laslett, P. and Harrison, J., 'Clayworth and Cogenhoe', in H. E. Bell and R. L. Ollard (eds), *Historical essays 1600–1750, presented to David Ogg* (London, 1963), pp. 157–84.

Laslett, P. and Wall, R. (eds), *Household and family in past time* (Cambridge, 1972).

Law, C. M., 'The growth of urban population in England and Wales, 1801–1911', *Trans. I.B.G.*, xli (1967), pp. 123–43.

Law, C. M., 'Some notes on the urban population of England and Wales in the eighteenth century', *The Local Historian*, x (1972), pp. 142–7.

Le Bras, H., 'Parents, grand-parents, bisaieux', *Pop.*, xxviii (1973), pp. 9–38.

Leibenstein, H., *Economic backwardness and economic growth* (New York, 1963).

Leibenstein, H., 'Population growth and the take-off hypothesis', in W. W. Rostow (ed.), *The economics of take-off into sustained growth*, (London, 1963), pp. 170–84.

Lennard, R., 'Statistics of corn yields in medieval England', *Economic History* (supplement to *Econ. J.*), iii (1936), pp. 172–92 and iii (1937), pp. 325–49.

Le Roy Ladurie, E., 'L'histoire immobile', *Annales, E.S.C.*, xxix (1974), pp. 673–92.

Lesthaeghe, R. J., *The decline of Belgian fertility 1800–1970* (Princeton, 1977).

Lesthaeghe, R. J., 'On the social control of human reproduction', *Pop. Dev. Rev.*, vi (1980), pp. 527–48.

Levasseur, E., *La population française: histoire de la population avant 1789 et démographie de la France comparée à celle des autres nations au XIXe siècle*, 3 vols (Paris, 1889–91).

Lewis, W. A., *The theory of economic growth* (London, 1955).

Lindert, P. H., *English occupations, 1670–1811.* Department of Economics, University of California, Davis, Working Paper 144 (1980).

Lindert, P. H. and Williamson, J. G., 'English workers' living standards during the industrial revolution: a new look', *Econ. Hist. Rev*, 2nd series, xxxvi (1983), pp. 1–25.

Lorimer, F. et al., *Culture and human fertility* (Paris, 1954).

McEvedy, C. and Jones, R., *Atlas of world population history* (London, 1978).

Macfarlane, A., 'Modes of reproduction', *J. Dev. Stud.*, xiv (1978), pp. 100–20.

Macfarlane, A., *Marriage and love in England. Modes of reproduction 1300–1840* (Oxford, 1986).

McInnis, M., 'The fertility transition in Europe and America', in J. Rogers (ed.), *Family building and family planning in pre-industrial societies*, Reports from the Family History Group, Department of History, University of Uppsala, no. 1 (Uppsala, 1980), pp. 1–15.

McKendrick, N., 'Josiah Wedgwood: an eighteenth-century entrepreneur in salesmanship and marketing techniques', *Econ. Hist. Rev.*, 2nd series, xii (1960), pp. 408–33.

McKeown, T., Brown, R. G. and Record, R. G. 'An interpretation of the modern rise of population in Europe', *Pop. Stud.*, xxvi (1972), pp. 345–82.

Malthus, T. R., *An essay on the principle of population as it affects the future improvement of society with remarks on the speculations of Mr Godwin, M. Condorcet and other writers* (London, 1798) [the 1st ed.].

[Malthus, T. R.], *An investigation of the cause of the present high price of provisions* (London, 1800).

Malthus, T. R., *An inquiry into the nature and progress of rent and the principles by which it is regulated* (London, 1815).

Malthus, T. R., *An essay on the principle of population; or, a view of its past and present effects on human happiness; with an inquiry into our prospects respecting the future removal or mitigation of the evils which it occasions*, 6th ed. (London, 1826).

Malthus, T. R., *The principles of political economy considered with a view to their practical application*, 2nd ed. (London, 1836).

Malthus, T. R., *The works of Thomas Robert Malthus*, ed. E. A. Wrigley and D. Souden, 8 vols (London, 1986).

Marshall, L. M., 'The rural population of Bedfordshire, 1671 to 1921', *Beds. Hist. Rec. Soc.*, xvi (1934), pp. 2–64.

Marx, K., *Capital: a critical analysis of capitalist production*, ed. F. Engels, translated from 3rd German edition by S. Moore and E. Aveling, 2 vols (London, 1887).

Mason, S. F., *A history of the sciences: main currents of scientific thought* (London, 1953).

Mathias, P., *The transformation of England. Essays in the economic and social history of England in the eighteenth century* (London, 1979).

Medick, H., 'The structures and function of population development under the proto-industrial system', in P. Kriedte, H. Medick and J. Schlumbohm, *Industrialization before industrialization*, (Cambridge, 1981), pp. 74–93.

Mendels, F. F., 'Industrialization and population pressure in eighteenth century Flanders', *J. Econ. Hist.*, xxxi (1971), pp. 269–71.

Mitchell, B. R., *European historical statistics, 1750–1975*, 2nd ed. (Cambridge, 1981).

Mitchell, B. R. and Deane, P., *Abstract of British historical statistics* (Cambridge 1962).

Morrow, R. B., 'Family limitation in pre-industrial England: a reappraisal', *Econ. Hist. Rev.*, 2nd series, xxxi (1978), pp. 419–28.

Nef, J. U., *The rise of the British coal industry*, 2 vols (London, 1932).

Newman Brown, W., 'The receipt of poor relief and family situation: Aldenham, Hertfordshire 1630–1690', in R. M. Smith (ed.), *Land, kinship and life cycle* (Cambridge, 1984), pp. 405–22.

O'Brien, D. P., *The classical economists* (Oxford, 1975).

Ohlin, G., 'Mortality, marriage and growth in pre-industrial populations', *Pop. Stud.*, xiv (1961), pp. 190–7.

Ormrod, D., 'Dutch commercial and industrial decline and British growth in the late seventeenth and early eighteenth centuries', in F. Krantz and P. M. Hohenberg (eds), *Failed transitions to modern industrial society; Renaissance Italy and seventeenth-century Holland* (Montreal, 1975), pp. 36–43.

Overton, M., 'Estimating crop yields from probate inventories: an example from East Anglia, 1585–1735', *J. Econ. Hist.*, xxxix (1979), pp. 363–78.

Palliser, D. M., 'Tawney's century: brave new world or Malthusian trap', *Econ. Hist. Rev.*, 2nd series, xxxv (1982), pp. 339–53.

Patten, J., 'Population distribution in Norfolk and Suffolk during the sixteenth and seventeenth centuries', *Trans. I.B.G.*, 1xv (1975), pp. 45–65.

Patten, J., *English towns 1500–1700* (Folkestone, 1978).

Petty, W., *The growth of the city of London*, in C. H. Hull (ed.), *The economic writings of Sir William Petty*, 2 vols (New York, 1963–4), ii, pp. 457–78.

Phelps Brown, E. H. and Hopkins, S. V., 'Seven centuries of building wages', in E. M. Carus-Wilson (ed.), *Essays in economic history*, 3 vols (London, 1954–62), ii, pp. 167–78.

Phelps Brown, E. H. and Hopkins, S. V., 'Seven centuries of the prices of consumables compared with builders' wage rates', in E. M. Carus-Wilson (ed.), *Essays in economic history*, 3 vols (London, 1954–62), ii, pp. 179–96.

Phythian-Adams, C., 'Urban decay in late medieval England', in P. Abrams and E. A. Wrigley (eds), *Towns and societies. Essays in economic history and historical sociology* (Cambridge, 1978), pp. 159–85.

Phythian-Adams, C., *Desolation of a city. Coventry and the urban crisis of the late middle ages* (Cambridge, 1979).

Pollard, S., *Peaceful conquest. The industrialization of Europe 1760–1970* (Oxford, 1981).

Pouthas, C. H., *La population française pendant la première moitié du XIXe siècle* (Paris, 1956).

Price, R., *An essay on the population of England from the revolution to the present time*, 2nd ed. (London, 1780), reprinted in *The population controversy*, compiled by D. V. Glass (Farnborough, 1973).

Reinhard, M. R., Armengaud, A. and Dupâquier, J., *Histoire générale de la population mondiale*, 3rd ed. (Paris, 1968).

Ricardo, D., *On the principles of political economy and taxation* in *The works and correspondence of David Ricardo*, ed. P. Sraffa with the collaboration of M. H. Dobb, i (Cambridge, 1951).

Roessingh, H. K., 'Village and hamlet in a sandy region of the Netherlands in the middle of the eighteenth century', *Acta Historiae Neerlandica*, iv (1970), pp. 105–29.

Rogers, J., 'The study of family planning in pre-industrial societies. Some methodological problems', in J. Rogers (ed.), *Family building and family planning in pre-industrial societies*, Reports from the Family History Group, Department of History, University of Uppsala, no. 1 (Uppsala, 1980), pp. 41–52.

Rostow, W. W., *The process of economic growth* (Oxford, 1953).

Rostow, W. W., *The world economy. History and prospect* (Austin and London, 1978).

Rozman, G., 'Edo's importance in changing Tokugawa society', *J. Jap. Stud.*, i (1974), pp. 91–112.

Runciman W. G., *Relative deprivation and social justice* (London, 1966).

Samuelson, P. A., 'The canonical classical model of political economy', *J. Econ. Lit.*, xvi (1978), pp. 1415–34.

Sauvy, A., *Théorie générale de la population*, 2nd ed. 2 vols (Paris, 1956-9).

Schofield, R. S., 'Dimensions of illiteracy, 1750-1850', *Explorations in Economic History*, x (1973), pp. 437-54.

Schofield. R. S., 'The relationship between demographic structure and environment in pre-industrial Europe', in W. Conze (ed.), *Sozialgeschichte der Familie in der Neuzeit Europas* (Stuttgart, 1976), pp. 147-60

Schofield, R. S., 'English marriage patterns revisited', *J. Fam. Hist.*, x (1985), pp. 2-20.

Schumpeter, J. A., *Business cycles: a theoretical, historical, and statistical analysis of the capitalist process*, 2 vols (New York, 1939).

Scott Smith, D., 'The demographic history of colonial New England', *J. Econ. Hist.*, xxxii (1972), pp. 165-83.

Scott Smith, D., 'A homeostatic demographic regime: patterns in west European family reconstitution studies', in R. D. Lee (ed.), *Population patterns in the past* (New York, 1977), pp. 19-51.

Sen, A., *Poverty and famines. An essay on entitlement and deprivation* (Oxford, 1981).

Sjoberg, G., *The pre-industrial city* (New York, 1960).

Slicher van Bath, B. H., *Een samenleving onder spanning: geschiedenis van het platteland in Overijssel* (Assen, 1957).

Slicher van Bath, B. H., *The agrarian history of western Europe, A.D. 500-1850* (London, 1963).

Smith, A., *An inquiry into the nature and causes of the wealth of nations*, new ed., ed. J. R. McCulloch (Edinburgh, 1863).

Smith, A., *An inquiry into the nature and causes of the wealth of nations*, ed. E. Cannan, 5th ed., 2 vols (London, 1961).

Smith, C. T., *An historical geography of western Europe before 1800* (London, 1967).

Smith, R. M., 'Some reflections on the evidence for the origins of the "European marriage pattern" in England', in C. Harris (ed.), *The sociology of the family: new directions for Britain* (Keele, 1979), pp. 74-112.

Smith, R. M., 'Fertility, economy and household formation in England over three centuries', *Pop. Dev. Rev.*, vii (1981), pp. 595-622.

Smith, R. M., 'Hypothèses sur la nuptialité en Angleterre aux XIIIᵉ-XIVᵉ siècles', *Annales, E.S.C.*, xxxviii (1983), pp. 107-36.

Smith, R. M., 'Some issues concerning families and their property in rural England 1250-1800', in R. M. Smith (ed.), *Land, kinship and life cycle* (Cambridge, 1984), pp. 1-86.

Smith, T. C., *Nakahara. Family farming and population in a Japanese village, 1717-1830* (Stanford, 1977).

Solow, R. M., 'Technical change and the aggregate production function', *Rev. Econ. & Stat.*, xxxix (1957), pp. 312-20.

Spagnoli, P. G., 'High fertility in mid-nineteenth century France: a multivariate analysis of fertility patterns in the arrondissement of Lille', *Research Econ. Hist.*, ii (1977), pp. 281-336.

Spagnoli, P. G., 'Population history from parish monographs: the problem of local demographic variations', *J. Interdisc. Hist.*, vii (1977), pp. 427-52.

Spengler, J. J., 'Mercantilist and physiocratic growth theory', in B. F. Hoselitz, J. J. Spengler, J. M. Letiche, E. McKinley, J. Buttrick and H. J. Bruton (eds), *Theories of economic growth* (Glencoe, 1960), pp. 3-64.

Stone, L., 'Social mobility in England, 1500-1700', *Past and Present*, xxxiii (1966), pp. 16-55.

Sundt, E., *On marriage in Norway*, translated with an introduction by M. Drake (Cambridge, 1980).

Tawney, A. J. and Tawney, R. H., 'An occupational census of the seventeenth century', *Econ. Hist. Rev.*, v (1934), pp. 25–64.

Thirsk, J., *Economic policy and projects. The development of a consumer society in early modern England* (Oxford, 1978).

Thomas, B., 'Escaping from constraints: the industrial revolution in a Malthusian context', *J. Interdisc. Hist.*, xv (1985), pp. 729–53.

Thomas, R. P. and McCloskey, D. N., 'Overseas trade and empire, 1700–1860', in R. Floud and D. N. McCloskey (eds), *The economic history of Britain since 1700*, 2 vols (Cambridge, 1981), i, pp. 87–102.

Thompson, F. M. L., 'The second agricultural revolution, 1815–1880', *Econ. Hist. Rev.*, 2nd series, xxi (1968), pp. 62–77.

Thompson, F. M. L., 'Nineteenth-century horse sense', *Econ. Hist. Rev.*, 2nd series, xxix (1976), pp. 60–81.

Thorold Rogers, J. E., *The economic interpretation of history* (London, 1888).

Thorold Rogers, J. E., *Six centuries of work and wages*, 9th ed. (London, 1908).

Tilly, L. A., 'The food riot as a form of political conflict in France', *J. Interdisc. Hist.*, ii (1971), pp. 23–57.

Tippett, L. H. C., *The methods of statistics*, 4th rev. ed. (London, 1952).

Titow, J. Z., *Winchester yields. A study in medieval agricultural productivity* (Cambridge, 1972).

Tönnies, F., *Community and society*, ed. C. P. Loomis (East Lansing, 1957).

Tooke, T., *A history of prices and of the state of the circulation*, 6 vols (London, 1838–57).

Turner, M., 'Agricultural productivity in England in the eighteenth century: evidence from yields', *Econ. Hist. Rev.*, 2nd series, xxxv (1982), pp. 489–510.

Uhlenberg, P. R., 'A study of cohort life cycles: cohorts of native born Massachusetts women, 1830–1920', *Pop. Stud.*, xxiii (1969), pp. 407–20.

Van de Walle, E., 'Marriage and marital fertility', *Daedalus*, xcvii (1968), pp. 486–501.

Van de Walle, E., *The female population of France in the nineteenth century* (Princeton, 1974).

Van de Walle, E., 'Alone in Europe: the French fertility decline until 1850', in C. Tilly (ed.), *Historical studies of changing fertility* (Princeton, 1978), pp. 257–88.

Van de Walle, E., 'France', in W. R. Lee (ed.), *European demography and economic growth* (London, 1979), pp. 123–43.

Van de Walle, E., 'Illegitimacy in France during the nineteenth century', in P. Laslett, K. Oosterveen and R. M. Smith (eds), *Bastardy and its comparative history* (London, 1980), pp. 264–77.

Van de Walle, E. and Lesthaeghe, R., 'Facteurs économiques et déclin de la fécondité en France et en Belgique', *Colloques Internationaux du CNRS*, no. 550, Valescure (1973), pp. 345–73.

Van der Woude, A. M., 'De omvang en samenstelling van de huishouding in Nederland in het verleden', *A.A.G. Bijdragen*, xv (1970), pp. 202–41.

Van der Woude, A. M., 'Demografische ontwikkeling van de noordelijke Nederlanden 1500–1800', in *Algemene Geschiedenis der Nederlanden*, v (Harlem, 1980), pp. 102–67.

Von Hayek, F. A., *The counter-revolution of science: studies on the abuse of reason* (New York, 1964).

Von Thünen, J. H., *Der isolirte Staat in Beziehung auf Landwirtschaft und Nationalökonomie*, 2nd ed., 2 vols (Rostock, 1842–50).

Von Thünen, J. H., *The isolated state*, English ed. of *Der isolirte Staat in Beziehung auf Landwirtschaft und Nationalökonomie*, ed. P. Hall (Oxford, 1966).

Von Tunzelmann, G. N., 'Trends in real wages, 1750-1850, revisited', *Econ. Hist. Rev.*, 2nd series, xxxii (1979), pp. 33-49.

Wales, T., 'Poverty, poor relief and the life cycle: some evidence from seventeenth-century Norfolk', in R. M. Smith (ed.), *Land, kinship and life cycle* (Cambridge, 1984), pp. 351-404.

Weber, M., *The theory of social and economic organization*, translated by A. M. Henderson and T. Parsons, ed. T. Parsons (New York, 1964).

Weinstein, F. and Platt, G. M., *The wish to be free: society, psyche and value change* (Berkeley, 1969).

Weir, D. R., *Fertility control in rural France, 1740-1829* (unpublished PhD thesis, Stanford, 1982).

Weir, D. R., 'Rather never than late: celibacy and age at marriage in English cohort fertility, 1541-1871', *J. Fam. Hist.*, ix (1984), pp. 341-55.

Wells, R. V., 'Demographic change and the life cycle of American families', *J. Interdisc. Hist.*, ii (1971), pp. 273-82.

Wells, R. V., 'Family size and fertility control in eighteenth century America: a study of Quaker families', *Pop. Stud.*, xxv (1971), pp. 73-82.

Wiebe, G., *Zur Geschichte der Preisrevolution des XVI and XVII Jahrhunderts* (Leipzig, 1895).

Wilkinson, R. G., *Poverty and progress* (London, 1973).

Wrightson, K., *English society, 1580-1640* (London, 1982).

Wrigley, E. A., *Industrial growth and population change* (Cambridge, 1961).

Wrigley, E. A., 'The supply of raw materials in the industrial revolution', *Econ. Hist. Rev.*, 2nd series, xv (1962), pp. 1-16. Reproduced as chapter 4 of this volume.

Wrigley, E. A., 'Family limitation in pre-industrial England', *Econ. Hist. Rev.*, 2nd series, xix (1966), pp. 82-109. Reproduced as chapter 10 of this volume.

Wrigley, E. A. (ed.), *An introduction to English historical demography* (London, 1966).

Wrigley, E. A., 'A simple model of London's importance in changing English society and economy, 1650-1750', *Past and Present*, xxxvii (1967), pp. 44-70. Reproduced as chapter 6 of this volume.

Wrigley, E. A., 'Mortality in pre-industrial England: the example of Colyton, Devon, over three centuries', *Daedalus*, xcvii (1968), pp. 546-80.

Wrigley, E. A., *Population and history* (London, 1969).

Wrigley, E. A., 'The process of modernization and the industrial revolution in England', *J. Interdisc. Hist.*, iii (1972), pp. 225-59. Reproduced as chapter 3 of this volume.

Wrigley, E. A., 'Some problems of family reconstitution using English parish register material: the example of Colyton', in D. E. C. Eversley (ed.), *Demography and economy*, Third International Conference of Economic History, Munich 1965 (Paris and The Hague, 1972), pp. 199-221.

Wrigley, E. A., 'Marital fertility in seventeenth-century Colyton: a note', *Econ. Hist. Rev.*, 2nd series, xxxi (1978), pp. 429-36.

Wrigley, E. A., 'Fertility strategy for the individual and the group', in C. Tilly (ed.), *Historical studies of changing fertility* (Princeton, 1978), pp. 135-54. Reproduced as chapter 8 of this volume.

Wrigley, E. A., 'Marriage, fertility and population growth in eighteenth-century England', in R. B. Outhwaite (ed.), *Marriage and society: studies in the social history of marriage* (London, 1981), pp. 137-85.

Wrigley, E. A., 'The growth of population in eighteenth-century England: a conundrum resolved', *Past and Present*, xcviii (1983), pp. 121–50. Reproduced as chapter 9 of this volume.

Wrigley, E. A., 'The means to marry: population and economy in pre-industrial England', *Qu. J. Soc. Affairs*, i (1985), pp. 271–80.

Wrigley, E. A., 'Introduction', in *The works of Thomas Robert Malthus*, ed. E. A. Wrigley and D. Souden, 8 vols (London, 1986), i, pp. *7–39*.

Wrigley, E. A., 'Men on the land and men in the countryside: employment in agriculture in early nineteenth-century England', in L. Bonfield, R. M. Smith and K. Wrightson (eds), *The world we have gained. Histories of population and social structure* (Oxford, 1986), pp. 295–336.

Wrigley, E. A. and Schofield, R. S., *The population history of England, 1541–1871. A reconstruction* (London, 1981).

Wrigley, E. A. and Schofield, R. S., 'English population history from family reconstitution: summary results, 1600–1799', *Pop. Stud.*, xxxvii (1983), pp. 157–84.

Wynne-Edwards, V. C., *Animal dispersion in relation to social behaviour* (Edinburgh, 1962).

Wynne-Edwards, V. C., 'Self-regulation in populations of red grouse, *Lagopus l. scoticus (Aves-galliformes)*', in J. Dupâquier, A. Fauve-Chamoux and E. Grebenik (eds), *Malthus past and present* (London, 1983), pp. 379–91.

Index

336

56f.

(57) SMOLETT

102 Price,

97 Rise in corn
    prices 1580

70

56-60

Agric / Trade + Credit